Elizabeth

J. RANDY TARABORRELLI

SIDGWICK & JACKSON

First published 2006 by Warner Books

First published in Great Britain 2006 by Sidgwick & Jackson
an imprint of Pan Macmillan Ltd
Pan Macmillan, 20 New Wharf Road, London N1 9RR
Basingstoke and Oxford
Associated companies throughout the world
www.panmacmillan.com

ISBN-13: 978-028-307007-5 (HB)
ISBN-10: 0-283-07007-2
ISBN-13: 978-0-283-07023-5 (TPB)
ISBN-10: 0-283-07023-4

1 3 5 7 9 8 6 4 2

A CIP catalogue record for this book is available from
the British Library.

Book design by Giorgetta Bell McRee
Printed and bound in Great Britain by
Mackays of Chatham plc, Chatham, Kent

For
Concetta, Antonetta, Rose Marie, Lena,
Roslyn, Michelle, Rosemaria
and Jessica

Contents

Contents ix

Elizabeth

I haven't had a quiet life. I've lived dangerously. Sometimes disaster has come at me like a train. There have been times when I've almost drunk myself to death. I've been in situations where I was perilously close to killing myself. I've almost died several times. Yet some instinct, some inner force, has always saved me, dragging me back just as the train whooshed past.

Miss Elizabeth Taylor, April 1997

Prologue

Even with all of the star treatment accorded her over the years, the truth is undeniable: It has never been easy being Elizabeth Taylor.

Gentle and caring at her core while often appearing to be petulant and self-consumed, Elizabeth is a complex woman who has usually been misunderstood, not only by others but, it would seem, by her as well. It's true that throughout her life she has claimed moments of clarity, times when she felt she was finally able to see her past in proper perspective. However, one must wonder, given the unique circumstances of her upbringing, if she could ever truly have the ability, the prescience, to see it all clearly.

In trying to understand Elizabeth's life, one must first turn to her childhood. Born into an affluent family in London, young Elizabeth possessed an engaging quality and stunning beauty that seemed to defy reason. From the beginning, her mother, Sara—a former theater actress—believed her daughter to have potential that was heaven-sent. In her mind, Elizabeth had the makings of a great star. However, Sara also knew it would never happen if Elizabeth didn't also believe it, and work at it. So from the time Elizabeth was about two, Sara endeavored to create in her the ultimate image of dignity, grace, and beauty. With the passing of the years, nearly every aspect of the young girl's behavior would be carefully considered and altered. Her speech. Her posture. Her gait. It was as if Sara was a director coaching the promising new star of a landmark movie—only she was a mom, and this was Elizabeth's life, not a film. Because Sara's optimism about Elizabeth's chances in show business came from the heart, it was inspiring, if also sometimes a bit alarming. Sara even orchestrated how her daughter would interact with others: If a broad laugh was too much, it would be replaced with a shy giggle. As a result, Elizabeth's early life soon became a marathon training session for succeeding in a business at which her mother had only found marginal accomplishment. For a young Elizabeth Taylor, perfection soon became the only acceptable option. Anything less would be considered failure.

The dissection of Elizabeth's self at her mother's hand also brought with it a legacy of irrationality. The belief that perfection's only alternative was failure left her feeling that life was, quite literally, unbearable. She felt out of control, so much that it seemed the only way she could seize some power over her world was to become deathly ill, to be hospitalized so that she didn't have to make movies, didn't have to take direction. Only she could know for certain if such reasoning explains her countless life-challenging sicknesses, but from the outside looking in it certainly seems plausible. At times, as will be explained in these pages, she would even see suicide as the only way to end her misery. Fortunately, the kindness and patience of those closest to her would save Elizabeth from several apparent attempts at taking her own life.

It wouldn't be until she was in her fifties that Elizabeth learned some invaluable lessons. Indeed, her work toward the treatment and cure of a deadly disease would ultimately lead her to some grand realizations. How ironic that after so many exhausting years of searching for a genuine connection with the world as an actress, she would find it in work that had nothing

to do with show business. As many around her suffered premature and cruel deaths, it finally became clear to her that life was
a gift. She came to realize that despite what her mother and the
movie studio system had taught her, between black and white
there is actually a whole spectrum of other shades—and perfection has a short shelf life.

In her later years, she would also come to understand that there
are certain inevitabilities to living. Life can be painful. Life can be
unfair. Life can be unpredictable. And it was only after accepting
those facts that Elizabeth Taylor came to the greatest realization
of all: Life was worth living.

Part One

———

CHILDHOOD

Sara and Francis

Sara Viola Warmbrodt was born on August 21, 1896, in the mill town of Arkansas City, Kansas. For all of her time on this earth, she would be quite a character, a memorable presence not only in her daughter, Elizabeth's, life but in those of nearly every person she would touch over the years. Through it all, good times and bad, she and Elizabeth would remain inseparable. Even during times of estrangement—for they did have their disagreements—they knew to whom to turn for unwavering support: each other. "My mother was my best friend," Elizabeth would later say, "my guide, my mentor, and my constant companion." Indeed, mother and daughter were life and breath to each other, and thus it would remain until Sara's death in 1994, just one month short of her ninety-ninth birthday.

Historically, Sara has been portrayed as a negative influence on Elizabeth's life, mostly because of her steely determination to mold her daughter into a star; indeed, so-called "stage mothers" are seldom viewed in a positive light. Like many parents who encourage their children into show business, Sara had once been an entertainer. In 1922, she had changed her name to Sara Sothern after relocating to Los Angeles from Arkansas City to pursue her dream career. Her mother—Elizabeth's grandmother—was a talented singer and musician who played both piano and violin. She was very encouraging of Sara's goals and didn't mind her dropping out of high school to pursue them and also study acting in Kansas City. After appearing in a number of small productions in the Midwest, Sara found herself in Los Angeles. There, she was cast in a supporting role in a theatrical revival of Channing Pollock's *The Sign on the Door*. (The silent movie released a year prior had starred Norma Talmadge.) After Pollock saw her in that show, he cast her in a key role—a crippled girl, miraculously healed—in his play *The Fool*, based on the life of Saint Francis of Assisi. The plot, a faith-healing concept, was very much in alignment with Sara's own spiritual belief as a Christian Scientist—that unwavering faith in a higher power could result in physical healing far beyond the reach and understanding of the medical profession.

The Fool first opened in Los Angeles to weak reviews but eventually made its way east to New York, where it opened on Broadway at the Times Square Theater in October 1922. There it played to full houses for nearly a year, even though the show continued to receive generally poor notices—except for Sara, who was singled out for her performance by some reviewers. She was faintly praised by the *New York Times* critic, who said, "In the final scene of the third act, a little cripple, well played by Sara Sothern, falls on her knees in prayer and rises to find that she can walk." When the show went to London in September 1924, Sara went with it, and caused quite a bit of pandemonium there. After the opening night, at least according to an interview Channing Pollock once gave, she even had to be extricated from a mob scene, with fans "clamoring for bits of her frock and locks of her hair as souvenirs. Later," Pollock recalled, "the Prince Royal went to her dressing room to present her with a diamond brooch the size of a belt buckle."

Margaret DeForest was the daughter of a friend of Sara's from Palm Springs, California, where Sara spent her elder years. She recalls of the Taylor matriarch, "Though she was a slight woman, Sara had a magnetic personality. People gravitated toward her, as they would one day her daughter. She was funny, smart and nobody's pushover. I knew her when she was much older, but I saw many pictures of her as a young woman. She had wonderful scrapbooks of her show business days, and loved to show them to me and my mother. She told us that Elizabeth had gathered the clip-

pings for her, compiled them herself, and then gave her the scrapbooks one year as a birthday gift. With her dark hair and blue eyes,
Sara was a real beauty. She was funny, too. She had a biting sense
of humor which, sometimes, people didn't know how to take. In
her later years, she used to be frustrated by Elizabeth's life. 'It
seems that someone forgot to teach that young lady manners,' she
used to say. Then she would add with a wink, 'And I guess that
would have been me.' I loved her. I just thought she was great, I
really did."

After *The Sign on the Door* closed, four more less successful theatrical productions in New York followed for Sara Sothern. By the
time she was thirty, she began reconsidering her options. It was at
just that time that Francis Taylor—a man whom she had dated
only casually back in Arkansas City—came back into her life.

The handsome and charming Francis Lenn Taylor was born on
December 28, 1897, also in Arkansas City, of Scotch-Irish descent. He had dropped out of high school and worked as an apprentice in an art gallery owned by his beloved, if also demanding,
uncle, Howard Young, in St. Louis. When Francis turned twenty-
one, his uncle gave him the opportunity to move to New York and
work at a gallery Howard opened there, the Howard Young
Gallery, which specialized in eighteenth- and nineteenth-century
European paintings.

Sarah and Francis became reacquainted one evening quite by
happenstance at the El Morocco nightclub in New York. Afterward, they began to enjoy each other's company on a regular basis.
She found him to be quiet and unassuming, so different in character and temperament from the many show business types she'd
known in recent years. True, he didn't have the kind of spark that
she usually required to stay interested in a man, but still, she
couldn't help but be fascinated by him. He'd been to Europe with
his uncle, had a wealth of interesting anecdotes to share about his
travels, understood art and could talk about it for hours, so there
was seldom a dull moment between them.

Francis Taylor was soft-spoken and easygoing. Tall and lean, with an aristocratic and refined bone structure, he had piercing blue eyes and light brown wavy hair, which was combed straight back. His was a scholarly air with his horn-rimmed glasses and natty three-piece suits, in which he always looked great. He was always dressed for presentation, never casually. He accepted life as it was and had little interest in changing things. He was whimsical and artistic in nature, not practical. Don't get the wrong impression of him, though: He wasn't exactly carefree. Quite the contrary—he was a contemplative person who often seemed uneasy and distracted. Elizabeth once said that as a young girl she would sit and stare at her father as he sat in his easy chair, his eyes closed and brow furrowed as if attempting to solve a complex, troubling problem. A gentle man, he shied away from confrontation and would do anything in his power to avoid an argument. Later in life, at the end of any conflict his fiery and decisive wife, Sara, would always be the victor. In fact, it's safe to say, at least based on the recollections of those who knew the Taylors well, that Francis never won an argument with her in their entire marriage. "She's the boss," he would say. "What she says goes, and that's fine with me." Indeed, he had great respect for Sara, thought her to be savvy and smart as well as talented, and never felt that he didn't have a place in her life. He knew his place.

Sara's zest for life had led Francis to lose all sense in her presence when he first met her. Inexplicably drawn to her, he confided to friends that he couldn't stop thinking about the ball of fire called "Sassy" by those who only spoke of her and not with her. He loved her unquenchable spirit, her joyous soul. In fact, Francis saw in Sara many qualities he had wanted for himself, such as charisma, a quick wit, and an ability to point a finger in someone's face and say—as she would quite often—"I know what the problem with you is, and here's how to fix it." It was when that finger was finally wagged in his face, as he would recall it, that he felt somehow reborn. Indeed, the first sign that he and Sara were perfect for each other was when she agreed with him about his faults. She could see right away that he lacked focus and confidence, that he thought of himself as somewhat of a social misfit. He was foggy and scattered and didn't "finish his sentences with strength," as she noted. "We can *all* change, darling," she would tell him, "and for you, that will prove to be a godsend." Her brash manner may have proved a sticking point for previous suitors, but Francis found it refreshing, even enlivening. He was filled with an intense inquisitiveness about her, and to be so fascinated by anyone was, for him, a unique experience.

Many people who knew Francis before he met Sara were dumbfounded by the changes they soon began to see in him. Her coaching led him to address many of his behavioral deficiencies, at least as she saw them. Under her influence, he began to walk with purpose and at a quicker pace. He shook the hand of every person he met with strength. He made firm eye contact. He spoke highly of himself to others; Sara loathed the British tradition of self-deprecating humor and wouldn't stand for it in her suitor. He took all of her advice seriously—and it worked for him. His transformation profound after just a few months, he knew he had one woman—Sara Warmbrodt—to thank for all of it. Indeed, he felt like a new man.

Francis and Sara were married in 1926. Then, after one more show in New York, *The Little Spitfire*, Sara Taylor made the fateful decision to leave show business.

Marrying and eventually raising children rather than having the career in show business she had originally planned was a decision Sara Taylor made for herself, not something she ever felt had been foisted upon her. "I gave up my career when I married Daddy," she once said (referring to Francis), "and all the king's horses and all the king's men couldn't have made me take it up again." As a Christian Scientist, she believed at a core, spiritual level that she could have her life exactly as she wanted if only she approached it with a positive and affirmative attitude. "Divine love always has met, and always will meet, every human need," she would say. Therefore, she rarely complained about her life or about her decisions. Rather, she felt empowered to handle anything that came her way, and she hoped to pass the same kind of belief system on to the children she might one day bear.

At this same time, a new branch of the Howard Young Gallery was about to open in London at 35 Old Bond Street in the heart of the British art center, and it was Howard's idea that Francis manage the new establishment. He absolutely insisted upon it, in fact, for Howard was an assertive man who almost always had his way. Francis and his new wife moved to London and settled into a suite at the luxurious Carlton Hotel, paid for, of course, by Howard Young.

Now that Sara had given up her career as an actress to be a wife, the rest of the world seemed to slip out of her view. Francis was her passion. For his part, he was just as devoted to her. While previously not a particularly effusive man, he now made an art out of romancing his wife. For instance, knowing Sara's favorite chocolatier was Fortnum and Mason, Francis would regularly stop at the high-class grocer's in search of the ultimate confection. He might surprise her with a bag of caramelized ginger, a tin of sweet-meats, or the traditional box of chocolates. He went to great lengths to show his devotion to her.

For the next two years, Francis and Sara would travel all over Europe in first-class style—London, Paris, Berlin, Vienna, and Budapest—thanks to Howard Young's generous underwriting of such excursions, many of which were business-related. In the process, they would traffic with the powerful and affluent of the art world and acquire from them old masters for the Young Gallery. It was a heady time, but it wasn't to last, because when Sara became pregnant at the end of 1928, the couple decided to take root in London. Howard leased a lovely nineteenth-century cottage for them at 11 Hampstead Way. With its beautifully manicured gardens and pathways and its gorgeous views of the verdant Hampstead Heath, it was an enchanted place.

In June 1929, Sara gave birth to their first child, a son named Howard (after his great-uncle). With the addition of the baby, the Taylors' home was suddenly too cramped with just two bedrooms.

The couple did have a nurse, a cook, and a driver, after all. It would make sense, Sara decided, if at very least the nurse and cook could live at the house. Howard quickly accommodated her and solved the domestic problem by purchasing nearby—with cash— a larger eighteenth-century home (with Tudor and Victorian influences in its architecture) known as Heathwood, at 8 Wildwood Road, again overlooking the Heath. Delightfully landscaped with aged trees and colorful wildflowers, the redbrick home came complete with a large kitchen, stately dining and living rooms, pool and tennis court, and live-in accommodations for all of the help.

Howard was a stunning baby who, his mother once proclaimed, "looked like a Botticelli angel." He really did, with large, expressive blue eyes, wavy blond hair, and perfectly placed features. He was his daddy's boy, though. Sara believed a father and son should share a special bond. Therefore, while she was an affectionate and effective mother, she would often abdicate parental duties to Francis. It was as if she saw the raising of her firstborn as an opportunity to further shape her husband into an even fuller, more responsible man. However, such devotion to Francis's betterment would not last forever. Things would change dramatically, beginning on February 27, 1932—the day Sara gave birth to a daughter, a baby she and Francis would name Elizabeth.

A Change in Sara

The new Taylor baby girl was named Elizabeth after both of her grandmothers and Rosemond after her paternal grandmother Mary's maiden name. To be clear from the outset: She's not fond of being called "Liz." She's disliked it ever since her older brother,

Howard, used to tease her when she was a little girl by calling her "Lizzie the Lizard." Also, the appellation had been appropriated by the press as part of the sensational "Liz and Dick" fanfare of the 1960s. She felt it was used as a way of thinking about her in reductive terms. She tolerated it then—and still does today—but, as she once told the present author, "People who know me and hope to get to know me better certainly do not call me Liz. They call me Elizabeth."

It's been said that as a newborn Elizabeth Rosemond was covered from head to toe with a soft down of dark hair, like a newborn kitten. Actually, that description exaggerates the reality of the situation. In truth, Elizabeth was born with residual hypertrichosis, an excessive body hair condition. For a memoir she penned for *McCall's* in 1954, Sara wrote, "As the precious bundle was placed in my arms, my heart stood still. There, inside the cashmere shawl, was the *funniest* looking baby I had ever seen! Her hair was long and black. Her ears were covered with thick black fuzz and inlaid into the sides of her head; her nose looked like a tip-tilted button, and her tiny face was so tightly closed it looked as if it would never unfold."

It's safe to say by her mother's description that poor Elizabeth was not exactly the prototypically beautiful newborn. This baby wouldn't even open her eyes; Sara would tickle her cheeks in hopes that she might do so. When the infant obliged, all that could be seen were their whites because the eyeballs would inevitably roll back in her head. Sara felt, understandably, that she had reason to be concerned. However, after about a month, things improved. Thankfully, the excessive body hair began to fall away, revealing underneath the most gorgeous infant. When she finally took in the world, it became clear that she also had unusually bright, lavender-blue eyes, and, it would seem, even a double line of eyelashes. Elizabeth Taylor historian and photographer Tom Gates recalls a conversation he had with Elizabeth, and then later with Sara: "I once asked Elizabeth how she felt about being tagged 'The Most Beautiful Woman in The World.' She answered, 'Oh, that's just silly. I see better-looking women every day just walking down the street.' I later mentioned her remark to Sara one day while we were at the Regency Hotel, shortly after the Burtons married. 'It's true,' her mom said, 'she has no idea how beautiful she is. But, I do remember shortly after she was born she gave us a good scare. The doctor told us that she had a mutation. Well, that sounded just awful—a *mutation*. But, when he explained that her eyes had double rows of eyelashes, I thought, well, now, that doesn't sound so terrible at all.'"

Indeed, with the birth of her daughter came a sea change in how Sara lived her own life. It was as if she saw Elizabeth's birth as a challenge to mold a life from the moment it began. It was odd, some thought, that she didn't feel that way about her son, Howard. She just didn't. Elizabeth was, for her, special. Sara enrolled her in singing and dancing lessons by the age of two. It was also at that age that the Taylors visited America with the children, and brought them to New Orleans. "It was fun for all of us to see the excitement on Elizabeth's face," Sara once recalled, "as she sat in a high chair at Antoine's, dining on Oysters Rockefeller and pompano baked in a paper bag—at 10 o'clock at night." She was two years old, and "dining on Oysters Rockefeller." The Good Life, indeed.

By the age of just three, Sara had taught Elizabeth how to curtsy, shake hands, speak to adults . . . and, as she put it, "be a lady." Some observers couldn't help but feel that Sara was rushing the child past adolescence and into an early adulthood. Elizabeth did seem much older than her years, attentive and sophisticated beyond her age, unnaturally so for some. However, she was her mother's daughter, and Sara was proud of her precociousness and refinement.

With the birth of Elizabeth, Sara even seemed to lose all desire to make Francis the ideal gentleman. Although most husbands would probably have been relieved to not have to hear opinions about their grooming habits, clothing choices, and even posture and gait, Francis was not one of them. He had actually come to rely on Sara's pointed criticisms. However, after Elizabeth entered their home, the Sara he had known began to drift away from him. While Francis was a proud father and himself captivated by his enchanting new daughter, he couldn't help but miss the Sara with whom he had fallen in love. She certainly had changed. Totally absorbed by her daughter, she was Elizabeth's now . . . not his. A story he would recount in great detail for many years can be viewed as relaying a defining moment in his relationship not only with his child but his wife as well. It happened when Elizabeth was just a toddler.

As he would tell it later in life, Francis stopped into Fortnum and Mason on his way home from the gallery one afternoon and bought a bright gold box of candies for the first woman in his life, Sara. She had so often lit up at the sight of such treats that he looked forward to seeing that flash of girlish glee come over her, even if just for a moment.

When he entered their home that evening, he closed the door quietly behind him, as Sara had previously instructed in case Elizabeth was napping. Upon entering the parlor he found his flawless daughter resting in a heavy, ornate crib that Sara insisted she hadn't yet outgrown, even though she was about three years old. He walked toward her and knelt down close, studying the face that would one day capture the world. He opened the box, and then broke off a small bit of fudge for the toddler, much to her delight.

At hearing her daughter's giggles, Sara descended the stairs and discovered her child and her husband on the floor of the parlor. In a flash, she saw it all: the opened shiny box, the empty wrapper, the tiny, discolored fingers. She became extremely upset, and in one swift motion swept the child up and away from the offending box. "She doesn't eat candy," she said angrily.

Sara's tone and quick action took Francis off guard. For a moment, as he recalled it, he was speechless. When he told her that he'd gotten the sweets for her, she said that the last thing she needed was another box of candy. She also told him that if he ever again dared to give their daughter sugary treats he would live to regret it. Then she rushed off toward the kitchen with Elizabeth, who was now whimpering because of the heated exchange.

Francis would later say that he gathered what remained of the gift he'd brought home for his wife and walked to a nearby wastebasket, where he dropped it. Clearly, the woman who had softened him, summoned him out of the shell he once called home, existed no longer. Luckily for him he hadn't emerged from that shell completely . . . and at that moment he began the process of pulling himself back into it.

A Family Held Hostage?

Elizabeth Taylor lived in and around London, England, for the first six years of her life, years she recalls as being "the happiest days of my childhood." No wonder. She and Howard enjoyed a privileged life with servants and nannies at their beck and call, but not really because of anything Francis Taylor had done to ensure their security. In fact, the Taylors' situation was an unusual one, because the family had been, in a sense, adopted by two wealthy men. The first of these benefactors, as we have seen, was Francis's uncle by marriage, Howard Young. The other was a trusted family friend named Victor Cazalet.

Howard Young was a remarkable man who ran away from his Ohio home at the age of ten with no money and by the age of eighteen was worth almost half a million dollars. He had made his fortune through photography, developing a chemical process that transformed old family photographs—certainly not of the best quality in his day, the late 1800s—into stunning works of art in convex oval frames. His invention became a sensation that soon swept the country. He then invested his money in oil, and as a result of his success in that endeavor, he was soon dealing in old masters in a new gallery in New York. The owner of homes in New York, Connecticut, Florida, and Wisconsin, he was responsible for relocating Francis and Sara to England in order that Francis might work at the art gallery he owned there.

The daughter of a close friend of Howard's wife, Mabel Rosemond, explains that "Uncle Howard came into the Taylor family when he married Mabel, the sister of Francis Taylor's mother. There was always a lot of angst about Mabel. She was tough and demanding, not a big fan of Francis's, whom she thought of as a very weak man. Sara and Francis were the poor relatives, so to speak, always traveling about with Howard, but, oddly, with Mabel never around. From my understanding, Howard and Mabel were estranged, but never divorced. They also never had children. Uncle Howard treated Francis as his own son but, though he was generous, it would be stretching things to say he was loving toward him."

It was when the Taylors relocated to England that they met the affluent Victor Cazalet, also in the art business and a Conservative member of Parliament who was known to speak out against anti-Semitism in England. A confirmed bachelor, at just five feet three inches tall, he had the nickname "Teenie." After he took the Taylors under his wing, the family would live in a succession of very large and beautifully appointed homes—and even *summer* homes in the English countryside—thanks to his largesse. For example, at one point, he lent the Taylors his sixteenth-century guest home on the property of his Kent estate, which was called Great Swifts. The Taylors happily moved in, had the electricity and water turned on (and the bills sent to Victor), and renamed the property Little Swallows. Francis did a great deal of remodeling of the home and, at Sara's direction, planted elm, linden, and fruit trees. The family then used this home for weekend getaways. It would be at this Kent estate that Elizabeth first learned to ride horses, on a New Forest pony named Betty that was given to her by Victor Cazalet.

Thelma Cazalet-Keir, Victor Cazalet's sister, recalled his affection for the young Elizabeth. "As a child, Elizabeth had a set of wooden block letters with which she first learned the alphabet," she remembered. "Victor and she would spend hours together spelling out various words. Then he would read to her. She liked best *The Secret Garden* by Hodgson Burnett and insisted he read it aloud over and over again."

These two men, Howard Young and Victor Cazalet, virtually seeded the Taylor family's prosperity, allowing them to remain unaffected by the worldwide depression. Francis fully understood what motivated Howard to subsidize his family: He was a pushy relative who wanted to coax his nephew into a successful life. He was domineering and tough—much like Sara—and never let Francis forget that he was in charge. Francis understood that much, and learned to live with it. However, he never quite understood what was going on with Victor Cazalet and what kind of relationship this man had with Sara. Theirs was a close friendship with a lot of questions attached to it. Were they having an affair? Many people in their circle suspected as much. Others were certain that Victor, unmarried with no children, was homosexual. From all accounts, Francis never knew for certain what was going on. Then, when Victor suddenly presented him one day with a brand-new red Buick automobile, he truly didn't know what to think. So he just accepted the gift. Something was very odd about the generous offering . . . But, then again, there were quite a few strange things going on at this time.

"Over the years, I heard a lot of stories about Sara suggesting that if Howard ever dropped the ball, Victor would pick it up and continue to support the family," said a family friend. "Yet, despite such maneuverings, my mother showed me many photos of everyone at dinner tables seeming to get along just fine. They were able to coexist, and I think it was Sara who was really controlling everyone in her midst—not Howard, not Victor, and certainly not

Francis. No matter what these men thought, it was Sara who was running the show.

"For instance, there were discrepancies as to who was paying for Elizabeth's and Howard's private schooling in England. Elizabeth went to Byron House, Howard to Arnold House. It was thought that Victor Cazalet paid for their educations. However, Mabel would insist that it had been Howard who had done so, and whenever the subject came up it was sure to become a hot dispute. Sara just kept mum about it, though, saying it was a private matter. Actually, I later learned that she got money from *both* men for those educations and then let them each think he was responsible for the schooling. Who knows what she did with the additional money? That was the kind of woman she was, very savvy but also manipulative."

"My family was held hostage by those men," Francis Taylor told his friend Marshall Baldrige many years later. "There's not much I could do about it. They were bigger . . . and stronger, too."

Actually, as it happened, the entire Cazalet family, not just Victor, became attached to Sara. Victor's sister Thelma took Sara to the coronation of George VI. His mother, Maud, arranged for little Elizabeth to deliver a birthday gift to the Dowager Queen Mary at Buckingham Palace on the occasion of her sixty-ninth birthday. They also shared a belief in the Christian Science faith; Victor and Sara spent many hours studying the writings of the teachings' founder, Mary Baker Eddy. Since Francis wasn't interested in the philosophy at all, he was alienated from what would become an important influence in the lives of his children.

For instance, much has been made over the years, by Sara and then by MGM, of an ear infection Elizabeth had when she was about three, which Sara believed was cured by Christian Science precepts. In one interview, she described what happened when the young girl ran a fever of 103 degrees for three weeks. Her abscessed ears had to be lanced twice a day. Sara says that she stayed up nights with Elizabeth, pacing the floors and meditating for a healing. Finally, Sara says, Elizabeth was concerned that her mother wasn't getting any sleep and, in her delirium, suggested that Sara summon Victor Cazalet. Then, Sara recalled, "When he arrived, Victor sat on the bed and held her in his arms and talked to her about God. Her great dark eyes searched his face, drinking in every word, *believing* and *understanding* [her emphasis]. A wonderful sense of peace filled the room. I laid my head down on the side of the bed and went to sleep for the first time in three weeks. When I awakened, she was fast asleep. The fever had broken."

Who knows if this story is true? Likely, certain elements of it happened—Elizabeth probably did have an ear infection—but did the three-year-old actually suggest that Sara summon Victor so that her mother might get some sleep? The story says a lot, though, about the importance of Christian Science and Victor Cazalet in Sara's and Elizabeth's lives. In fact, from that point onward, Sara was even more devoted to the faith, and medicine would only be allowed in the household when Francis absolutely insisted upon it, and usually for his own care, not the children's. The tale also said a lot about Sara's vision of her daughter as being wise and thoughtful, even as a tot. And of course, it speaks to Sara's theatrical ways. She was an actress at heart, and always knew how to tell a good story. In years to come, her daughter would be influenced by Sara's dramatic nature: Certainly, no one could ever spin a better yarn than Elizabeth Taylor.

"Bravo!"

The Taylors enjoyed a very comfortable lot in life. But what good was comfort, Sara Taylor maintained, without a sense of accomplishment? Francis enjoyed his work at Howard's art gallery, even if he wasn't making enough money to support his family in the lifestyle to which they'd become accustomed. However, Sara did not have much in her own life to motivate and excite her. She certainly wasn't like many other women of her time, content with the usual path of the homemaker, soup and sandwiches at the ready for the little ones when they returned home from school for lunch.

Sara had style and grace to spare. A thin but shapely brunette, she shimmered when she entered a room. She had impeccable taste, scrutinizing every decorating detail of the homes in which she and her family would live—fabric, paint, wallpaper—making sure everything was of the highest quality. She was also the consummate party-giver. She loved and knew good food, though she herself was not much of a cook. (The family always had a chef or some other functionary to prepare meals.) Sara enjoyed hosting carefully choreographed evenings of dining and entertainment in the family home. She was meticulous in the planning of such events; tapers on the table were always burned for five minutes ahead of time so that the wicks would be black rather than waxy white. Every piece of flatware would be polished until it gleamed. Conversations at dinner were always spirited, about politics, the arts, music, and current events. At such gatherings, the Taylors would mix with celebrated figures such as Winston Churchill and Sir Anthony Eden. Sara and Francis thought of themselves as Anglophiles, both developing—or maybe affecting—subtle British accents. They also attended Royal Ascot, the major racing event at which smart fashion was the required dress: top hat and tails for the men, formal wear and hats for women. At one such function, Elizabeth and Sara wore matching blue silk and lace creations by Mainbocher, a famous American designer. Indeed, Sara was used to the best life had to offer, and she believed that she probably would have been a great theater star if she had continued to work at it. But despite her worldliness, she did crave a greater sense of purpose. Her interest in Elizabeth's future soon became the primary focus of her life.

By the time she was four, Elizabeth truly was lovely, her alabaster complexion offset by dark curls and luminescent blue eyes that, in a flattering light, seemed violet. Also, there was a certain vibrancy about her, an energy, a driving force. She wasn't like other children. She had something other tots didn't possess, a precociousness that wasn't cloying or irritating. She was smart, conversational . . . seeming like an old soul in the body of a small child. Her glowing youth and cameolike beauty were often the subject of attention. Just to help Mother Nature along, Sara would accentuate a mole on Elizabeth's cheek with an eyebrow pencil. "People would stop me in the streets," Sara had said, perhaps exaggerating just a bit, "and they would tell me, 'My God! That child should be in pictures. Why, she's the spitting image of Vivien Leigh!'"

Elizabeth was used to a privileged lifestyle; it was all she and her brother, Howard, knew. With their nursemaid and cook in tow, Sara and Francis would take the children on jaunts across the English countryside, spending weekends only in the expensive bed-and-breakfast establishments in Devon or Suffolk that would allow the presence of their golden retriever, Monty. Of course, the children were spoiled. They were used to attention, and expected it wherever they went. Indeed, both were beautiful and, as such, constantly lavished with compliments. However, they were also well-behaved and polite to all who encountered them. Sara would have it no other way.

In 1936, Sara overheard some cocktail chatter that Princesses Elizabeth and Margaret Rose—later Queen Elizabeth II and Princess Margaret—attended classes at the noted Vacani Dance School on Brompton Road, near the famous Harrods department store. The next day, she went about the business of enrolling four-year-old Elizabeth in the same school. Many years later, MGM would put forth the story that Elizabeth had attended classes with both royals. In fact, what actually happened was that when Elizabeth began ballet lessons at Vacani, Sara took a look around, only to find that none of the dozen or so students looked very royal.

When she questioned Madam Pauline Vacani, who had co-founded the school, she learned that, yes, Princesses Elizabeth and Margaret Rose did take classes—but the young ladies did not come to the school. Rather, the instructors went to them. That was a big disappointment. Still, Elizabeth supposedly continued at Vacani. Years later, someone—Sara?—told the MGM press department that Elizabeth had, indeed, taken her lessons with the young royals . . . and thus a legend was born.

At Vacani, Elizabeth was said to have taken to ballet quickly—giving flight to even more whimsy. As the story goes, she was selected from her class to be one of the many youngsters to participate in an annual charity recital. It was a memorable night because the Duchess of York (the future Queen Mother) brought her daughters, Elizabeth's "fellow students" Elizabeth and Margaret Rose, to the show. Thank goodness she had, because Sara and MGM would play up their royal presence to the hilt for decades to come. It probably really was a big night for Elizabeth and Sara. However, it was *not* the "Royal Command Performance" the public was later led to believe it was when Elizabeth became famous. Even Bosley Crowther, in his history of MGM, *The International Motion Picture Almanac*, wrote that "when three years old, Elizabeth danced before Princess Elizabeth and Princess Margaret Rose" as if she were the only one on that stage. Actually, there were dozens of youngsters flitting about the stage in little tutus, and Elizabeth and Margaret Rose just happened to be in the audience. The show was not presented in their honor. Later, MGM decided that Elizabeth had performed for the King—at a Royal Command Performance at the Hippodrome. Of course, no matter how many press releases they decided to distribute with that stunning revelation, the truth was that it never happened.

In her 1963 memoir, Elizabeth recalls that night and the applause washing over her after her dance, the acceptance of the crowd making her feel as though she were born to be on a stage. "It was a marvelous feeling," she wrote, "the isolation, the hugeness, the feeling of space and no end to space, the lights, the music—and then the applause bringing you back into focus, the noise rattling against your face." (Shades of Sara! That's quite a memory considering she was only four.)

In 1954, Sara also wrote about that night in a memoir for *McCall's*: "I knew then that there would come a time when she would want to follow in my footsteps. I could still hear the applause of that wonderful night years before when *The Fool* had opened in London at the Apollo Theatre and I, playing the part of the little crippled girl, had stood alone in the middle of the stage and had taken a dozen curtain calls, while a reputedly staid British audience called, 'Bravo! Bravo! Bravo!'"

Interestingly there are no existing records of Elizabeth ever having attended Vacani. A diligent private investigator could find no one still alive who worked there at the time, or whose relatives had anything to do with the school, who has any memory at all of Elizabeth, or of Sara. People connected to Vacani certainly don't deny that Elizabeth attended classes there, but her name could not be found on *any* program for *any* performance given at *any* time. Was the entire Vacani experience just the result of someone's imagination? Beatrice Edmonds's mother, Edna, attended Vacani in 1936 and, says Beatrice, had once held firm to her memory that Elizabeth was not a classmate. "However, by 1960, she had not only convinced herself that Elizabeth had been a classmate, she'd pretty much made up her mind that she, too, had been in the Royal Command Performance, standing right up there next to her," says Beatrice with a laugh. "It was just harmless fun . . . a way of having some peripheral connection to a major movie star. Look, if MGM could make up stories, I always said, then why not my mom?"

"*Missing a Father's Love*"

Where his children were concerned, Francis Taylor was rarely demonstrative; he seldom gave Elizabeth and Howard the kind of guidance and attention they would later say they had craved from him. Though they—and especially Elizabeth—had more than enough affection from Sara, with the passing of the years, they couldn't help but feel sad and disappointed that Francis had maintained a certain emotional distance. It wasn't that he didn't love his children. From what he would tell friends and relatives about them—and especially from the way he would boast about Elizabeth when she was on her way to stardom—he did care about them, and deeply.

There were actually very good reasons for Francis's apparent lack of affection toward his children, particularly Elizabeth, because he did spend more time with Howard. First of all, he was a man who simply didn't know how to show his feelings. He felt that overt demonstrations of love were embarrassing. However, a bigger problem had to do with Sara, who had become so absolutely territorial where Elizabeth was concerned that there was almost no way for Francis to have free access to her. Sara had taken Elizabeth for her own, coddling her and treating her like a prized possession. The dynamic between Francis and Sara was such that he really had no power over the situation. The years of being married to Sara—and of being overpowered by Howard Young and Victor Cazalet—had weakened his resolve. He didn't feel free to express himself because he knew he would be leveled by a criticism or a contradiction. Sara was a formidable woman, and Francis seldom viewed anything as being worth going up against her, even when it came to his own children. With the passing of time, he seemed to shut down emotionally. He'd also mastered the art of appearing to be paying attention when actually he wasn't listening to a word Sara—or even Howard or Victor—was saying to him. "Years of practice," he would say, only half joking.

It's been reported that Francis Taylor was an alcoholic, and even Elizabeth has suggested as much in interviews. Considering what was going on in his life, it's probably not surprising that he might seek relief in alcohol. At the time, though, his drinking wasn't given a label. If anything, he was a functioning alcoholic. (Because Mabel Young was also an alcoholic, the family knew a bit about the disease.)

"Though Francis was able to conduct business and day-to-day activities without interruption, he started drinking at noon and usually didn't stop until he went to bed," recalled Stefan Verkaufen, a young Viennese apprentice art dealer, just twenty at the time, who knew Francis well. "Sara was concerned about it and sometimes quite angry about it, as well. I remember being invited to their home for a dinner party, and Francis was not present when I arrived. She was pacing the floor angrily. He showed up two hours later, telling her that he was in a meeting. I knew Francis and I knew he had been drinking. How? Because that was the only time he truly seemed happy, when he'd had a few drinks. And he was smiling from ear to ear. Sara, however, was not. He later told me that he and Sara had often fought about the drinking. Still, Francis wasn't going to stop. He made that much clear. He couldn't manage much in his life, but the one thing he could control was how much he drank when Sara wasn't around to monitor it. Sara would just have to accept his habit, not easy for a woman who was used to always having her way."

Many Elizabeth Taylor biographers over the years have reported that Francis Taylor had homosexual leanings, and that the resultant inner turmoil was yet another explanation for his melancholy in life. Certainly, Sara and Howard would have made his life very difficult if they were ever to have learned such a secret—if, in fact, it was true.

Marshall Baldrige was a young blond and blue-eyed employee of Howard's at the art gallery in London. Their relationship was unusual in that Marshall was just a teenager in 1938 when he met Francis, who was forty-one, at the Victoria and Albert Museum in London. (The Victoria and Albert, which is housed in Aston Webb's grand building, is a museum of the decorative arts, founded in 1852 to support and encourage excellence in art and design.) Marshall, who is now in his mid-eighties, says that he and Francis were, for years, "inseparable," though he insists the relationship was strictly one of mentor and protégé. Baldrige hoped to one day open his own art gallery. Shortly after Francis met him, he offered the teenager an apprentice position at Howard's gallery, and he also told him that he had part ownership in the establishment (the veracity of which remains unclear).

Francis often complained to Marshall that he felt useless in the household, that he didn't believe Sara needed him. He feared that if he were to die, Sara would just go on without missing a step. Yes, she would have a period of mourning, he felt, but it would probably last a short time before she would continue with her life, with the help of Howard Young and Victor Cazalet.

"The Christian Scientist philosophy that Sara had adopted basically taught her not to dwell on her mistakes but to move past them quickly, and I think it caused even more of a barrier between her and Francis," says Baldrige. "Francis sometimes wanted to talk about their problems, but she felt that even talking about them gave them too much focus. She was not the type of woman to spend a lot of time reflecting on things. She would say that she was too busy for self-examination, always moving forward onto the next thing. So, in terms of communication, Francis didn't have much in his marriage. Eventually, he wasn't even interested in trying."

Baldrige vividly recalls a Saturday morning that began with an animated telephone call from Francis. He explained the he had asked Sara for a day alone with Elizabeth. Sara's hold over the family's seemingly most prized possession had been eating away at him for some time, not just challenging his already questionable place as head of the household, but creating a wedge between him and the child he longed to know. While Sara may have felt that Elizabeth's blossoming poise and charisma was mainly due to her tutelage, Francis believed that his daughter's gifts were, at least in part, a product of his bloodline too. In her, he saw the zest for life his mother had, the drive toward perfection that his father possessed. Though he rarely spoke of his theories regarding his daughter's powerful persona, at his most candid he would tell all who would listen, "She's my child first, really. She's a Taylor, inside and out." He wanted to spend more time with her. Much to his surprise, Sara granted him her charge for the day. "But her hair needs brushing hourly," she warned him, "and if she's touching her face too much, simply say her name very loudly. She'll know exactly what it means."

Marshall heard the excitement in Francis's voice when he rang. Francis said that he was apprehensive about being alone with six-year-old Elizabeth for an entire day, so he had decided that they would spend it shopping. He couldn't go wrong there, he reasoned. Then he planned to take her to the Theatre Museum, which houses the world's leading collection of material relating to the British stage. He asked Marshall to meet them afterward for lunch at the famous Harrods department store, and to bring along his younger sister who was about Elizabeth's age.

"When we got there, they were already seated and waiting for us," Baldrige recalled. "Elizabeth was such a pretty girl with long ribbons in her hair that matched her white dress. Francis was in his usual three-piece suit with a bow tie. He was very distinguished-looking, as always, but he also looked uncommonly tired. After we joined them, I watched them interact for an hour at the table. They seemed to adore each other. There was no strain between them. Still, I recall Francis nervously crushing out one cigarette after another, as if he was on edge. Elizabeth and my sister got on famously, talking about dance classes. Elizabeth was completely animated and, I thought, very mature and adult-seeming for such a young girl, quite the little conversationalist. She was very proper in her eating, the perfect young lady. I thought she would be much more reserved, from what Francis had told me about her. He had said she was very shy. I didn't think that of her at all.

"After the meal, we took the girls shopping. Elizabeth found a hat that she said she just had to have, a big white, floppy thing totally inappropriate for a little girl and much too big for her head. It was on sale for a couple of pounds. Francis said, 'I'll buy it for you as a treat,' and she said, 'No, Daddy, I have my own money.' She opened her purse and gathered a few pence that she had saved. He told her to keep her money, and bought her the hat. After he paid for it, he knelt down and placed it on her head. He gave a quick peck on the cheek. She then ran off with my sister to a full-length mirror. The two of them took turns trying on the hat and giggling at their reflections as they made funny poses."

As the girls played, Marshall asked Francis how he felt the day had thus far gone for him.

"This is both a happy and sad day for me," Francis answered, according to Marshall's memory. "Happy because I have a chance to spend some time with my daughter. Sad because I know this is a rare opportunity for me."

"Why do you say that?" Marshall asked.

"Because my dear wife won't let me near her," Francis answered, his expression now grim. He took a handkerchief out of his pocket and mopped the back of his neck as he often did when he was upset, an old habit. "She wants her all to herself. She dotes on her day and night. It infuriates me." He concluded that he might actually be able to have a wonderful, nurturing relationship with his only daughter, "if only I could steal her away from Sara for five minutes."

Marshall reminded Francis that Elizabeth was his daughter as well as Sara's. He warned him that he should endeavor to change the situation because, truly, Elizabeth would one day be the one to bear the consequences of it.

"It's no use," Francis said, the pessimism apparent in his voice. "Please don't think I haven't tried."

Suddenly, Elizabeth and Annabelle came running up to them.

"We want ice cream now," Elizabeth announced, grabbing her father's hand.

"Then ice cream we shall have," Francis told her.

And off the two happily went, with Marshall and his sister following close behind.

"I Think I Might Want to Be an Actress"

In the spring of 1939, the American embassy in London sent a disturbing notice to all citizens of the United States residing in Britain, warning them that a war was about to break out, that they were in imminent danger, and that they should return to America as soon as possible. It was not an easy decision for the Taylors to make. They had a good life in Britain. Should they stay there and hope for the best, or should they return to their native home? Marshall Baldrige recalls, "Francis did not want to go. He liked his life in England. But Sara had decided that the family should move to California. At the same time, Howard decided that the gallery should move to America. Once they decided as much, it was all over for Francis. 'I guess I have to go, but I want you to come with me,' he told me sadly. 'I need your support. Sara and Howard will completely destroy me in America.' I didn't want to leave London, my family, my sister, who I adored. 'My God, Francis, I just can't go,' I told him, 'but maybe one day I will meet you there.' He had tears in his eyes. I felt awful. I knew that I was throwing him to the wolves. My heart went out to him.

"A couple of weeks later, a customer of ours came into the

gallery and said that Sara had told her that Francis had received a personal telephone call from Joseph Kennedy, who was the American ambassador to the Court of St. James's and, of course, patriarch of the famous American Kennedy dynasty. She said that Kennedy had encouraged Francis to relocate his family as soon as possible. She said that this call had made the family realize that they had no choice but to move to the States, and she was so grateful that Kennedy would have taken the time to care about their fate. I was stunned by that bit of news. I couldn't believe that Francis hadn't mentioned it to me. 'What's this about?' I asked when I next saw him, 'Joe Kennedy calling you and telling you to move to the States?' He looked at me as if I was out of my mind. 'What are you talking about?' he asked me. 'I have never talked to Kennedy in my entire life.' When I told him what I had heard, he was exasperated. 'How Sara ever came up with that one, I'll never know,' he said. 'But that's a whopper, all right, isn't it?'"

On April 3, 1939—weeks after Hitler took over Czechoslovakia—Sara, Elizabeth, and little Howard (along with a nanny named Gladys) sailed to America aboard the SS *Manhattan*, but without Francis. He stayed behind to wrap up loose ends with the art business.

It was during that eight-day journey to the United States that a new Hollywood film called *The Little Princess* starring Shirley Temple was shown as part of the activities schedule for passengers. Sara took her children to see the movie in the cruise ship's theater. Elizabeth, seven years old now, hadn't seen many films in London and was excited to go to this one. It's a little startling, in retrospect, to note that *The Little Princess* was Shirley Temple's *fortieth* movie—and she was just eleven!

If any child ever had star quality on the screen, it was Shirley Temple. She is easily the most famous child star of all time. Elizabeth, as she has recalled it, sat in the dark theater in rapt silence, watching the young curly-haired star with awed fascination. She could sing, dance, act . . . she had an infectious personality. She truly was a wonder. *The Little Princess* was Shirley's first Technicolor film, which made it all the more exciting to watch. When the lights came up, a thoroughly impressed Elizabeth Taylor turned to her mother and said the words Sara had longed to hear: "Mummy," she whispered urgently, "I think I might want to be an *actress*. A movie star!"

A New Life in America

In April 1939, after arriving in New York, Sara Taylor, her children, and their nanny boarded a train to Pasadena, California, where her father lived. (Her mother had died about two years earlier.) Sara had loved Southern California when she worked in the theater there years earlier and, with her heart now set on some kind of career in show business for Elizabeth—though she didn't yet know what that would be exactly—she felt that settling near the entertainment capital of Hollywood made the most sense. The Taylor family showed up at the doorstep of Sara's father on May 1, 1939. For the next six months, Elizabeth and Howard were enrolled in the private Willard School outside of Pasadena.

In December of that same year, after closing his London gallery, Francis followed his family to America. Darryl Mitchell's father, Edward, was a dealer on Bond Street who knew Francis, though he had apparently never met Sara. "My dad always said that Francis had seriously considered not joining the family in the States. He had mulled over the possibility of staying in England with Marshall Baldrige's family," said Mitchell. "Francis told my dad that the marriage to Sara was troubled, and that once Sara was gone he was able to breathe freely.

"There was also a strange dynamic between Francis and Victor

Cazalet, a lot of confusion as to what Victor's role was, not only in Sara's life, but also in Francis's. He certainly appeared to be happier with Sara gone. However, Francis could not imagine leaving his children. He loved them too much. I often wondered, though, what impact the vague and unusual interpersonal relationships her parents had with Victor Cazalet had on Elizabeth and Howard.

"Anyway, Francis went to America, but only for the children. Also, at this time, Howard gave him the gallery business to operate as his own. So finally Francis owned the gallery business, and that gave him some incentive to start a new life in America."

Marshall Baldrige continues the story: "Once his mind was made up, Francis was determined to make a go of it in America with an exclusive offering of paintings by the artist Augustus John. I know Elizabeth would say in later interviews that he had to start all over again with just a couple of paintings, but in fact we packed about seventy of the John oils in crates and sent them ahead to the States, using the transport firm of Pitt & Scott. The intention was that he would open a gallery at the Chateau Elysee in Hollywood, which he did [in 1940]. He also had one very expensive painting, a Frans Hals, which he took with him to America and which the family, and later Elizabeth, would own as part of their collection."

If anyone thought Sara Taylor would have been happy living on her father's chicken ranch in Pasadena for very long, that person would have been daft, or so says Stefan Verkaufen. "In fact, as soon as Francis arrived, the family settled in Pacific Palisades, California, in an expansive home leased for them by . . . who else? Howard Young, of course," he recalls. "A year later [in 1941], Howard bought the family a home in Beverly Hills, a Mediterranean-style estate at 703 North Elm Drive. It was then that I received an excited telephone call from Francis telling me that he had relocated his art gallery to the nearby Beverly Hills Hotel on Sunset Boulevard. It was a prime location, one of the most famous hotels and a virtual crossroads of the world with potential clients from all over the globe. He was very excited. 'It's mine now,' he told me of the gallery, 'and, finally, I have something that belongs to me, and that no one can ever take from me. Not Howard. Not Victor. And not Sara.' He also said that he and Sara were getting along better, and that he was happy to see her again. I wasn't sure whether to believe him or not."

Sara had always had vision, brilliance, and enthusiasm like few others. That didn't change once her family was ensconced in Beverly Hills. She immediately enrolled Elizabeth in singing and dancing lessons after her school day at the Hawthorn Elementary School. Elizabeth's riding lessons also continued, and thus she would have something in common with the affluent children Sara had envisioned as her friends. Howard, for his part, was clearly not interested in show business and seemed better at sports. That was fine with Sara. As long as Elizabeth had the motivation, she was eager to promote it. At this time, she also enrolled both of her children in Christian Science studies.

Sara also arranged an important "audition" of sorts for Elizabeth with Hedda Hopper. At the time, Hedda, along with Louella Parsons, was one of the leading gossip columnists in show business, renowned almost as much for her outrageous headwear as for her scoops. A mere mention in her column for a young hopeful entertainer all but guaranteed that studio heads and recording company executives would take notice. When Francis came home one day in the fall of 1940 with the news that Hedda had come into his gallery—at the behest of Victor Cazalet, a friend of Hopper's ex-husband—to purchase an Augustus John, Sara was thrilled. She probably couldn't contain herself when Francis then presented her with the columnist's telephone number. (Smart man! Imagine the scene if he had neglected to get her number!) And so, faster than Sara could say, "Make my daughter a star!" she had arranged a meeting between her eight-year-old daughter and the fifty-year-old showbiz journalist and socialite—at Hedda's home, no less! Unfortunately, it did not go well.

Hedda was unsettled, as she would recount many times in subsequent years, by the manner in which Sara, whom she described as "bursting with ambition," insisted that Elizabeth stand in the middle of her drawing room and sing. The young girl, her face clouded with worry and tears about to fall from her eyes, sang a sweet song—"Blue Danube"—in a weak and thin tone. As she sang, she nervously fingered her hair and stared into space, careful not to make eye contact with Hedda or even her mother. After her "performance," Hedda felt she had no choice but to applaud and act as if the heavens had opened up and dropped the sweetest little angel this side of Deanna Durbin. In truth, she found it all a bit disconcerting. "It was one of the most painful ordeals I have ever witnessed," she later recalled in her autobiography. She said that Elizabeth was "clearly terrified, but I felt that the mother was never going to rest until this child was famous, and I wasn't having any of it. She wanted to have a glamorous life through her child. I had seen too much misery in child stars. Let a child be a child, that was my motto. And I told Sara Taylor just that: 'Let a child be a child.'"

Be that as it may, Hedda Hopper was gracious enough to give Sara and Elizabeth a mention in her column. She took credit for discovering, as she put it, "a new find—eight-year-old Elizabeth Taylor, whose mother was Sara Sothern, the lame girl in the play, *The Fool*, and whose father, Francis Taylor, has just opened an exhibition of paintings by Augustus John in the Beverly Hills Hotel."

"But I Want to Be with MGM!"

As weeks turned into months, Sara Taylor continued her show business networking in Hollywood, hoping to meet someone in some social situation who might actually be able to assist her in her quest to make her daughter a star . . . at something. Elizabeth and Howard continued to attend school, while Elizabeth maintained a schedule of singing and dancing lessons. Both children also continued their Christian Science studies: No audition would ever take place for Elizabeth until she and her mother had prayed for a positive outcome to it.

Sara also continued as the consummate dinner-party and cocktail-hour hostess. Because people gravitated toward her anyway, it wasn't difficult for her to find her place in Beverly Hills high society, and even assist Francis in securing affluent new clients for his art gallery. To inspire conversations about Elizabeth's beauty, Sara had photos of her daughter taped to the refrigerator in the kitchen, next to pictures of Vivien Leigh. The idea was that, hopefully, guests would remark on the similarities in their features. "Oh, Elizabeth put those photos up there," she would lie. "But do you really think so?" she would ask. "You know, you might be right about that. I never really noticed."

Coincidentally, it happened to be at Francis's place of business that Sara met Andrea Cowden, wife of J. Cheever Cowden, at that time chairman of Universal Pictures. Cowden had come into the Howard Young Gallery to examine the Augustus John paintings she'd heard that Francis had on exhibit there. Sara and Andrea hit it off immediately—especially after Andrea wrote out a check for $20,000 for a few John paintings and sketches. A week later, Andrea attended a formal exhibition of the artist's paintings at the gallery. She mentioned in passing that she had once actually posed for Augustus John (in London, from which she hailed), and both Taylors were impressed by the revelation. It was at that time that Sara invited the Cowdens to the Taylor home for tea. Of course, she had an ulterior motive: She wanted the Cowdens' assistance with Elizabeth.

The afternoon tea party—in February 1941, just before Elizabeth's ninth birthday—was a great success. Sara had the cook prepare filet of beef Wellington with potatoes and caviar, which, even though it was presented after tea, seemed a lot more like dinner than lunch. It was impressive, just the same. For dessert, there was raspberry parfait with coffee.

Afterward, Francis offered a discount on another Augustus John painting for which Andrea Cowden had expressed great admiration. Sara then told J. Cheever how much she believed in her daughter and how much time and energy she had devoted to seeing her become a success in show business. He was impressed; Sara was difficult to resist. Then, she brought out her precocious daughter, Elizabeth. Many years later, Andrea Cowden would recall, "She was the most beautiful child I had ever seen. She did not walk, she danced. She was so merry, so full of love for every little thing, whether it was a person, an animal, or a flower. She had a lovely singing voice, too. At that time, you didn't know what she'd be, but you knew she'd be something." Be reminded: People's memories do seem to take on a nostalgic glow when it comes to the young Elizabeth Taylor. It's a bit difficult to believe that Andrea Cowden would have been able to glean so much about the youngster after just one tea party. Suffice it to say, though, that she and her husband were impressed enough; J. Cheever offered to sign Elizabeth to a contract at Universal. One can only imagine Sara's elation after the Cowdens left the Taylor home that day!

The deal was signed on April 21, 1941: a hundred dollars a week for five months, the money to go to Sara—not Francis, incidentally—on Elizabeth's behalf. Ten percent of that amount went directly to Sara, as Elizabeth's "manager," or, as the contract read, "to assist in the performance of such services as shall be required by the studio." The contract could be renewed with the agreement of both parties. Sara would be absolutely diligent in depositing Elizabeth's balance in an account for her, and it's fair to say that her husband had virtually nothing to do with any of this business.

There was one big surprise in this scenario, upon which no one had counted. Suddenly, little Elizabeth had an opinion, and who would have imagined that to be the case since she had been so agreeable up until this time? However, it was just a matter of time before her mother's example was bound to influence her and encourage her to at least hint at a decisive nature. When told about the deal with Universal, she dug in her heels and said, "But *I* want to be with MGM!"

Elizabeth's interest in MGM had come after a chance encounter a couple of months earlier. She had a playmate whose father, John W. Considine Jr., just happened to be a producer at Metro-Goldwyn-Mayer Studios. When Sara found out, she sprang into action and invited him and his wife, Carmen, to the requisite meal at the Taylor home. After dinner and drinks and no small amount of persuasion from Sara, John finally agreed to take the entire family on a tour of the MGM lot. It was an exciting morning when the Taylors, Elizabeth with her dark hair bound in pink and white ribbons, showed up at MGM. She was enthralled by the actors and actresses she met, most of them in colorful, whimsical costumes. The bright lights and imposing cameras, the elaborate sets . . . it all seemed like some kind of miniature fantasy world, and before she knew it she wanted to be a part of it. "Everyone looked so happy and seemed to be enjoying themselves," she would later remember. "The child actors ran about playing tag. It was like a little playground, but somehow so much more exciting because, well, it was the *movies*. It was noisy and bustling and chaotic and . . . thrilling. Oh, yes, I was hooked. And my mother? Her eyes were darting about even more than mine." As for her father, Elizabeth recalls his walking about with his hands thrust in his coat pockets and an expression on his face that suggested a certain amount of bemusement, not so much at what he was seeing but at his wife's and daughter's reaction to it. Elizabeth said he didn't share their enthusiasm for the magical world of picture-making, "but we didn't expect that he would. But Howard had fun," she added.

Amazingly—and if anyone ever doubted the Taylors' good fortune, all they needed to hear was this story from Sara, and she told it every chance she got—who should walk onto one of the sets being visited by the family but the head of the studio himself, the fearsome and legendary L. B. Mayer. Momentarily humbled by his presence, Sara soon recovered her senses and took command of the situation. She was about to suggest that Elizabeth sing for him, when he beat her to it. "I want to hear this little girl sing," he decided. So sing she did—"Blue Danube" in a high-pitched voice—and . . . well, she was not very good. No matter how you packaged it—a pretty dress, deep blue eyes, luxurious black hair, and loads of enthusiasm—the fact of the matter was that the young Elizabeth Taylor was not a singer. Still, she gave it her all, and Mayer must have been at least a little impressed because he turned to Considine and said, "Sign her up!" Everyone was elated. However, in the weeks to come, the Taylors were taught their first tough lesson about show business: Nothing is a done deal until it's a done deal.

After that day, John W. Considine suddenly became difficult to reach. The MGM contract was not forthcoming. Could it be that Mayer had told Considine to sign Elizabeth just to avoid an embarrassing moment? His words—"Sign her up"—rang in Sara's ears for weeks. She couldn't fathom what might have occurred to change his mind. When Mayer then refused to take her telephone calls, she went from sad and confused to indignant and angry, and then she abruptly pushed L. B. Mayer and his MGM Studios out of her mind altogether. She wasn't one to dwell on an empty promise and had already, in her view, spent far too much time lamenting one. "Oh, the heck with him," she told Elizabeth. "He doesn't know what he's missing. One day *he* will come to *us*. And then, we shall see what we shall see." True to her determined nature, Sara was then off on her next mission—the next important contact for whom she would plan the next big meal. To all outward appearances, Elizabeth, too, never gave MGM another thought—until she was presented with the opportunity to sign with Universal, and so it was a bolt from the blue when she announced her desire to be with MGM. It shouldn't have been a surprise, though, since Elizabeth had actually *seen* MGM and didn't really know much, if anything, about Universal. However, it didn't much matter what Elizabeth wanted in this regard. She was nine. She'd get over it.

By the end of the summer of 1941, Elizabeth Taylor was on a soundstage at Universal Studios making her first "short" film, a forgettable, sixty-minute trifle first called *Man or Mouse* but soon renamed *There's One Born Every Minute*. It would be released in the summer of the following year. In it, Elizabeth would portray a misbehaving little brat. Years later, on *The David Frost Show*, she would describe the role as "a beastly child who runs around slinging rubber bands at fat ladies' bottoms." Though not much of a screen debut, it was probably as good as any place to begin a storied film career. But then, in what must have seemed like a cruel plot twist to her real life, Elizabeth was dropped by Universal two weeks after she finished the film. The upper-level executives simply didn't find her that special, and they thought her brief performance was adequate but certainly didn't qualify as one that suggested a new star in the making. "The kid has nothing," noted Universal's casting director, Dan Kelly, in an oft-quoted memo. "Her eyes are too old. She doesn't have the face of a kid."

Everyone in the Taylor household was disappointed by the surprising turn of events; even Francis and Howard acted as if they were dismayed by the news. Elizabeth could see through her father's disappointment, though. When asked by one of her Hawthorn schoolteachers at this time what she had planned for her future, the ten-year-old prodigy remarked, "My father is very much against my being an actress." However, as everyone well understood, it didn't much matter what Francis thought, for it was Sara who was in charge of things. She and Elizabeth had now been given a taste of the movie business, and it was all they needed to whet their appetites for more. For all of their efforts thus far, Elizabeth had $1,800 in the bank, Sara $200. It was a start. They didn't need the money anyway. At night, Sara would pull out her dog-eared script from *The Fool* and have Elizabeth act out the part of the crippled girl, which she had played on Broadway. Mother would rehearse daughter repeatedly in the role. It had to be perfect; nothing else would do. Every night, Sara worked with Elizabeth assiduously, forcing her to stay awake when she was exhausted so she could rehearse the script . . . over and over. Finally, Elizabeth began to cry on cue for the scene in which such emotion was required. Sara was well pleased. One wonders, though, if those tears might not have been generated more by the young girl's sheer exasperation with her mother than by her ability to make believable her acting.

A year went by, during which time, in 1943, the Taylors received the horrifying news that Victor Cazalet, a major in the British army by this time, had been killed in a plane crash in the harbor of Gilbraltar. Of course, all of the Taylors were devastated. Sara and Francis did not attend the funeral due to safety concerns during wartime, but it would be many months before either of them would be able to reconcile their close friend's sudden and tragic passing. To this day, Elizabeth remains very friendly with extended members of the Cazalet family. "My biggest regret," she would say many years after his death, "is that Victor never had a chance to see my success. Oh, how he would have smiled at it." Actually, Victor Cazalet did know that Elizabeth had been signed to Universal. He was thrilled with the news when Sara called to deliver it before the contract was even signed. "Imagine excitement of Taylors," he wrote in his diary on April 16, 1941. "Elizabeth has contract for seven years from big Cinema group." (Note that Victor had apparently been told by Sara that the contract was for seven years, when actually it was for six months. But, alas, that was Sara's way.)

It would be in the same year as Cazalet's death, 1943, that Elizabeth would get her next big break. Her mother would later recall, "She sang and danced and begged Daddy and me to please, please, *please* sign a contract with MGM." That's not exactly how it happened, though Metro-Goldwyn-Mayer staff producer Sam Marx recalled the story in a 1975 interview he did with Peter Lawford for a documentary about Elizabeth:

"I was an air raid warden in, of all places, Beverly Hills. At this point in the story, people generally break up laughing, and I don't blame them. We were pretty far from the action, you know? One of the other air raid wardens in the unit was Francis Taylor. In addition to being an air raid warden, I was also a producer at MGM. He knew it and he began talking to me about his beautiful daughter. I was starting a film called *Lassie Come Home*. In it was a charming little girl named Marie Flynn [who had appeared with Ingrid Bergman in *Intermezzo: A Love Story*], and for that reason I had no need for any other girl. So, I wasn't being very nice to Francis in putting him off. Then, when the first rushes came in, I found that the girl was a head taller than Roddy McDowall. In those days you couldn't have the girl be taller than the boy, you just couldn't do it. So, unfortunately for her, we had to take her out of the part. MGM had just made a film [in which] there were seven charming little girls. The casting office agreed to get them to my office at five o'clock. And then I remembered Francis Taylor. I called him at his gallery and told him what was going on. He reported that his daughter was in Pasadena with her mother [visiting Sara's father], and possibly would get to the studio, but he wasn't sure. At five o'clock, the casting director ushered in the six girls, all English with their mothers and schoolteachers to watch them, and the whole crowd gathered in my office. I started looking them over to see who we would get to fill this part when my secretary called from outside and said there was another girl who had just arrived. Elizabeth, with her mother. She walked in and was wearing—I still recall—a blue velvet cape. Her blue eyes, the dark hair, the cape, it was like an eclipse of the sun, blotting out everybody who was in the office. This gorgeous, beautiful young girl. We never even tested her. We never even *thought* to make a test." Elizabeth had won the role.

It would be on the set of this film that Elizabeth would meet one of her lifelong friends, Roddy McDowall, who was the thirteen-year-old star of the movie. "On her first day of filming, I recall, they took one look at her and said, get that girl off the set. She has too much eye makeup on, too much mascara," Roddy once recalled. "So they rushed her off the set and started rubbing at her eyes with a moist cloth to take the mascara off. Guess what? They learned then that she had no mascara on. She has a double set of eyelashes. Now, who has double eyelashes except a girl who was absolutely born to be on the big screen? And the wonderful thing about Elizabeth was that she was so totally unaware of her beauty. At a place, MGM, that was full of gorgeous women, she did stand out as a young girl. She was the most beautiful child I had ever seen."

Renowned for its movie-star glamour queens, such as Joan Crawford and Greta Garbo, prior to Elizabeth's arrival, and Judy Garland, Katharine Hepburn, and Lana Turner during the time of Elizabeth's signing, MGM was the most powerful and influential of all the film studios at the time. Under the rule of the legendary Louis B. Mayer, the Culver City, California, studio pretty much invented the so-called "star system" whereby its contract players were turned into movie stars by having their entire lives taken over by MGM. They were told how to act, not only onstage but off it as well, and harshly penalized if they misbehaved. An indiscretion could result in the artist being fined, put on suspension, or, worse, having his or her contract canceled altogether. For years, Mayer ruled with an iron fist, manipulating the professional and private lives of everyone who signed on with MGM, pulling strings as if the actors and actresses were mere puppets under his control. He was as feared as he was loved. The actresses were called Metro Girls, and as such they weren't allowed to smoke, drink, swear, or have sex before marriage. There was no bending of those rules, and as far as Sara was concerned, nothing wrong with them, either. For now, though, her daughter was just a ten-year-old making a *Lassie* movie. "I had a great imagination," Elizabeth recalls, "and just slid into being an actress. It was a piece of cake." She only had four scenes in the movie—less than ten minutes of screen time. When it was released, she was pretty much ignored by the critics. Still, on the strength of that one film appearance, MGM signed her to a seven-year contract, starting at $300 a week.

As if to reaffirm the correctness of their decision regarding Elizabeth's talent, MGM then loaned her to 20th Century-Fox for one film, *Jane Eyre*. She received no credit and was only seen in the film for less than three minutes as a friend of Jane's—but they were three minutes that revealed the undeniable power of her screen presence. There was something about Elizabeth's brief performance in *Jane Eyre* that exhibited the inexpressible onscreen magic that would be Elizabeth Taylor's for the rest of her career. In the movie, young Elizabeth even had a death scene that was so poignant and real, it is worth repeated viewings. A staggering amount of wisdom was apparent in her acting, far exceeding her years. Suddenly, for no good reason other than just maybe fate and providence and luck, she now seemed to be an actress. She had no formal training other than her mother's tutoring, yet, she . . . was . . . an actress. She would also appear ever so briefly as a shy country girl in another soap-opera movie, *White Cliffs of Dover*, again with Roddy McDowall, who in the film grows up to be Peter Lawford. She said "hello" in one scene and "good-bye" in another, and that was pretty much it. Still, she and Sara were not disheartened in the least. It was one of the year's most popular films.

As Elizabeth started making headway in the film business, her father became more disenchanted by the prospects. Marshall Baldrige remembers, "If I recall, he started drinking even more when he got to America and Elizabeth began to take off as an actress. At that time, if it were left to him, he would just as soon she do something more practical with her life than be an actress. A 'real' career of some kind would have met with his approval after she had entered adulthood, but he would also have been just as satisfied if she decided to marry, have children, and be a home-maker. He wasn't at all devoted to her blossoming career in movies, and had a sense—and a foreshadowing one, as it would happen—that she was growing up too fast. He didn't want her to completely miss out on her childhood, and he suspected that she'd already lost a good portion of it to Sara's ambition. He told me one story I'll never forget, which happened during a night when, I guess, he'd been drinking."

"Is it really worth it," Francis asked Sara one night at the dinner table, according to what he later recalled to Baldrige, "all the years you and Elizabeth have invested in this endeavor?"

Sara, as usual, tried to ignore her husband's cynicism.

Francis continued by observing that if one were to add up all of Elizabeth's time on the screen in the three movies she'd thus far made, it would probably amount to less than fifteen scant minutes. He was being completely dismissive of the progress Sara had thus far made with Elizabeth and her film career. Sara probably couldn't believe her husband's lack of insight. "Daddy, I thank you for your support," she said, glaring at him. "I thank you for your kindness. And I thank you for minding your own business." She then rose and left the table.

"You're giving our child away, you know?" he called after her.

Sara returned to the dining room. "*Elizabeth.*" That's the only word she spoke, yet her daughter knew exactly what it meant. The little girl stood and obediently followed her mother out of the room, leaving Francis and Howard to their dinner. Father and son would spend many nights in the future just that way—sharing their meals together while the ladies of the house planned for the future.

Under the circumstances, it was not surprising that Francis Taylor would not have a positive reaction to *Jane Eyre*. Exiting a private screening room following a preview of the film, he is said to have walked right past the outstretched hands of studio executives, leaving his wife and daughter to accept all of the glory.

National Velvet

*N*ational *Velvet* was one of thirty pictures released by MGM in 1944. It was one of only four films given the Technicolor treatment, evidence of its prestige and the importance of the production to the studio. Its road to the Culver City back lot was circuitous, to say the least. In 1935, Pandro S. Berman, as RKO's production chief, had tried to buy the book for Katharine Hepburn, twenty-eight years old at the time. He apparently didn't move quickly enough and the film rights were acquired by Paramount. But they couldn't cast it, and sold it to Metro in 1937. Nothing happened with it until Berman, no longer at RKO, arrived at MGM in 1941. He became obsessed with bringing the beloved best-selling novel to the screen. Pre-production would take almost two years, and with a beautifully written script and a cast that included Andy Hardy himself, Mickey Rooney, one of the studio's most important stars, the only thing remaining was the casting of the film's central character, Velvet Brown. If Berman was unsure as to who would portray the twelve-year-old girl who disguises herself as a fifteen-year-old boy in order to ride in the Grand National Steeplechase, there were at least two people on the lot—Sara and Elizabeth—who were absolutely sure of who would play that part: Elizabeth Taylor

Elizabeth had always loved horses, and had ridden before she came to the United States from England. She was about three when she first mounted the horse named Betty, given to her by Victor Cazalet. She was, she recalls, wearing a "little organdy dress." The horse threw her off, and she landed in a thorny bush. True to her nature, she got right back on and little time elapsed before she became quite skilled as a rider. She felt that being on a horse, riding bareback, provided her greatest and only sense of freedom from the studios, from her school studies, from her work in films, and even from her mother who often had business on her mind. No one could tell her what to do when she was on a horse galloping away from her responsibilities.

Looking back on *National Velvet* today, Elizabeth believes she got the role in that movie by "sheer willpower." She could be right about that. She'd read Enid Bagnold's book and decided in her young and fertile mind that she wanted to star in the movie version as the fabled Velvet Brown. She and her mother then went to MGM and talked to anyone they could find who was even remotely involved in the project, spreading the word that Elizabeth would be perfect in the role. Finally, they found their way into Pandro S. Berman's office, the producer of the film, and gave him the pitch. Elizabeth said that she totally identified with the main character—an ambitious young girl who dreams of entering her horse in the Grand National and disguises herself as a boy in order to ride. She was an actress . . . she had the appropriate English accent . . . she could ride horses . . . what else did he need? The problem, as told over the years, was that Elizabeth was too slight in build to pull off the notion that she could masquerade as a boy. She was just a little girl, after all, and she looked like one. Berman just felt that it wouldn't work out for her. But "I am going to play that part," the youngster said with steely determination.

It's been famously reported over the years that Elizabeth actually "willed" herself to grow three inches for the part. Elizabeth still believes this is true. Of course, it's not the case, but it did make for some fun reading back when MGM was promoting the film. In fact, she pretty much ate her way to an additional weight that actually made her look bigger, but not necessarily taller. She recalled, "There was this place called Tips, where they had a thing called a Farm Breakfast—two hamburger patties, two fried eggs, a great big mound of hash-brown potatoes and after that a whole bunch of silver-dollar pancakes. I used to have two Farm Breakfasts every morning at one sitting. For lunch, I'd have steaks and salads, then swim and do exercises to stretch myself." All of the foregoing is probably true. But a ten-year-old child growing an inch a month for three months by stretching herself and eating an abundance of carbohydrates would have been somewhat of a medical miracle. Still, Elizabeth continued: "In three months, I'd grown three inches. That single-mindedness, or stubbornness if you will, is as much a part of me as the color of my eyes."

By the time the film was in production, nothing was more important to Elizabeth and her mother than *National Velvet*. In it she would appear opposite Mickey Rooney, who played the role of the young wanderer who appears at the Brown home one day and winds up training the Pie for the Grand National Steeplechase. They knew that it was the movie that could make Elizabeth a star, and they were right about it. She really was a natural. She has recalled, "The first time I ever had to cry [on film] was in *National Velvet*. The horse was supposed to have colic, and of course he was Velvet's life. When the character Mickey played said he didn't think the horse would live, Velvet cries. I knew the scene and it hadn't worried me in the slightest. Anyway, when we rehearsed the scene, Mickey put his arm around me and said, 'Honey, you know in this scene you have to cry.' And I said, 'Yes, Mickey, I know.' 'Well,' he said, 'you should think that your father is dying and your mother has to wash clothes for a living and your little brother is out selling newspapers on the street and he doesn't have shoes and he's cold and shivering, and your little dog was run over.' It was meant to make me cry. Instead, I started to laugh. I didn't have the heart to say anything to him. The more I tried, the more I could not stop the giggles. When I did the scene, instead of imagining my father drunk and dying and my mother doing the laundry in a snowy stream, all I thought about was the horse being very sick . . . and the tears just came. But how generous of Mickey to try to help me." (Of course, Elizabeth is entitled to her own memory about her first screen cry, but the truth is, she was called upon to cry in both *Jane Eyre* and *Lassie Come Home.*)

Another humorous story Elizabeth enjoys telling has to do with her hairstyle in the film. The director, Clarence Brown, felt that when the time came in the script for Velvet to cut her hair in order to look like a jockey, the only way to achieve realism would be for Elizabeth to actually shear off her own hair. Not in a million years was Elizabeth Taylor going to cut those flowing locks, and she told Brown as much. (And she had good reason: The year before in *Jane Eyre*, playing a foundling in an orphans' home, she had to endure a devastating haircut by Henry Daniell, who portrayed the home's merciless headmaster.) Back and forth they went, director and star, with, of course, Taylor's mother siding with her. Finally, Elizabeth and Sara went to Sydney Guilaroff— who would become famous as the MGM hairstylist—and asked for his advice. Guilaroff saved the day by constructing two wigs for her—one that matched her own hair and that Mickey Rooney would be shown whacking at with scissors in the film, and another, a boy-bob, that she would wear over her own unshorn tresses as the jockey who rides the Pie to victory. She went back to Brown wearing the bobbed wig, and of course he said, "You see, I told you that you had to cut your hair in order for this to work." It was a sweet moment for Elizabeth when, the crucial scene shot and in the can, she was able to pull that wig off.

Rescreening the newly released DVD of *National Velvet* today, it is as irresistible as when it was made more than sixty years ago. There is nothing dated about the film, nor one false note in Elizabeth's performance. Its popularity has endured, and in 2003 it was selected by the Library of Congress for its permanent film collection. Watching it, one is struck not only by the timelessness of the story, but also by its parallels to the life experiences of Elizabeth and her mother: Dreams can become reality despite the intervention of fate—or perhaps because of it. As a young girl,

Velvet's mother—played by the wonderful Anne Revere—dreamed of swimming the English Channel. Nothing or no one could dissuade her. She swam the cold and choppy Channel in a competition—and won! Mrs. Brown never spent the prize money of 100 sovereigns, keeping the gold coins in a leather pouch in a trunk in the attic. Now it is Velvet's time to dream—of entering the Pie in the Grand National. She has no doubt that she will win. The entrance fee would be paid by Mrs. Brown's secret treasure, which she turns over to a breathless Velvet in a powerfully emotional scene. "Everyone should have a chance at a breathtaking piece of folly at least once in his life," she says.

Dark-haired, willowy, and ineffably graceful on and off her four-legged costar, young Elizabeth beautifully acquitted herself in this, her first major film. As twelve-year-old Velvet, she seems like an old soul, but when she runs about the seaside Sussex pastureland (actually Pebble Beach in Northern California) chasing after the Pie dressed in her middie-blouse and pleated skirt or riding the handsome gelding sans saddle, jumping the stone fences at full gallop, she is the very embodiment of the child that Enid Bagnold must have envisioned as Velvet Brown. Though she was still a few years away from the kind of fully ripened femme fatale that ancient nations went to war over, the movie's called-for hair bob and racing silks were unable to fully transform her into a jockey-boy. With her oh so delicate features, including her heliotrope eyes and the apple pinkness of her cheeks, plus the simple sweetness of her disposition, she just could not erase the line separating little boys from little girls.

Unfortunately, it was because of her work on *National Velvet* that Elizabeth would be doomed to spend the rest of her life dealing with torturous pain in her spine. She took a fall from her horse during the filming of the movie. It was, actually, a scripted fall. Most theatergoers assumed that the studio had used a stunt double for Elizabeth when Velvet Brown took that spill. However, it truly *was* Elizabeth. She hit the turf on her back and actually bounced off it. Unfortunately, the damage done to her back during the tumble would be the catalyst for a myriad of very serious spinal problems that would plague her for the rest of her days.

National Velvet was released in New York City on December 14, 1944, in order to qualify for the Academy Awards of that year. It was issued nationally on January 26 the following year and was an immediate hit, grossing over $4.25 million, equal to about a third of all the money brought in by the remaining twenty-nine MGM releases in 1944. The film's reviews and Elizabeth's personal notices were glowing. "[She imbued] the character with such a burning, tempered with a sweet, fragile charm, that not even a splendidly restrained Mickey Rooney could steal scenes from her," enthused the *New York World-Telegram & Sun*. At Academy Award time, the film copped two of the three statuettes for which it was nominated, including a Best Supporting Actress Oscar for Anne Revere, as the wise prophetess/ Brown family matriarch. Director Clarence Brown received the fourth of five nominations he would eventually get as Best Director, but he would go winless every time. MGM rewarded Elizabeth with a lucrative long-term contract, establishing her as one of its top child actresses, along with the younger Margaret O'Brien. Elizabeth now wryly says that if she had known that she would have to sign a contract with MGM, she might not have grown the necessary three inches for the film. "I had no idea what I was getting myself into," she says. "Slavery!"

Legend has it that L. B. Mayer was so excited about his success with her that he even gave her the horse she rode in the film as a gift for her thirteenth birthday. In truth, she had demanded it, and made it clear that she would not rest until it was hers. A theme of her life had begun: What Elizabeth wants, Elizabeth gets. Pandro Berman told Brenda Maddox, who wrote one of the best Taylor biographies ever published (*Who's Afraid of Elizabeth Taylor?*), "All the while we were making the picture, this kid is pestering me to give her the horse. 'Can I have the horse? Can I have the horse?' I couldn't give it to her. It wasn't my horse. It was L. B. Mayer's horse. So I asked Mayer and he said, okay, let her have the horse.

Now fade out and fade into 1959 when we're doing *Butterfield 8* and she is now Elizabeth, the cold-eyed dame. She says to me, 'Aren't you the guy who gave me the horse after *National Velvet?*' And I say, 'Yes, I'm afraid that I am.' And she says to me, 'You son of a bitch. I'm still paying for feed for that goddamned horse.'" (Berman was not a big fan of Taylor's, and the reasons for his ill feelings about her will become clear later. Plus, it should also be noted that she may have been joking; not everyone gets her biting humor.)

Throughout the history of the film business, people have tried to describe and categorize and duplicate that indescribable quality, that certain something that is the stuff of screen legends, and Elizabeth Taylor certainly has it in *National Velvet*. Sara saw it on the screen when she went to see the movie, and as she would recall, she couldn't help but cry at her daughter's performance. Racked with sobs in the darkened theater, it was clear that she felt an emotion not simply born of the impact of her daughter's acting ability. Her almost mournful reaction to that now historic movie might be likened to a bride's mother—happy that her daughter had found love, someone with whom she would spend the rest of her life, but with full knowledge that the bond they once shared was being replaced by a new, more powerful connection. Elizabeth Taylor was hers no longer. She belonged to Hollywood. She belonged to the world.

Making a Star . . . a Star!

By the age of thirteen, Elizabeth Taylor had become a major movie star thanks to *National Velvet*, earning a salary of $300 a week—not much today, but at the time a reasonable amount to pay a child actress. In what may have seemed like a nice gesture from the studio, Sara, now forty-nine, continued on the payroll, earning about 10 percent of that amount a year as her daughter's chaperone and, really, only acting teacher. If in the films Elizabeth would make in the years to come she wasn't delivering her lines with conviction, Sara, standing on the sidelines, would put her hand on her heart to signal more emotion. If Elizabeth seemed tired during a scene, Sara would smile broadly at her, baring her teeth to indicate a more upbeat demeanor. If she forgot her lines, Sara would tap her head to suggest that Elizabeth needed to concentrate. She also constantly tried to coach Elizabeth to lower the timbre of her speaking voice, but was unsuccessful in that regard.

If Sara had proceeded with such tactics in a good-natured way, it may have been easier for Elizabeth to digest her ideas and incorporate them into her acting. However, it simply wasn't possible for Sara to conduct herself in a way that might be considered relaxed or lighthearted when she was present on the set of one of her daughter's films. During the course of just a couple of years, Elizabeth's career had become serious business to Sara. The sense of fun that had been integral to her personality had been replaced by a sense of urgency. It was as if she felt that Elizabeth had to be perfect in each moment because one mistake could ruin everything they'd so far achieved. Of course, that wasn't the case. No one expected such precision from a thirteen-year-old actress—no one, that is, but her mother. If Elizabeth made a mistake, Sara would visibly stiffen. The expression on her face, grim and irate, would signal to everyone present that she was displeased. Such displays of emotion made it all the more difficult for a young girl who was already under enormous pressure. If only Sara could have been just a little more understanding it would have made everything so much easier. Upon seeing that Sara was upset with something that had occurred, Elizabeth would drop her eyes and become flustered and anxious. Eventually, of course, she would rise to the occasion and do whatever it was she was supposed to do—she was a quick study and did have natural ability—but at what cost to her psyche?

While it was without a doubt her great beauty that initially attracted audiences to her and her films, it was Elizabeth's honesty as a performer that kept them coming back, this according to Richard Brooks, who later directed Taylor in *Cat on a Hot Tin Roof*:

"Here's a girl on the big screen—bigger than life—idolized in thousands upon thousands of dark theaters all over the world by men and women, some who want to emulate her, some who love her, a fantasy, a dream. But she is also so vulnerable that she could easily be hurt. Vulnerability is a counterpart of humility, and Elizabeth really was a humble person. That's one of the things that made her such a great star. One could ask, well, who could hurt Elizabeth Taylor? She has wealth, she's affluent, she has men, she's a power, a turret, a fortress. But she wasn't, and the audience knew it. It came out of the screen, this vulnerability, and the audience reached out to her and wanted to protect her. That was Elizabeth."

Of course, like most child stars, Elizabeth would become a bird in the gilded cage of the MGM studio system, totally controlled by the adults in her life at the studio. Luckily, her parents—mostly Sara, but at times even Francis—were both strong-willed and protective, traits that would serve Elizabeth well in years to come and prevent MGM from always having its way with their daughter. After *National Velvet*, Sara returned from a meeting at the studio and informed Francis that it was time for him to step up and join her in forging their daughter's future at MGM. "It's a gentleman's club," she told him. "If I smoked cigars, I might have half a chance with Mr. Mayer." Francis may not have had the showbiz savvy his wife had gained in recent years, but he did look forward to having a more active role in Elizabeth's new and exciting life. "I think he felt that he may as well join them since he surely wasn't going to beat them," said his friend Stefan Verkaufen. Therefore, with an agenda clearly set by his wife, Francis had a face-to-face with one of the most powerful men in Hollywood, Mayer, and it couldn't have gone better.

In an interview with Helen Gurley Brown for *Cosmopolitan* in 1987, Elizabeth recalled, "When they wanted to change my name to Virginia—don't ask me why—my father said, 'no, she was christened Elizabeth and that's what she'll be called.' They said my hair was too dark, that it would photograph blue-black. My father said, 'You're not dyeing my child's hair.' They wanted to pluck my eyebrows, and again he said, no. L. B. Mayer, none of them, could have fought with my dad and won. They wanted to remove the mole from my face. They wanted to change the shape of my mouth with heavy lipstick. That's when *I* said no."

She later wrote in her book, *Elizabeth Takes Off*, "Luckily, my strong sense of self enabled me to deal with tyrannical studio bosses like Louis B. Mayer. While I defied the studio and wouldn't let anyone push me around, Judy Garland never talked back; she followed the studio's orders. They pumped pills into that poor girl to keep her awake, to put her to sleep, and to keep her slim. Judy, an eager, loving and trusting person, never questioned the company's motives."

Indeed, even though Elizabeth was one of the major stars at MGM, she wasn't like the other actresses there who constantly subjugated themselves to the irascible studio boss. In fact, she wasn't fond of L. B. Mayer at all; she thought him a hypocrite. She would point out that he constantly encouraged all of the children at the studio to think of him as a benevolent father and come to him with their problems, "but just try to get an appointment with the man. It will simply never happen." She loathed duplicity in people, even at an early age.

"People often express sadness that the studio system doesn't exist any longer, but those are usually people who were not in it," Elizabeth told Whoopi Goldberg when she appeared on her talk show in September 1992. "People like L. B. Mayer were monsters, actually. If you got pregnant, you were put on suspension. If you didn't like a script, you were put on suspension. So you had to live your life according to what they wanted you to do, otherwise you couldn't live because you were paid by the week. If you were a bad girl your pay was cut off. Bad girl meaning if you got pregnant, for instance. I didn't like having a gun at my head. I didn't then and I don't think I ever will. I have tried to behave in my life . . . but it's not working."

When she was about fourteen, Elizabeth could no longer contain her feelings about the much-feared studio boss. It's one of Elizabeth's oft-told stories: She and her mother were having a meeting with Mayer about a newspaper article that suggested Elizabeth was being considered for a role in a musical. Sara told Mayer she thought Elizabeth would need more singing and dancing lessons. For no reason anyone could think of, Mayer suddenly blew up at her. He began swearing at her, calling her a stupid woman and berating her; every other word from his mouth was a curse word as he reminded her that he had pulled her and her daughter "from the gutter." As he went on, Sara just sat before him with her eyes closed, apparently trying to remain centered and calm as her Christian Science background would have dictated during such a crisis. However, Elizabeth couldn't take it. She stood up and yelled at him, "Don't you dare speak to my mother like that. You and your studio can just go to hell." Mayer stood up and shouted, "You can't talk to me that way, young lady." She countered with, "I most certainly can. You can take your studio and you know where to put it." Then she stormed out of the office. Sara stayed behind and tried to smooth things over with Mayer. Later, she was proud of Elizabeth for defending her, but she was also concerned that her daughter had shown her temper in front of the man who controlled just about everything at MGM. She tried to convince her to apologize, but Elizabeth stubbornly refused. She never did apologize and she also never set foot in L. B. Mayer's office again. It's amazing, in retrospect, that Mayer continued to give her work. "He must have needed me badly," she has said by way of explanation, "very badly."

Still, despite her independent steak, notwithstanding what she recalls about her "strong sense of self," she actually did make some important concessions to the studio. First, it should be said that she certainly had what it took in terms of looks to be a movie star, even if her acting wasn't always the best during these years. As she passed through her teenage years, she became even more beautiful, her dark, brooding looks taking on a sexy, ingénue quality. At 110 curvaceous pounds and with a nineteen-inch waist, she had a killer body. Tom Gates tells a humorous anecdote about Elizabeth's budding figure and its impact on sister MGM contract player Esther Williams. "I knew that Esther and Elizabeth never worked together and asked Esther if they had ever met," says Gates. "'Some execs at M-G-M thought it would be a good idea if I taught Elizabeth Taylor, who was about fourteen at the time, to swim,' she told me. 'So they trotted her out in a swimsuit to my swimming pool. I took one look at her in that suit and said, 'I may never teach you to swim but, believe me, you'll never drown!'"

Though just a petite five feet two—Elizabeth fibbed to the press and added two inches to her height—she appeared taller and more willowy onscreen than in person. She also, of course, had the bluest, most expressive eyes, which looked as if they were somehow illuminated from within. They were the focal point of a face that seemed sculpted from marble. Even the mole on her right cheek looked as if it had been applied by design, and this after her mother stopped coloring it in with the eyebrow pencil. The entire picture was framed by dark, luxurious hair. Everywhere she went, heads turned. Photographers fell over themselves trying to snap her picture, and she loved posing for them.

That said, no matter how great a beauty a woman was at MGM, L. B. Mayer felt that there was always room for improvement. For instance, when you look at early pictures of Elizabeth, it's obvious that the studio had begun to pluck her hairline to neaten it. Also, and importantly, they would reshape her eyebrows into what would become the famous "Taylor arch." Naturally, she was born with rounded eyebrows, like nearly everyone else in the world. It was the studio that created the more sensual look, and it would make a tremendous difference in her appearance. Moreover, though she will never admit to it or confirm it, people who know her well insist that she would have had rhinoplasty surgery— when she was in her twenties. There was certainly nothing wrong with her nose, but the powers that be at MGM apparently thought it a little too thick at the bottom, so they took care of it. It's been said that the surgery was performed by the same doctor who did Natalie Wood's and Marilyn Monroe's noses and also gave Monroe a chin implant.

One has to wonder what such tinkering does to a young woman's awareness of herself. She looked perfect in photographs, but there was constant "improvement" going on behind the scenes from her mother and the studio. Some who knew Elizabeth well felt that the constant nagging at her to be and act a certain way did cause a sort of psychological tear in her personality. She began to feel, as she got older, that it was *all* acting: photography, public appearances, accepting awards . . . her *life* . . . and not just the part when she was making movies, either. She learned to *play* at being Elizabeth Taylor, and it was a full-time job

Another of the challenges Elizabeth faced at MGM concerned the schooling she received on the lot, where the studio had its own little red schoolhouse for the child stars. It was really the most rudimentary of educations, or, as she recalls it, "a ridiculous way of schooling us. Between takes, you had to study for a minimum of ten minutes." There have been stories reported about the young thespian's lack of interest in her studies and her decision, made early in life, that the world of movies was the only one about which she needed to know. It was particularly difficult for her when she was a teenager and was required to attend classes for three hours every day before 3 p.m. or the production she was working on would have to be closed. Later, at sixteen, when she was making *Conspirator* with Robert Taylor, her teacher would literally pull her out of a romantic scene, grabbing her by the shoulders and telling her to "march" to her lessons. If she had a problem with it, Taylor would remind her that his wife, the great

Barbara Stanwyck, was a true professional and would never balk at anything the studio told her she had to do. Elizabeth, in the interest of being polite to her costar, who was old enough to be her father, would bite her tongue.

Though she was now making a good deal of money, she didn't know how to keep track of it. So poor was she at mathematics, she had to count by using her fingers when she was seventeen. Her reading and spelling skills were also weak. Still, the studio pushed her along in its school system, passing her from one grade to the next, just to get her through the distraction her "education" was to her movie career. She would always feel inferior about her schooling, and this inferiority complex would come into clearer focus in years to come when she would find herself the wife of the very scholarly Richard Burton.

Despite her great fame and popularity, the young Elizabeth Taylor would become an extremely antisocial teenager, not knowing how to mix and relate to people—mostly adults—who did not make their living in front of movie cameras. She often wondered what it might be like to go to a regular school, to be able to have friends who were not actors, who did not always seem to be performing for cameras even in their personal lives. She also couldn't help but notice the lack of classmates her own age at the studio school—Margaret O'Brien and Butch Jenkins were five years younger, and Roddy McDowall was four years older. She felt isolated, which probably prompted her interest in animals as pets. MGM certainly made a lot of her fascination with small animals; countless photos were taken of Elizabeth with a golden retriever named Monty; a spaniel called Spot; a cocker, Twinkle; a cat she named Jeepers Creepers; not to mention her horses, King Charles and Prince Charming—and even Howard's horse, Sweetheart. There was also a squirrel in the lot, which had to be given away after it bit Francis! In years to come, there would be speculation that the reason Elizabeth gravitated to her pets was the unconditional love she felt from them. Her friend Michael Jackson, who also feels that his childhood was robbed from him, would have a collection of animals as well—in fact, an exotic zoo at his Neverland Ranch—with whom he says he had better relationships than with the people in his life. Of course, it's entirely possible that Elizabeth felt that she could better relate to her pets, considering the circumstances of her life at the time. Or . . . perhaps she just liked animals.

Among the menagerie there were also eight chipmunks, the most famous of the bunch in 1946 being one named Nibbles. Elizabeth actually published a popular book, *Nibbles and Me*, about her friendship with the small animal. The book was telling, too, of her longing for love and companionship, and suggested a deep need for intimacy that, in retrospect, is aching. "Oh, he is so cute," she wrote of the chipmunk. "He's gone again, but not before he kissed me. He stands on my neck with his front feet on my chin and stretches himself so that he can reach my mouth. He is happy with me. He keeps showing me that he is—and can you wonder that I love him so much?" Mind you, she was fourteen when she wrote those words, originally as an essay for her teacher at the MGM school.

Actor Robert Wagner is two years older than Elizabeth but was a friend of hers when they were children. He recalls, "The business she was in could be very disillusioning. She would be needed for a picture, and all efforts would be made for just her. Everybody would be delighted to have her there because they knew she was going to perform; she was going to be that *star* for them. They would become like a family, in a sense, the cast and crew. But really it was an illusion because when the movie was over . . . forget it. Those people would scatter to the winds. She would never see a lot of them again. That's just the nature of the business, but if you are doing as many films as she was doing, it hurts—especially for a kid. It puts you in a place where you never really feel secure, you start thinking everyone is a big phony, their interest and even affection is not real, and they are just kissing your butt to get the job done. And, in fact, they usually are doing just that."

In so many ways, she was not a child—but obviously not an

adult, either. She was stuck in a weird netherworld, and would therefore always feel like a misfit. But, really, if one looks at it objectively, she had been living in such a world for years before she even got to MGM. After all, it was Sara Taylor who had begun shaping Elizabeth into a young woman back when she was about two, so to be fair, one can't hold MGM or L. B. Mayer solely responsible for any damage to Elizabeth's psyche.

Nothing became more important to Elizabeth Taylor than her career, because it was all she had, and all she felt that distinguished her. A note to her mother written when the actress was a teenager illustrates this point. As the story goes—and it was Sara who started this particular legend, maybe in reaction to rumors that she was a difficult stage mother—Sara was concerned about the overwhelming impact show business was having on her daughter, and she suggested that perhaps the whole family should "go back to our old life in England." Even in Sara's telling of it, it sounds more like a threat than a helpful suggestion—and it doesn't stretch credulity to think that it may have come as a consequence of a mother-daughter disagreement. Such a conclusion is even more plausible given Elizabeth's response, in a private letter to her mother that—surprisingly enough—Sara made public by quoting in one of her many personally penned features about life with her daughter for a women's magazine. "I've done a lot of thinking," Elizabeth wrote, "and I realize that my whole life is being in motion pictures. For me to quit would be like cutting away the roots of a tree—I'd soon wilt and become dead and useless. I also like to think maybe I have brought a little happiness to a few people—in my way—but more than anything I would like to have made you happy. But I'm afraid I haven't succeeded very well. I'm not going to stop trying, though."

It was only natural that Elizabeth and Sara would begin to butt heads as Elizabeth got older, each mirroring the other's stubborn nature. Elizabeth, for instance, wanted to essay older roles, while Sara, despite her daughter's growing physical maturity, insisted that she be a child onscreen for as long as possible. She managed to keep Elizabeth in children's parts until she was about fifteen. *A Date with Judy* was the 1948 film that marked the first time Elizabeth, now sixteen, wore makeup onscreen and had, as she puts it, "a leading man who wasn't four-legged." Robert Stack, twelve years her senior, played her love interest in that film and gave her the first "adult" onscreen kiss—not a polite peck on the lips, as given her by Jimmy Lyndon in *Cynthia* the prior year. "I think in real life I got my own first kiss about two weeks before, she once told Barbara Walters. "Oh, I was in a panic, that I'd be kissed on the screen before I was kissed in real life, and that would have been such a terrible humiliation."

Though she enjoyed her career, Elizabeth would be conflicted about it for years to come. From time to time, she would feel resentment toward her mother for having made her the breadwinner of the family. But in some ways, their mutual affection and understanding made what might have been a very difficult and complicated working situation for many other mothers and daughters a winning one for them. They gave color and depth to each other's lives, basking in Elizabeth's achievements, sharing her great success because they'd earned it as a mother-daughter team. However, their relationship was as complex as Sara herself. Studio executives described Sara's ability to manipulate others as "stellar." L. B. Mayer once told Hedda Hopper, "Sara Taylor could talk you into a bank heist over a telephone line." Elizabeth would sometimes want to scream out in vexation at the chokehold her mother had on her during her important, formative years. She couldn't even go to the restroom at MGM without someone following her, at Sara's and also at the studio's direction.

While Sara's ability to steer her daughter's interests and desires was viewed by some people as ingenious and others as destructive, her husband's opinion of it had not been altered over the years: He absolutely didn't like it. It's interesting that when Francis first met Sara he found endearing her skill for guiding those around her down the path she thought best. However, with Elizabeth, he was much less appreciative of her penchant toward manipulation. By the end of the decade, it had caused many marital difficulties for the Taylors. In fact, earlier, in November 1946, the two had even separated for a time.

It's been reported by several Elizabeth Taylor biographers that Sara was at this time having some kind of romantic involvement with Michael Curtiz, director of Elizabeth's movie *Life with Father*, and that it spurred a separation from Francis. Stefan Verkaufen, the Viennese art dealer who was very close to the Taylors, had by this time moved to Los Angeles. He says, "If you knew Sara, you knew how preposterous it was to think that she was having an affair with anyone in 1946. She simply would never have done it once Elizabeth was a star. She would have been too concerned about the damage it might have caused Elizabeth's career if it was discovered. Image—not just Elizabeth's but her own—was everything to Sara, and it was a concern that most certainly trumped any desire she may have had to have an affair. She was very fearful of L. B. Mayer's reaction to her personal life and endeavored to make sure he never knew of Francis's alcoholism, for example. She lived in fear that a personal scandal would ruin everything she had worked to achieve.

"However, there *had* been whisperings about Sara and Curtiz. When a photograph turned up in a magazine of the two of them at a beach, it did upset Francis. I don't think it was the reason for the separation, though. I think it was Francis's enragement over Sara's constant nagging of Elizabeth. He was quite unhappy about it, especially when Elizabeth started acting in a very bratty and spoiled manner. As she started making more films, she became more superior-acting, and Francis hated it. So, yes, he and Sara split up. Sara tried to smooth things over because she certainly did not want a separation, but in the end she and Elizabeth moved to a beach house in Malibu, while Francis and Howard stayed behind at the home in Beverly Hills. However, I also remember Sara saying, 'There will never be a divorce in this family. I can assure you of that.' "

Predictably—and much to Sara's disconcertment—the studio

was concerned about the estrangement of Elizabeth's parents. The news made the papers, as expected considering the famous daughter. "Maybe they loved me too much," Elizabeth later said. "They had no life of their own, especially my mother." (Her comment foreshadows a similar observation that she would make almost thirty years later when announcing the end of her first marriage to Richard Burton: "Maybe we loved each other too much.")

L. B. Mayer gave Sara a check, which he called a bonus, and told her to take Elizabeth and leave the country. So off they went to England on the *Queen Mary*, in the last week of July 1947. At the same time, Howard Young took Francis and little Howard on a long fishing trip, ostensibly to forget their troubles. Elizabeth and Sara spent about two months in the Southampton area before they received a telegram from L. B. Mayer telling them to return for a new movie, *A Date with Judy*.

Within about a year, the couple would reconcile and be living together again, but Francis remained unhappy with Sara's decisions concerning Elizabeth. But the pattern had been set in stone years earlier. While Francis's responsibility was Howard, Sara's was Elizabeth, and her attitude about their talented daughter remained unchanged: hands off. Francis once told Stefan Verkaufen that during the production of *A Date with Judy* Elizabeth complained to him that she was exhausted from all of the hours she had been working on the set. It was her first musical, and she was worn down by the rigorous rehearsals. "Mummy won't listen," she told him. It was rare for Elizabeth to go to Francis with her problems. It practically never happened. She must truly be desperate, he reasoned, or she never would have come to him. He decided not to waste his time talking to Sara about it, instead going straight to the movie's director, Richard Thorpe. Thorpe told him that he should take up the matter with Sara, that it was she, not him, who was pushing Elizabeth too hard. It's not known if Francis did mention it to Sara, but if he did the matter still remained unresolved. Then, late one night Elizabeth approached both her parents as they were preparing for bed. She complained that she was sick and tired of making movies and that she just wanted to be a regular child—a request that seemed appropriate for a young woman in her position. Sara, though, took her daughter's cry for help as a sign of ingratitude. "But you're *not* a regular child, and thank God for that," she told her. "You have a responsibility, Elizabeth. Not just to this family, but to the country now, the whole world."

Elizabeth looked to Francis for help, but he just didn't have it in him. The only way for him to be there for his child would have been to stand up to his wife, and apparently he couldn't bring himself to do it. Instead, he held his tongue, not saying a word. Elizabeth fled from the room, crying.

When recounting this upsetting story, Francis later told Stefan that he viewed the moment as defining for all concerned. It was painfully clear to him that Sara had become so invested in the future of Elizabeth Taylor, *movie star*, that nothing would stand in her way of even bigger success with her—even her daughter's own happiness. Also, Elizabeth's feelings for him had also come into focus. "I could see that she'd lost all respect for me that night," he told Stefan. "It was as if a dagger had pierced my heart." Years later, Elizabeth would blithely state, "You know, my *real* fathers were Benny Thau [a top-level MGM executive], and Jules Goldstone [her agent]." How sad that she would end up feeling that way, especially considering her father's understandable problems and his utter inability to address them. He wouldn't have hurt her intentionally for the world. Yet he had done just that, and she would never forget it.

Part Two

FINDING HER WAY

Early Suitors . . . and Howard Hughes

Elizabeth Taylor has said that one of the biggest challenges she faced during her adolescent years was her lack of peers. Youngsters her own age seemed too immature when contrasted with the adults in her world. She didn't know how to respond to them. Older children somehow seemed too worldly to her. She presumed that their experiences were more varied than any she'd known, her having been locked up within the walls of MGM for so many years. Therefore, without anyone to help define her personality, she really was on her own. She was her—and her mother's—own creation, not just on the screen but in her private life.

By the time Elizabeth was about sixteen, Sara had become preoccupied with her daughter's social life—her dating life, specifically. True to her complex nature, there were a couple of paradoxes at work with Sara: As much as she wanted Elizabeth to remain a little girl, she also wanted her to be viewed by the public as popular and desirable. Moreover, it was as if she wouldn't let Elizabeth out of her sight for ten minutes, yet she wanted her to date. Or perhaps it would be more accurate to state that she wanted people to *think* Elizabeth was dating. In other words, she was concerned about Elizabeth's public image and worried that unless she was photographed on some young man's arm soon, the public would begin to think that maybe she wasn't dating material, and how would *that* look?

The problem was that the roles played by Elizabeth's costars—

usually not even the costars themselves—had become the only "people" with whom Elizabeth had developed relationships, and those parts were scripted by adults. In the real world, young men were immediately unsettled upon first contact with her. While not impervious to her beauty, they were fearful of her, reluctant to approach her. Plus, everyone knew about her mother's protective nature, and no one wanted to tangle with her. Today, when asked if she ever had to deal with the "casting couch"—giving out sexual favors for movie roles—Elizabeth laughs and says, "By the time I was old enough, no one dared."

Despite her formidable image, she was actually extremely naïve when it came to romance. She had a screenwriter's view of it. All she wanted was to fall in love and have the kind of head-over-heels experiences she'd acted on the screen, to know that by the end of the story everyone would be forever happy. Indeed, when it came to matters of the heart, a film's fantasy was truly her only frame of reference. She wasn't going to be finding boyfriends on her own, that much was clear—not that anyone wanted her to do so anyway. It was at Sara's urging that MGM set Elizabeth up on her first date, when she was sixteen. It was to be with a young chap they found for her, an all-America football player, the tall and handsome Heisman Trophy winner Lieutenant Glenn Davis, just out of West Point. Tall, with reddish brown hair, he was all muscle and swagger. Doris Kearns, wife of MGM publicist Hubie Kearns, brought Davis to the Taylors' new Malibu retreat for a Sunday brunch. For Sara, as soon as she met the twenty-three-year-old Davis it was true love—even if Elizabeth seemed at first shy and ambivalent. "When I saw that frank, wonderful face, I thought, 'This is the boy.' I felt such a sense of relief," Sara later wrote. "My worries were over."

At this time, the summer of 1948, Elizabeth was making *Little Women*, Louisa May Alcott's autobiographical account of her life with her three sisters in Concord, Massachusetts, in the 1860s. Taylor would appear in the film (which turned out to be fairly mediocre), with June Allyson, Margaret O'Brien, Janet Leigh, and

Peter Lawford, as the snooty and anxious Amy, complete with strawberry blonde wig. "I liked playing the role of a young girl in love," she said of her part. During filming, she and Glenn saw each other from time to time, mostly at the Taylors' summer home. One weekend, he bought Elizabeth her first gift of jewelry. Oddly, the piece somehow ended up in Sara and Francis's joint will in the 1960s: "To our beloved grandchild, Liza Todd, we bequeath the cultured pearl necklace with 69 graduated pearls, given to Elizabeth by Glenn Davis." When Elizabeth told a reporter that she and Davis were "engaged to be engaged," it became a big story and no one questioned it at the time, not even Davis (who years later would say, "We were not engaged, nor were we engaged to be engaged.") It was as if Elizabeth was easily able to glide from the role she was playing in *Little Women* to the one she was playing in real life, without anyone taking issue with it or even thinking twice about it.

In September, the affable Glenn Davis was shipped off to Korea. He left Elizabeth with a little gold football around her neck and his picture on her dressing table to help keep their "love" alive. She promised to wait for him. Touching photographs of the two of them kissing good-bye were published around the world. "Letters came in bunches from Korea," recalled Sara Taylor in one of her many articles, "and she spent half her time hanging over her desk writing in return. All of which proves that my daughter's movie career has given her no degree of sophistication." Though the meaning of Sara's observation is unclear, something about it seems oddly critical. In any event, the situation with Glenn Davis was innocent enough, even if it had all been a public relations ruse.

In November 1948, the Taylor women went to England so that Elizabeth could film *Conspirator* there with Robert Taylor; Francis and Howard stayed behind in California. In the film, Elizabeth played a twenty-one-year-old debutante who unwittingly marries a communist spy, played by Taylor. It seemed odd casting at the time due to the difference in their ages—she was sixteen, he was thirty-eight—yet it somehow made perfect sense on the screen. At this point, Elizabeth was earning about $1,000 a week for her work in films. When the movie was released in 1950, it would bomb at the box office, though the young actress would be praised for her work, with *Variety* saying she "comes out with flying colors."

Sara and Elizabeth had a wonderful time together in London. From photographs taken during the trip, it's clear that Sara—still a real beauty with her dark hair and dancing eyes—enjoyed the attention of the press, as if perhaps reliving her glory days in London when she was a theater star appearing in *The Fool*.

Mother and daughter returned to America in February 1949, with Francis meeting them in New York City. From there, they went to Howard Young's winter home at Star Island, Florida, where Elizabeth would celebrate her seventeenth birthday. It was at Young's, during a dinner party on March 3, that she met the wealthy William Pawley. At twenty-eight, he was more than ten years her senior, from a socially prominent family. With coal-black hair and deep, penetrating eyes, he had the chiseled face of a Hollywood actor, complete with pencil-thin mustache. Gregarious, funny, and unfailingly polite, he was the kind of young man any mother would approve of for her daughter, and he was wealthy as well. Elizabeth was immediately infatuated with him, and Sara had to admit that he did appear to be a more suitable beau than the financially challenged football player. Therefore, she encouraged Elizabeth in her crush over Pawley, and after a couple of weeks it actually seemed as if the two might have some sort of romance.

A dilemma arose, however, when in March 1949 Glenn Davis was granted a furlough from his tour of duty and of course wanted to see Elizabeth. What transpired next may not reveal Sara's best moment, but it does demonstrate how easy it was for her to become swept away by the cyclone of excitement and publicity her daughter's career could generate at any time. Glenn telephoned the Taylors from California to ask if he might fly down to see Elizabeth. Sara picked up the phone and, according to a Taylor relative who is very familiar with what transpired, did not at first know how to treat his request. "She knew that Elizabeth was finished with him," said the relative, "but as she was about to tell him not to come, something came over her, as she would later tell it. She referred to it as an epiphany, something she didn't have a chance to think through but rather just act upon in the moment. It hit her that his arrival at the airport would present a valuable photo opportunity for Elizabeth. Before she knew what she was doing she had told him to come on down to Florida. Then she hung up and telephoned MGM's press department to arrange to have the media positioned at the airport so that the very moment Elizabeth and Glenn were at long last reunited could be the subject of photo essays all over the world. After it was all arranged, she said, she sat down in a chair and thought, 'Dear Lord, what have I just done?' But, then she remembered that Davis had film aspirations and had actually played himself in a low-budget film called *The Spirit of West Point*. So she figured, well, he'll get some publicity, too, so everyone wins."

In Sara's view, what she'd done was probably comparable to what publicists did every day at MGM for their contract players. Movie studios embellished the truth all the time, so it's understandable that she would feel that her idea was valid if her goal was just to generate publicity. The problem, though, was that she was a mother, not a publicist, and as such had put herself in a position of exploiting her own daughter's naïveté and trust, not to mention Glenn Davis's. If Elizabeth and Glenn had actually been in a legitimate relationship and he was coming home from war to resume his romance with her, then, yes, that would have been a legitimate story to feed to the press. But that was not at all the situation—at least not as far as Elizabeth was concerned. Elizabeth had no experience at all with romance; this was a delicate time for her and surely Sara must have recognized as much. Indeed, according to Taylor family history, Sara wasn't totally comfortable after she had a chance to consider all of the ramifications of her actions. However, once she put the idea into motion with MGM, there was really no turning back, for her or her daughter.

Elizabeth had no problem going to meet Glenn Davis upon his arrival in Florida and acting as if she anticipated a happy future with him in her life. Why would she? She had no frame of reference for real relationships and didn't even know enough to realize that what she was doing was disingenuous. For her, the experience with Davis at the airport would be just like any number of situations she'd thus far had with the actors she'd worked with at the studio. She was acting, as she saw it, and none of it was real anyway.

As expected, the scene at the airport turned into a mad one, with photographers jostling for position to get the best photographs of MGM's winsome star with the all-American boyfriend she had missed so much, and Elizabeth put on the expected good show of chirpy, girlish emotion at the very sight of the slack-jawed Glenn. The next day, photographs of the two were published in newspapers all over the country, the captions indicating that Glenn would probably be offering Elizabeth an engagement ring in the near future, an embellishment that was MGM's, not Sara's.

"I think it was a roller coaster of emotions for Sara," says the Taylor relative. "She was happy that she had gotten the press she wanted, very impressed with herself for having pulled it off, but also feeling a bit guilty about how easy it had been to manipulate things. I knew her. She was not a venal woman but rather a focused person who, once she set her sights on something, went about the business of doing it, no matter what. I can tell you that Francis was not pleased about any of it. It may have been good publicity, but to Elizabeth it was much more . . . it was her life. Or was it? The lines of distinction were quickly becoming blurred, even for her. She was just sixteen, after all."

When Glenn Davis figured out what was going on, he turned around and went back to Los Angeles feeling betrayed and hurt—and with a ruby-and-diamond engagement ring in his pocket, a miniature of his class ring from West Point. As it happened, he had actually intended to ask Elizabeth to marry him and when he saw her obvious enthusiasm for him at the airport he knew that her answer was going to be an unequivocal yes. However, once the couple was away from the panting press, he found that Elizabeth was distant and totally uninterested in anything he had to say. She had changed. The scene was over. What did he expect of her? "I was pretty devastated by the whole thing," he recalled. He was followed in Los Angeles shortly thereafter, on March 23, by Elizabeth and her parents. The next day would mark the Academy Awards presentation and Elizabeth was scheduled to present the statue for costume design. Someone had to escort her to the awards, and it would, obviously, have to be the young man who'd just been pictured with her in newspapers all over the world: Glenn Davis. He did not reject MGM's suggestion when the studio called with it. (It's been reported that Elizabeth was the one to ask him to accompany her, but that does not appear to be true.) Like Sara, he was also caught in the whirlwind of Elizabeth's life and career, and even he would have to admit to a certain thrill about it. While he and Elizabeth appeared to be the idyllic young couple at the awards show, it was all as much make-believe as one of her movies. However, Elizabeth pulled it off without much of a problem. Anyone who had been watching would have thought that she really did have an emotional attachment to Glenn Davis. Again . . . all acting. This was her first exposure to the notion of dating a member of the opposite sex, and already it had become quite easy for her to separate herself from the truth of it. For her, dating and acting had quickly become interchangeable. Meanwhile, this orchestrated fantasy with Glenn Davis was also her first relationship melodrama, setting the stage for many more in years to come in which she would be involved with one man while on the arm of another.

It can also be fairly speculated that the fact that Glenn Davis agreed to take Elizabeth to the Oscars might have helped assuage any guilt Sara felt about her original strategy to generate publicity for her daughter. She probably reasoned that he must not have been that hurt by her plan or he wouldn't have agreed to MGM's request. Of course, with MGM's idea he had been in on the joke, whereas with Sara's he had not. After the Academy Awards show, he and Elizabeth shook hands; it was the last time he would ever lay eyes on her.

At the end of May 1949, Elizabeth and Sara were houseguests of the Pawley family in Florida. The day after they arrived, William presented Elizabeth with a three-and-a-half-carat, emerald-cut solitaire diamond ring—for which he had paid $16,000—her first "white diamond." Now they were officially, and quite suddenly, engaged. MGM organized a press conference to announce the engagement, and during it Sara reminded reporters that Elizabeth had never really been engaged to Glenn Davis, which was true. "She just wore his gold football, like all the girls out there were doing," she said. Still, these sudden romantic experiences all must have seemed a tad on the disposable side for Elizabeth: out with one boyfriend and in with the other, and, truly, without much consideration for either of them. In retrospect, it was not a very good impression to make on a naïve seventeen-year-old. At the press conference, she sat with Pawley and didn't say much other than to describe her ring to one reporter as "a nice piece of ice."

Elizabeth's engagement to William Pawley ended a few months later when he tried to persuade her to give up her career for him. Of course, she would never do such a thing for him—or anyone else—at this time. When the engagement ended, Elizabeth wasn't upset about it, not in the least. In fact, she told the press that it had to end because she was about to start two new movie projects—*The Big Hangover* and *Father of the Bride*—and would be preoccupied with both commitments, which was an odd way to explain the end of a romance but does demonstrate that she hadn't taken it very seriously. Already there seemed to be many consequences of her having been influenced to play so loosely with people's emotions, not the least of which was that Elizabeth

Taylor, after just two boyfriends, had become a good deal less sentimental and a little more detached from true, genuine emotion.

There was another suitor still on the horizon. It was in the fall of 1949 when the very wealthy and eccentric Howard Hughes became a customer of Francis's Beverly Hills art gallery. Hughes, owner of the successful Hughes Aircraft Company and a stockholder in TWA, had just recently acquired RKO Studios and was anxious to carve out a niche in the film industry. In his mid-forties at the time, he was a lothario who had already had a number of older famous women in his bed, such as Lana Turner, Ava Gardner, Joan Crawford, Bette Davis, and Katharine Hepburn. He wasn't well, though, with a myriad of health problems. Though regarded as handsome, he was six feet three and weighed just 150 pounds. Francis wasn't fond of him at all, and found him cold and calculating. However, he obviously had deep pockets and was a good customer, so Sara encouraged Francis to tolerate him. "Hughes was staying in one of the bungalows at the Beverly Hills Hotel," recalled Stefan Verkaufen. "He was reclusive, very strange. One day he came into the gallery, purchased some very expensive paintings, and asked Francis to have dozens more shipped to Los Angeles from Europe. Then he mentioned that he had seen Elizabeth coming into the gallery, and wanted to meet her. He invited the Taylors to Reno for a weekend getaway at one of his hotels there. 'And bring your daughter,' he said. Francis told him that they would talk to Elizabeth about going, but that she probably wouldn't consent to it. He also mentioned that she was studying the script to a new movie she was just about ready to start filming, *A Place in the Sun*. It was the first time I had heard about that film, so I remember it specifically. Howard smiled and said, 'Well, it doesn't hurt to ask.'"

When Francis asked Elizabeth to go to Reno at Hughes's behest, she declined the invitation. It became a point of contention between mother and daughter, as one might imagine given recent events. Still, this was Howard Hughes, and, knowing how Sara was, could anyone blame her for at least trying one more time to orchestrate what could have been one of the biggest PR stunts ever? In the end, it seems that the only reason she didn't force Elizabeth to go was because she came down with a bad cold—she really could will herself to be ill, or at least that's how it often seemed. So the Taylors went without her, and took four other friends, including Stefan Verkaufen.

After Francis, Sara, Stefan, and the others got to Reno, Howard took the Taylor parents aside and made them an offer. According to what Francis later told Stefan, Hughes said that if the Taylors persuaded Elizabeth to marry him, he would finance a movie studio for her. It was over the top, but such was Hughes's way. Sara was more excited by these prospects than anyone had seen her in some time. "She telephoned Elizabeth and told her to get to Reno immediately, and she didn't care how sick she was or what script she was reviewing," says Verkaufen. "Time was of the essence. 'I can't believe that this is our life,' Sara said later. 'I feel as if I'm dreaming.'" It's telling of Elizabeth's evolving personality that not only was she was becoming more annoyed by Sara with each passing day, but she had also come not to feel restricted in expressing her opinion about it. It was at around this time that she said of Sara, "She's a large pain in the ass."

When Elizabeth arrived in Reno the next day, Sara told her about Howard's offer. "Absolutely not," Elizabeth immediately decided. "I don't want anything to do with him. I don't care how much money he has." Her position seemed unreasonable. After all, she didn't even know Hughes well enough to have an opinion of him, and it felt to observers like the real problem was between her and her mother rather than with him. "Or," offered Stefan Verkaufen, "maybe she was just afraid of him because Howard was a bit on the frightening side." For whatever reason, Elizabeth had made up her mind, and even Sara could not convince her to, in a sense, prostitute herself for Howard Hughes. Francis—who was said to be secretly happy about his daughter's decision—broke the news to Hughes. Still, Hughes insisted upon meeting Elizabeth anyway, hosting a cocktail party for her. She attended, but reluctantly.

Nicky Hilton

As a suitor, men didn't come much better than Nicky Hilton, or at least that's how it seemed at first blush. Shortly after the Howard Hughes encounter, Elizabeth met twenty-three-year-old Conrad Nicholson Hilton Jr., son of the millionaire socialite hotel owner Conrad Hilton and one of the wealthiest and most eligible bachelors in Los Angeles. The Hilton empire was worth more than $75 million. Elizabeth, at seventeen, was introduced to Nicky, as he was called, on the set of *A Place in the Sun*, and began dating him in the fall of 1949. She was quickly swept off her feet by his charm, magnetism, Texan drawl, and rakish good looks. Six feet tall, with brown hair and eyes, broad shoulders, and a reed-thin waist, he was, as Elizabeth later put it, "spectacular in every way." Besides his looks, Elizabeth couldn't help but be bowled over by his wealth—or at least that of his family—and by the sixty-four-room Bel Air manor in which he lived, furnished with choice antiques, crystal chandeliers, fine carpets, and museum-quality art. She was also impressed by the troupe of uniformed butlers, maids, and other servants at the Hiltons' beck and call. It was apparent that Nicky was as spoiled as Elizabeth—maybe even more so.

In late winter of 1950, after a brief courtship, Nicky asked Elizabeth to marry him, and she accepted. That was also the month she graduated from high school . . . in a fashion. MGM orchestrated the idea of Elizabeth donning a white cap and gown and actually attending a graduation ceremony with students she didn't know at University High School in Los Angeles. Like almost everything else in her life, it was all illusion, but this one really had a purpose behind it. Debbie Reynolds, who actually was a student at the school, recalls, "I believe that how it happened was that Nicky wanted to marry her, he asked her father for his permission, and her father laid down the law and said, not until she graduates high school. As it happened, the state board of education required that she graduate from a real school, not any MGM kind of school, and that's how she ended up at our school. But it was sad and lonely for her that day, and my heart went out to her. She told me how unhappy she was in her life and that she felt like such a misfit standing there with all of those kids who really just wanted her autograph because they knew they could never have her friendship."

After she got to know Nicky, Elizabeth believed she was in love with him. Of course, she had no experience against which to measure such feelings, and no one to guide her. Even her own mother now feared that Elizabeth had mistaken the romantic illusion she had played in the twelve movies she'd so far made as being somehow comparable to real-life experience. "When other teenage girls were reading romantic stories and imagining themselves as the heroine," Sara had said, "Elizabeth was living her dream world, by acting the role of the heroine—that is, at the studio."

At the time, Elizabeth just wanted to marry Nicky, and that was the end of it. All she could see was that he seemed strong and powerful, that there was something about her dynamic with him that made her think he was the boss. It was different than what she'd seen in her mother's marriage, and she wanted it for herself. Was Nicky more self-reliant than Francis Taylor, though? Probably not . . . even if Elizabeth did think so at the time. After all, it was only because of his family's money that he was wealthy, much like the relationship Francis had with his uncle Howard. So, in a sense, Francis and Nicky had at least that much in common.

A primary reason why Elizabeth wanted to marry at just eighteen, though, was that she was absolutely frantic for some distance from Sara. Her mother's refusal to let her out of her sight had been wearing Elizabeth down for some time. It was only natural at her age that she be able to put some emotional distance between herself and her mother. However, she knew full well that Sara would not let go easily, and so marriage seemed a good way to win her freedom. She wrote in 1987 that she was "desperate to live a life independent of my parents." It would seem, though, that she was referring only to Sara, because she never had those kinds of issues with Francis.

Marriage also represented an outlet for Elizabeth's adolescent urges, which she'd lately felt, to explore her sexuality. She was still a virgin. As she later wrote, "I had always had a strict and proper upbringing, and that was absolutely necessary, living the existence I did. The irony is that the morality I learned at home required marriage. I couldn't just have an affair. I was ready for love, and I was ready for lovemaking."

Sara, who was now fifty-four, and Francis, fifty-three, were not happy about the impending marriage, or so says a relative of Elizabeth's. "I've read over the years that they were thrilled with it, but my memory of it was that there was a lot of ambivalence surrounding it. Sara wanted Elizabeth to date for purposes of publicity, yes, but marry? Well, girls did marry young back then, but I think Sara would have preferred that Elizabeth wait until she was maybe twenty-one. But still, if she was going to do it, Sara felt that Nicky Hilton was probably not a bad choice in that he would give them even greater access to the social strata that she valued. When he gifted Elizabeth with a hundred shares of stock in the Hilton hotels, as well as a few diamond baubles, Sara figured he might not be so bad, after all. In truth, I think she was just attempting to make the best of what she thought was a bad situation, looking at the bright side as had always been her way. Francis even began to think exactly as Elizabeth would later say she'd been thinking all along: that his unhappy daughter could finally escape his wife's stranglehold if she was a married woman, and that Nicky might even be able to do the thing that Francis hadn't been able to do, which was to protect her.

"I've also read that Nicky demanded that Elizabeth convert to Catholicism and that Sara was unhappy about that as well," says the same Taylor relative. "In fact, my memory of it was that he only wanted Elizabeth to sign a document saying she would agree to raise the children as Catholic, not convert to one herself. She and Sara agreed that the document was unnecessary, and she didn't want to sign it. So round and round they went over that issue, and I believe she didn't sign it until about ten days before the wedding."

Just as her marriage was being discussed, Elizabeth was in the midst of filming Vincente Minnelli's *Father of the Bride*, a light-hearted romp in which Joan Bennett and Spencer Tracy played her parents. Elizabeth finished the movie just hours before her engagement to Nicky was announced. As if to further blur the distinction between reality and fiction and undoubtedly to exploit the occasion, MGM then decided to delay the film's release to coincide with Elizabeth's wedding, over which the studio took complete charge. MGM's wardrobe mistress, Helen Rose, created Elizabeth's $3,500 bridal gown, a gift from Louis B. Mayer. Ceil Chapman designed her trousseau, and Edith Head her many honeymoon outfits . . . all of which were presents to their star from the studio. MGM even paid for Sara's wardrobe for the happy occasion. Was it any wonder that young Elizabeth had such trouble distinguishing between her film career and her real life?

In the days before the wedding, Elizabeth became ill and very depressed, much as she would in years to come when she had to appear on the set of a movie she didn't want to do. Many of her relatives felt that she believed she was making a mistake, that her intuition told her that there was trouble ahead, but that she also knew it was too late to change her mind. Therefore, on May 6, 1950, the Church of the Good Shepherd in Beverly Hills was filled with MGM executives and movie stars, as well as Hilton hotel executives, for the wedding of eighteen-year-old Elizabeth

Taylor. The morning had begun with the kind of random and un-expected melodrama that would typify so many of Elizabeth's romantic entanglements. The doorbell rang at the Taylors' Beverly Hills home, and when Sara went to answer it she found Elizabeth's previous fiancé, William Pawley, standing before her looking quite stern. Inexplicably, she let him into the house, and then upstairs to confer with Elizabeth. Fifteen minutes later, he angrily bolted from the room and left the premises. Shortly thereafter, Elizabeth emerged from her bedroom in tears. It's not known what Pawley said to her, but it wouldn't be difficult to surmise at least the parameters of their conversation, considering that Elizabeth had rejected him as a suitor. Pawley even had the temerity to show up at the wedding!

"I closed my eyes to any problems," Elizabeth recalled, "and walked radiantly down the aisle." It was a happy day. As Elizabeth was escorted down the aisle by Francis to Wagner's Wedding March, the excitement and anticipation she felt was evident on her face. Her eyes were aglow with anticipation. After the ceremony, she confidently announced that she was so happy she would probably now retire from making movies. In the years to come, she would make that proclamation many times over.

In truth, though she put on a brave face for the world, privately Elizabeth was scared. "I was terrified," she later recalled. "So was Nick. I remember taking out my handkerchief and mopping the sweat off his face during the ceremony. There was a big reception and, for the first time in my life, I had two glasses of champagne. Then the time came to leave and I had a third glass. And I became more and more afraid. My bridesmaids dragged me off and stuffed me into my going-away suit. I wanted to run, I was so scared. I really had no idea what was coming."

For their honeymoon, the newlyweds would embark on a three-month European vacation to the south of France on the *Queen Mary*—but not right away. Mother's Day was just around the corner and Elizabeth had never been away from Sara on that special day, so Nicky would have to wait it out before he would be able to honeymoon with his new wife. Also, Sara wasn't at all happy with some of the wedding pictures, so in the best tradition of Hollywood image-making, she arranged that they be reshot. Thus all of the principals in the immediate family had to get dressed again in their wedding finery and pose for new photographs at the house. "Oh, please, Daddy! Just pretend that it's last week," Sara suggested to Francis, who was visibly annoyed by the exercise. "A smile. Is that so hard?" Once all of that was taken care of, the Hiltons were able to depart for their honeymoon on the *Queen Mary*, where they were properly ensconced. Making matters even more surreal, Elizabeth brought her maid with her on the honeymoon. (Well, *someone* had to unpack the seventeen trunks she'd brought for the trip.)

The next day, Elizabeth woke up still a virgin. Nicky hadn't slept with her in the intervening week, and then they spent their first night on the cruise at a bar, drinking. It would actually be two more nights before the marriage was consummated. "Then came disillusionment," Elizabeth later recalled, "rude and brutal. I fell off my pink cloud with a thud."

The story of Elizabeth's honeymoon with Nicky has almost become the stuff of legends. The way he gambled and drank while in Monte Carlo, leaving his bride alone and sobbing until the wee hours of the morning, has been told numerous times. Indeed, people who saw them on their honeymoon have recalled Nicky's belligerent behavior toward his new wife. He was suddenly angry at her and jealous of the attention she generated wherever they went. Some of Elizabeth's faults were now more noticeable to him, and he wasn't happy about it. She was stubborn, a consequence of being told what to do and how to do it from as far back in her life as she could remember. She was maddeningly late for everything, probably due to having to always be "on the set on time" from an early age. She was sloppy, a repercussion of having been constantly nagged by her mother to be the ever so prim and proper movie princess.

However, for every one of her problems, Nicky had ten of his own, and they were a good deal more serious than anything she presented. After the honeymoon, as the weeks turned into months, it became clear that he was an alcoholic with serious drug and gambling problems. He and Elizabeth had violent quarrels. While they were out on the town one evening, witnesses watched him give her a forceful shove that sent her reeling backward. She stumbled and fell, landing with a shattering impact that knocked the wind from her. "That'll teach you," he said, standing over her menacingly. Then he walked away, not even looking back at her on the floor, where she lay sobbing. To think that he would hit her was more than she could imagine or bear. She certainly wasn't prepared for such treatment; she'd never been shoved like that in any of her movies, that much was certain.

There also had been no hint at Nicky's violent temper when Elizabeth was dating him. He had a Jekyll-and-Hyde personality— Jekyll before the wedding and Hyde after the nuptials. Who knows what had gone so wrong in Hilton's life to spur him into such violence? All that mattered was Elizabeth needed to get away from him. It's fascinating, in retrospect, that her first marriage was such a breeding ground for so many of the problems that would be significant in her later life. Nicky was an alcoholic, a drug addict, and physically abusive . . . all issues that Elizabeth would have to deal with in years to come.

Elizabeth hadn't made a single important decision on her own in her entire life. Now, as Nicky's victim, she was faced with a real-life drama the scope of which would have been devastating to even the most experienced of women. At first, it was important to her that Sara believe the marriage to be perfect. Perfection had always been of paramount importance to her mother, and Elizabeth certainly did not want to disappoint her. She was also afraid of being embarrassed and harshly judged. She blamed herself for the marital discord, not knowing how else to explain something that was not an ideal situation except to accept culpability for it. It's Elizabeth Taylor legend that she did not share her misery with anyone, including Sara. Even Elizabeth has said as much, numerous times. It now seems, though, that Sara did learn what was happening to her daughter, at least according to one of Elizabeth's closest relatives. That relative explained:

"As I recall it, when Elizabeth returned from her honeymoon, she and Nicky had a stopover in New York. Sara had a very bad feeling about things, just a mother's intuition. She just . . . *knew*. She asked Ivy Hewett, who was one of Uncle Howard's secretaries, to call upon Elizabeth at the hotel the newlyweds were staying at, just to check up on her, and then report back everything she saw. So Ivy made a date to meet with Elizabeth at a restaurant. When Elizabeth showed up, she was wearing a long-sleeved blouse with a see-through sort of material and, sure enough, you could see bruises and black-and-blue marks all over her arms. It was as if she knew that Sara had sent Ivy to check on her and was deliberately passing on a message. Surely she could have worn a sweater if she really didn't want the bruises to be seen. Ivy was shocked. She immediately reported it back to Sara. As soon as Elizabeth returned to California, Sara confronted her, and she readily admitted that Nicky was hitting her. However, Elizabeth insisted that she could handle it and she begged her not to tell Francis. As far as I know, Sara did so promise, and she kept that promise. For the duration of the marriage, Sara and Elizabeth tried to figure a way out, but it wasn't as easy as just ending it. There were concerns about MGM, about divorce, about Elizabeth's public image. Also, Elizabeth was terrified that Nicky would kill her if he knew she was thinking of leaving him. It was a nightmare. During this time, Elizabeth's suffering was also Sara's."

Within a short time, Nicky let it be known that he was uncomfortable with the relationship Elizabeth had with Sara, and was also threatened by it. Earlier, while on their honeymoon, Elizabeth was unpacking her things when Nicky teased her about a floppy hat she had brought along with her.

"My mother gave it to me," Elizabeth said, "so I'll need to wear it in a few pictures."

"But it's a hat for a little girl," he remarked.

"I must always be a little girl for my mother," she told him. It was just the kind of sentiment that infuriated Nicky Hilton.

The same Taylor relative who related the story of Sara's learning of her daughter's abuse relayed this story as it was told to him by Sara:

A few weeks into the marriage, Elizabeth and Nicky went to the Taylor home in Beverly Hills for dinner. Francis was in New York visiting his uncle Howard. One can imagine that it must have galled Sara to have Nicky Hilton in her home considering what she knew about him, but when a mother is in such a difficult situation with her daughter she does what she has to do to at least keep an eye on things even if she can't change them.

While Sara was in the kitchen, Nicky began to argue with Elizabeth. At first she responded in hushed tones, attempting to keep the row private. That became impossible, however, as Hilton's voice bellowed through the house while he laid into his teenage bride. He was drunk and out of control. Sara was eavesdropping out of concern from the kitchen.

"You make me sick," Nicky hollered at Elizabeth. As he turned to walk away from her, Elizabeth grabbed him by the arm and, in one quick and violent move, apparently twisted him around and slapped him across the face with everything she had in her. She hit him so hard that he nearly lost his balance. Looking in from the kitchen, Sara was shocked beyond measure.

Elizabeth locked eyes with Nicky and snarled, "Don't you ever turn your back on me. Ever!"

Nicky took Elizabeth in from head to toe. Then, with a thunderous sound, his opened hand landed on his wife's beautiful face. At that moment, Sara said, she burst into the room just in time to see her daughter aloft from yet another blow. Elizabeth landed in a heap in the corner of the room. "You hit me," she managed to say through her tears. "How dare you!"

"Get out of my house, now, you bastard" Sara screamed as she ran to her daughter's side. "And don't you ever come back!" she added. "You're nothing but a coward. You hit a lady."

"No I didn't," Nicky said plainly. "Tell her, Elizabeth. Tell her you're no lady."

Nicky showed no regret as he walked out the front door, leaving mother and daughter on the floor and in tears.

After seven months, the Hiltons separated. They divorced in February 1951. Elizabeth, who was making about $2,000 a week, did not ask for alimony. "I don't need a prize for failing," she remarked at the time.

Failure. It was a word Elizabeth wasn't used to having applied to her, in any way. Her mother had been pushing her toward excellence for so many years that the idea of actually not succeeding at something was enormously upsetting to her. It filled her with the most intense feelings of inferiority, of worthlessness. In fact, she would never forget the way it made her feel and would often think back on this time as the beginning of all of the true heartache in her life. Not surprisingly, her perceived failure at being a good wife and at having a happy marriage took its toll. Her divorce would be the first in the Taylor family. By the time she began work on the set of *Father's Little Dividend* (the sequel to *Father of the Bride*), she had lost twenty pounds, become a chain-smoker, and was suffering from high blood pressure, colitis, and an ulcer—all in just a few months. In time it would become clear that whenever there was turmoil in her life, she would inevitably become extremely ill. Indeed, for decades to come, a vicious pattern would be repeated: deathly sicknesses and dramatic recoveries almost always linked to upheavals in her personal life.

"The collapse of my marriage was a dreadful blow to my self-esteem," Elizabeth said many years later. "And like everything else in my life, the entire fiasco was played out before the public. I reported back to the studio and found comfort in keeping busy. If I could not be the perfect wife in reality, I could continue to create illusions on the screen. *Father's Little Dividend* followed *Father of the Bride* and in the sequel my celluloid counterpart became a mother. I was doing exactly what I wanted to do, only it was in 35-millimeter rather than life."

It would actually take years before Elizabeth would hint at the horror she experienced as Nicky's spouse; in her 1965 memoir she didn't mention any of the beatings. Because she wanted to maintain some privacy about the matter—and also because she was ashamed—she didn't even tell the judge all of the awful details when he asked why she was divorcing Nicky. She just said that he had been "mean" to her, had told her to go to hell, and had called her mother derisive names. She got her divorce, but she wondered what the press would have thought about her decision—which was, for the most part, criticized—if they had only known the truth.

Many years later, Elizabeth finally revealed a secret she had kept for almost half a century: The final beating she endured as Hilton's wife had caused a miscarriage. "I left him after having a baby kicked out of my stomach," she said sadly. "I had terrible pains. I saw the baby in the toilet. I didn't know that I was pregnant, so it wasn't a malicious or on-purpose kind of act," she hastened to add, seeming to want to protect Nicky, even after all this time. "It just happened. He was drunk. I thought, 'This is not why I was put on earth. God did not put me here to have a baby kicked out of my stomach.'"

Elizabeth's Anger

After her marriage to Nicky Hilton ended, Elizabeth Taylor was not only physically ill but also angry . . . at herself, at Nicky, at fate . . . and at everyone around her, including her parents. In fact, she was now more argumentative than ever with Sara, their relationship straining at the seams. Elizabeth, who would turn nineteen in February, was in full-fledged rebellion mode and would seemingly do anything she could think of not only to horrify Sara, but also to assert her independence from her. She was definitely changing. For instance, she had in the past employed colorful language in expressing herself—and often shocked her fellow students and teachers with it during classes at the MGM schoolhouse. But now she was swearing more than ever, and out of anger rather than just to surprise and shock others. She had also started smoking cigarettes and, even more disturbing given her father's problem, drinking alcohol. Though she suffered terrible stomach problems as a result of the stress in her life—and she was on a strict diet of baby food!—she refused to rest. She seemed to be careening out of control. "At this time, my efforts to climb back on my cloud were failing," she recalled. "I was still on a treadmill, breathlessly running too fast—full of panic, fear, self-doubts. I was floundering, doing impulsive things, not caring whether I was headed for disaster, letting myself get swept along."

Once she was divorced from Nicky Hilton, there would be a string of brief romantic entanglements for Elizabeth, including one with married suitor Stanley Donen, the director of the film she was making at the time, *Love Is Better Than Ever*. The movie is a black-and-white marshmallow of a musical in which she plays, of all things, a dance teacher. It would be shelved for two years because Larry Parks (her costar) was in trouble with the House Un-American Activities Committee, after admitting he'd flirted with the Communist Party when he was younger. (Parks had become a major box-office star with *The Jolson Story* and its sequel, *Jolson Sings Again*.) Finally released with little fanfare in 1952, if remembered at all it is mainly for bringing together Elizabeth and Stanley.

Stanley was separated from his wife, but that didn't make it any easier for Sara to accept him in her daughter's life. She felt strongly that Elizabeth was taking a terrible chance with MGM by being so open about her relationship with Donen, such as attending the Academy Awards show with him in March 1951, and then the premiere of *Father's Little Dividend* in April. After all, her contract did include a so-called "morals clause," which was supposed to discourage her from doing anything that might embarrass the studio. Therefore, mother and daughter had more than a few heated discussions over Donen. However, Elizabeth was not trying to hide anything from anyone, obviously, or she wouldn't have been so public with Donen. She liked him and wanted to be with him, and that was the end of it, as far as she was concerned. He'd been of great assistance to her during the making of *Love Is Better Than Ever*, especially on days when she could barely imagine getting through the day, let alone a scene. The romance did not last long, especially since MGM decided to cast her in the film *Ivanhoe*, which would shoot in England—far enough from Donen, the studio reasoned, to keep her from getting into more serious trouble with him.

At this time, in 1951, there was a good deal of discussion in private circles as well as speculation in the media as to whether or not Elizabeth would even re-sign with MGM since her contract with the studio was about to expire. It was then that the eccentric Howard Hughes made a return appearance to her life, obtaining entrée via an unlikely and rather surprising source: her father, Francis Taylor. Hughes again approached Taylor about the availability of his famous daughter, repeating a familiar refrain: He wanted to start a film company that would finance Elizabeth's next movies, the next six, he said, to be specific. Whether Hughes did in fact have a plan to resume making films after selling his successful RKO Studios to Desilu, it was clear that he was trying to once again get close to the elusive Elizabeth, who had earlier decided not to give him the time of day. This time, Francis heavily promoted the idea with his daughter until—given her present indecision about MGM—she eventually told him she would "probably agree" to working for a company in which Hughes was invested, at least preliminarily. Therefore, Walden Productions was quickly formed—named after a street near the Taylors' Beverly Hills home—to be owned by Francis Taylor, Howard Hughes, and Jules Goldstone, Elizabeth's attorney at the time. Hughes made it clear that he intended to recruit Francis as an executive producer on Elizabeth's films, which would basically put him in the driver's seat in a way that would trump anything his wife had ever done with Elizabeth's career. People in Francis's life couldn't believe that he was actually going to be involved in such an enterprise; it was just so unlike him. "I'm simply trying to carve a little something out for myself for a change," he explained at the time. "Is there anything wrong with that?"

Howard Hughes was—as is well-known now—extremely paranoid, so much so that he had a telephone line installed in Jules Goldstone's office to which only he had the number. Its purpose was so that he could negotiate and do business on Elizabeth's behalf with no one listening in on the calls. He also did everything he could think of to get a meeting with Elizabeth to discuss future projects. He called her and left messages; she never called back. He sent roses; she never acknowledged them. Many observers at the time remained puzzled as to why Elizabeth had such animosity toward this man, whom she really did not know very well. "He needed a bath," she later explained. "I always knew what I wanted and what I didn't want. Somebody hitting on me made no difference to me, unless I was interested." Francis even pleaded with her to, at the very least, consent to having dinner with Hughes. "How are you going to make movies for him if you don't even know him?" he asked. Elizabeth countered that she had never been social with L. B. Mayer and, in fact, loathed the MGM studio head, "but that hasn't stopped me from making movies for him, has it?" With Hughes, if they were to work together, she decided, it would be a matter of strictly business. She knew where to draw the line, and she wasn't afraid to draw it.

However, all of the discussion about Howard Hughes would turn out to be for nothing. When Elizabeth chose to renew her contract at MGM, her decision spelled the end of Walden Productions. It had been Francis's one chance to do something for himself that would have given him a real sense of purpose, of achievement. Also, it would have involved himself in his daughter's life and career. He was terribly disappointed that things hadn't worked out. It was a big blow, and it would take some time for him to get over it. He got no sympathy from Elizabeth, though. She seemed somewhat blasé about the entire affair, as if she hadn't really expected any of it to work out anyway.

With her future at MGM rectified, Elizabeth left Los Angeles for New York on business, and then was scheduled to depart for London to film *Ivanhoe*. While in New York, she stayed for a brief time with her uncle Howard in a suite at the St. Regis Hotel. She'd always had a good and loving relationship with Howard, but Taylor family history has it that their easy rapport was truly tested during this visit.

Everyone in the family felt that Elizabeth could have acted a little more contrite that Walden Productions hadn't worked out for Francis, and it was his uncle Howard who decided to take it upon himself to talk to her about it. In a surprise altercation with his niece as soon as she got to New York, he attempted to defend Francis and even hint at what he had been up against for so many years by being married to the overbearing Sara. It was a bad idea. "Daddy has no one to blame but himself," Elizabeth countered angrily, "if he's allowed Mummy to control him all of these years. It's too late to come crying to me about it now. I won't hear of it." She further stated that she wasn't going to continue to listen to Howard Young plead Francis's case because, in her view, if her father really loved her, he would have explained himself to her personally by this time—and he hadn't done so, "so what does that tell you?" She also said that it was too late for Francis to start taking an interest in her career by suddenly becoming involved as a producer of her films. "Where was he when I was starting out and Mummy and I were looking for work?" she demanded to know. Indeed, during the course of this very heated, thirty-minute discussion about her parents, Elizabeth became angrier, it's been said, than Howard had ever before seen her.

Upset by the scene, Howard immediately telephoned Sara in Los Angeles—note that he did not call Francis—to inform her that Elizabeth was harboring a good deal of anger over Francis's neglect of her. He said that he was actually afraid for her future emotional well-being. "It's no good, that kind of anger," he told Sara, according to a later recollection. Sara thought this analysis was probably the most preposterous thing she'd ever heard. After all, she said, if her daughter actually felt that way, she would be the first to know about it, and she didn't, so it must not be the case. Before hanging up on him, she told him that he had unnecessarily antagonized Elizabeth, who was already overworked, exhausted, and, actually, still quite ill—so much that there was concern that perhaps she shouldn't even go to England to film *Ivanhoe*. "She's eating baby food, for God's sake," Sara told him. "Have some compassion. Who told you to talk to her about this?" she demanded to know. For the record, it's not known at whose behest Howard decided to have this discussion with Elizabeth, but some Taylor relatives seem to believe that Francis had asked him to intervene. That stands to reason. When word of all of this unpleasantness got back to Francis, he was understandably distraught about it but, true to his nature, did nothing to change the situation

Uncle Howard Gets Rid of Nicky Hilton

It was while she was in London in the summer of 1952 making *Ivanhoe* that Elizabeth began to date charming matinee idol Michael Wilding, whom she had first met back in 1948 when she was in England for *Conspirator*. Wilding was a major star in his native England, a sophisticated man who was listened to and respected in the intellectual, theatrical circles in which he spent his time. When he first met Elizabeth, he was immediately taken by her. He had seen pictures of her, and some of her films, of course, and he knew she was gorgeous. But the reality of Elizabeth, the realness of her person and flesh, left him speechless, as he has recalled it. Actually, she was used to that sort of reaction from people; few who met her for the first time had a different response. There was usually a moment, and she could spot it instantly even if a person tried to hide it, of stunned recognition of her beauty, of her presence . . . and especially of her eyes. She'd gotten used to people looking at her cobalt-blue eyes with great fascination as if trying to determine if they were really that blue, or was it just the way they caught a certain light? It was the way it had always been for Elizabeth Taylor, and the way it would remain.*

As they got to know each other, Elizabeth remembers feeling that Michael was the kind of man who could "take care of me, make me feel good about things, about the world." His conversation was witty and, to a twenty-year-old, profound. In her eyes, and over a very short period of time, he became infallible, just as in the eyes of a child, a father—or at least other fathers, certainly

---

*Tom Gates recalls the first time he met Elizabeth Taylor, in the spring of 1964: "Ever since I first began seeing images of her on magazine covers, I wondered if she could possibly be as beautiful in person. During a chance meeting with her publicist, John Springer, while I was still in school, he told me that among his many clients were both Elizabeth and Richard Burton. I literally begged him for an introduction. He said that he could invite me to a party that both would be attending. This was shortly after they married and were staying in Manhattan at the Regency Hotel. We were introduced, and I remember that as we shook hands I scrutinized her face. Amazingly, it was even more perfect than in her photographs. No matter how she turned her head it was like looking at a perfect sculpture; a sort of living work of art. Not knowing what else to say, I finally said something like, 'It's very nice meeting you, Miss Taylor,' and with somewhat wobbly legs I walked over to a sofa and practically collapsed. One of the guests came over to me and asked if I was all right. 'I guess so,' I said, 'I just met Elizabeth Taylor.' 'Oh,' he said, 'I know exactly how you feel. It happens to all of us the first time. After a while you get used to it.' Well, I never quite got used to it."

not her own—could do no wrong. "He represented tranquillity, security, maturity—all the things I needed in myself," she has recalled.

At the time, Michael Wilding, who was twenty years Elizabeth's senior, was married to actress Kay Young, but they were separated, and in fact he hadn't even seen her in a number of years. Distinguished, with his receding hairline and his tweed suits, he certainly seemed more the fatherly type than the lover. He suffered from epilepsy, a closely guarded secret at the time because of the stigma attached to the condition, and this very likely was at the root of his timid demeanor and cautious nature in public settings. He was soft-spoken and retiring and, like Francis Taylor, loathed confrontation. In time, when he and Elizabeth fought, he would always let her win the argument. He would simply be no match for her and would inevitably let her have her way, which suited her just fine. Indeed, it seemed clear to anyone paying attention that Elizabeth was entering a relationship that would strongly resemble that of her parents. Like Sara had done to Francis for years, Elizabeth was easily able to run roughshod over Michael. But, unlike Francis, Michael was also quite nurturing, caring, and protective. In a sense, he was her father . . . only *better*. Taylor family history also has it that Elizabeth saw a lot of Victor Cazalet's personality in Michael Wilding, his charming banter and debonair manner, for instance. When she told Sara as much, Sara apparently said, "There will only be one Victor, and he's gone now forever, so don't try to replace him in your life. It's no good, Elizabeth."

Elizabeth and Michael dated throughout the summer of *Ivanhoe*, and he helped her tremendously by lending emotional support and doling out fatherly advice during what turned out to be a very difficult production for her. Based on the classic novel of the Crusades by Sir Walter Scott, *Ivanhoe* would also star Robert Taylor and Joan Fontaine. It was just the kind of historical, Technicolor epic that MGM did better than any other studio. Elizabeth was unhappy with the script, though, because there were two leading ladies in the film—she and Joan Fontaine—and only one got the hero in the end. And it wasn't Elizabeth. To add to her unhappiness, because she was in London making this movie, she was also unable to attend the wedding of her brother, Howard, to Mara Regan. Howard had just received his Army induction notice and wanted to be married before he was shipped off to war. He and Mara originally had a date in mind that would have made it possible for Elizabeth to attend, but then moved the ceremony up to June 23, 1951. Elizabeth was disappointed that she could not be present for her brother and his new wife, especially since both had been in her wedding party to Nicky Hilton.

Ivanhoe would be well-received when it was finally released in 1952. But Elizabeth had no interest in this movie at all, primarily because she simply wasn't emotionally or physically equipped to make it. Every day was torture for her. She gave such a lackluster performance in her scenes that the vocal track of practically every one had to be rerecorded by her in Hollywood later during postproduction just so that she could be properly understood.

During this time, Elizabeth began to feel that she was falling for Wilding, and over a few weeks he started to reciprocate. Though some in his circle felt that he was only becoming interested in Taylor to further his career and public image in America, Michael insisted that his motives were genuine and that he was drawn to her because he'd simply never met anyone like her before. Besides, he didn't enjoy acting anyway, or so he said during one dinner conversation; when asked about his future ambitions, he said he just wanted to retire to a country home and live a quiet and peaceful life. Of course, the question posed whenever he made a statement like that one was: What are you doing with Elizabeth Taylor, then? Actually, he would say, he didn't really like actresses very much, as a rule.

When Elizabeth decided she wanted him as her second husband, Michael wasn't so sure about the sensibleness of such a move. He was more mature and experienced in his reasoning and resisted taking the relationship to the next level, saying that he felt they were moving too quickly. *Ivanhoe* wrapped production in October, and by that time Elizabeth was frustrated that she'd not been able to get the answer from him that she wanted, which was yes to a marriage proposal. By this time, she was used to having her way, and few people could deny her when she desired something. To merely conclude that she was selfish, though, would be too simplistic a conclusion. She was a world-famous movie star and, as such, a woman who had grown accustomed to entitlement. The world revolved around her—she didn't ask it to do so, or try in any way to spin it in her favor, it just always had, for as far back as she could remember. It was the only way she knew it. Moreover, as she got older she began to feel that she simply could not be alone. She had always had someone watching over her, be it Sara Taylor or the movie studio, and she was used to it. She didn't know how to be an independent woman.

To her credit, at least she had the courage and spirit to try love again after the bloodbath of her marriage to Nicky Hilton. She could have easily abandoned the notion and become permanently disillusioned about her future, but she didn't. Her imagination had been inflamed, her emotions stirred by the possibility of having a life's companion, and maybe even raising a family with him. She was her mother's daughter, after all, and as such, she was nothing if not tenacious. She believed she could achieve anything if she set her mind and heart to it—even a good marriage.

After finishing *Ivanhoe* in October, Elizabeth returned to the United States uncertain as to where she stood with Michael Wilding and even considering the possibility that perhaps it was not meant to be. She still had business with Nicky Hilton, unfortunately, concerning stock in the Hilton hotel chain that she'd received as a wedding present from the Hilton family, as well as some other issues relating to the divorce settlement. Obviously, she didn't wish to see him. However, on another level, she had to admit that she also couldn't wait for him to be able to look at her and recognize that not only had she survived his brutality, she had continued to thrive as well. Once in New York, she checked into the Plaza Hotel.

Sara and Francis decided that they would not allow their daughter to meet with Nicky Hilton alone, so they flew to New York with Elizabeth's attorney and also took a suite at the Plaza. When Nicky showed up at the first meeting with Elizabeth and her parents, he seemed to be the same calm, well-mannered young man he'd been before the wedding. After all, no one would have been able to guess during his courtship of Elizabeth that once he had a few drinks in him he could explode in horrible violence against any woman. Now he seemed to be that same person again, laughing it up with Francis as if he'd never laid a hand on the man's daughter. Immediately after that meeting, Elizabeth began to despair that she was the one responsible for bringing forth such unspeakable violence from Nicky, actually taking responsibility for what had happened in their marriage. "He's just the way he was before he knew me," she said through her tears, "so I must have done *something* or said *something*..." It is said that during this emotional breakdown Francis Taylor first learned that his only daughter had been viciously beaten during her marriage. He was, understandably, devastated by the revelation.

This was the 1950s. Spousal abuse was not yet the subject of discussion and debate in public forums, such as on televised afternoon talk shows, that it is today, and Sara and Francis truly did not know how to deal with its psychological complexities and ramifications. There was just no way that the Taylor parents were equipped to deal with the trauma Elizabeth had suffered and the post-traumatic stress she apparently continued to experience. They decided that they needed a few days to come up with a strategy to handle things, but then, much to their dismay, Elizabeth began sneaking out with Nicky on dates! They feared that the situation, left unchecked, could easily evolve into their daughter agreeing to a second marriage to a wealthy batterer. Knowing her impulsive nature and confused emotional state, it was not a far-fetched notion. They had to put a stop to it.

It was Francis Taylor who made the first move toward a solution: He telephoned his uncle Howard at his home in Connecticut and asked for his advice, explaining the full scope of the problem—or at least as much as he understood at the time. It's not known if Howard Young had been aware of the beatings Elizabeth had suffered, but it's likely that this conversation with his nephew marked the first he had been exposed to this family secret. Howard promised that he would take care of the problem. Indeed, he was a man accustomed to having the final word in any disagreement, a person some considered a bully, and, certainly, one who had cowed Francis for most of his life. However, his personality and temperament would serve the family well in the troubling and ongoing problem Nicky Hilton presented in their lives.

Howard telephoned Elizabeth at the Plaza Hotel and invited her and Nicky to his estate in Connecticut for dinner and an overnight visit. She was surprised by the invitation, considering what had happened between them before she left for England, but also happy that he was not holding a grudge against her. She eagerly agreed to see Howard and bring along her ex-husband. A Taylor family member who was not alive at the time but who has heard the story many times recalls, "The family history has it that Uncle Howard treated Elizabeth and Nicky to a sumptuous meal and delightful evening. Then, the next morning before Elizabeth had awakened, he met with Nicky privately. He offered him $20,000 to disappear from Elizabeth's life forever, never see her again, never contact her again, never have anything to do with her, and only deal with her through his and her attorneys from that moment on. Well, $20,000 was peanuts to Nicky Hilton. He laughed in Howard's face and said, 'No deal.' You didn't laugh in Uncle Howard's face and get away with it. Howard hauled off and punched Nicky in the gut and leveled him right onto the floor. Then he said that if Nicky didn't leave his niece alone he would get on the phone and call every columnist he knew in Hollywood and tell them that Nicky had beaten Elizabeth during their marriage, thereby ruining him and the Hilton family name forever.

The threat of being revealed as a man who had beaten America's sweetheart—Velvet Brown from *National Velvet*, Kay Banks from *Father of the Bride*—was the only thing that made Nicky stop and think. He backed off and said he would take Elizabeth back to New York and leave her alone. Then, according to the way I heard the story, he said, 'Can I still have the $20,000?' And Howard said, 'Fuck you. You should have taken it when I offered it. That offer is now rescinded. Now get out of my house, you little bastard.' An hour or so later, Nicky drove Elizabeth back to New York. I understand that on the way back, he told her he was serious about a German actress named Betsy von Furstenberg, and he wouldn't be seeing her again, ever. I don't know how she took it, probably not well, knowing Elizabeth. I only know that it was finally the end of Nicky Hilton in her life. I am pretty sure she never saw him again."

Michael Wilding

When Elizabeth and her parents returned to Los Angeles after the Hilton-related business meetings in New York, Elizabeth telephoned Michael Wilding in London to ask if he might want to come to the States to visit her. He agreed to do so, and the two spent the winter months of 1951 in California dating and getting to know each other away from public scrutiny. On December 12, Wilding was granted a divorce. That night, he and Elizabeth were dining at Romanoff's restaurant in Los Angeles when he pulled from his vest pocket a sapphire-and-diamond ring. He intended it to be a simple token of his feelings—a commemoration of his new freedom and a commitment that he was indeed interested in pursuing a future with her. However, when he went to put the ring on her right hand, she snatched it from him and put it on her left hand, third finger. "That's where it belongs," she told him, beaming. Then she kissed him and said, "Now, that makes it official, doesn't it? Or shall I spell it out for you? Will you marry me?"

At first, Sara and Francis were unsure as to whether or not Elizabeth should marry again, or at least so soon. Marianne Lincoln worked for Francis Taylor in his Beverly Hills art gallery at the time and recalls that the Taylor parents both made an effort to learn what they could about Wilding during his time in Los Angeles because they felt much guilt over allowing Elizabeth to marry Hilton, even though they could not have stopped her if they wanted to. They made it clear that they thought Elizabeth should wait before jumping into another marriage. They had no problem with Wilding and thought he was a decent person who would treat her well, but they were conscious that they had thought the same about Nicky Hilton. Simply put, they were worried about their daughter and just wished that she would be more cautious with her heart.

Lincoln, who now lives abroad, recalled a conversation she had with Francis as they were preparing for a Los Angeles exhibit in the spring of 1952. "She has everything, yet she faces, I fear, a life of heartbreak," Francis told her, according to her memory. "You can thank Sara for that, for pushing this life on her." He was, clearly, still angry at his wife, blaming her for Elizabeth's lot in life, and not even trying to hide his feelings about it. "Look at her," he said of his daughter. "She's nineteen and will be married twice already."

"Maybe this time it will work," Marianne offered hopefully.

"He is twenty years older than she is," Francis reminded her. "How is it possible that it will work?" Still, he said that he and Sara would dutifully attend the wedding in London, as soon as Elizabeth sent word back to them that it had been officially scheduled.

On February 21, 1952, Elizabeth and Michael were married

in a brief, ten-minute service in Westminster at the Caxton Registry Hall. She had ultimately decided not to give her parents enough warning to allow them to make the trip abroad, explaining privately to a Taylor relative that she didn't want them present, "because I know they aren't supportive of me and Michael, and I'm just not going to put up with it from them. I have enough on my mind with the picture I'm making." Sara was heartsick, Francis not so much. He seemed distant and pensive during this time, as if he'd found a place of calm within and wasn't about to leave it to cross swords with anyone. However, Sara couldn't stop crying about the missed opportunity to see her daughter marry again, and also couldn't comprehend why Elizabeth would have such animosity toward her, especially after she had been so supportive during the nightmare of Nicky Hilton. It just didn't make any sense to her. "[Uncle] Howard told me that she's secretly mad at Francis," she told one relative, "but she can't be mad at me, too, can she? What did I ever do to her?"

Of course, considering what Elizabeth had just put her parents through with Nicky Hilton, it would have been a nice gesture to invite them to her wedding. However, she knew they were ambivalent about the marriage, and she didn't want them to spoil her day. They had to settle with taking photos of themselves holding a picture of Elizabeth and Michael on their wedding day, which MGM then sent the media. It was a very odd thing to agree to do, but they did it anyway.

According to Elizabeth's new contract with MGM, Sara Taylor was still on the payroll, but she had much less to do with Elizabeth's career by this time. It was a juggernaut now, traveling along on its own power and speed and no longer requiring Sara's people skills to keep it on track. Plus, Elizabeth was not exactly open to helpful suggestions at this time in her life, and even Sara knew better than to try to tell her how to act out a scene on a soundstage. The days of Sara standing on the sidelines and making faces at Elizabeth as she tried to work were long gone. Because Elizabeth's new contract also guaranteed a three-year deal for her new husband, Michael, at MGM—at her direction, of course—it must have seemed to her as if everyone in her midst was profiting from her success, except her father, who, she may also have felt, had also tried to do as much with the recently failed Howard Hughes enterprise.

The Wilding marriage started out on an easy and romantic note, but their peace would not last long. They had rented a small, two-bedroom home in Los Angeles, but then in the summer of 1952 Elizabeth learned that she was pregnant. Her new MGM contract gave her roughly $5,000 a week, but she was being taxed in the 90 percent bracket. When attorneys and agents and publicists took their shares, she was left with about $20,000 a year. In the early 1950s, that was considered a good living—unless you were Elizabeth Taylor. As soon as the studio learned she was expecting—which was just after she finished her film *The Girl Who Had Everything*—it placed her on suspension: She would not be paid for pregnancy leave. Around the same time, Wilding—who now had a three-year deal with MGM, secured by Elizabeth for him—rejected the studio's script for *Latin Lovers*. As a result, he too was placed on suspension. (The role ultimately went to Ricardo Montalban, which made a lot more sense, anyway.) Compounding matters, leaving England had cost Michael just about every cent he owned: Inland Revenue billed him the equivalent of about $100,000. The couple was now living on Elizabeth's savings. These were show business people, though, and very practical. When Elizabeth found the home they decided they wanted, she went about the business of securing it for them even though they simply didn't have the money to be able to afford it.

Elizabeth decided, against the advice of her attorney and accountant, that she wanted to pay for the estate in cash. She explained that she wanted to know that the house was hers and that no one could take it from her if she decided to stop working and could no longer afford the mortgage payments (which, if anything, shows how insecure she was about her future). The house was listed at $75,000. She had about $20,000 in her bank account, but she didn't want to spend it because, after all, she and her husband were living on it. Therefore, she went on a mission to raise the balance of the asking price. First she went to the Los Angeles courthouse to finally collect the money that had been put aside for her from her childhood earnings, as per the Coogan Act that stipulated that her earnings during those years had to be deposited in a special account with the courts by Sara (who always did exactly as she was supposed to where this important matter was concerned). At the end of the day at court, Elizabeth walked away with another $47,100. It was still not enough, though. Taylor family history has it that she considered telephoning her uncle Howard on the East Coast to ask him for a loan. "Francis told me that she had second thoughts about that," said Marshall Baldrige, "because she'd learned that Howard had been the one to get rid of Nicky Hilton, and she wasn't a hundred percent sure how to feel about it. She took it the wrong way. She said, 'If he was going to tell the world that Nicky beat me, was he considering what that would have done to me and my reputation? How could he do that to me?' She didn't get it that, really, Howard was bluffing. He wouldn't have done it for precisely that reason. However, as shrewd as Elizabeth was in so many ways, she could be just that dense. She would see exactly what was in front of her, and not look any deeper for hidden meaning or a person's true motivation. So she was actually unhappy with Howard for what he'd done, and decided not to call upon him for a loan."

Elizabeth then decided that she would find another way to raise the money, and she did just that from an unnamed executive at MGM. It seems difficult to imagine that she would have asked L. B. Mayer for it, given their tense relationship, but who else would have been able to authorize such a payment? At any rate, she did raise the required funds, further demonstrating that when she wanted something, she was the kind of woman who would find a way to get it. "Yes, I got the money," she later confirmed, "but only on the condition that I would make an exhausting tour—pregnant, mind you, to promote a picture. I vowed then and there that I would never have to ask anybody for anything."

Elizabeth's pregnancy marked the first time her weight had become an issue. She'd always been thin, but with her pregnancy she gained fifty pounds. She'd lose most of it when the baby was born, but her figure was never quite the same, and neither was her appetite. From this time onward, the scale would be one of her greatest foes.

Her first child, Michael Howard Wilding, was born by cesarian section on January 6, 1953. The middle name of Howard was in honor of her brother, who had returned home from Korea just in time for the birth. The baby was beautiful, with dark curly hair and deep blue eyes. Elizabeth was thrilled, saying that the newborn had given her a new sense of purpose. "I've never felt so important in my life," she said.

The studio, eager to capitalize on the publicity of motherhood for one of its biggest attractions, arranged for Elizabeth Taylor to begin giving interviews as soon as she returned home from the hospital. "We brought a nurse from the hospital to take care of little Mike," she told a reporter from *Screen Life*. "But she will leave as soon as I finish my next picture [*Rhapsody*]. I intend to take care of him full time, all by myself. Part of the fun is taking care of your own child. Mike and I just simply adore taking care of him. Yes, we still have our five cats and two dogs, and we are trying to get a third dog, a coach dog, to grow up with the baby. They say they are very good with children. You know, I have always loved animals," Elizabeth said wistfully. "Remember my horse, Prince Charles? And my chipmunk? And my dogs and cats?"

When Elizabeth ran off to tend to the crying baby, Michael pulled the reporter aside. "Elizabeth has only one regret living up on this hilltop," he said, referring to their estate. "There's no street where she can take Michael in a perambulator and wheel him for an airing. She's such a proud little mother. Isn't she just the loveliest thing you've ever seen?"

Two close family friends were guests at a small gathering at the Wilding home in February, during which Elizabeth introduced the new baby to her friends and to those of her parents. Neither wished to be identified, but their story is significant just the same. Sara, now fifty-nine, and Francis, fifty-eight, were also present, as was their son, Howard, now twenty-six.

"It was like a christening, only more informal, maybe fifty people," said one of the guests. "Things were changing with the Taylor family. It had been hard for Sara to relinquish control of Elizabeth's career. At the party, she told me that she felt she'd done her part and done it well. She was tired, anyway, or so she said, and ready to let it go. Just a simple gesture of gratitude from time to time from Elizabeth would have been nice, especially as Sara got older. I know that Sara felt underappreciated but, as she put it to me, 'You can't go through life expecting your children to show gratitude. If you do, you will be destined to live with constant disappointment, and have no one to blame but yourself.' The truth was that Elizabeth was holding on to a lot of anger having to do with the way she was treated as a child."

There was one moment during the festivities that the two family friends will never forget. Even today, more than fifty years later, both say it makes their hearts clench achingly to recall it. It started when Sara picked up the new baby from the bassinet and began to cradle him in her arms, rocking him. "You will be the most perfect child," Sara said to little Michael in a soft and loving voice. "Just like your mother. Perfect, in every way."

"Mummy, no!" came the voice from behind her. It was Elizabeth. With a look of anger on her face, she rushed over to Sara. "Give him to me, now!" she ordered.

"What did I do?" Sara asked, shaken almost to tears. "What in the world . . ."

"Just give him to me," Elizabeth repeated, according to the later recollection. Sara then gently handed little Michael to his mother.

Elizabeth stared at Sara for a moment. Perhaps remembering that they had guests, she collected herself and said in a voice so calm it sounded eerie, "Why, you did nothing, Mummy. Every-thing is fine. It's just time for his nap." Then, without another word, she quickly took the baby upstairs.

"We all stood in the living room with our mouths open, not knowing how to react to such an outburst," recalled the family friend. "Clearly embarrassed, Sara took a deep breath to calm her-self and then announced, 'Francis. Howard. It's time for us to go.' After Howard retrieved his mother's wrap and assisted her with it, the three of them walked out the front door without saying good-bye to anyone. But they had left the door open, and I happened to be the one to close it. It was then that I saw them standing maybe ten feet from the house, huddled together. Sara was in Francis's arms. She was crying."

A Marriage Devoid of Passion

Despite the children they had together, Elizabeth Taylor's mar-riage to Michael Wilding was in trouble after the first couple of years. Not surprisingly, the two had lost their way. There were a myriad of problems, not the least of which was that Michael had begun to take his wife's illnesses less seriously than he had in the past. By this time, Elizabeth had all sorts of health issues, includ-ing a sciatic nerve problem that kept her wheelchair-bound for days at a time. Michael joked that she used hospitals as if they were resorts. However, he was serious when he said that he be-lieved that there were underlying reasons for Elizabeth's poor health—even if he wasn't exactly sure what they were at the time. At least as he saw it, his wife always managed to find a way to make her life a misery. For instance, he recalled being stung by a bee in the backyard and said he pulled out the stinger, "and that was the end of it." However, when Elizabeth was similarly stung, she swelled up and came down with a fever, "and it turned into a major hospital event. If she gets a cold," he continued, "she reacts so violently she's almost dead from pneumonia. She stubs her toe, it's broken. She bumps into something, she ends up in a cast. It makes no sense. No person is that fragile. There's something else at work."

It's not so much that Michael believed his wife's illnesses were psychosomatic—she really *was* in pain when she said she was—as that he felt there was some subconscious reason for her to continue to find ways to prolong her physical despair. Her Christian Scientist mother, Sara, agreed with him, but she had learned long before to not discuss such matters with Elizabeth. The two of them—Michael and Sara—may have been on to something in trying to understand Elizabeth. It's also possible that on some level, Elizabeth realized that being terribly ill was one way to control her life. When she was sick and hospitalized, she was away from the studio, didn't have to make movies she didn't wish to make—and was also absent from any of the complex responsibilities of her personal life. Being ill also got her the attention of her mother, and she knew that this interest from Sara was focused on her well-being instead of on her career. On some level, it must have made her feel loved. Truly, though, only Elizabeth could know the real reasons for all of the sicknesses in her life—and her public comments about the subject seem to suggest that she hasn't given it much thought. "Richard says I'm prone to *incidents*, not accidents," she would say in years to come, referencing her seventh husband, Richard Burton. One certainly can't blame observers from speculating about the matter, though. After all, few people have suffered in their lives as much as Elizabeth Taylor—and there does have to be *some* explanation for it other than being "prone to incidents."

Meanwhile, Michael simply stopped caring about Elizabeth's physical problems, and she began to feel abandoned and unloved.

Their communication had not only begun to sour, it had even become violent. For instance, while they were dining with Frank Sinatra one evening on the Sunset Strip, she insulted Michael about his wardrobe. He told her to shut up. She went to slap him but he seized her wrist in midair and gave it a sharp twist. Elizabeth screamed out in pain. "You broke my wrist! If I have to miss a day of filming because of this, I'll sue you!" Wilding was indifferent to her outburst. "Oh, screw you, Elizabeth," he said before walking out of the restaurant and leaving her with Frank. A few nights later at another restaurant in Hollywood, Michael said something that once again displeased her. She swung her arm in a wide arc, her fist finally striking him on the jaw. She wasn't much more than five feet tall, but her hand could really pack a wallop when she decided to put all of her strength and fury behind it. Michael fell to the floor, as if *he* were smaller than *she*—and he wasn't. In some ways, it seemed that Michael was getting acquainted with the part of Elizabeth that was finally getting even with Nicky Hilton. She was the aggressor now—and somehow to her it felt right.

Elizabeth even tried to compel Michael to rise—or sink, as it were—to the level of a Nicky Hilton by inciting him to anger. He once recalled a morning when he was quietly doing a crossword puzzle and not paying attention to her. "She snatched the paper from my hand, tore it in half, and threw it into the fire," he remembered. "'So much for you and your stupid games,' she said, adding, 'Go on, hit me! Hit me, why don't you?' I told her, 'I've never gone in for hitting hysterical females.' She moaned, 'Oh God, if only you would. At least that would prove you are flesh and blood instead of a stuffed dummy.'"

There were many of these kinds of dramatic interactions with Michael, as if Elizabeth had begun to equate melodrama with intimacy. At the very least, she was acting as a character might in one of her more overblown films because, to her mind, that was how people engaged with each other in offscreen relationships as well. Everything was heightened, all emotions raw and unabated as she mistreated her husband, encouraged reciprocity at home, and then acted out similar scenarios at the studio with her costars. The fact that she'd seen such violence in her first marriage didn't help when it came to differentiating what was and was not acceptable behavior between people.

During an interview and photo session the couple did with *Photoplay*, Elizabeth's public façade seemed to crack. In the pictures, her blue eyes are shrouded by large sunglasses. The lovely nose, red lips, and perfectly sculpted face had always translated into spectacular photographs, and her features did not let her—or the photographer—down on this day. Michael, in a natty black suit and tie, was at her side. "Elizabeth, dear, move slightly over, I don't think you're in your best light," he said, trying to be helpful.

In front of the reporter, she snapped at him: "Don't tell me what to do, Michael. I'm not your daughter, I'm your wife."

"But dear . . ."

It was clear from her curt attitude that more was at issue than just the photograph they were taking at the moment. "I know how to pose for a picture," she said through a frozen smile. Then, in remarks that seemed reminiscent of Sara Taylor, she said, "When you have taken as many pictures as I have, then you can tell me how to pose. Meanwhile, just be quiet . . . *Daddy*."

"The happiest years of my marriage were when Elizabeth was dependent on me," Michael admitted later. "Now I follow her around, and I hate it. And," he added, "I thought I'd be the one to guide this trembling little creature along life's stony path. It didn't turn out that way. Not at all. Lately, I'm told to shut up."

"Her father, Francis, was concerned enough about stories about her bad temper to mention it to her," recalled Paul Young, an attorney in Beverly Hills who began working for Francis and Sara at this time. "He and I were having a drink at the Beverly Hills Hotel where he had asked Elizabeth to join us. He was upset. He'd heard that she slapped Michael in public and wanted to ask her about it. She showed up in a foul mood after having a bad day at the studio. 'That bastard Mayer,' she said, 'I swear to God, one day

I will put my hands around his throat and strangle the life out of him.' She sat down without even saying hello to me. 'What is it you want to talk to me about?' she demanded of Francis. 'I'm worried about you,' he told her. 'Your temper. I've been reading things . . .' Elizabeth said, 'Daddy, you should know better than to believe what you read about me. They're all lies. Every word.' He kept pushing. 'Well, did you slap Michael the other night at dinner?' She shot back with, 'So what if I did? That's *my* business.'"

At that point she began to cry. Again, Francis was seeing first-hand the effect Nicky Hilton's brutality was still having on his daughter. While Elizabeth sobbed quietly, hiding her face as best she could, Young excused himself. "I thought it best that I leave. As I rose she didn't even acknowledge my presence.

"I was gone for about twenty minutes; by the time I got back she was gone. Francis was very emotional. 'I'm worried about her,' he told me. 'She's out of control. I think Hilton ruined her. She hasn't been the same since she married that bastard.' At that moment, Sara walked into the restaurant and joined us. 'Did you speak to her?' she asked Francis. 'What did she say?' Francis told her what happened. She slumped forward in her chair a bit and seemed on the verge of crying. 'She won't listen to either of us,' Sara said, turning to me. 'I don't even know why we try anymore.'"

In the midst of her emotional disarray, Elizabeth still had to continue making movies for the studio without any kind of break. She was about to replace Vivien Leigh in a movie called *Elephant Walk* for which MGM loaned her to Paramount for $150,000; Elizabeth received her contracted salary of $42,500. In it, she would portray a bride who embarks on an adventure to the jungle with her husband (Peter Finch), a man who has built a plantation right smack in the middle of the ancient path of the elephants' walk. One had to wonder how she found herself in these kinds of movies . . . but . . . according to the script, once in the jungle, Elizabeth is tempted by Dana Andrews to leave her alcoholic husband, but in the end decides to stay with him. Then the elephants go wild and destroy everything in their path. The movie is filled with metaphors. During the course of making it, Elizabeth suffered an injury that almost left her blinded in one eye, but she recovered just in time to make *Rhapsody*, from May through July of 1953. Elizabeth calls this soapy drama another of her "films that never should have been made by me or anyone else."

The marital problems continued to mount on an almost-daily basis. Still, the couple did not abandon the relationship, determined to make it work, if only for the sake of their young son. By the summer of 1954, Elizabeth was again pregnant. At this time, they decided to purchase a new property, again funded by her savings since Michael no longer had any money of his own. The architect George MacLean had designed an estate in Beverly Hills, close to David O. Selznick's home, that he thought was ideal for them. Elizabeth was anxious to see it. But when they got to the address, there was no one present to meet them and give them access to the estate, which was walled and gated. That didn't stop her. She asked Michael to help hoist her up, and the next thing he knew she was over the wall. She then unlocked the front gate and let Michael into the property. Inside the sizable estate, the garden was landscaped with huge old trees of every variety, from pine to fir. There, the two immediately felt a sense of peacefulness. It was the first time in a while that their problems seemed lifted from them. The couple sat in the garden and enjoyed an impromptu romantic picnic with potato chips and an uncorked bottle of wine left by workers who'd been tending the property. "I think it was one of the most beautiful moments of my life," Elizabeth later remarked. She bought the house, and within a month reality had once again set in to replace any magic she'd first felt about the property: the mortgage of $2,000 a month.

"Look, she couldn't afford it," said Paul Young. "Jules Goldstone [her attorney] and I met with her and explained to her that something like 75 percent of her nearly $200,000 annual income was going to taxes, and she would never be able to afford the mortgage on her lifestyle. 'I'm not used to being told I can't have something,' she told us. 'From the time I was a little girl, my mother told me I could have anything I wanted, and I always have and I'm most certainly not going to stop now. So your job is to figure out a way to get me this house.' Still, Sara told me that after Elizabeth and Michael moved into the estate, Elizabeth would lose sleep agonizing over finances and wondering how much more money she would have to make before she would be able to afford her lifestyle. Obviously, the fact that her husband was not contributing a dime did not help matters, and I think it ruined him in her eyes. One day, she brought him into the office to go over some insurance policies, and I have to say that it was a most unpleasant experience. At one point, she handed him a pen and said, 'Jesus Christ, Michael, stop asking so many questions and just sign the goddamn policy. You make me sick.' He took the pen and obediently signed. She then stood up and said, 'Now, let's go. I have things to do.' And he followed her out the door like a little puppy. Afterward, I called Francis and said, 'Pal, I don't care if your kid is the great Elizabeth Taylor, I wouldn't want to be married to her for all the tea in China.' He laughed and said, 'Oh yeah? Well, just try being married to her mother!'"

Elizabeth's second child, Christopher, was born on February 27, 1955, which was also Elizabeth's twenty-third birthday. By that time she and her husband were barely speaking. When Michael turned down the opportunity to tour with a production of *My Fair Lady*, in the role of Professor Higgins, which made Rex Harrison a star, Elizabeth couldn't believe it. He was afraid that his epilepsy would get out of control if he were to take on such a grueling schedule, but she thought he was just being lazy and cowardly. "I can't believe that I would marry a coward," she screamed at him one day. From that moment on, the marriage was pretty much over, or so said Michael later. "I still loved her," he said, "but a barrier of silence and rejection had grown between us." In fact, the Wildings' marriage was so clearly devoid of passion that sleeping in the same room had become a laughable concept. Though he had his choice of guest rooms, Michael chose to sleep in the living room, on a big violet-colored divan, while Elizabeth occupied the master bedroom. She would cry herself to sleep, heartbroken that another marriage was about to end for her. "I was dead, old at twenty-four," she later said. "It was just smog and no sunshine. We would wake up in the morning without hope, with nothing to do or talk about, with no reason for living out the day."

The summer of 1956 found Elizabeth Taylor restless and ready to find entertainment outside her crumbling marriage. Kevin Mc-Clory, an assistant to movie producer Mike Todd, took a bold move in asking her out. In the guise of a business meeting to discuss a future film project, McClory began to wine and dine Taylor. Soon they were seeing each other on a regular basis. She may not have felt a deep romantic connection with him, but just the possibility of a life beyond her loveless marriage gave her a newfound energy. "I'm in a restaurant with my wife, and who walks in but Elizabeth with this other guy," says Paul Young. "I thought that he was a business associate until I saw them holding hands and kissing over their meal. My wife thought it was a shocking display coming from both a married woman and a celebrity. However, she couldn't keep her eyes off it. Elizabeth seemed a little tipsy, and at one point she got up to go to the ladies' room, bumped into someone else's table, and spilled a bottle of wine all over it. She signed a napkin and handed it to the couple as an apology. 'I can't believe you represent her,' [my wife] told me, very bothered by it all. 'Well, I don't,' I said. 'I represent her father.' My wife said, 'Well, he needs to take her over his knee and give her a good spanking.' Later, as they were walking out of the restaurant, Elizabeth made a point of bringing the man to our table. Holding hands with him and being very affectionate, she introduced him as Kevin Mc-Clory. Then she said, 'It's time for Mr. Wilding to go back to England where he belongs, don't you agree? Therefore, my father will be in touch with you shortly about the dissolution of my marriage to him.' Very formal, ice cold. So, my wife, never one to hold her tongue, looked Kevin up and down, head to toe, and said to Elizabeth, 'Oh really? So, you're still married, are you, my dear?' Elizabeth gave her a look that could boil water, and shot back, 'Obviously, my *dear*, or you would have read about it in all the papers.' And with that, she turned and walked away. Her gentleman friend followed, trying to keep up. Before she left the restaurant, she turned back to us and gave my wife another killer look. The next day, I got a telephone call from Francis, who said, 'My daughter is absolutely furious with your wife for insulting her last night. She told me, "Mr. Young's wife has a big fat mouth and I hate her."' I explained what happened and he said, 'Well, if she's going to date before she's even divorced, she deserves everything she gets.'"

On June 30, Kevin invited her to join Mike Todd and a group of his friends for a weekend of sailing on the *Hyding*, a 117-foot yacht that Todd had chartered. She was happy to go, Elizabeth said, eager to escape the degenerating situation at home. Somehow or another, no one seems to remember exactly how, there was one guest on board whom Elizabeth did not expect: Michael Wilding. Leave it to Elizabeth to find herself on a cruise with both her husband and the man she was dating, but such was her life at the time. Even though she was just twenty-four, her world had never been short on intrigue.

When they boarded, Elizabeth recalls that Mike Todd went straight for the bar, while most of the guests greeted her, cooing over the young star. Her husband wandered about the yacht, trying his best to avoid his wife. She spent most of the cruise talking to Kevin, and occasionally catching the eye of their host, Mike Todd, who seemed unable to keep his eyes off of her in her pink toreador pants and pale blue sweater. As the ship headed out into the open sea, Elizabeth began to feel seasick, "and since I've never been shy about complaining, I'm sure I carried on a bit." Todd heard that she was unwell and suggested she have a cocktail to treat her symptoms. After he escorted her to a bar in the ship's cabin, the two were seen in animated conversation. At one point he sarcastically told her, "Honey, you are a latent intellectual."

She froze for a moment, then announced, "That wasn't very nice."

"Yes, I know," he responded. "I figure you've had your fill of nice."

Elizabeth was speechless for a moment, but eager to continue the easy conversation with Mike Todd. Occasionally, when her husband would happen by, she would laugh just a bit louder at Todd's jokes. As the day wore on, Elizabeth and Mike enjoyed each other's company while she continued to drink champagne, despite her headache and nausea. At one point she handed her empty glass to Todd and asked for another. He smiled at her, saying, "Suit yourself. It's your head." When he moved off to grant her request, Elizabeth once again noticed Michael Wilding sitting alone in a corner. She knew then that she would be moving on from him. The kind thing to do was to set this miserable man free.

In July 1956, MGM announced that Elizabeth Taylor and Michael Wilding were separating. Elizabeth tried to convince herself that the marriage was not a complete failure, since it had lasted more than four years, and produced two handsome children. But she knew it had truly ended long before the world was told of its demise. It was the avoidance of that truth that had wasted the latter years of her life with Michael. "I am afraid that the marriage with Michael had become the relationship for which we were much more suited—brother and sister," she later observed. "He was one of the nicest people I'd ever known. But I'm afraid in those last years I gave him rather a rough time, sort of henpecked him and probably wasn't mature enough for him."

Movies

*O*f course, amid all of the personal upheaval in her life, there was Elizabeth Taylor's astonishing movie career. Many books have been written about her films with her private life as a backdrop to her prodigious career. Entire books have been written about *Cleopatra*! Important as many of her films may have been, though, it has to be said that a great many of them were inferior projects that she only made either because she was forced to do so by the studio or because she needed the money. In truth, it's not from those movies that one really learns much about Elizabeth Taylor, other than her growing ability as an actress in a succession of bad films. "Don't ask me about acting," she would say. "Someday, I hope to be really good. I'm not learning and developing. I'm trying. I've always been an intuitive actress as opposed to an instructed one. I have no technique. I just try to become the other person. Some people act by charts or by the Stanislavski method. I can only do it by forgetting myself completely, even moving or picking up things by impulse. I've been good so few times, but I'd like to be good always."

That said, Elizabeth was, as everyone well knows, a singularly unique and great movie star, no matter the ratio of good films to bad in her career. By the early 1950s, her talent and undeniable box-office appeal, not to mention her breathtaking beauty, had caught the attention of other movie studios. One such studio was Paramount, who contracted with MGM for Elizabeth's services to appear in George Stevens's *A Place in the Sun*. Based on Theodore Dreiser's popular novel of more than two decades earlier, *An American Tragedy*, it had been given an unsatisfactory production under that title by Paramount in 1931. (MGM had previously loaned her to Warner Bros. in 1947 for its big-budget film version of the stage hit *Life with Father* and would let Warner's have her again in 1956 for *Giant*.)

It was in *A Place in the Sun*, magnificently filmed on location in

Lake Tahoe and under George Stevens's insistent and dogged direction of her, that Elizabeth finally rose to the challenge of her craft. In fact, she has said that she really didn't take acting seriously until she did this movie. Playing opposite Montgomery Clift, her performance as the beautiful, wealthy Angela Vickers was inspired. When Academy Award time rolled around, the black-and-white film received nine nominations, including Best Picture, Clift for Best Actor, and Shelley Winters for Best Actress. It wound up with six Oscars, including one for Stevens as Best Director. Finally, and despite her own Oscar snub, Elizabeth had arrived as an actress, her performance hailed by critics as being the equal of Winters's. And as a star, she would for the rest of her career be billed above the title.

Montgomery Clift became one of her best friends during this time. Handsome, with a shock of dark brown hair and piercing blue-gray eyes, sensuously full lips, and a strong jawline, Monty, as he was called by his friends, was twenty-eight years old when he arrived in Hollywood to star for director Howard Hawks in the classic western *Red River* opposite big John Wayne. Those who knew of Clift's sexual orientation had serious misgivings that he could carry off the part of the belligerent foster son of the Duke. But the sensitive-looking Clift not only held his own against Wayne, but earned his grudging respect along with excellent notices from film critics. Clift was cast by George Stevens to star opposite Elizabeth in *A Place in the Sun*, and audiences fell as hard for him as she did in his unsympathetic role of the ambitious suitor who is sent to the electric chair for murdering his pregnant girlfriend (Shelley Winters) when her condition threatens to disrupt his cushy new life. Taylor and Clift were achingly beautiful and their love scenes were so convincing that they will forever rank as classic examples of young love on the silver screen.

Despite the closeness of their personal relationship following this film, Clift's sexual orientation kept him from giving himself to her. They got along so well, it seemed unfair that he preferred men over women. Some have reckoned that Elizabeth's attraction to Clift (and his to her) was based in a large part on their mutual physical beauty, which could reasonably be compared—the same dark hair, the same thick, dark eyebrows over light-colored eyes, the perfectly shaped faces, the full, kissable lips—he a male version of Elizabeth, she his female counterpart. If Monty had been heterosexual, there's little doubt that he and Elizabeth would have married. "We really loved each other," Elizabeth once told Barbara Walters, "in the fullest, complete sense of the word."

In another interview, this one with the gay magazine the *Advocate*, she explained, "I was 18 or 19 when I helped him realize that he was a homosexual, and I barely knew what I was talking about. I was a virgin when I was married, and not a world expert on sexuality. But I loved Monty with all of my heart and just knew that he was unhappy. I knew that he was meant to be with a man and not a woman, and I discussed it with him, introduced him to some really great guys. It was very hard for men who wanted to come out of the closet in those days. The men I knew—Monty and Jimmy [Dean] and Rock [Hudson]—if anything I helped them get out of the closet. I didn't even know I was doing it. I didn't know that I was more advanced than most people in this town. It just never occurred to me."

On May 12, 1956, Monty left a gathering at the Wildings', which had also been attended by Rock Hudson. On his way down a treacherous canyon road, he got in a terrible automobile accident. Elizabeth arrived on the scene shortly afterward to find her friend bloodied almost beyond recognition. His teeth had been knocked down his throat, preventing him from breathing. Without a moment's hesitation, Elizabeth plunged her hand down his windpipe to clear the blockage. She would have done anything to save him. While she was at his side, photographers began to arrive on the scene. "If you take one picture of this man in this condition," she told them through her tears, "I swear to God, I will not pose for another photo, ever!" Rock Hudson once recalled it this way: "She prevented the photographers from taking Monty's picture by the foulest language I have ever heard. She shocked them out of taking it. She was saying things like, 'You son of a bitch! I'll kick you in the nuts.' The photographers were saying, 'Miss Taylor, you shouldn't be talking like that.' And then six of us formed a line to hide Monty, and we said to the photographers [Hudson bared his teeth viciously], 'Take a picture of us. We'll smile.'" The paparazzi backed off. "His head was so swollen it was almost as wide as his shoulders," Elizabeth later said of Clift's injuries. "His eyes had disappeared. His cheeks were level with his nose . . . and his upper lip—it was like a spoon had gouged a great big chunk out of his mouth and teeth." She accompanied Monty to the hospital, not about to leave his side. The incident showed many people another side of her, a facet of her personality that is giving and totally selfless. Though she could be tremendously self-absorbed, she could also be a good and loyal friend, especially to the downtrodden and confused people in her life—as she would demonstrate countless times in the future.

In 1956, Elizabeth appeared as Leslie Benedict in the Warner Bros. film version of the best-selling Edna Ferber novel *Giant*. Her costars were Rock Hudson and James Dean, both of whom she developed a deep feeling for. It was on that set, in Marfa, Texas, that she and Hudson became close friends; the two spent a great deal of time together, drinking and partying. In fact, they created what Elizabeth now remembers as the best drink she'd ever tasted: a chocolate martini made with vodka, Hershey's syrup, and Kahlúa. "How we survived," she says of their late nights together and early mornings on the set, "I'll never know."

Elizabeth would talk to Rock for hours about her struggles in trying to have both a career and family life, and he confided in her about his life as well. "We used to sit up all night talking about everything," she has said. "We had no secrets from each other, ever, all through the years." Of course, as we well now know, Hudson was gay and closeted, his entire life and career an emotional complication for him.

Perhaps their bond had something to do with the gravity of the high-profile project they were in Texas to film and bring to life:

George Stevens's sprawling, 197-minute, multigenerational saga detailing some thirty years in the life of cattle baron Jordan "Bick" Benedict (Hudson), his beautiful wife Leslie (Taylor), and their family as they go about their daily routine on their half-million-acre ranch, Reata. No sooner have Leslie and Bick married than Bick's sister Luz (Mercedes McCambridge) and Leslie lock horns over the way the new mistress of the house takes over what had always been Luz's province. Among their differences is Leslie's intention to break down the walls of prejudice against the Mexican workers at Reata. But the real antagonist in the proceedings is Jett Rink (Dean), who goes through a gradual transition from dirt-poor farmer to millionaire after he strikes it rich in oil. Leslie's and Luz's differences are nothing compared to those that develop over the years between Bick and Jett.

The film is an epic in every meaning of the word and would not only be popular with moviegoers, but would wind up winning for Stevens his second Oscar as Best Director in a film starring Elizabeth Taylor, the first having been for *A Place in the Sun*. Was she his muse, or merely his good-luck charm? Perhaps she was a little bit of both. *Giant* was Warner Bros.' highest-grossing film of the year, earning back seven times its original cost of $5.4 million and garnering nine Oscar nominations. (Sadly, Dean never saw the release of the film; he died in a car accident a year before its release.)

Although Elizabeth demonstrated a wide range in her acting, going from nubile teenager to handsome, sixtyish, matronly grandmother, she once again came up undeservedly empty at Oscar time, while her costars Hudson and Dean were both nominated for Best Actor, as was Mercedes McCambridge in the Supporting Actress category. Although nominated, *Giant* failed to gain the Best Picture Oscar. That would go to Mike Todd for *Around the World in 80 Days*.

Between the emotional high of the commercial and critical success she enjoyed in 1951 with *A Place in the Sun* at Paramount and the epic, widely praised blockbuster *Giant* with Warner Bros. in 1956, Elizabeth had to endure a grueling schedule of seven films in five years, many of them unworthy of her talents, and none of them deserving of a place on her résumé. There were a couple of problems going on at the same time. First of all, having been robbed of her childhood, Elizabeth would have little sense of her self or of her self-worth as she entered adulthood. Therefore, she did not know what kinds of movies to make, which scripts were viable for her and which were not—who she was as an actress, let alone as a woman. Her confusion would become clearer in the future with the movies she'd make with Richard Burton, but in these earlier days it's obvious that Elizabeth didn't really have a career plan, or any idea at all as to what she would be best at in terms of acting. This uncertainty was compounded by the fact that she didn't really have much choice anyway during these years. Because of contractual obligations, she had to make what was thrown at her or risk being suspended by MGM. Ironically, it seemed that she would always end up off the MGM lot for projects of substance. For instance, in the midst of her emotional disarray in her private life with Michael Wilding, MGM insisted on loaning her to Paramount as a replacement for an ailing Vivien Leigh in *Elephant Walk*. Then she made *Rhapsody*, from May through July of 1953. But wait, there were others, some of which have already been covered in this text: *The Girl Who Had Everything*, an inept remake of 1931's *A Free Soul*; the big-budget historical spectacle *Ivanhoe*; *Love Is Better Than Ever*, a B-grade musical that was released two years after it was made (due to costar Larry Parks's being blacklisted); and the Technicolor sudser costarring Van Johnson about lost love in post–World War II France, *The Last Time I Saw Paris*. (Actually, this one has a lot to commend it; Elizabeth's performance is haunting and it's filmed beautifully.) And there was one more that she would rather have not done—*Beau Brummell*, the movie with which she finished 1953 and began the new year of 1954. Though these are terrible films, it has to be said that Elizabeth Taylor always did her best with such mediocrity, and she was always a riveting screen presence. Even when there was no reason for her to invest herself emotionally in the work, she gave it her all and transcended these mostly inferior projects.

Mike Todd

Elizabeth Taylor had never met anyone quite like Mike Todd. A good-looking guy with a firm, square jaw and jet-black hair, he had lean cheeks beneath steady brown eyes. He had the build of a prizefighter. His skin was ruddy, described by one magazine as "like a rock granite quarry, after a dozen years of being battered by rainstorms." It wasn't his appearance that set Todd apart, though. It was his unquenchable spirit. He loved his life and lived it to the fullest, and after so many years with the dour Michael Wilding, Elizabeth couldn't help but be attracted to someone like him. Being in his presence somehow filled her with hope for the future. She would find, in talking to him, that he had a brilliant mind, always with a project in the offing or a great idea in development. His was a steely determination to succeed. He was also a man of unquestionable integrity, she would learn, his word his bond. In a sense he was a combination of the best traits of her two husbands: Nicky Hilton's drive and ambition and sense of financial security, with Michael Wilding's patience and understanding. He was also a powerful and self-sufficient man, very much, it could be said, unlike her own father. On paper, it looked like Elizabeth couldn't go wrong with Mike Todd, even if he was twice her age.

If there's one thing Mike offered Elizabeth that no other man before him could, it was his scathing, even mischievous wit. Elizabeth likes to tell the story of the time, before the world knew they were a couple, when Todd took her to a dinner party and introduced her as "Tondelayo Schwartzkopf." The hostess couldn't take her eyes off her. Finally she went over to Elizabeth and said, "I have to tell you, you look a lot like Elizabeth Taylor . . . only heavier." Todd got a kick out of that and slapped Elizabeth on the rump. "See that, I told you, you were getting fat," he said.

Mike Todd was born Avrom Hirsch Goldbogen on June 22, 1907, in Minneapolis. He was a busy man when he met Elizabeth. With only a sixth-grade education, Todd had made a name for himself, first as a Broadway producer in 1940 with *The Hot Mikado*, a takeoff on the Gilbert and Sullivan operetta. He produced nine more shows between 1942 and 1946, and in recent years he had produced about twenty musicals, burlesque shows, and strip revues. He'd also developed a revolutionary camera system called Todd-AO (Todd American Optical), which basically gave the viewer a widened screen experience. The first film to utilize the process, and to great success, was *Oklahoma!* in 1955. He had two prior marriages, one to actress Joan Blondell.

Todd had had business problems in the past—he was bankrupted twice—but in recent years he had amassed quite a fortune. He had just finished making the epic *Around the World in 80 Days* when he met Elizabeth. Based on Jules Verne's 1873 novel of the same name, Todd's last film was in many ways a reflection of the man himself— a big, brassy, costly, colorful, larger-than-life epic. With this his valedictory picture, he broke all the rules, using his legendary charms to attract top international stars—from Marlene Dietrich and Frank Sinatra to Noël Coward and Peter Lorre, plus more than forty others—to perform for scale, the minimum pay that the Screen Actors Guild allowed its members to accept. The title says it all—a Victorian gentleman makes a bet that he can orbit the globe in eighty days. At a cost of $6 million, a paltry amount by today's standards but quite a sum for its time, the film went on to gross in excess of $42 million ($403.8 million in today's dollars). In addition to a Best Picture Oscar, it would earn four others.

After his latest round of success, Mike Todd would never look back—not that he was ever the kind of man who did so, anyway.

He was like Elizabeth in that respect: always moving forward, never taking the time to reflect on the past. Or, as his biographer Art Cohn wrote about Todd: "He is reborn each day without knowledge of the past. He has no yesterdays, no reminiscences or regrets. The man he was the day before or twenty years before is a stranger to him and he has no interest in knowing him. What is done is done for; he must start clear at each moment."

The day after MGM announced Elizabeth's separation from Wilding, Todd said he wanted to meet with her at MGM. He was late arriving, and she sat in the commissary sipping a Coke and steaming about his tardiness. When he finally showed up, he grabbed her by the hand and dragged her to an empty office, without saying a word. He then sat her down and, for the next hour, proceeded to tell her how much he loved her, and how determined he was to make her his wife. He would not take no for an answer, he said. "Don't horse around," he finally concluded. "You know you're going to marry me." Elizabeth expressed surprise. "If this was what getting swept off your feet was like," she said later, "well, I must admit, as much as a brute as I thought he was, I was still quite flattered."

From there, things moved quickly. Before she was even divorced, Elizabeth accepted a $30,000 pearl "friendship ring" from him. It was soon replaced by a 29.4-carat diamond engagement sparkler, for which Mike paid $92,000—a huge sum at that time for a piece of jewelry. It was so large, she liked to call it her "ice skating rink." It was actually Mike who started Elizabeth down the road of collecting expensive jewels. She'd always enjoyed a good piece, but with Mike she took that simple enjoyment to a whole new level of admiration.*

---

* Elizabeth would develop a vast knowledge of jewels, understanding the geographical origin of all of the pieces in her vast collection and appreciating their great beauty. Her book *Elizabeth Taylor: My Love Affair with Jewelry* is a must-have for any fan of Elizabeth's who wants to know the stories behind her many beautiful pieces of jewelry. "I don't believe I own the pieces," she wrote. "I believe that I am their custodian, here to enjoy them, to give them the best treatment in the world, to watch after their safety, and to love them."

As a suitor, Mike Todd was obviously a good deal more exciting than Michael Wilding. A charming rogue, he was crass and sometimes vulgar, but also extremely rich, generous, and romantic. For instance, every Saturday he celebrated the weekly anniversary of their meeting, gifting Elizabeth with rubies, emeralds, sapphires, pearls, and designer clothing. Elizabeth fondly recalls the day Mike presented her with a ruby-and-diamond set she cherishes still. It was about three months into their marriage and they were staying at La Fiorentina, a lovely villa outside Monte Carlo near St.-Jean-Cap-Ferrat. She had been swimming laps in the pool, wearing her (circa 1880) diamond, platinum, and gold tiara (of course!). Mike came out of the villa holding a box. He went to the edge of the pool, and she swam toward him to greet him. His eyes full with warmth, he knelt down before her and opened the box. In it was the most beautiful ruby-and-diamond necklace she'd ever seen. Elizabeth let out a squeal as Mike put the baubles, from Cartier, around her neck. Then he brought forth from the box two matching ear pendants. Still on his knees, he fastened them to her earlobes. But he wasn't finished yet. He went back to the box for a matching bracelet, which he attached to her wrist. "I shrieked with joy," Elizabeth recalls, "put my arms around Mike's neck, and pulled him into the pool after me. It was a perfect summer day and a day of perfect love."

One story famously told through the years has it that when Mike first presented her with the delicate diamond tiara she would wear while swimming, she went into another room to try it on and then emerged nude, except for the tiara. They then had sex, it's been reported, while she wore the tiara. Who knows if that story is true? However, there was something inherently sensual about the jewels and the furs and the boats and the liquor and everything else about Elizabeth that was over the top. One can actually imagine her running around naked in her tiara, making love to a sexy man, and then playing with her jewels in bed afterward, all the while sipping a flute of the best champagne. Few people thought critically about the behavior of movie stars back then, when it came to alcohol, anyway. For instance, Mike would boast, "She drinks champagne at breakfast every morning," as if it was a badge of honor, a glamorous thing to do . . . not as a possible indication of a drinking problem. (All Elizabeth has said about the tiara publicly is that Mike gave it to her because he viewed her as his queen, "and I wore it because he was my king." It adorned her head at the Academy Awards when *Around the World in 80 Days* won Best Picture.)

Mike treated his raven-haired beauty not only to expensive gifts, but also to a whirlwind life that included private planes, yachts, fancy automobiles, and extravagant estate living with Picassos and other works of fine art. He was also a passionate lover, giving her the kind of powerful intimacy and connection that had been missing from her life with both of her previous husbands. When she wanted tenderness, he was as gentle as a puppy in spite of his outward roughness. But his gentleness was never, and could never, be mistaken for weakness. "Mike was strong, which was very good for me," she once observed. "I will get away with murder if I can. I used to try, out of my perversity, sometimes to drive Mike mad. I'd be late, deliberately just fiddle around and be late, and I loved it when he would lose his temper and dominate me. I would start to purr because he had won."

It's interesting that Elizabeth sought such dominance, especially since she had felt so manipulated as a child star. One would have thought that as an adult she would have rebelled against the notion of any kind of domination. But instead she began to mirror her parents' relationship and endeavor to rule her husbands in much the way Sara had Francis. But still, as her mother's daughter, she would never allow herself to submit to any such mastery. The predictable result in her life—from Mike Todd onward—would be, for the most part, sheer chaos. Of course, it's easy for outsiders to see as much, especially retrospectively. At the time, Elizabeth was just enjoying herself—and she would never really be one for self-examination anyway. "Every woman should have a Mike Todd in her life," she wrote in her 1987 memoir *Elizabeth*

Takes Off. "God, I loved him. My self-esteem, my image, everything soared under his exuberant, loving care."

"He was a very rebellious sort of guy who went against the grain and he taught her to be that way," observed the columnist and friend Liz Smith. "She was quite different after meeting Mike Todd. He said, 'Audacity makes the star' and she began to live that motto. They had big fights, and they made up and fought again, loudly and blatantly. Then they made up again and he would spoil her with presents. After Mike, she would always have these sorts of relationships that had a lot to do with fighting and making up."

Mike would also be physically abusive from time to time. He wasn't brutal, like Nicky Hilton, but if she stepped terribly out of line, in his view, he would not hesitate to shove or push her, or even smack her across the face. Violence was definitely an element of the relationship.

Still, there were many good times with Mike Todd. Though Elizabeth lived with him on a grand scale, the small moments with Mike are the most memorable to her, and also to the people who knew them. Albert Skinner was a young paralegal in 1957, whom Mike Todd had taken under his wing. "I helped handle everything from the business surrounding Todd-AO to the big party at Madison Square Garden," he recalled. "I don't think Todd has ever been understood, historically. He was a lot more fun than people know. He, I, and Elizabeth did a lot of crazy things in Chicago, me just tagging along for the ride.

"For instance, I remember how much fun we had running from paparazzi. Once, we were coming out of a restaurant and, as always, the photographers were waiting. We had a car there, but Mike grabbed Elizabeth and said, 'No. Let's make a run for it!' She said, 'But to where?' He said, 'It's Chicago, baby. Who cares?' Off they went, with me following. Mike and I were in our suits, Elizabeth in a cocktail dress, her high heels in her hands, running barefoot. We ran for blocks with the media guys in hot pursuit on foot, in and out of alleys, down crowded streets. She was squealing and laughing the entire time. Finally, we ducked into a dark nightclub and tucked ourselves into a corner where we had drinks and watched the performance of a drunken blues singer. I remember suddenly noticing that everyone in the club was looking at us. When Elizabeth had to go to the ladies' room and got up and walked off, all eyes were on her. She knew it. She carried herself as if she knew she was on display, very regally with an air about her. There was something about her, though, that made people feel unable to approach her. She later told me that it was an art, looking accessible but making people understand that you were totally inaccessible. 'Never look anyone in the eye, ever,' she would say. 'You have to walk with your vision about two inches above the heads of everyone in the room, and with a smile that is as meaningless as it is broad.' In the club, Elizabeth and Mike got up to dance in each other's arms, and I watched them knowing that they were meant to be together and would probably always be together. It just seemed like a perfect fit to me.

"We left the club and went back on the lam. 'Let's go!' exclaimed Elizabeth, and off we went, running through the rain-slicked streets of Chicago, followed again by the paparazzi. She was whooping it up and laughing and taunting them, saying, 'Catch us if you can, you bastards!'

"We ducked into a dark movie theater, where they were playing, much to our astonishment, *Giant*. So we sat in there watching it for a while and the whole time I was thinking, 'What if these people in here knew that Elizabeth Taylor was in here with them?' She leaned over to me and said, 'Isn't Rock the most gorgeous man you have ever seen? I think he's homosexual, though. What a shame for all of the women in this theater.' Then she said, 'Come on, let's get out of here.' And off we went for more running and being chased."

Mike had brought a frivolity to Elizabeth's life that she hadn't known before, but as was often the case in her complex story, the joy was often interrupted by the insatiable curiosity of the public. The press was intent on chronicling the evolution of Taylor's romantic life. Trying to figure out what drove her from one man's arms into another's with such rapidity and regularity became sport for many journalists. She wasn't living in a way many people could relate to, which made things all the more exciting.

It was impossible, though, for Elizabeth to clarify to anyone, perhaps even herself, just how tremendous an influence Mike was in her life. She was feeling brand-new, reborn. Yet her flair for the dramatic had made her seem like the girl who cried wolf. She had vowed her deep love and undying affection twice before, and so convincingly, that people weren't able to see that with Todd, it really *was* different.

In November 1956, Elizabeth took a fall and hurt her back. She'd experienced spinal problems in the past, but after the accident matters became much worse. She was forced to undergo a four-hour operation. "Three disks were absolutely gone," she later recalled. "They cut away all the dead bone right down to the nerve center. They took bone from my hip, my pelvis, and from a bone bank and made little matchsticks and formed clusters that finally calcified and became one long column, six inches long." She was in tremendous pain for, as she put it, "longer than I can remember. It was agony. I was in a hospital bed for two months and had to learn to walk all over again."

A barely recovered Elizabeth finally married Mike Todd on February 2, 1957, at the beachfront estate of Todd's friend Fernando Hernandez (who was a friend of former Mexican president Miguel Alemán). Mike was forty-nine; Elizabeth, twenty-four. Of course, Sara and Francis were present, as were Howard and Mara. In fact, Mara was again one of Elizabeth's attendants, the other being Debbie Reynolds. Debbie was married to Eddie Fisher, Mike's close friend and also one of his best men, along with Michael Todd Jr. At this time, Debbie, Eddie, Elizabeth, and Mike were absolutely inseparable; their close friendship was well-known by all.

A humorous family story: Two days earlier, when Francis, Sara, Howard, and Mara were leaving Los Angeles for Acapulco, they were, as always, descended upon by the media. "I'm not saying a word about this one," Sara told the reporters. However, the press was unrelenting in its desire for some comment from the family. Suddenly, without warning, Francis—who had never said a single word to any media person—grabbed one of the microphones. "I wish for my daughter the same thing that every father wishes," he announced, "and that is that she will finally find happiness." Sara, Howard, and Mara looked at him with dumbstruck expressions, as if they simply couldn't believe he had opened his mouth to a reporter! "I hope that this time her dreams will come true," Francis concluded, handing back the microphone to its owner and suddenly looking very uncomfortable about the whole thing. "That was very nice, Daddy," Sara was heard to say as the family walked toward their waiting plane. "But if I had known you were going to make a statement, I would have been happy to write one for you." It was everything Howard and Mara could do to suppress their giggles. Who knows what possessed Francis, but it was the first and last time he ever talked to a member of the press . . . at least that anyone can remember.

Seven months later, on August 6, 1957, Elizabeth gave birth to a girl, whom she and Mike named Elizabeth Francis, after her father, and nicknamed Liza. When doctors said that Elizabeth should not have any more children, Mike gave them permission to perform a tubal ligation on her. Elizabeth later said she was very upset by the decision, calling it "a huge shock to me."

A few months later, to mark the one-year anniversary of *Around the World in 80 Days*, Mike hosted a party at Madison Square Garden for 18,000 of his closest friends. It was "invitation only"! The cake was fourteen feet high and thirty feet in diameter. CBS-TV broadcast the party live—even though it eventually deteriorated into a food fight. In fact, Walter Cronkite, who covered it as if it was a serious news story, later referred to it as the nadir of his career as a reporter.

Meanwhile, of course, Elizabeth's film career soared. In 1957, MGM hoped to replicate the success of *Gone with the Wind* by putting into production the big-budget Civil War epic *Raintree County*, in which she would again costar with Montgomery Clift. Elizabeth had to take Monty under her protective wing just to get him through the picture due to his many emotional and physical addictions. Not even the best plastic surgeons money could buy were able to restore his face to what it was before his accident. Only a glimmer of his former beauty remained. Although it fell short of the David O. Selznick masterpiece on all counts, *Raintree County* earned Elizabeth an Oscar nomination as Best Actress.

Mike Todd's Sudden Death

In March 1958, Mike Todd was selected by the Friars Club of New York as Showman of the Year. A dinner was planned in his honor at the Waldorf-Astoria Hotel on the twenty-second. Elizabeth has always said that she was bedridden with bronchitis and was therefore unable to accompany him. She had arranged time off from *Cat on a Hot Tin Roof*, which she'd just begun two weeks earlier, in order to recuperate. Her director, Richard Brooks, says that Mike told him that she was actually feeling better and was going to go with him to New York. Brooks says he convinced Todd that the movie's insurance carrier would be upset that Elizabeth had taken time off the film but was well enough to go on a trip to New York. So it was decided that she would not go. Whichever way it happened . . . she didn't go with Mike.

On March 22, feeling on top of the world, Mike soared off in *The Lucky Liz*, his private plane, into dark and stormy skies. He had kissed Elizabeth good-bye numerous times before leaving, in a manner that could only be described as desperate. "I'm too happy," he told her, according to her later recollection, "and I'm afraid that something's going to happen because I'm too happy." Elizabeth would say that when Mike left her, she had a vague but nonetheless disturbing feeling, a premonition of danger. Perhaps Mike felt the same way.

It was pouring rain with thunder and lightning throughout the night—"very Macbethian," she has recalled—and as the hours passed, Elizabeth's fever increased. The children's nurse came into her room at five in the morning to apply rubbing alcohol to her back—she was that hot. Mike had said he would call at six in the morning when his plane was set to land in Albuquerque for refueling. However, the call never came; Elizabeth's instincts would prove to be painfully acute: Mike had been in a fiery plane crash en route to the East Coast. His wedding ring was about the only thing that survived the crash; it was eventually returned to Elizabeth. Also killed in the horrifying tragedy was Todd's biographer, the journalist Art Cohn, who was very nearly finished with a book he was writing about Mike. (That book, *The Nine Lives of Michael Todd*, was later completed by Cohn's wife, Marta, and released posthumously under his name in 1958.)

"I'm sure Mike conned those pilots into taking that plane up," said his friend the Hollywood columnist James Bacon. "No self-respecting pilot would have taken the plane up in that kind of weather. The next morning at seven o'clock, my phone rings. It was the AP bureau chief in Albuquerque, New Mexico. He said, there's a plane down here that's crashed and everybody's dead. Mike Todd's plane. So I had to call up Dick Hanley, who was Mike's secretary, and Rex Kennamer, who was Elizabeth's doctor, and the three of us converged on her home. We told her. She started running and screaming through the house, into the street. Doctor Kennamer grabbed her and shot her with a hypodermic and knocked her out."

Elizabeth recalled, "All I could do was scream 'No, no, no!' I ran downstairs crying, frantic, out of my mind and all through the house and out into the street, screaming and crying in my nightgown. ["It was a 'baby doll,' you know, with the little panties," she told Larry King thirty-five years later in 2003, adding just a bit of a fancy flourish to the horrifying story.] I fell to my knees in the middle of the street. Screaming, 'No, no not Mike. Not Mike. Dear God, please not Mike.' Rex picked me up and carried me into the house. That's all I can remember because he knocked me out with a hypodermic needle."

Elizabeth, just twenty-six at this time, was truly inconsolable. Her mourning was so great that her very life appeared to be in jeopardy as she repeatedly declared she would never be able to live without Mike. There seemed no rescuing her from the emotional abyss. Her director from *Cat on a Hot Tin Roof*, Richard Brooks, came to visit her. When it had been decided that Elizabeth would not go on the trip, Mike had asked Richard to accompany him; luckily for him, he had declined the invitation. "Dick [Hanley] took me up to her bedroom where she was in a state of absolute screaming nerves," he later told Peter Lawford.

"You bastard, you. You're just like the rest of them," she screamed at him. "You just came over here to find out when the hell I'm coming back to work, didn't you? That's why you're here, isn't it?"

"Elizabeth," he said, "it's a movie. That's all it is. It's a movie. And it doesn't mean a goddamn thing as to what you're going to face now. If you want to come back to work, come back. If you don't, don't." She appreciated his words so much, she melted in his arms.

Her friend Shirley MacLaine recalled, "I went over there just after Mike died, and Sydney Guilaroff [Elizabeth's friend and hairdresser] was there feeding her vodka and helping her to the bathroom. She was shrieking and screaming."

"Well, I couldn't leave her alone," Guilaroff told Cathy Griffin, his biographer. "There was no point in putting a nurse with her because she was sedated, and when she would wake up she would just scream. I held her whenever she was awake. I just stayed with her, tried to make her eat."

Of course, Sara, Francis, and Howard were at Elizabeth's side during this entire ordeal. Photographers who were staked outside of Elizabeth's home spent their days waiting to take candid pictures of the grim-faced Taylors as they came and went from the house. All three appeared grief-stricken; at one point Sara collapsed as she walked from their automobile. Howard grabbed her by an elbow just seconds before she would have fallen to the pavement. On their way back to their car that evening, the media descended like locusts upon the Taylors, demanding comments from them about the tragedy. Of course, true to their natures, Francis and Howard wouldn't utter a single word about any of it. Sara, though, realized that the reporters wouldn't rest until they got something from them, so she gave them what they wanted. Trembling, she stood before their microphones and cameras, seeming very small and frightened. "Of course, she's absolutely devastated," she said of Elizabeth. "Why, it's the worst day of her life, isn't it? Of all of our lives. Please pray for us all. That's all I can say, really." Sara slowly backed away from the attention, and was then helped away from the scene by Francis.

In the next few days, Elizabeth became obsessed with trying to figure out what she was doing the very moment Mike lost his life in the plane. Had she been awake? Asleep? Had she been dreaming? If so, about what? In her grief, she took pills to sleep, pills to stay awake, pills for depression, pills for anxiety . . . so much medication, actually, that few in her circle seemed to be able to keep track of their purposes. Today, when Elizabeth looks back on it, this time is a blazing haze of deep sorrow, abject fear, and seething fury.

Howard Hughes heard of Elizabeth's loss and lent her a TWA jet, complete with crew, so that she could fly to Chicago in privacy for the funeral. (Hughes was by this time a friend of Elizabeth's; after the two got to know one another better, she began to view him as sad and emotionally fragile.) At the funeral, Elizabeth had to be restrained by Howard, lest she literally hurl herself onto the casket. A mob of perhaps 10,000 people pushed forward as the grieving young widow dressed in black with dangling diamond earrings was escorted to her limousine. They shouted out her name, took photos, pushed and shoved for a better view of her. There was never a private moment for Elizabeth Taylor, even in grief. Her brother appeared to be just as tormented by all of the attention. At the cemetery, the hordes packed picnic lunches and laid their tablecloths among the tombstones so that they could watch the show—in the freezing March weather! It was a big, popcorn-eating sensation for the masses. Elizabeth Taylor: "I remember seeing bags of potato chips in the wind. And empty Coca-Cola bottles. And children crawling over tombstones. And as the car pulled up, they all broke away from their picnic lunches and came screaming like blackbirds to the car—all squawking and screaming and yelling in our ears as if it were some sort of premiere." When the graveside service was over, things got even worse. The crowd descended upon Elizabeth and Howard as they tried to make their way back to their waiting car. They began ripping at Elizabeth's clothes as Howard shouted at them to "Get back! Get back!" Finally, when brother and sister got into their car, they discovered that they had somehow lost their driver in the fracas. "They swarmed like insects all over the car so you couldn't see out the windows," Elizabeth later recalled of the crowd. The unruly mob then began rocking the car back and forth. Inside, Elizabeth began to scream at the top of her lungs, like a caged animal. It was a terrible scene. One wonders what Mike Todd would have thought of it.

Mike had always been the man who had helped Elizabeth view the eager throng as just a silly distraction to her true existence, like on that night in Chicago, laughing and dodging fans and paparazzi. That magical evening had ended just as the sun rose, Albert Skinner recalled. The three of them, after slipping into a small diner, shared one giant slice of chocolate cake. Skinner recalled, "Elizabeth watched her new husband for a moment, then said, 'I've never been alone, my entire life. Yet I've always felt lonely. But tonight, I feel like I have friends.' She smiled, then leaned her head softly on Mike's shoulder. What a moment that was."

One talent Mike Todd had with Elizabeth was his ability to present her with another perspective on her life. He somehow managed to create a comic farce of the media whirlwind in which she had been caught up since childhood. What she had seen previously as a never-ending battle could, for a few moments at least, become a game worth playing with Mike leading the way. As powerful a man as he was, Todd was able to treat Elizabeth like the child she'd never really been. And it was during experiences like that crazy night in Chicago, when her cocoon of celebrity was being parodied, that Elizabeth knew for certain that Mike was the man for her. He could make her oppressive world go away and a new, more happy one appear in its place. As grandiose a life as she had led thus far, escapism—true freedom from the stresses and pressures of constant public scrutiny—was invaluable to her. For that reason, she saw Mike Todd as a savior of sorts. And now her savior was gone.

As her car finally pulled past the fanatical crowd and out of the cemetery that day, it stopped for a moment while the police escort cleared a path at a nearby intersection. It was then that Elizabeth spotted a young girl standing alone at the curbside, holding a single wilted rose and looking appropriately mournful. Elizabeth lowered the darkened window. As soon as it went down, a myriad of hands bearing large floral offerings waved in her direction—it was as if they had come from nowhere. Undaunted, Elizabeth seemed somehow transfixed as she leaned out just a bit and pointed to the girl. "That one," she said. The little girl's mother excitedly led her to the waiting car, offering her own more plentiful floral arrangement and cooing her praise for the movie star. Elizabeth ignored her and focused on the child. In a sea of confusion and hysteria, she had finally found a bit of humanity: a sad, or maybe even just frightened, youngster reaching out a trembling hand. Elizabeth took the flower, locking eyes with the child. "You're sweet," she said quietly. "It's you I'll try to remember."

Eddie Fisher

Elizabeth Taylor almost didn't make Mike Todd's funeral. She got the courage to do so from an unlikely source, Mike's best friend, Eddie Fisher. The two had been inseparable. Eddie considered Mike a father figure and even named his son (born just three weeks before the plane crash) after him. When Elizabeth began dating Mike, the couple continued to enjoy the company of Eddie and his wife, Debbie Reynolds. A waiter who once worked at Chasen's recalled the ritual of their meals together: "First the women would order, then Todd, then Fisher. Whatever Todd selected, Fisher would ask for exactly the same. If Todd said steak, medium rare, Eddie wanted steak, medium rare. If Todd wanted sole slightly underdone, Eddie wanted the same thing. Then he would talk Debbie into changing her order to what he and Todd were eating, and when it came, Fisher even ate the way Todd did—fast. Elizabeth Taylor, though, was something else. She had a mind of her own. Nobody dared tell her what to have."

Eddie had been emotionally devastated by the sudden loss of his good friend, and was one of the few people in Elizabeth's life who truly grasped the deep impact his death had on her. Early the morning after Todd's death, Eddie's limousine passed the throng of reporters and fans outside the Todd estate. He had arrived to escort Elizabeth to Chicago.

The night prior, he had come to the same home, only to find Elizabeth wandering in a daze, almost unable to function, appearing drugged and confused. That night he and Debbie explained the plans that had been made for the trip back to Chicago. Elizabeth at first said she was unable to go, contending that her children needed her. Reynolds, though, generously offered to stay behind to look after them, and Taylor was left with little reason to avoid the event. So it was agreed. Elizabeth and Eddie would fly together, and Debbie, the dutiful wife and dependable friend, would remain in Los Angeles.

Eddie was greeted at the door by the Todd housekeeper, who informed him Elizabeth would not be making the trip. Eddie pushed his way past the woman and climbed the stairs to Elizabeth's bedroom—the door was open. She was sitting on the bed, fully dressed in black, staring off at nothing in particular. Fisher walked into her field of view and lifted a packed suitcase that sat nearby. She looked at him through dull eyes.

"I thought I could do it," she managed.

"Well, you thought right," he responded. He was surprisingly harsh with her.

"No . . ."

Minutes later, Elizabeth descended the stairs on the arm of Eddie Fisher. Not a word was spoken as they entered the waiting limousine.

On the flight to Chicago, Howard Hughes had directed the crew to give the grieving passengers their privacy, so there was a palpable silence on the long trip. Elizabeth clung to Eddie for much of that flight, the turbulence reminding both just how they had lost the man so dear to them. They could identify with each other's pain better, perhaps, than anyone else they knew. It was understandable. They both loved Mike. Talking about him was a way of keeping him alive in their hearts. It was also a way for Elizabeth to keep her soul from going into complete atrophy because, as she put it, "I knew that with each passing day, I was getting harder inside, building a resistance to love. I was afraid I would never love again, and then Eddie came into my life and I began to think, maybe . . ."

James Bacon succinctly put it this way: "Eddie Fisher performed the most dangerous duty known to man, he dried a widow's tears."

Edwin John Fisher, with his meticulously combed dark brown hair and somewhat foxlike face, was born in 1928 in South Philadelphia, the son of Russian Jewish immigrants. From those humble beginnings, he rose to the top rung on the pop music ladder before he was old enough to vote. With an easy smile and an ingratiating demeanor, he was considered "cute" and a snappy dresser. He was a genuine teen idol by 1954—having sold more than eight million records—when he met America's girl next door, Debbie Reynolds, a five-foot-two, eyes-of-blue, energetic and ever so wholesome entertainer. Fans overwhelmingly approved of their relationship, which was covered in exacting detail by all the movie magazines. "Never," said gossip maven Hedda Hopper, "have I seen a more patriotic match than these two clean-cut, clean-living youngsters. When I think of them, I see flags flying and hear bands playing."

As if to accede to their fans' demands, Eddie and Debbie were wed in 1955 in a Catholic ceremony. Despite the birth of their daughter, Carrie, during their first year together, the marriage was in trouble almost from the beginning. Still, they muddled through and were inspired by the marriage of their close friends Elizabeth and Mike—that is until Mike died. Eddie was so sad about his friend's death that Elizabeth's heart went out to him. Since the source of their mourning was the loss of the same man, a bond grew. Within about five months—by August—both began to consider the unthinkable. Could the two of them be a couple?

Elizabeth knew that going after Eddie Fisher would make for a huge scandal in her life. However, she simply couldn't chase away that feeling that Eddie might bring back some of the magic she had felt with Mike. After all, Todd and Fisher had been joined at the hip for so many years that they were able to finish each other's sentences. Maybe this was how she could climb out of the abyss left after Mike's death, with the help of his best friend. In other words, still so much a child at heart, she would replace Mike in her life with Eddie, just as she had Nibbles the chipmunk in her book *Nibbles and Me*, written when she was just fourteen. In the story, when the chipmunk dies (and apparently this really happened, since it was originally a school essay), "My heart was broken. Mummie and I went up into the woods and cried it out. We walked and walked and talked about life. And then I knew just as I knew before, that in reality there is no death. I knew that he would always live in my heart, and that another one would come to me. Not to take his place, but to bring the same sense of love to me, and he did—and I knew him immediately, and I named him Nibbles . . . not Nibbles the second, but just Nibbles—my favorite chipmunk."

Eddie's marriage to Debbie didn't seem to be working out anyway, Elizabeth rationalized. After all, Debbie had already filed for divorce—twice—so how content could she be in the relationship? Of course, Debbie had two children at home, one a newborn, so that did present a bit of a complication. "However," Elizabeth explained to one friend, "she's in show business and didn't get to the top of her profession by being weak-kneed. She must have some inherent strength, like every other dame in this goddamned business." Debbie would survive, Elizabeth decided. She'd known her for many years, and she wasn't worried about her at all. In fact, the end of her marriage might be just what she needed to find the right man for her, someone who might make her happier than she'd ever been with Eddie Fisher.

The bottom line, though, was that Elizabeth Taylor, though still naïve in many ways, was a grown woman who didn't play by the rules. She was a star, living a different reality, as was Eddie Fisher. "Look, we felt we could get away with anything," Eddie now says. "After all, we had climbed to the top of our professions and achieved more than we ever dreamed possible, so we felt invincible. We did whatever the hell we wanted to do and then waited for the consequences. That's just the way we were back then. Young, rich, famous . . . and irresponsible. *Ahhhh*," he sighed. "Good times."

It didn't take long for the tempestuous Liz-Eddie-Debbie triangle to make international news. Once the sensational headlines began to surface, they continued for the biggest story in the land—not the biggest show business story, *the biggest story* . . . period. One Swedish newspaper best summed up the public sentiment with the headline, "Blood Thirsty Widow Liz Vampired Eddie." Editorials closer to home denounced Elizabeth; fan magazines encouraged readers to boycott her films. The press seemed to completely forget that she was a recent widow and now painted her solely as a calculating homewrecker. Images were quickly set in stone: Debbie was America's fragile, put-upon sweetheart, while Elizabeth was the evil siren in search of yet another sexual conquest. With the passing of time, everyone—or at least that's how it seemed—had a strongly held opinion about the affair, and most of those were against Elizabeth. In just a few months, her status had changed from sainted widow to shameless hussy.

The two left Musso and Frank's Grill in Hollywood one evening, shortly after deciding to unveil their forbidden love. The press flashbulbs were clearly accompanied by a sound that was brand-new to Elizabeth: the unmistakable grumble of a disapproving public.

"Shame on you," one said.

"Whore!" yelled another.

Eddie recalled that the two huddled together, ducking into the black sedan. As the driver headed off, Elizabeth looked back at the angry mob.

"Oh, dear Lord," she said, "what the hell have we done?"

Elizabeth and Eddie Marry

Interestingly, despite the imbroglio in which she found herself at this time, Elizabeth Taylor's career as one of the world's leading actresses did not suffer. By the end of the 1950s, she was one of the most beautiful and sought-after women in film. Her place in the history of motion pictures was irrevocably fixed and firmly secure, even if she were never to make another movie. Everything about her promised excitement. Bad publicity, good publicity, triumphs, tragedies . . . it all blended together to create a Hollywood personality the likes of which the public could seemingly not get enough of. She was like a comet blazing across the sky, only there was no burnout for her. Instead, she seemed to only get brighter, bigger, and better with time, a woman whose beauty was matched by her ability as an actress. The film version of *Cat on a Hot Tin Roof*—in which, happily for the studio, she played a woman with a voracious appetite for sex—was a box-office success; she was nominated for another Oscar for her work in it, this time losing to Susan Hayward (in *I Want to Live*). Still, Elizabeth was a hot commodity. Her success despite the affair with Eddie only emboldened her, in a sense, to believe that she could do no wrong, even when she was very wrong in what she was doing.

Debbie, as the woman scorned, also saw her career take flight. Eddie's sank into serious decline, at least for the time being.

Six months after the affair started—and a month shy of the one-year anniversary of Mike Todd's death—Debbie filed for divorce again. When it was finally granted, custody of the couple's children and a large financial and property settlement were Debbie's. It had been acrimonious, though, and by the time all of the mudslinging was over, Debbie truly loathed Eddie—and the feeling was mutual.

With Eddie's divorce at last finalized, he and Elizabeth were free to marry after a suitable, and legally directed, waiting period. First, though, Elizabeth wanted to formally convert to Judaism. She says that her decision to do so was not influenced by Eddie, and is eager to set the record straight in that regard since so many accounts in the past have said that she converted for him. She explains that she first thought she wanted to convert when she was married to Mike Todd, who was also Jewish. He suggested that she wait and make a careful decision about it. After Mike's death, Elizabeth felt a "desperate need for a formalized religion" and recalls that she wasn't feeling spiritually fulfilled by Catholicism. Christian Science, her faith when she was a child, also didn't address many of the questions she had about life and death, at least not to her satisfaction. After studying the Reform philosophy of Judaism for about nine months, she says, she felt an immediate connection to the faith. She never was much for attending synagogue, though. She says, "I'm one of those people who think you can be close to God anywhere, not just in a place designed for worship and built with millions of pesos while people are starving outside." That particular observation is intriguing because, truly, it's more a Christian Scientist's philosophy than a Jewish one. It seems safe to say that Elizabeth took elements of both faiths, and tried to live by their tenets. At the formal religious conversion ceremony, with her parents at her side as witnesses in full support of her decision, Elizabeth repeated the words of Ruth. "Entreat me not to leave thee, and to return from following thee," she intoned, "for whither thou goest, I will go; and where thou lodgest, I will lodge; thy people shall be my people and thy God my God." Her Jewish name would be Elisheba Rachel.

On April 1, Eddie opened a six-week engagement at the Tropicana Hotel in Las Vegas. It was a terrific show; Fisher could always be depended on to deliver as an entertainer and still seemed to have the loyalty of a paying audience, no matter the scandal in his life. Sitting ringside that night was Elizabeth—smoking her cigarettes from a diamond-encrusted holder—along with Francis, Sara, Howard, and Mara. Elizabeth seemed elated, her family members a bit less so. After the performance, everyone congregated backstage with press members, friends, and coworkers. Displaying a gleaming diamond bracelet given to her by Eddie, Elizabeth announced that she hoped they would be married within six weeks. Everyone applauded the news, except for Sara and Francis. According to witnesses, they urgently pulled Howard and Mara aside and went into a huddle in a corner, seeming very concerned. Without saying a word to anyone, the four then quietly slipped out of the backstage area, suggesting that perhaps they weren't in total alignment with Elizabeth about Eddie. Still, a hastily arranged press conference was assembled backstage. "Eddie and I are proud of our feelings toward each other and we have never tried to hide them," Elizabeth said to the assembled members of the media. "We have been accused of being indiscreet, and rightly so, but we haven't tried to cover up anything. We have been honest in what we have done, and we have ourselves to live with."

Whatever reservations her family may have had about the union, Elizabeth and Eddie were married on May 12, 1959, in a Jewish ceremony. She wore green chiffon and looked radiant. Mike's son was best man. At just twenty-seven, Elizabeth had now been married four times. Eddie and his new bride then sailed off to Spain for their honeymoon. "When Elizabeth loves she loves better than any woman in the world," he said. "She gives more love than any human being I have ever known in my entire life. Gives more and takes more, and that's love and loving."

So devoted to Eddie was Elizabeth that she would rearrange her busy schedule so that she could continue to sit ringside at his nightclub appearances. Though she tried to act oblivious to the fascinated stares of other audience members, surely she had to know that she was as much on display as her husband, and probably even more so. Toward the end of the show, Eddie would customarily acknowledge friends and family members. Afterward, he would walk slowly toward Elizabeth's side of the stage. "Liz! Liz!" the audience would chant. "Oh, have I left anyone out?" he would ask teasingly. Finally, he would point to her and say, "I am honored to be graced with the presence of the most beautiful woman in the world, my wife, the light of my life, Mrs. Eddie Fisher." Held in a large halo of ice by a blue-white spot, Elizabeth would stand and allow the audience's approval to wash over her. Then Eddie would swell into full voice for his big finale, "That Face," which he would dedicate to Elizabeth. However, Eddie's encore number was eerily prophetic: the Richard Rodgers–Oscar Hammerstein II song of lost love from *South Pacific*, "This Nearly Was Mine."

Alas, it took Elizabeth just a few months to come to the conclusion that she had made a big mistake. Eddie was not Mike, nor did he have the older man's strength, determination and know-how in the care and handling of a complicated woman like Elizabeth Taylor. She finally had "an epiphany," she said: Their mutual grieving over the terrible loss of Mike Todd in their lives was what had actually brought her and Eddie together, not any true feelings of romance. Lately, whenever she looked at Eddie, she saw Mike's ghost standing behind him, as if taunting her to recognize the truth of her fourth marriage. Or, as she later told her friend, the producer Joseph Mankiewicz, "I somehow believed that I could keep Mike's memory alive through Eddie. Instead, I now find that all I have is Mike's ghost. How can I be his wife," she asked, "when I am still married to a ghost?"

Those who remember Elizabeth on the set of *Suddenly, Last Summer* recall seeing her and Eddie constantly entwined and demonstrative of their affection for one another. In retrospect, their passionate display seems more like an act, played strictly for the crew. Offstage, but not always in private, her obvious contempt for the man she chose to replace Mike Todd would today probably be considered spousal abuse, with her hurling withering epithets at a cowed Fisher. It was not unlike the relationship between Brick and Maggie in *Cat on a Hot Tin Roof*, only in reverse. For most of that film, Brick (Paul Newman) humiliates and ridicules Maggie (Elizabeth) when she unashamedly begs him to make love to her. Her pleadings are met with an utter disdain that borders on hatred. In angry frustration, she blurts out the name of Skipper, Brick's running buddy, who may or may not have been in a sexual relationship with her husband: "Skipper is *dead*. I'm alive. Maggie the Cat is *alive*." The parallels are uncanny, even if they are coincidental.

Despite the emotional tumult in her life at this time with Eddie, Elizabeth Taylor's work on *Suddenly, Last Summer* is captivating just the same. Appearing with a stellar cast—Katharine Hepburn, Montgomery Clift, and Mercedes McCambridge—she would be nominated for an Academy Award for her button-pushing work in this film. Adapted from Tennessee Williams's one-act play, it's a difficult, challenging movie to watch, involving electroshock therapy, homosexuality, murder, and even cannibalism. Elizabeth gives one of her best performances in it; contemporary critics noted that even at a time in her life when she seemed out of control, she managed to pull herself together for her work on film. It's because acting remained her great passion, and when she loved a role, as she did in *Suddenly, Last Summer*, she would gladly give herself to it completely. It was a place for her to go to escape her private demons, a sanctuary from the chaos of her jumbled world.

Butterfield 8

Elizabeth Taylor's next movie, *Butterfield 8*, was one she truly did not want to make. In fact, she did everything she could to get out of it. As it happened, she and her agent, Kurt Frings, had just agreed with producer Walter Wanger to star for 20th Century-Fox in the epic *Cleopatra*, for a million dollars. Legend has it that Wanger called Elizabeth on the set of *Suddenly, Last Summer* and related the offer through Eddie Fisher, who had answered the phone. As a joke, Taylor supposedly replied, "Sure, tell him I'll do it for a million dollars." Elizabeth told the story that way in her 1965 memoir. Of it, Eddie says today, "Maybe it happened that way, maybe it didn't. Who can remember? But if it gets me in the story, then, yeah, that's how it happened." Elizabeth's salary for *Cleopatra* was indeed astronomical for the times, the most any actor or actress had ever been paid. However, none of her movies had ever lost money, so she was well worth it.

Still high from that achievement, she was brought back to earth with a thud when she learned that she still had one more film to do for MGM. She'd thought her deal with them had expired. It hadn't. The studio demanded that she make one more film, and that would be *Butterfield 8*—based on John O'Hara's novel—for which she would receive only $125,000. Because she was being forced to do something she truly did not want to do, there was no way it would go well for her, or for the studio. She promised producer Pandro S. Berman that she would be trouble and that she would make not only his life but those of all the actors a living hell. She'd known him for most of her life—he had produced *National Velvet*—so one might have thought she would at least be nice to him . . . but she wasn't. She was too angry to be nice, and made production on the film very difficult for everyone involved.

Eddie was given a small part in the film (which he essayed very well), but not for his acting ability so much as for his ability to babysit the star. It was, he says, "the worst job of my life, trying to deal with my hellion of a wife."

By this time, Elizabeth Taylor had become the strong-willed, sharp-tongued powerhouse her mother, Sara, had been years earlier. However, at the same time, she had no one to regulate her penchant toward self-consumption. Those closest to her were often her handlers—agents, publicists, assistants—and rarely would she be scolded for her temperamental nature.

There was one tremendous difference between Elizabeth and Sara, though. Her mother's single-mindedness and drive was focused outward, on her daughter. Elizabeth, on the other hand, even after her children were born, still saw herself as the one who most needed tending. She firmly believed what her mother had told her all those years earlier: She was special. She deserved the finest. By now, though, she had gotten the best of everything, quite literally. If material goods and public adoration were all that were factored in, there's nothing Taylor could have wanted. She had it all.

Of course, she didn't really have it all, did she? What she lacked was a genuine, supportive relationship. She craved a strong man.

However, she found herself in a serious conundrum. While looking for a fighter, she ultimately still needed to win. She craved both the strong man her mother never had, and the sense of righteousness her mother had in great abundance. It was a complex tug-of-war between dueling desires, a battle that would be impossible to win.

While Mike Todd had the wherewithal for the conflict she so desired, Eddie did not. His supplication at her feet would inevitably fill her with rage. She became abusive during the making of *Butterfield 8*, trying to spur him into anger to get a rise out of him so that he might prove to her that he really was a man. It never worked. Instead of engaging in battle, Eddie was unfailingly sweet, his every reaction to her couched in careful gentleness . . . which only infuriated her all the more. Sometimes, if she had been particularly vicious toward him, the poor man would retire to his bed and draw the blankets over his head. She couldn't help but connect his avoidance of the sparring bouts she would instigate with the weakness of her father, Francis. "Wimp!" she would at times shout toward Eddie as he headed away from the growing tornado that was Elizabeth Taylor.

Eddie, of course, had his own issues. "My father was a tyrant who treated my mother like a slave," he explains. "I wanted my mother to fight back, and because she never did, I thought she was weak." In Elizabeth, he had certainly finally found a strong mother figure, one who fought back . . . and how.

In *Butterfield 8*, John O'Hara expertly wove Depression-era history with speakeasy culture. It's based on the true story of Starr Faithful (her real name!), who'd been found dead on June 8, 1931, in Long Beach, on Long Island. After her death, it was learned that hers had been a hard-living, hard-drinking life of loose morals, mostly spent in speakeasies. She was tough, but sympathetic. In his colorful portrait, O'Hara reimagined Faithful as Gloria Wandrous, a tragic antiheroine whose turbulent life ends in a senseless death. The script was rife with illicit sex and rampant boozing; it was, arguably, the perfect Elizabeth Taylor vehicle.

O'Hara later said that in Gloria Wandrous he created Elizabeth Taylor before there even *was* an Elizabeth Taylor, just as in *Pal Joey* he had created Frank Sinatra before Frank Sinatra. (Butterfield 8, incidentally, was a telephone exchange in Manhattan's Upper East Side.)

Production on *Butterfield 8* began in New York on January 4, 1960. Eddie did what he could to get Elizabeth to work on time and act as an intermediary between her and everyone else, but in the end she was determined to have a terrible time, and so she did . . . as did everyone else.

When it was finished, there was a screening of a rough cut for studio executives. During it, Elizabeth hurled a drink at the screen. Then, in lipstick, she scrawled "NO SALE" on the office door of producer Pandro Berman (wickedly re-creating the memorable opening scene in the film in which her character does the same thing on the living room mirror after spending the night with Laurence Harvey).

The irony of this story is that, in the end, despite all of the melodrama that had surrounded the making of *Butterfield 8*, Elizabeth was terrific in it. As always, it was her talent that would redeem her—and, of course, the vulnerability of which her *Cat on a Hot Tin Roof* director, Richard Brooks, speaks and that now had another level of humanity to it. In a 1975 interview Brooks said that, in his view, her work had been enhanced by the experience of Mike Todd's death: "What it did mainly was it helped her grow up. Death and anguish were things she'd read in a script and she could emulate from other performances or from being told about. But when Todd died, it was something happening to her in the moment, and she was enough of a pro, enough of an actress, to know that this was something that you use honorably and to the best of its advantage. That was what she did. She used everything in her life from that moment on, and consciously too—the joys as well as the sorrows."

Despite her bravura performance, however, Elizabeth still felt that the movie had been a complete waste of her time. "This picture stinks," she said succinctly. As it turned out, most of the country's film critics agreed with her bitter assessment when the movie was finally released to the public. Undaunted, though, Elizabeth's devoted audience flocked to the theaters to see her star in *Butterfield 8*: The film wound up tripling its $2.5 million cost, earning more than $7.5 million for MGM.

Part Three

***

HER DESTINY

A False Start for Cleopatra

With *Butterfield 8* finally out of the way, Elizabeth Taylor was finally free to do something she really wanted: make the film *Cleopatra*. September 28, 1960, was the day scheduled for the beginning of principal photography on that film. For the production, an eight-acre outdoor lot at Pinewood Studios, some fifteen miles northwest of London, had been majestically re-created as the ancient city of Alexandria at a cost of about $600,000. Peter Finch had been cast as Julius Caesar, Stephen Boyd as Mark Antony. After numerous revisions, the script was now being honed into a final draft by screenwriter Dale Wasserman, who had been instructed by Walter Wanger to focus all of his attention on the development of Elizabeth's role. "The film was about Elizabeth Taylor, and I was to write it as a vehicle for her, with only her in mind throughout," he recalled. "That was made clear to me at the outset." Though she now occupied a big part of his creative world, Wasserman had never even met Elizabeth. He based his work on his observations of her after repeatedly viewing most of her movies.

On November 13, Elizabeth's health took a turn for the worse. She awakened with a terrible headache. So bad and persistent was the pain that a doctor had to be summoned. Before long, Elizabeth was checked into a hospital, now suffering from spinal meningitis. Out of the blue and without warning, it was as if her pain, misery, and anger continued to have no outlet other than through the slow and utter destruction of her body.

Sara, with her Christian Scientist background, was not surprised by this latest turn of events. "I was afraid this kind of thing might happen to her," she told one of Elizabeth's friends at the time. "I mean, look at how unhappy she is. It has to manifest somehow." Needless to say, those kinds of comments did not sit well with Elizabeth.

After a week's stay in the hospital, Elizabeth, Eddie, and the children abruptly took off for Palm Springs, where she would recuperate, leaving those invested in *Cleopatra* in London to wonder if she would ever return to the set, and if so, when. By this time, $7 million had been spent on the film. The movie was already proving to be a financial disaster, and Elizabeth had stepped before a camera only a handful of times, giving the studio about twelve minutes of usable footage for its millions. At the rate she was going, it promised to be many months before she would find her stride as an actress in this film. Elizabeth's absences had already cost Lloyd's of London, the production's insurer, millions of dollars. Therefore, 20th Century-Fox made the decision to shut down the production, as if they had any other choice with its star an ocean and a continent away.

A Near-Death Experience and Then an Oscar

March 4, 1961—a day Elizabeth Taylor would never forget. She, Eddie, and the children were in London staying at the Dorchester Hotel. She was getting ready to finally begin work on the almost forgotten *Cleopatra* film and would shortly be leaving for Rome. On this day, though, something in her body had gone very wrong, and without warning she collapsed. She was found on the floor, suffocating, her face turning blue, her fingernails black. By sheer coincidence, down the hall from Elizabeth's room, a bachelor party was being given for a young medical student. The hotel operator figured that a doctor would be at that party, and made a call to the room. Sure enough, a noted anesthesiologist was there. He ran down the hallway to Elizabeth's room, where he found her on the bed, nearly unconscious. He tried to dislodge the congestion in her throat with his finger, but to no avail. Then he pushed his finger against her eye, pressuring it to ensure that she would not go into a coma. She woke up instantly, took one look at him, hurled an epithet at him, and then passed out again.

Arrangements were made for Elizabeth's immediate transportation to The London Clinic. There, an emergency tracheotomy was performed. While she was on the operating table, though, she says, she woke up. Looking at all of the doctors and nurses around her, she tried to speak. However, the air from her lungs just went straight out the gaping hole in her throat. When a nurse noticed that Elizabeth had come out of the anesthesia, she saw the terror in her eyes and leaned over to comfort her. Elizabeth asked her for a piece of paper and a pen. In scrawled handwriting she wrote, "Am I still dying?" Then she lost consciousness again.

After the tracheotomy, it still did not look good for Elizabeth. By this time in her life, she'd had a nervous breakdown, colitis, three cesarian sections, a tonsillectomy, anemia, a crushed spinal disk, bronchitis, meningitis, phlebitis, a broken leg, torn knee ligaments, double pneumonia, food poisoning, a splinter in her eye, three vertebrae replaced in her spine, a tracheotomy—illnesses and accidents by the score, and she wasn't even thirty. Again, certain questions are unavoidable: Why so much misery in her life? What was behind it? Did she feel so out of control that she believed her only safe haven to be a hospital? This time, though, she didn't seem to have the will to go on, so exhausted was she from her . . . life. In fact, Eddie was told that she was dying. It appears that Elizabeth was not totally unaware, at least by this time, of the possibility that something in her mentality may have been responsible for her illness. Later, in 1965, in her first memoir, she would write, "When I became sick with pneumonia, I think it was my subconscious which let me become so seriously ill. I just let the disease take me. I had been hoping to be happy, pretending to be happy. But there was something deeply desperate inside me and I was consumed by self-pity. My despair became so black that I just couldn't face waking up anymore."

Sara Taylor flew to England to be at her daughter's side with, of course, Francis. Again, the attention from Sara was focused, as always during times of crisis, on Elizabeth's physical well-being rather than on her film career. Did that make Elizabeth, on some level, feel more loved by her mother?

"I remember Francis calling me in tears to tell me that Elizabeth was dying and that he and Sara were going to be with her," says Stefan Verkaufen. "I asked how Sara was doing. He said, 'Not good at all.' I knew that she'd already been very upset about the business with Eddie Fisher. It hadn't been an easy couple of years for the Taylor parents. I don't think people were aware of how difficult Elizabeth's romantic life and her illnesses had been on them. It was a constant heartache. Now this."

When the news got out that Elizabeth Taylor was in her final days, thousands gathered in the streets in front of the hospital to hold vigil for her. There were prayer services all over the world. It doesn't overstate it to say that the possibility that Elizabeth might die was major, worldwide news; some news outlets even erroneously reported that she *had* died—much to her later glee. Many historians have pointed to this time in her life as the period during which Elizabeth garnered the most sympathy thus far, thereby softening her image as a tempestuous homewrecker. It's true; she certainly now seemed more fragile and vulnerable than ever before.

Of course . . . she recovered. She always, somehow, recovered, didn't she? One day she just looked up at Eddie and, because she couldn't speak, her eyes did the talking for her: *I'm alive*, they seemed to say. *I can't believe it. How wonderful!*

Her mother later told Peter Lawford in a television interview, "We were there for three nights, we didn't leave the hospital. We sat on a bench outside her room. And the doctors kept coming out and saying it looked like the end. And I was praying with all of my heart, and so was Daddy. And I knew it wasn't the end, and she knew it. She told me afterward that she could hear all of this. They had machines all around her, yet she could hear everything they were saying . . . and she knew that it wasn't the end."

For the next week Eddie sat at her side, watching over her, aware of her every breath. She seemed so fragile lying in her bed, her arms stuck full of needles, her body connected to all sorts of beeping machinery. She looked so young and innocent without her makeup, nothing at all like the hellion she'd been with him in recent months. Now she actually resembled the young lass from *National Velvet*, as if her most recent tragedy had somehow brought her back to her youth. Sympathy for her surged up in Eddie. He was so moved and frightened, there were times he would put his head on her breast and sob. He did love her, no matter what she thought of him.

"I remember wondering, without her anger, what would she be?" he recalled many years later. "It occurred to me that I'd never known her when she wasn't angry. At me. At the studio. Her mother. Mike, for dying and leaving her. At the world. Without her anger to keep her going, I wondered if she would just fall limp and be . . . nothing. I just didn't know."

One day, he glanced at her and caught her staring at him. When she forced a weak smile, he knew she was back.

The late novelist Truman Capote once remembered his visit to Elizabeth in the hospital: "She was very lively, though one could see she had gone through a massive ordeal. She was whiter, by far, than the hospital's bed sheets. Her eyes, without makeup, seemed bruised and swollen, like a weeping child's. 'My chest and lungs were filled with a sort of thick black fire,' she told me. 'They had to cut a hole in my throat to drain out the fire. You see,' she said, pointing to a wound in her throat that was stopped with a small rubber plug. 'If I pull it out, my voice disappears,' she said and pulled it out and indeed her voice did disappear—an effect which made me nervous, but which made her merry. She was laughing, but I didn't hear her laughter until she had reinserted the plug."

When she left the hospital to go back to Hollywood on March 27, Elizabeth credited Eddie's devotion for her return to—not good, but reasonable—health. For Elizabeth, it was one step forward, three back when it came to any recovery. She would stay in California for a six-month recuperation before resuming work—finally—on *Cleopatra*.

Later, in July 1961, Elizabeth would be honored at a fund-raiser at Cedars of Lebanon–Mt. Sinai Hospital in Los Angeles (now Cedars-Sinai). It was at that event, in a speech written for her by Joseph Mankiewicz about what had happened to her in Rome— leave it to Elizabeth to have someone write a speech for her about her own near-death experience—that she demonstrated her flair for the dramatic that she'd inherited from her mother. Although there is no way to be sure, it is quite likely that Mankiewicz also directed this emotional soliloquy. Remember, he is the only person in the history of the movies to win two back-to-back Oscars for directing *and* writing: *People Will Talk* (1949) and *All About Eve* (1950). Standing alone at a microphone in front of a rapt audience, she intoned:

"Throughout many critical hours in the operating theater [*Operating theater!* Pronounced by Elizabeth as *THEE-uh-tah*], it was as if every nerve, every muscle were being strained to the last ounce of my strength. Gradually and inevitably, that last ounce was drawn, and there was no more breath. I remember I had focused desperately on the hospital light hanging directly above me. It had become something I needed almost fanatically to continue to see, the vision of life itself. Slowly, it faded and dimmed, like a well-done theatrical effect to blackness.

"I died."

With that, a collective gasp could be heard from her audience. "Shall I tell you what it was like?" Elizabeth asked.

People in the audience nodded eagerly.

"Being down a long, far tunnel, and there was a small light at the end. I had to keep looking at that light. And I heard the voices, urging me to come back. *Come back, Elizabeth. Come back.*" She also said that she saw Mike Todd on the other side, and he too urged her to turn around and return to her life. Indeed, she was more than just an actress, through and through. She was her mother's daughter. "The experience I had was painful, but beautiful," she said dreamily. "It was like childbirth."

Earlier in the year, Elizabeth had received an Oscar nomination for Best Actress for her work in *Butterfield* 8. She had already received three previous consecutive nominations, but had lost each time. However, she had garnered such worldwide sympathy in recent months that winning the prized statuette her fourth time at bat seemed a foregone conclusion. At the awards show, held at the Santa Monica Civic Auditorium on April 17, Yul Brynner, as the previous year's Best Actor Oscar winner, had the happy task of announcing that, indeed, Elizabeth had won the Academy Award. Finally, at long last, her Oscar wait had ended. What a victory for her and her mother, Sara, who was in the audience with Francis.

When Elizabeth's name was called out as the winner, she appeared genuinely stunned. The applause was thunderous. Eddie helped her to her feet and escorted her to the top of the stairs leading to the stage. After kissing Eddie, Elizabeth, resplendent in a white Dior gown, her tracheotomy scar clearly visible, made her way unsteadily to the podium as the audience of twenty-five hundred rose as one, roaring its approval in a boisterous ovation. Once there, she stood shaking as the demonstration continued. Despite all that had happened to her in her life—and all she had done to provoke the public's confusion and even its scorn—she was still very much the beloved icon, that much was clear. Indeed, she was one of the world's greatest stars, and though the price of such acclaim had been dear, this truly was her shining moment. Finally, in a soft, whispery voice, she said that she didn't know how to express her gratitude, except to say, "Thank you. Thank you with all of my heart." She then turned, walked shakily across the wing and to the backstage ladies' room—and fainted.

Marianne Lincoln watched the awards presentation on television. "I was so excited for her," she recalled. "Of course, everyone was, but . . . dare I ask? No one ever has, in all of these years, at least not publicly: Why, oh, why could she not have at least thanked her devoted mother? That was what immediately came to my mind. Of course, she was weak and disoriented, that was clear, and it was what Francis would say when I asked him about it. But can you imagine the joy Sara would have felt in that moment if Elizabeth had just acknowledged her, in some way? I so longed for that moment for Sara. I think everyone did, but it didn't happen. 'Yes, it would have been nice,' Francis told me. 'But don't worry about Sara. She's okay. She's just glad Elizabeth is still with us.' It was a joyous time just the same."

Elizabeth wasn't so naïve as to think that her Oscar win was purely because of her work in *Butterfield 8*. She firmly believed that a major reason for it was that the Academy felt sorry for her for all she'd been through with the near-death experience in London. Calling this one "a sympathy award," she felt that her work in the previous three movies had been much more deserving of such Academy recognition. "It was all clear to me," she would recall. "I knew it wasn't my acting, but rather my *life*, which won me the award." However, she was grateful for the acknowledgment just the same, and heartened by such an important validation of her talent. Debbie Reynolds would later remark, "Hell, even *I* voted for her!"

Indeed, Elizabeth Taylor had survived, but, even more, she had thrived. Her great achievement at this difficult time in her life brings to mind a scene from *Cat on a Hot Tin Roof*. In it, Elizabeth, as Maggie, tells Brick, played by Paul Newman, "Oh, I'm more determined than you think. I'll win all right."

"Win what?" he asks. "What is the victory of a cat on a hot tin roof?"

She fixes him with a soulful yet defiant look, and answers, "Just stayin' on it, I guess. Long as she can."

Cleopatra Begins Filming

It was September 25, 1961, the first day of principal photography on the newly revamped production of *Cleopatra* at Cinecitta Studios outside Rome. This day had certainly been a long time coming, with so many writers, directors, and producers having careened in and out of the project with such rapidity that it had become difficult for industry trade publications to keep track of all of the players. By this time, Peter Finch, whom Elizabeth had personally selected, the two having starred together in *Elephant Walk*, was out of the cast as Caesar, replaced by Rex Harrison. Stephen Boyd was also replaced as Mark Antony by Richard Burton. (Both Finch and Boyd left the production to fulfill other commitments.) A big problem, though, was that the script remained unfinished. Four-time Oscar winner Joseph Mankiewicz had by this time replaced Rouben Mamoulian as director. Mankiewicz—who was being paid more money ($600,000) than any director in history—had done what he could to rewrite the script on his own, but now he and a team of writers would be forced to do the best they could with what they had, scripting the rest of the movie on the spot. (Mankiewicz had wanted Marlon Brando in the Richard Burton role, but Brando was still making *Mutiny on the Bounty* at the time.)

Even when Elizabeth Taylor was not being filmed for a star turn in one of her movies, she had a way of making the smallest incidents of her life memorable. One can't help but wish she'd always been followed by a camera crew, if only for posterity. Her entrance onto the set of *Cleopatra* on the first day of shooting is a good example of how this woman could take the routine and turn it into a *moment*. Wearing a full-length black mink coat, Elizabeth walked with purpose onto the busy set, fully aware that all eyes of cast and crew were riveted upon her. She was followed by a phalanx of functionaries: two hairdressers, two costume designers, a seamstress, secretary, assistant, maid, and, of course, a press agent. With her jet-black hair in an elaborate upswept style, her eyes heavily circled with black eyeliner, the rest of her makeup meticulously applied, she was most certainly ready for her close-up as monarch of the Nile. She walked past her costars, Rex Harrison and Richard Burton, without so much as a glance in their direction, though she must have known they were smiling at her, hoping to distract her for a few seconds of attention. She would soon have scenes with Rex, but it would be months before she would work with Richard. However, at this time, her attention was focused on her director, Joseph Mankiewicz, who was standing about fifteen feet away. She stood before him. Taking her in head to toe, he bowed. She extended her hand, palm down. "Are you ready, my Queen?" he asked. He took her hand and kissed it.

"I was *born* ready, dear sir," she said. She then dropped her mink to the floor, where it fell behind her. Someone swooped it up and out of the way. Elizabeth took one step forward, a vision in gold brocade, sequins, and beads. For a few seconds, Joe appeared stunned. "My dear, you leave me breathless," he told her.

"Of course I do," she said.

Joseph Mankiewicz had directed Elizabeth to an Oscar nomination in *Suddenly, Last Summer*. She got along well with him, though he treated her with great deference, like most people in her life at this time. After many discussions about the movie over dinners with him and from reading so many script variations, Elizabeth believed that Cleopatra was a strong and ambitious role model for women, a worthwhile person to bring to life on the screen. She also felt that there were certain parallels between the Queen's life and her own. For instance, as she would explain it, she felt that Mike Todd had been to her what Julius Caesar had been to Cleopatra. After Caesar's death, Cleopatra was attracted to Mark Antony in much the same way, she felt, that she was drawn to Eddie Fisher after Todd's death.

For the movie, the Roman forum site had been constructed at Cinecitta, while the Alexandria set, which would be utilized later, was built on a private beach at Anzio in southern Italy. At Cinecitta, Elizabeth's dressing rooms were so large that they comprised an entire small building, which was soon dubbed "Casa Taylor." Even Eddie had an office there, as well as dressing quarters.

Elizabeth's deal for the movie was a masterwork of negotiation on her and her agent's part. It contained some of the most startling concessions given to an actress by a studio up to that time. Of course, she was the biggest star in movies, it could be argued, and deserved whatever she asked for from the studio—her million-dollar fee was broken down into about $125,000 a week in salary, as well as other financial disbursements along the way. She also got $3,000 a week in living expenses, plus food and lodging, and first-class round-trip airline tickets to the movie's locations for herself, three other adults, and her three children. She required two penthouse suites at the Dorchester in London, plus a Rolls-Royce Silver Cloud limousine at her disposal at all times. Her contract said that the movie had to be made in Europe, not in the United States, for tax purposes. Elizabeth also demanded that it be shot in Todd-AO, rather than 20th Century-Fox's own trademark widescreen process, CinemaScope, so that, as owner of that company—she had inherited it from Mike Todd—she would derive royalties from its use. (Expansive sets had to be built to fill this widescreen process, which accounted for a lot of the movie's budget.) She actually also owned a third of *Cleopatra* through her own corporation, MCL, Inc. (the initials of her three children, Michael, Christopher, and Liza). She would also receive 10 percent of the film's gross receipts. In the end, Elizabeth would make a fortune from this movie—more than $7 million, and in the early sixties that was *a lot* of money. Richard Burton put it best to historian Brad Geagley when he said, "Elizabeth taught me how to squeeze the studio executives by the balls."

"The studio was always on me about the money being spent," recalled Joseph Mankiewicz. "But Elizabeth's lifestyle was extravagant; she had to have the best of everything—the best linens, the best wines, the best champagnes . . . there were maids and butlers and other servants, which the studio was paying for. She had a villa she was living in with Eddie [called Villa Papa] which had fifteen rooms, a heated swimming pool, and a tennis court—all of which the studio paid for. It was a walled estate on about eight acres, seven miles from Rome and some fifteen minutes from the studio. There were dogs and cats and rabbits, kids living there, secretaries and publicists. Two of the kids were in school. [Michael and Chris were in the fourth and second grades, at the American Day School in Rome; Liza, three, was not yet in school.] It was a mad scene to go there and see her and Eddie."

Actor and producer Chris Mankiewicz, Joseph's son, celebrated his twenty-first birthday on the set of *Cleopatra*, working on the film as an assistant director. Part of his job was to hustle the actors around and get them to the set on time. "I was principally one of those people, being the son of the director of the movie as well, who was charged with dealing with Elizabeth if there was something very unpleasant or something that people were afraid they would not be able to get her to do. But there'd be no hiding the fact that it was a very tough experience in the sense that people were very . . . well, you know, she was just resented by almost everybody.

"Most European movies are shot under French hours, which is, they shoot from twelve o'clock in the afternoon until eight o'clock at night, without stopping. They have food available on the set but they don't have any breaks for lunch. The result is that they work straight through, and then they can take their makeup off, have a pleasant evening, and sleep fairly late the next morning. The difference is that we had some actors, mainly Elizabeth and her friends, who bucked that system and would go off in the middle of the hot day for lunch and a bottle of wine. All of a sudden they had to deal with actors coming back to the set after lunch and acting a little tipsy. It affected the rhythm and ability to work quickly.

"When she didn't show up for work, they'd send me to fetch her. They figured I had an advantage with her that others didn't have, given my relationship with the director. I was a kid and she was a star, so I tried to be as pleasant as possible. I have to say my relationship with her was excellent. She was infallibly polite. I would say, 'Elizabeth, please, they're waiting for you.' She would say, 'Thank you, Chris,' and then she would show up . . . usually. In truth, despite my best efforts, hundreds of hours were spent waiting for her. We joked that the movie should have been called *Waiting for Elizabeth*. But still, she was a fabulous star and when she gave you that smile . . . wow. Remember, she was at the height of her power. She was the most powerful woman in movies, the first actor—male or female—to get a million dollars. She had the studios kneeling in front of her and could do virtually anything she wanted. She was impervious to any kind of discipline, and completely enjoying it."

After greeting director Joseph Mankiewicz on that first day of filming, Elizabeth Taylor stood in place as people swarmed busily about her. A makeup artist applied powder to her face while a hairdresser fussed with her coif and someone else adjusted her formfitting and revealing costume. Another person did nothing but stare at her, looking very worried. She acted as if she didn't notice any of them. Meanwhile, her costar Richard approached. Once he was standing next to her, he leaned in and breathed on her neck. "You're much too fat, luv," he said, his voice a soft murmur, "but I admit, you do have a pretty little face."

Elizabeth might have been insulted had the comment been made by anyone other than Richard Burton. However, coming from him, in that intoxicating Welsh accent of his, it somehow seemed like a compliment. She couldn't help herself. She had to laugh. It erupted from her in the way a good laugh always did, like a horse's whinny, loud and shrill, and full of joy. "Why, the nerve!" she said, punching him on the shoulder. She then hurried over to Eddie Fisher and sat on his lap, as if to send a message to Richard that she already had a husband, thank you.

Richard Burton

It's not hyperbolic to say that the movie industry had never seen anything quite like Richard Burton—and to this day, no one has really replaced him in the business. Not only was he a singular man, he was a one-of-a-kind actor, his sheer presence filling the screen like no other. Certainly, few people expressed themselves like Burton, with his Welsh accent so musical in tone, his voice clear, rich, and distinctive. He was smart and witty, sexy and passionate—he had a smoldering quality about him that was irresistible, it seemed, even to many of the men in his life. Certainly he was an object of desire for most women with whom he crossed paths. His face was angled and, usually, serious. Even the pockmarks that scarred his face somehow worked for him, making him seem weathered, knowledgeable beyond his years. He had forever-tousled brown hair, piercing blue-green eyes, and a rugged frame, though he was no more than five feet nine (which is astonishing when one considers his enormous onscreen presence).

To know Richard Burton was to either love or hate him; there was usually no gray area when it came to one's reaction to him. However, friend and foe alike had to agree that, on his good days, he was an electrifying man filled with a great zest for life, love, and work. He was a smart, mostly self-educated scholar who spoke four languages and had such an amazing memory that he could easily recite nearly any passage of Shakespeare—and many other literary works as well. However, though he had a bright personality, there was always a deep and profound sense of anguish about him, especially in later years. On his bad days, he was sullen and depressed, a dark person who could be cruel to even his closest of friends. In the end, despite all he would make of himself from meager beginnings, there was always something rather tragic about Richard Burton—which may be one of the reasons he remains so vividly alive in the memories of everyone he touched in his lifetime.

He was born Richard Walter Jenkins Jr. on November 10, 1925, in Pontrhydyfen, Neath Port Talbot, Wales, approximately ten miles east of Swansea. (Pontrhydyfen is pronounced *Pont-reader-ven.*) He was the twelfth of thirteen children. He never knew his mother, Edith; she died giving birth to his youngest sibling. His father, known as Dic Bach, was fifty when Richard was born. He was a hardworking coal miner who did his best with what he had—a backbreaking job that yielded little money to support his large family. The family was used to accepting rations of free soup from different charities in the neighborhood. Perhaps it was the anxiety in his life that drove Dic Bach to drink; he was an alcoholic.

On what usually amounted to five shillings ($1.25 at the time) a week, Dic Bach was unable to support all of his children, so Richard was shipped off to live with his oldest sister, Cassie, and her husband. Attending school in Port Talbot (a town that was later to spawn another great Welsh actor, Anthony Hopkins), Richard spoke only Welsh until about the age of ten. Once in high school, the young man was taken under the wing of a teacher, Philip Burton, who brought the seventeen-year-old into his home and taught him drama and literature. He also worked on the tonal quality of his voice, giving him a strong and rounded sound, minimizing his strong Welsh accent and teaching him English in the process. Richard changed his last name to Burton, in honor of his teacher. He felt that the adopted name would afford him a better opportunity in the theater world in London, and hide the Welsh background he felt would be frowned upon by a class-obsessed British society. The name change was also a way to distance himself from a father he believed never cared for him. When Dic Bach died in 1957, Richard elected not to attend his funeral.

Burton began doing theater in England in 1943 before spending three years in the Royal Air Force. In 1948, he made his British film debut in the Welsh yarn *The Last Days of Dolwyn*. It was on the set of this film that he met eighteen-year-old blonde Welsh actress Sybil Williams, whom he would always call "Syb." He would take her as his wife in 1949, after which she gave up her career as an actress.

During his rapid climb to stardom, Richard was rarely faithful to Sybil. He especially fancied actresses, and there would be plenty on his list of conquests, such as Tammy Grimes, Susan Strasberg, Zsa Zsa Gabor . . . the list seemed endless. "He did *Alexander the Great* and *Look Back in Anger* with Claire Bloom," recalled his good friend Joe Sirolla. "And had an affair with her. Sybil would come to the theater and Claire would say, 'Oh, Sybil, I'm so desperately in love with your husband. Why, I don't know what I'm going to do.' And finally, after weeks and weeks of this, Sybil said, 'Darling, you *must* find something to do, because for me to hear this every night, well, it's not very pleasant.' She was wonderful. Richard adored her. We never dreamed he would ever leave her. He would often say he was nothing without Sybil."

Sybil decided to accept Richard's infidelity as part of their life together. Like a lot of women of her time, she looked the other way, though she wasn't happy about it. Also, from a practical standpoint, Sybil had to consider the well-being of her two daughters, Kate and Jessica. Kate Burton would grow up to become a successful actress; she would appear with her father in the television miniseries *Ellis Island* in 1984. Sadly, Jessica was diagnosed as both autistic and schizophrenic. She would be institutionalized on and off from the age of six, a heartbreaking situation and one that neither Sybil nor Richard would ever be able to fully reconcile.

The real challenge that faced Richard, though, and one he was unable to resolve in his lifetime, was that he was an out-of-control alcoholic. When sober, he was a delight, kind and generous, a good and loyal friend to many. However, after a few drinks, he sometimes became belligerent and difficult, and also very guilty about his many indiscretions. During this time—the 1950s and 1960s—a dependency on alcohol wasn't thought of as a disease but, rather, just an expedient way to get through the difficult day. It was also glamorized, not demonized.

In 1952, Richard left London for Hollywood, signing a contract with 20th Century-Fox. He was immediately hailed as a force to be reckoned with following his star turn in 1952 for his first U.S. film, *My Cousin Rachel*, opposite Olivia de Havilland. The movie earned him a Golden Globe and his first Academy Award nomination. As a reward for his work in that film and as confirmation of his box-office appeal, Fox cast Burton in its most important film in years, *The Robe*, a biblical epic based on the Lloyd C. Douglas novel. It was the studio's first film to be shot entirely in its new widescreen process, CinemaScope. *The Robe* turned out to be 1953's top-grossing film and earned Richard his second Oscar nomination. More movies followed. By 1961, he was starring in the Broadway hit *Camelot* (for which he would win his first Tony). He would leave that show in order to make *Cleopatra*.

To begin his work in *Cleopatra*, Richard arrived in Rome with his wife, Sybil, their daughter Kate, Roddy McDowall (who had also been in *Camelot* and would play Octavian in *Cleopatra*), and friend and actor John Valva. The contingent checked into a villa about two miles away from the Fishers. "I'm getting $250,000 for being in *Cleopatra*," he said. "Of course, the girl who plays Cleopatra is getting quite a bit more," he added with a wink.

Actually, Elizabeth had first met Richard years earlier at the home of actor Stewart Granger in Los Angeles, when Granger and his wife, Jean Simmons, hosted what has been described as "a Sunday cocktail brunch." Richard was in attendance with Sybil. Elizabeth was there with her spouse Michael Wilding. Her first impression of Richard, as she has recalled it, was that he was an egotistical lout. She barely paid attention to him. Instead, she sat in a deck chair by the pool, reading a book and feeling very antisocial. Every now and then, she would notice Burton as he recited Shakespeare in a big booming voice, or gave a long oration about some political matter, commanding the attention of everyone present. She's said that she had to give him "the cold fish eye," meaning that she was taken aback by his self-involvement.

The two would only have a couple of brief exchanges in the next few years, one at a cocktail party hosted by Tyrone Power at his Manhattan penthouse, another at a chance meeting in a restaurant in Los Angeles. Strangest of all her encounters with Burton, though, was in September 1959 when Elizabeth and Eddie Fisher attended a luncheon held on the set of the musical *Can-Can*, then in production at 20th Century-Fox, with hundreds of stars and executives invited to meet Soviet premier Nikita Khrushchev. After lunch, Spyros P. Skouras, president of Fox, engaged in a lively debate with Khrushchev over communism. Burton, also present, became so outraged by Khrushchev that he had to be held back from storming the stage. Elizabeth says she stood on her chair for a better look at the fracas.

Indeed, whenever Elizabeth happened upon Richard Burton, he was always at peak emotion, as she would put it, "giving a lecture about something, or singing a bawdy song that was completely inappropriate for the evening, or just going on and on and on about something or the other. I thought, my goodness, does the man ever shut up?"

Elizabeth was well aware of Richard's reputation as a lothario. However, that didn't matter to her because she was sure he would never have her. "I didn't want to be another notch on his belt, I knew that much going in," she has recalled. "I wasn't going to let him have that kind of power on me."

Given as much, if Elizabeth knew what Richard had said about her earlier in the week, she would not have been pleased. At the party organized to bid him farewell from *Camelot* in New York, in which he had been appearing on Broadway, he predicted to friends that in just two days' time he would have Elizabeth in his bed. "I just need two days with her," he said. "It's guaranteed."

Publicly, Richard's Burton's view of Elizabeth Taylor was not exactly flattering. "All this stuff about her being the most beautiful woman in the world is absolute nonsense," he said after first meeting her. "She's a pretty girl, of course, and she has wonderful eyes. But she has a double chin and an overdeveloped chest and she's rather short in the leg."

Everyone knew, though, that what Richard said publicly was often part of his act of bravado. Privately, he would say that, in the first seconds he laid eyes upon her on the set of *Cleopatra*, he was, this time, really taken by her. She was shorter than he remembered, but also slimmer and more curvaceous. More than anything, he loved her laugh. It was genuine and irresistible. "I will never forget that first laugh," he'd say.

Though she had a low opinion of the way he conducted his personal life, Elizabeth couldn't help but be impressed, if not also intimidated, by Richard Burton's well-earned standing as a brilliant Shakespearean actor. When it came to his craft, he was studied and deliberate and—at least usually—disciplined, despite his problems with alcohol. She would later recall how astonished she was that he would not only know his lines, but everybody else's as well . . . and he would have them all memorized the day before they even began working on camera. Friends such as Roddy McDowall had told Elizabeth Taylor that she was fortunate to have Richard Burton in her film . . . and from a creative standpoint, it was true. The question would be whether or not she would be equally fortunate to have him in her life.

Elizabeth Adopts a Baby

At the time that she was preparing to make Cleopatra, Elizabeth decided that she wanted to adopt a child with Eddie. Because she'd had a tubal ligation after her third baby, she was no longer able to bear children. Elizabeth and Eddie agreed that their marriage was in trouble, and they thought that adopting a baby might help to salvage it. Eddie had greater confidence in that scenario than did Elizabeth, though. While she did begin to investigate her options where adoption was concerned, she never had complete faith that a new baby would save her marriage. But it was worth a try, she decided.

Prior to the start of filming on Cleopatra, she and Eddie had asked a friend of theirs, Maria Schell (sister of Maximilian Schell) to assist them in adopting a baby of Swiss, German, or Viennese descent. They explained that they hoped to bring into their family a child who was ill, or in some other way disadvantaged, so that they might share with him or her their good fortune.

Well-meaning friends had a litany of concerns about Elizabeth's possibly adopting a child. After all, how much time had she spent in hospitals in recent years, practically at death's door? How much time had she spent on movie sets? Traveling? At awards shows and other banquets? From a purely practical standpoint, it did seem that she was not available, nor was she emotionally equipped, to be a mother—as much as she may have wanted to do so, as much as she yearned for it. Just wanting something badly doesn't mean one should have it. After all, even at her best, Elizabeth seemed never far from her worst. Though she spent as much time with her children as possible, her three natural offspring were for the most part being raised by nursemaids and other capable functionaries.

The desire to nurse and care for a sick baby was not a matter of noblesse oblige. Elizabeth was genuine in her desire to share her love and wealth with a child from unfortunate circumstances. It became her great wish, and she was determined to see it through—no matter what anyone thought of it. She told people that she had a strong and nagging feeling that there was a child "out there, somewhere" who needed her. She said that she didn't feel it fair to deprive that child of what she might be able to give it. "Why should a small child somewhere suffer just because I can't make my marriage work?" she asked.

It's fascinating, in retrospect, that Elizabeth would have such a strong sense of destiny where the adoption of a child was concerned, because, as it would happen, there actually *was* a baby being raised in a far-off land, a little girl who would end up the very needy beneficiary not only of her love, but her largesse as well. In the small village of Mering, Germany, thirty miles north of Munich, an impoverished family was barely scraping by, living an existence that was in stark contrast to anything Elizabeth had ever known.

In Mering, a hardworking couple was raising two young daughters—six and two years old—in a one-room apartment with a tiny stove, a small sink, and one bed. Though the father was employed at the local feed store, delivering sacks to farmers for their livestock, money was in short supply. The cost of raising their two children had become such a strain on his salary that his young wife also began working at the same store as a cashier. When she discovered she was pregnant in 1961, it was, she recalled, "a great shock to us. There was certainly no more space in our one room for another child, and we wondered where the extra money for food and clothes would come from. It was probably because of my anguish and worry that [the baby] was born prematurely," she said. "For the first few months of her life, this tiny baby struggled for her life in a special hospital for premature children in Augsburg. It was with mixed feelings of intense elation and anguish that we learned the crisis had passed: She would live." (Note: The mother did not speak English; her words here are translated.)

The young couple was torn about their new daughter's fate. They were told that she would have to spend months in the hospital, but they simply did not have the money to pay for her care.

After four months of hospitalization, they became desperate. The baby would have to be discharged because they could not pay the bills. "Then, one day in August 1961," the child's mother said, "I saw an ad in *Heim und Welt* (*Home and World*) that seemed to leap right out of the magazine and hit me in my heart. It said: 'I seek for my acquaintance to adopt a very young boy or girl.'" After a week of indecision about it, the couple decided to answer the ad. The mother recalled, "We were then contacted by Maria Konigs-bauer, the private secretary to famous actress Maria Schell, who told us that she was acting for none other than Elizabeth Taylor. She asked if the baby could be brought to Munich. It was arranged."

The couple took their daughter, whom they had named Petra, to a hospital in Munich, and left her there with the understanding that Elizabeth would soon visit her. They then went back to Mering and waited to see what would happen next. However, in a few days, they received more devastating news. Doctors in Munich had discovered that the baby had a congenital hip injury, one that had gone undetected by the medical staff in Augsburg. The injury would take a great time and lots of money to treat. "My heart was breaking as I realized that certainly there was no hope for Petra's adoption now," recalled her mother, "and I contemplated the future life of my baby. But then word reached us from Rome, like a ray of hope in the darkness of our misery: Miss Taylor had seen the baby, and though she had been warned not to adopt her because of the nature of her injury, she thought better of it. Elizabeth saw Petra and loved her and told Maria Schell that she wanted her not in spite of her injury, but *because* of it. More than anything this convinced us that we were doing the right thing and had made the right choice."

That night the couple decided that they would give their baby to Elizabeth Taylor. "It was as if it was prearranged by some power greater than us," said the child's mother. "How, in a million years, could we ever have imagined that Elizabeth Taylor, of all people in the world, would come into our lives? We felt that it was meant to be because it was just so . . . amazing. We had to do it. We had to let the baby go."

They knew they had made the right decision when, three days later, they received a letter from Elizabeth. Elizabeth wrote that if money was needed for the child, "I have plenty of it to give." She had been told, she said, by doctors that she could not have any more children, and she "longed for another," she wrote. "Not only do I have the money," she added, "I also have the love to give, and I so want to give it."

The necessary paperwork was quickly signed for Elizabeth and Eddie's adoption of the nine-month-old baby, and it was finalized in January 1962.

Elizabeth later recalled, "She was covered with abscesses, suffering from malnutrition, had a crippled hip that was going to cripple her for life—and I just loved her. She didn't cry and she didn't laugh. She was in a laundry basket with two pillows stuffed in the bottom. She had very dark eyes. She watched everything and I held her and I bathed her and I changed her for three days and finally she started giggling, and finally she would cry when she wanted her bottle. This funny little introverted person that was just sort of half asleep responded so much to love—the warmth, I think, of two arms. I was hooked by the end of a few days. The German officials wanted me to have a 'perfect baby.' I had to fight like a tiger to get her. To me, she *was* perfect. Her first word was 'Mama.' I guess that's universal, but when it happens you just die."

The child would be renamed Maria, in honor of Maria Schell. In an ironic foreshadowing of the future of Elizabeth's union with Eddie, considering that one of the reasons the baby was being adopted was to save the marriage, the infant was referred to in adoption paperwork as "Maria Taylor."

In years to come, Elizabeth would spend a small fortune on corrective surgeries for Maria. Though the child would spend agonizing years in body casts, she would grow to be healthy and happy, thanks to Elizabeth's largesse, as well as her devotion.

"Love, in All of Its Mystery, Unfolds"

Elizabeth Taylor and Richard Burton began their celebrated affair in much the same way they would conduct their relationship for the next twenty-some years: fearlessly, carelessly, passionately . . . and publicly.

Yes, Richard was a married man. However, as she had proved in the past, Elizabeth was not willing to turn down the opportunity for love just because the circumstances surrounding it were inconvenient. She longed for love in her life—always had—and not just a poor imitation of it, which is how she viewed what she had with Eddie. Or, as she told Helen Gurley Brown many years later, "Eddie and I resurrected Mike, and that's sick. Boy, did I realize how sick it was. And then along came Richard, and I realized it wasn't gone, it hadn't dried up, that Mike's legacy to me had been love."

From the outset, Taylor and Burton had one thing in common at their core: They were two people who had grown accustomed to living their lives on their own terms—working hard to achieve their goals in their own time, in their own way. No doubt, as they would both insist, they didn't mean to hurt their loved ones in the process of fulfilling their hearts' desires, but if feelings had to be hurt and hearts had to be broken, they eventually decided, so be it. They would just have to work twice as hard, Elizabeth would say, to make sure their relationship was a success so that all of the pain they had caused others would not be in vain. "I knew what I was doing, loving Richard, was wrong," she wrote in her autobiography. "But I couldn't help loving Richard. I don't think that was without honor. I don't think that was dishonest. It was a fact I could not evade."

Between September 1961 and January 1962, Elizabeth filmed her scenes in *Cleopatra* as Richard concentrated on his. They weren't scheduled to appear on camera together until the third week in January, but by that time they had gotten so close—with daily luncheons and nightly dinners together, and then late-night partying—that many on the set had begun to speculate that something was going on between them. Since Sybil Burton had been dividing her time between Rome and London, and Eddie between Rome, New York, and California, they were not around to prevent their spouses from spending plenty of time together.

In just a matter of days, Richard began to have a better understanding of Elizabeth and what she was going through at this time in her life. He gently brought to her attention certain things she hadn't really thought much about, such as the impropriety of having so many photographs of Mike Todd around the villa she shared with Eddie Fisher, the fact that she was still wearing Mike's wedding band (and, often, not Eddie's), and that she would sometimes talk incessantly about Mike, to the exclusion of Eddie. She said that she began to realize how "selfish" it had been for her to live in the past, and that it was Richard who had finally brought it all to clarity for her. He began to represent to her, as she put it, "Prince Charming kissing the sleeping princess."

Elizabeth has a memory of a night she, Eddie, Richard, Sybil, and Roddy McDowall went to dinner after a long day at the studio. Richard sat across the table from her. At about 9:30, Eddie decided that it was time for them to leave since Elizabeth had to be on the set early the next day. She protested, asking if they could stay just a while longer. She didn't want to leave. Elizabeth, never one to be vague about her feelings when it came to something she did not want to do, began protesting loudly. "I don't want to go," she said. "We're having so much fun. Please, Eddie."

"No, we should leave now," Eddie said, reaching for her wrap. At the time, he was being paid $1,500 a week to keep Elizabeth away from alcohol and get her home and into bed at a reasonable hour . . . then back to the set the next day on time. However, as far as Elizabeth was concerned, he might as well have been just another insolent employee.

Richard began talking busily to Eddie, obviously trying to prolong the evening. "So, chap, what are your plans for the future?" he wanted to know. "Any movies on the horizon? Television, perhaps? Theater?"

As Eddie answered his questions, Richard took Elizabeth's empty glass of wine and exchanged it stealthily for his full one. The two shared a conspiratorial look. Roddy McDowall took it all in with a disapproving eye. Before the group knew it, they were all involved in another conversation. Twenty minutes later, Richard again swapped his full glass of wine with Elizabeth's empty one. The two winked at one another. This went on for about another two hours.

Everyone knew that Eddie didn't want Elizabeth to have more than one glass of wine at dinner if she were going to be able to properly perform the next day. However, he did nothing to stop Richard. Though Richard may have thought he was being clever about exchanging the wineglasses, how surreptitious could he have been with only five of them sitting at the table?

Finally it was Roddy who said, "We have to go." When Elizabeth started protesting again, he was firm. "That's it," he said. "We are going. *Now*."

As the small party rose to leave the restaurant, Elizabeth and Richard were so tipsy that they had to hang on to each other just to walk. "Oh, we're all a bloody mess now, aren't we?" she said with a cackle of a laugh. "See, Eddie? It's all your fault. You should have made us leave sooner."

Elizabeth's reaction to Richard that night: "I absolutely adore this man."

January 22, 1962, was the first day that Elizabeth, then thirty, and Richard, thirty-six, would work together in front of the camera on *Cleopatra*. In many ways, the events of that memorable day would foreshadow some of the dysfunction in their relationship, with Richard showing up for rehearsal so hungover from the previous night's drinking binge that he could barely walk. In fact, as Elizabeth would recall it, she had never before seen a man so com-

Elizabeth and her second husband, British actor Michael Wilding, whom she married on February 21, 1952. She was twenty years younger than Wilding, but the marriage would last for four years. (PHOTOFEST)

Elizabeth with her sometimes troublesome but always loyal mother, Sara. (PHOTOFEST)

The marriage to Michael Wilding would produce two sons. Michael Howard Wilding was born on January 6, 1953. (The middle name, Howard, was in honor of her brother, who had returned home from Korea just in time for the birth.) Then on February 27, 1955, Elizabeth's twenty-third birthday, she had a second child, Christopher. (PHOTOFEST)

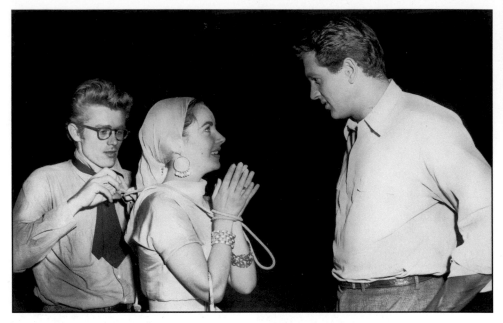

Twenty-three-year-old Elizabeth, sandwiched between her *Giant* co-stars James Dean (left) and Rock Hudson, appears all tied up during a break in filming at the Warner Bros. Studio lot, where she was "on loan" from MGM. (PHOTOFEST)

In 1957 Elizabeth appeared in *Raintree County* with her very good friend Montgomery Clift. Their chemistry was based in large part on physical attraction but also on mutual respect. Some have speculated that if Monty didn't "bat for the other team," he and Elizabeth would have married.
(TOM GATES COLLECTION)

Third husband Mike Todd gazes lovingly at his Elizabeth, who was half his age. He was the first of her husbands to shower her with furs, jewels, and museum-quality works of art. (TOM GATES COLLECTION)

Elizabeth and Mike. They adored each other, and she still thinks of him as one of the two loves of her life (the other being Richard Burton). Here they are with their daughter, Elizabeth Frances—named after Elizabeth and her father, but nicknamed Liza—who was born on August 6, 1957. (TOM GATES COLLECTION)

Mike and Elizabeth and Eddie Fisher and his wife, Debbie Reynolds, were inseparable during the Todd-Taylor marriage. Here the foursome attends a race at England's Epsom Downs in 1957. (TOM GATES COLLECTION)

March 1958: Elizabeth is escorted by her brother, Howard (right), to Mike Todd's funeral. Todd was killed en route to New York in his private plane, *Lucky Liz*. Only a very bad cold kept Elizabeth from joining him. After much grieving, she returned to finish filming *Cat on a Hot Tin Roof*. (BETTMANN/CORBIS)

Elizabeth made her first public appearance after Mike's death at Eddie Fisher's opening in Las Vegas in June 1958. Backstage, Debbie seems a bit perplexed at the rapport her husband has with Elizabeth. (PHOTOFEST)

Elizabeth was forced to make *Butterfield* 8 by MGM in 1960. She hated the script, hated the movie, did everything she could think of to get out of it . . . and then ended up winning an Oscar for it! (PHOTOFEST)

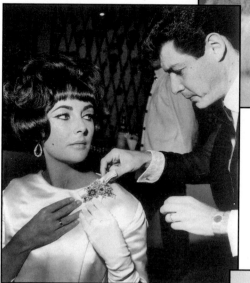

Eddie Fisher, here adjusting the brooch on Elizabeth's evening coat before attending a party at Rome's Grand Hotel, must have been relieved that he survived the Liz-Eddie-Debbie scandal of several years earlier. Little did he realize that the Fisher-Taylor-Burton scandal lay just around the corner. (TOM GATES COLLECTION)

This is a very rare shot from the first production of *Cleopatra*, September 1960. Many Taylor historians feel that the costumes in this version were much better than the ones later designed for the Italian production. The London footage was scrapped, though, when Elizabeth became deathly ill. (J. RANDY TARABORRELLI COLLECTION)

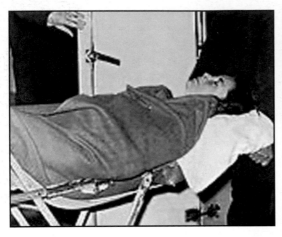

March 1961: Wrapped in a blanket, Elizabeth is rushed to The London Clinic, where the twenty-nine-year-old would fight for her life after contracting pneumonia and having an emergency tracheotomy. News of her illness–and even erroneous reports of her death–spread around the world like wildfire. (BETTMANN/CORBIS)

No one was more concerned about Elizabeth during this dark period than Sara and Francis Taylor, seen here leaving The London Clinic on March 6, 1961. By this time, these two had endured more heartache from their daughter's many challenges than most parents could ever fathom. (BETTMANN/CORBIS)

Of course, she recovered. Some-how, Elizabeth *always* seemed to recover! Here she is on the set of *Cleopatra* (now in Rome), with Sara and Francis, ebullient at their daughter's seemingly miraculous healing.
(RETROPHOTO)

Richard Burton in a rare publicity photo from the late 1950s. In 1961 he was cast in *Cleopatra* as a replacement for Stephen Boyd. It was a decision that would forever change the course of his life. (J. RANDY TARABORRELLI COLLECTION)

Though Elizabeth and Richard were both married to long-suffering spouses, they could not resist each other. Within weeks of working together on *Cleopatra*, they were having a complex and often very painful love affair. (SUNSET BOULEVARD/CORBIS)

April 13, 1962: A sobbing Elizabeth is escorted from a Via Veneto nightclub amidst a barrage of photographer flashes. The Vatican had charged her with "erotic vagrancy" because of her scandalous affair with Burton. (TOM GATES COLLECTION)

By the time Elizabeth and Richard married on March 15, 1964, most of their friends and family were drained by their wild, personal adventures and tempestuous romance. "We shall have no more marriages," Richard said, quoting Shakespeare. Here they are, a couple of years later on the set of *The Sandpiper*. (PHOTOFEST)

The newlyweds caused pandemonium wherever they went, with people just wanting a glimpse of them. In Boston, where Richard opened in *Hamlet* weeks after their wedding, the couple was mobbed. Elizabeth suffered injuries to her arms and spine in the fracas. (TOM GATES COLLECTION)

In 1966 Elizabeth and Richard filmed what is arguably their best movie, *Who's Afraid of Virginia Woolf?* Elizabeth would win an Oscar for her work in the movie, though Richard was unfairly overlooked. (COURTESY OF ACADEMY OF MOTION PICTURES ARTS & SCIENCES)

pletely debilitated from alcohol consumption. "He was kind of quivering from head to foot," she recalled, "and there were grog blossoms [blemishes]—you know, from booze—all over his face."

"Oh Christ, I need a cup of coffee," Burton said, trembling.

When someone handed him a cup, Elizabeth observed that Richard was so jittery he couldn't even raise it to his mouth without spilling the coffee all over himself. "Oh, you poor dear," she said as she helped him steady his hand. "Let me help you." As she held the cup for him, he gingerly sipped from it. "Thank you, my dear," he said weakly.

One may have thought that Elizabeth would have been aghast that a costar would show up for work on the first day of such an important film in seemingly no condition to perform. Certainly in the past she would never have allowed such an unprofessional display on the set of one of her films without making a big issue of it. However, such was not the case on this morning with Richard. Rather, she was drawn to him because of what she immediately perceived as a tantalizing conflict in his personality. He was a strong man, very much unlike her father. Yet he had an extreme vulnerability—very much *like* her father. "That just endeared him so to me," she would recall of the moment she helped him drink his coffee. "I thought, well, he really *is* human. He was so vulnerable and sweet and shaky and terribly giggly that with my heart I *cwtched* him." (That's Welsh for "hugged" him.)

Others more critical of Richard may have viewed him in a very different light. However, Joseph Mankiewicz probably said it best when he observed, "It's in one's first perception of another—skewed though it may be—that love, in all of its mystery, unfolds, isn't it?"

In their first moment onscreen together, Elizabeth, as Cleopatra, whispers urgently to Richard's Mark Antony, "To have waited so long, to know so suddenly. Without you, this is not a world I want to live in."

"Everything that I want to hold or love or have or be is here with me now," Burton, in character, responded.

When the two then embraced and kissed, the electricity was almost palpable. Eddie was not on the set that day, which was probably for the best. They filmed the scene a few times. The final time, they held the kiss so long that some observers actually began to feel a little uncomfortable. "Cut!" Joseph Mankiewicz said. They continued kissing. "I said, cut!" he repeated. "Don't the two of you have any interest at all in eating lunch?"

They broke their embrace and, after a few self-conscious moments, walked their separate ways, Richard with his few handlers and Elizabeth with her coterie of hairdressers, makeup artists, and others who were always fussing over her.

About a week after they finally began working together, Richard and Elizabeth were on a beach in Torre Astura, where an elaborate replica of the royal palace had been built. The day began at noon, as was the custom in Italy, and the weather was not making production easy on anyone, especially the frustrated Joe Mankiewicz. His son, Chris, was responsible for keeping the mercurial Taylor in line as a threatening storm ground production to a crawl. They would shoot for two minutes of sunshine, then the clouds would roll in and everything would stop. At one point, Taylor and Burton were called to the set, extras were being placed, and cameras were about to roll, when a tremendous clap of thunder shook the ground, a torrential downpour fell, and everyone scattered. Richard grabbed Elizabeth's hand and pulled her toward the plaster façade of a palace wall. Entering a tremendous door, they closed it behind them before the director's son spotted them. Hank Lustig, a jeweler from London, had flown in to present some pieces to Mankiewicz and Taylor for the production, and had sought shelter in the same spot. Above their heads were about six stories of scaffolding with leaky wooden planks—probably not the best place to stay dry.

"Have you lost your mind?" Elizabeth asked Richard. "We'll get drenched here. They call them façades for a reason, numbskull."

Richard climbed a painter's ladder and reached into a bucket. From it he retrieved an open bottle of wine.

"Do you know how long it takes to get this makeup done if it gets wet?" Elizabeth continued complaining.

"Well, it's already wet, isn't it?" Burton said as he took a swig and handed the bottle to her. In the distance, an umbrella-toting Chris Mankiewicz joined a chorus of production assistants calling Elizabeth's name in increasingly panicked voices. "Have a nip," Burton prodded. "Who's the boss here?" She looked at him blankly as he continued: "Besides me, I mean?"

Elizabeth spotted Hank Lustig, huddling in a relatively dry spot. "You there!"

"Me?"

She yanked the bottle from Burton's grasp and brandished it. "Did you bring this here?"

"Certainly not!" Lustig responded.

"Good. This man is *not* to be drinking on duty," she said quite seriously of Richard. "By order of the Queen."

Lustig was unsure how to respond as the two stars watched him for his reaction, then burst into spontaneous laughter. He backed away a bit, slipping behind a piece of equipment as Elizabeth and Richard passed the bottle back and forth. He recalls, "They spent about the next twenty minutes or so peering through cracks in the façade, or peeking out the door. They laughed almost the entire time, or at least mostly she did, from things he would whisper to her. It was like they were children hiding from their parents."

At one point, a suspicious silence led Lustig to check if the two had left. They hadn't. They were passionately kissing. The silence was broken in a strange, less-than-romantic way.

"Ouch!" Elizabeth shouted.

"What the hell is it?" Richard asked.

"There are hairpins in this," she shouted. "You can't just take it off like a hat!"

"You scared the daylights out of me."

"Well, you're pulling my hair out!"

The two continued bickering until, again, silence fell. Lustig knew they were back at it, and didn't need to spy this time.

When the rain subsided, the calls for the two stars had built to near pandemonium. It was decided that it would be best for Elizabeth to depart first, so that they wouldn't be seen leaving together. She fluffed her wardrobe away from her damp skin and gathered herself to go. She started out, then turned back to Richard. "You truly are a horrible, horrible man."

"If I was twice as awful," he said, returning the volley, "I'd be perfect for you."

She smirked a bit before stepping back into the real world. Richard pressed his face close to the crack in the door and watched her go. "You still with us?" he then bellowed. Hank Lustig leaned out from his hiding spot. "You know, if you weren't here that might have ended differently," Richard said.

"I'm sorry . . ."

"No. You did me a favor. You see, once you screw her, she makes you marry her."

Lustig was stunned to silence.

"I'm still weighing my options," Richard Burton quipped. As he headed off he said, "Stay dry, chum. And mum's the word."

Elizabeth Confesses to Eddie about Richard

By the end of the third week of January 1962, Elizabeth Taylor and Richard Burton had worked together for about five days on the set of *Cleopatra*. One morning, Richard walked into the makeup trailer at Cinecitta and made a startling announcement. Chris Mankiewicz happened to be present. "Gentlemen," he said in those stentorian tones of his, "last night, I screwed Miss Elizabeth Taylor in the backseat of my Cadillac." His proclamation was met with awkward silence. One wonders if he expected applause?

"The sense of it from everyone was, 'Uh-oh, here we go,'" Chris recalls. "Richard was famous for having sex with his leading ladies in almost every movie. Some on the crew had joked about having a betting pool on how long it would be before he and Elizabeth would have become involved. But, you know, Italians can be very sex-obsessed anyway, at least certainly in those days. There was a lot of sexual badinage, people making jokes about one another as well, not just about the stars.

"Elizabeth was infinitely more prudish than Richard, even though she'd had already a number of husbands. She wasn't as easy as people thought. I remember, years later, my father said, 'I could have had an affair with Elizabeth, but what people don't know about her is that she won't just sleep with you, she'll make you promise to then marry her.' At some point, I think he tried to go to bed with her. But she said, not unless you marry me, and he walked away from that. But I remember he always used to say, she'll have you but you've got to marry her."

One might want to imagine that the consummation of such an important, life-changing relationship in the lives of two worldly people like Elizabeth and Richard would have occurred in some ceremonial fashion, perhaps in an exotic and wildly romantic location. However, from all accounts, it does indeed seem that the love affair of Richard Burton and Elizabeth Taylor was consummated when he had his way with her in the backseat of his Cadillac. It's not likely she got a promise of marriage out of him, either. For Richard, she would, apparently, make an exception to that rule . . .

Joseph Mankiewicz talked the situation over with producer Walter Wanger. "I've been sitting on a volcano all alone for too long," he told him, "and I want to give you some facts you ought to know. Liz and Burton are not just *playing* Cleopatra and Antony."

Chris Mankiewicz recalls, "To be honest, my father encouraged, to some degree, the affair, or at least he didn't try to stop it. He had his reasons. He felt that Richard was, as a British-trained actor, more disciplined than Elizabeth. He and Rex Harrison were theater people. You didn't have a second take with him. They were used to doing it in one take, on a stage, in front of an audience. So making movies with them was a bit easier. The feeling was that Elizabeth was often not so well prepared. By having the two of them spending the evenings together, there would be, he hoped, opportunities for them to rehearse. He also hoped that there would be opportunities for her to get into the habit of being more disciplined, of rehearsing her lines with him, memorizing her script and being more prepared for the following day's work."

It didn't take long before Louella O. Parsons, the Hearst newspapers' Hollywood reporter, was reporting that Elizabeth's marriage was in trouble, and that the ever-tempestuous actress was in the midst of yet another torrid affair that could possibly lead to the dissolution of not only her marriage but someone else's as well. More than a thousand reporters swarmed onto the *Cleopatra* location, a veritable army of media, all after the big story that Elizabeth was involved in a romance, maybe with her costar Richard Burton. The widowed Mankiewicz tried to downplay the rumors by joking that Elizabeth's affair was actually with him. It didn't work. The media was on to a story, and would not let it go until it was confirmed. When Joe went to Walter Wanger and told him that it was possible that their Cleopatra and Mark Antony were carrying on away from the camera's view, Wanger's biggest concern was whether such a thing would help or hurt the movie. During a meeting with Richard, he asked what was going on with Elizabeth. Richard downplayed the significance of any pairing, though he did not deny it. "Actually, it might just be a once-over-lightly," he said.

The story got to Eddie, who was in New York at the time on business, within days. He telephoned Elizabeth to ask her to hold a press conference and deny any kind of romance with Richard

Burton. "It needs to stop, all this talk," he told her. "And you're the only one who can do that."

"I'm sorry, Eddie, but I can't," she told him.

"Why?"

"It's just not the right time," she said, being guarded.

"Thanks a lot," Eddie said, before slamming down the telephone.

By the time Eddie got back to Rome a few days later, it seemed as if everyone on the set of *Cleopatra* knew what had been going on behind his back. He couldn't help but notice the way people averted their eyes when he walked into a room.

That night, Eddie and Elizabeth had a quiet meal and some uneasy conversation before retiring for the evening. As they lay next to each other, Elizabeth drifted off almost immediately. Suddenly, the phone rang. Eddie picked it up quickly, so as not to have it awaken her. It was Bob Abrams, a friend of his who had come to Rome to visit him. "There's something you need to know," Bob said, according to a later recollection. "Elizabeth and Richard are having an affair."

Coming from Bob, Eddie knew it was true. Just as he hung up the phone, Elizabeth stirred. "A friend just called me to tell me that you and Richard Burton are having an affair," he said. "Is it true?"

Elizabeth exhaled deeply, as if to suggest an imminent confession. "It's true," she said, her voice nearly a whisper.

The two then lay in bed, side by side, staring at the ceiling and not saying another word about it.

Unadulterated Drama

Once it was clear on the set of *Cleopatra* that Elizabeth and Richard were involved, there was simply no way for it to be concealed from the press. It quickly erupted into a worldwide news event, even though the two stars continued to deny it. Of course, just about anything Elizabeth Taylor did in those days made international headlines, so an affair with a handsome, married costar was sure to generate its share of sensational copy. It wasn't her first affair, after all, and considering that she was still blamed by many for breaking up Eddie Fisher's marriage to Debbie Reynolds, it seemed to her critics that she was just a wanton woman who simply didn't give a damn about anyone other than herself. She wasn't perceived as a person trying to take hold of any small bits of happiness a troubled life offered, that's for sure, even if it was true. The headlines were horrendous, the scandal bigger than anything Elizabeth had created in her life up until that time—and that's saying a lot.

Finally, after about a week of indecision as to how to handle things, Elizabeth made a choice. "I had to be with Richard," she said many years later. "I knew it was wrong. I knew it would hurt people. I knew. *I knew.* But I also knew what I had to do. God help me, I had to be with Richard."

"With the obvious becoming even more so, it was decided by Joe [Mankiewicz], Walter [Wanger], and Roddy [McDowall] that someone had to do something about Sybil," a friend of Burton's in London recalled. "They liked her very much and felt it was wrong for her to not know what was going on with Richard. Roddy, it was decided, would be the bearer of bad news. He screwed up his courage, flew to London, and told Sybil that Richard was having an affair with Elizabeth. She reacted by slapping him heartily across the face."

Once the Burton-Taylor romance was out in the open, Richard seemed to suddenly feel he had license to behave as inappropriately in public as he liked where Elizabeth was concerned, and she was—or at least she seemed to be—a willing participant in the torture he inflicted upon Eddie Fisher. It certainly seemed to be the case the night Burton showed up unexpectedly at a dinner party at the Fishers' villa in Rome, as Eddie recalled it. When confronted by Eddie, Richard became belligerent. "Why don't you just go home to your own wife?" Eddie shouted at him. He seemed on the verge of strangling him with his bare hands. "*She's* your woman, not Elizabeth. Elizabeth is mine."

"Oh yeah? Well, guess what? They're *both* my women," Richard spouted back. He could barely stand, and the aroma of liquor surrounded him. He turned to Elizabeth, who seemed to be hiding a smile at this display. "Are you my woman?" he demanded to know. "*Well, are you?* If so, then come over here and stick your tongue down my throat and prove it."

The moment hung, as both men watched her, waiting for her next move. Guests present at the Fisher villa were uncomfortable, stunned to silence by the sheer audacity Burton displayed. Elizabeth stood motionless for a moment, her eyes locked on Richard. Then she began to move toward him, holding her glass of champagne. Some observers assumed that she was going to walk over and toss the drink on him. However, she surprised everyone, except perhaps Richard. He knew what Elizabeth would do. With all eyes on her, she leaned into this man who seemed to have a hypnotic effect on her, and she pressed her lips firmly against his.

Humiliated in front of his guests, Eddie stepped past the kissing couple in the doorway and went outside the house. By this time, even the pianist had stopped playing and all eyes were on the passionate display that seemed almost scripted. Richard was the first to break. He turned to walk out, past Fisher. Richard halted a moment, turned to Eddie, and said almost politely, "Keep her warm for me, won't you?" Then he was gone.

Elizabeth, feeling the eyes on her, gathered herself a bit, then whirled around and glided toward a grand marble staircase. She tipped her champagne glass high, taking one last big American gulp before the mainly upper-crust Italian crowd in attendance. She plopped the empty glass on a butler's tray and floated up the stairs.

The next day, Elizabeth and Richard had scenes together on the set of *Cleopatra*. There was an odd tension in the air, and all on the set could feel it. Elizabeth avoided eye contact with Richard—some opined that her aversion to him was disdain, others that it was her building desire for her leading man that she couldn't face. There were innumerable delays in shooting. Elizabeth claimed that she was ill, or exhausted, or simply menstruating (according to her contract, she didn't have to appear for work during the first two days of her cycle).*

Eddie Fisher felt very strongly at the time—and still does today—that Richard's sole motivation in pursuing Elizabeth was to further his career. That's too simple a conclusion. Even if he *had* planned to catapult himself to stardom with the help of a great star like Elizabeth, the sheer complexity of the couple's dynamic didn't seem like a simple means to an end for Burton. Inexplicably drawn to each other, the two began a dark journey where love and contempt were often interchangeable. He may have begun the odyssey with Elizabeth thinking of his own career, but once the two had created the enigmatic union, neither was truly captain of that ship. Elizabeth and Richard were led by something

---

* Some reports have had it that this clause was the result of Elizabeth's experience on the film A *Place in the Sun* as a teenager. Director George Stevens had made her jump into a freezing lake repeatedly, over her mother's objections, while she was having her period. Sara Taylor, it was said, feared—perhaps somewhat unreasonably—that her daughter would not be able to bear children as a result of that shoot. She then had it written into her daughter's contracts that she did not have to work for the first two days of menstruation, and the clause stayed in Elizabeth's deals for about the next twenty years. However, upon closer inspection of the facts, it seems that Sara got the idea that Elizabeth should not have to work during her cycle from the earlier example of Irene Dunne, who was permitted to miss work during her period. In fact, Sara began to withhold Elizabeth from working during those troublesome days as early as 1946, when Elizabeth was fourteen and making *Life with Father*.

bigger than the both of them . . . their desire for pure, unadulterated drama.

Elizabeth Attempts Suicide?

Eddie Fisher made up his mind that the only thing he could do to salvage what little dignity he had left was to get as far away from Elizabeth and Richard as possible. He planned to take the green Rolls-Royce she had given him as a gift and drive to Milan, where he would sort out his jumbled thoughts and twisted emotions. However, before he would take his leave, he decided to have a little chat with Sybil Burton, Richard's long-suffering wife. It was February 17, 1962.

"You know, they are having an affair," Eddie told Sybil. Of course, she already knew, and certainly didn't need to be reminded. "I know," she said simply.

"What are you going to do about it?"

"Nothing," she said. "Richard has been having affairs for years, and he always comes back to me. This will be just like all of the others. He'll be back. It will blow over. Trust me. I know my husband."

Eddie laughed in her face. "Clearly, you don't know my wife," he said bitterly. "We are talking about *Elizabeth Taylor* here, not some chippy from one of Burton's pictures. She wants your husband, and I can tell you from experience that she's a woman who *always* gets what she wants." He delivered the lines as if he was starring in a bad movie, and, this being his first acting job in years, he took full advantage of the scene.

"But . . ."

"Listen to me, sweetheart," he said, playing the tough guy to the hilt. "Your marriage? It ain't gonna recover. Trust me."

For a moment, the two stared at each other, a silence hanging between them. Previously, Sybil had said that she believed the affair would just blow over, and that she and Richard would "be a million dollars richer because of it." Now she wasn't so sure. It was as if a wave of recognition had suddenly swept over her. She began to sob, the tears flowing uncontrollably. She ran from the room.

Eddie left the Burton villa, jumped into his Rolls, and took off for Milan. The problem, though, was that he was as obsessed with Elizabeth as she was with Richard, and there could be no clean break. He stopped three times along the way to call her, but couldn't locate her. Finally he tracked her down at her secretary Richard Hanley's apartment. Very upset with him, she told him that Sybil had appeared unannounced at the studio and confronted her and Richard. The argument turned so volatile that no one was even able to work after it. The production had to be canceled for the day, at a cost of half a million dollars to 20th Century-Fox. "And it's all your fault," Elizabeth said angrily. Then Richard grabbed the receiver.

"What are you doing there?" Eddie asked

"What do you think I'm doing here?" Richard shouted into the phone. "And I'm going to kill you for what you have done to Sybil."

"What *I* did to Sybil?" Eddie screamed back. "Are you crazy?"

After he hung up, Richard, worn out by the juvenile exchange, told Elizabeth that it was over between them. It was too difficult for everyone concerned, he said. He told her that she should just go back to Eddie and he to Sybil. Besides, he said, Elizabeth was too combative a person. He was used to more passivity from a woman. After all, "Syb" had put up with a lot from him, he pointed out, and probably more than Elizabeth could ever tolerate in the future. It was better, he said, if he and Elizabeth now cut to what he called "the inevitable conclusion" of their brief but combative romance.

"But, Richard. No!" Elizabeth protested. Unfazed, Richard turned and walked out the door.

By the next morning, everyone at Cinecitta had heard that Elizabeth had had some kind of a breakdown over Richard. Walter Wanger went to Villa Papa to see if he could be of any assistance, and also to gauge his star's ability to continue working on the movie. When he arrived, Elizabeth was in her bedroom, being tended to by her physician, Dr. Rexford Kennamer. Dick Hanley told Walter that the star would greet him shortly. About an hour later, she appeared, looking distraught. "I feel dreadful about this whole thing," she said, her hands trembling. She poured herself a brandy and sank into a chair. "I don't know what to do," she said, according to Wanger's memory.

She seemed out of it, slightly loopy. After a few minutes with him, she rose and excused herself. Wanger, Roddy McDowall, Dick Hanley, and Elizabeth's hairdresser, Vivian Zavits, retired to a reception room where they could discuss Elizabeth's condition privately. After some time, Wanger went upstairs to check on her. "I'm fine," she said from the other side of a closed door. "I've taken some sleeping pills. But perhaps I should eat before I doze off," she added weakly. Wanger then went back downstairs to see about her lunch. The meal was prepared. A maid took it to Elizabeth.

Five minutes later, the maid's screams reverberated throughout the household. "Miss Taylor has taken too many pills," she cried out. "I can't wake her!"

Pandemonium erupted. An ambulance was called. A snitch in the household called the tip into a newspaper. By the time she got to Salvatore Mundi International Hospital, the paparazzi were present in full force. Elizabeth had her stomach pumped; she survived an overdose of sleeping pills. Maybe it was accidental. However, the reports were that she had swallowed thirty pills, so . . . maybe not. People in her circle were split as to what they believed. The studio issued a statement that said that she had suffered from a stomach ailment. The public bought it.

How she could work herself into such a state over someone

she'd only known for about six weeks, and try to take her life without, apparently, even considering her children, was very upsetting to everyone who knew her, even Richard. He was about as self-loathing as anyone he knew, but Elizabeth now proved to him what many in her circle had known about her for years: She was in a league all her own when it came to the cataclysmic. In retrospect, it seems impossible to reconcile the fact that in just a week, on February 27, 1962, she would turn only thirty. Just look at the punishing life she had lived up until this time!

Her friends who believed it to be true were stunned that she had tried to commit suicide over Richard. However, it's impossible to isolate Elizabeth's behavior and choices from her apparent alcoholism and addiction to prescription drugs. In reviewing her life and trying to understand it, it has to be remembered that it was, for the most part, played out in a haze of either depression or euphoria, both extremes having often been chemically induced.

Also, just as one can't isolate her vices from her life, the recognition of her celebrity as an important factor is key to understanding her. By thirty, she'd lived a life of entitlement for more than twenty years. She'd made thirty-three movies and was a major star who always got exactly what she wanted, a star who inspired awe everywhere she went and in whatever she did. On the sets of her films, she was treated with reverence and deference. In public, she was idolized by the masses. In private, her men gave her jewels, even when she truly didn't deserve them. For instance, Eddie, for her thirtieth, would gift her with a ten-carat yellow diamond ring (for which, he said, he got "zip reaction"), and a folded mirror that opened into an emerald-studded serpent, which he'd had designed by Bulgari. It's not as if she deserved such presents from him while she was cheating on him with Burton! While it may have been thrilling for her to live this way, it was also very corruptive. However, the notion that fame corrupts is not exactly revelatory.

More important, by this time, Elizabeth Taylor had still not yet figured out how to extract any knowledge she may have gleaned from past experiences to assimilate into her behavior in some meaningful way. Despite her life-altering moments, even facing death a couple of times, she hadn't exactly become a pensive, deep-thinking woman. Her inner life remained undeveloped. Still her mother's daughter, she also strove for perfection in everything she did and, especially in the case of her latest married suitor, against the greatest of odds. After Richard told her she couldn't have what she wanted in that very moment—*him*—and it became clear to her that things would not, and might never be, ideal for her with him, she reacted in a terrible and self-destructive way. If the overdose was indeed intentional, it's horrifying to think that she would do such a thing to herself and to her family. "Well, I believe that in that very second, she just didn't want to live," says someone who knew her very well back then. "It wasn't rational, of course. But people who want to commit suicide are not rational in their darkest of moments, now are they?"

"Le Scandale"

On April 2, 1962, it was announced that Elizabeth Taylor and Eddie Fisher were divorcing. By this time, just about everyone who cared about such things knew that Elizabeth was having an affair with her costar Richard Burton. There were photos of the two movie stars in bathing suits, taken by the legendary photographer Bert Stern, looking very much in love while sunning themselves on the deck of a boat—Elizabeth particularly fetching in a bikini—that had circulated around the world. It was the biggest story in the land, or, as Richard dubbed it, "Le Scandale." Photographers hid in bushes and scaled walls as they followed their every move in public. A distant and grainy shot of the two love-birds simply standing next to each other on the set of *Cleopatra* could guarantee a huge payday for the lucky paparazzo who managed to sneak the photo. "Photographers dressed up like priests used to come to the door," Elizabeth has recalled, "or they'd get inside as workmen or plumbers. They were on the wall, climbing up with stepladders from the outside. The servants would come rushing out with brooms and rakes, and the kids would turn the hose on those maniacs."

One bodyguard of Elizabeth's had the unusual job of literally beating the bushes with a police nightstick at regular intervals, in order to locate and then chase away photographers who might be hiding there. Some of Elizabeth's guests, such as Audrey Hepburn, who'd just gotten the role in the film version of *My Fair Lady* and had gone to share the good news with Elizabeth, found it more than a little unnerving that a man was swatting the bushes behind her as she sipped her tea.

Martin Landau, their costar in *Cleopatra*, recalls, "We were sitting having drinks waiting to do a scene, and there was a big wall behind us, and they were lighting this scene and when they turned the arcs on, the big lights, it revealed about thirty photographers hanging on to cliffs and scaffolds. If any of them had dropped, they would have fallen forty feet, up there with their long-lensed cameras, and I assure you they were not taking pictures of me."

Predictably, international headlines blasted Elizabeth for her "wanton" behavior. What she and Burton were now doing to Eddie Fisher and Sybil Burton promised to be even more sensational in the news cycle than what she and Eddie had done to Debbie Reynolds three years earlier. Some felt that Eddie finally got what he deserved when Elizabeth left him, especially after the way he had treated Debbie. It also seemed to a lot of people that Elizabeth always ended up on top, at the expense of anyone who got in her way. People wondered if there were any way she could be committed to any one person for a decent period of time. Did she feel that there was always someone better for her just around the corner?

Stephanie Wanger, who is Walter's daughter and was on the set of *Cleopatra* for much of the filming, recalled, "The bottom line is they were deeply in love. It was the real thing. As a couple, they fit well together. They had a rapport, and all Rome seemed to be caught up in the romance. It became what Camelot ought to have been for Jack and Jackie Kennedy." (When one considers that the Arthurian legends contain a story about a faithless wife, Guenevere, in love with her husband King Arthur's favorite knight, Lancelot, it may have been a particularly apt analogy, given the misery that was Jackie Kennedy's private life with the President's unfaithful behavior in their marriage.)

Stewart Wilson and Victor Zellman were the accountants working for Elizabeth whose task it was to iron out a settlement with Eddie. Wilson met with Elizabeth in Rome. Also at the meeting was Mike Todd Jr., who was the president of the Michael Todd Company, founded by his father. Elizabeth was the board chairman. "She was exhausted when we met with her on April 2, the day the announcement was made," he said, "but ready for business when we got to her dressing quarters."

Elizabeth came swirling into the room in a white caftan with matching turban, in full Cleopatra makeup, her violet eyes heavily etched with black liner, lids blushed with a pink color. Her lips were painted a deep crimson. She was in between scenes for the movie, smoking a cigarette from a diamond-encrusted cigarette holder. "So, boys, what do I have to do to end it with Eddie?" she said, getting to the point quickly.

"Give him money," said Stewart Wilson.

"How much?"

"A lot," said Wilson. "We just met with him, and he's saying he wants millions."

Elizabeth took a deep drag from her cigarette. "I can not *believe* that I have to pay this man money," she said, now seeming upset. "How is it that the *wife* has to pay the *husband*? How did that ever happen in this world? Eddie Fisher had a career long before I came along, did he not?"

"He says his career was ruined because of you," Todd Jr. explained.

"Oh, that is such bullshit," Elizabeth said. "It's easy to blame Elizabeth Taylor for every goddamn thing that happens to every goddamn person in Hollywood, isn't it?" She then decided that she would give Fisher a million dollars if he would just sign the divorce papers, and that would be the end of it. "Tell him that. And then when he gets up off the floor, have the papers ready for him to sign, and a check ready to give him," she instructed.

"But, Elizabeth—" Todd Jr. began.

She held her hands up to stop him and said that she didn't want to hear another word about it. "It's worth it to me to end this," she concluded. Then she extended her hand to shake theirs, thanked them, and told them that the meeting was over. Before she left the room, she embraced Mike Todd Jr. and whispered something in his ear that made him smile. With that, she left the room.

The next day, Elizabeth's attorney in Los Angeles, Mickey Rudin, called Eddie to present him with the offer. He turned it down. (Today, Eddie insists that no such offer was extended, or rejected.) Stewart and Victor had to go back to Elizabeth and give her the bad news. Again, they caught her between scenes. This time, Richard was with her.

"You've got to be kidding me," Elizabeth said when told the news. Richard sat in a chair, looking amused.

"He said he wanted more," said Stewart Wilson.

"Well, he's not getting more," Elizabeth said angrily. "And, in fact, now he's not getting the million, either."

"Unbelievable," Richard said. "Taking money from a woman."

"That's what *I* said, yesterday," Elizabeth remarked. "Tell him to get a job. How about that? Try working. Like the rest of us."

By the time the final decree was handed down (not until March 1964), Eddie would end up with roughly just half a million dollars—a significant amount of money in 1964, if not now. It's difficult to understand why Elizabeth still, to this day, holds such hostility toward Eddie or exactly when her animosity started. When she wrote her first book in 1965, she still seemed to have some warm feelings for him. "I was not a very healthy girl," she wrote at that time. "Poor Eddie. What hell that must have been for him." In years to come, though, Eddie would write a couple of autobiographies of his own and would be very critical of Elizabeth in them, especially in the second, the truly sensational *Been There, Done That* (1999). Those books, combined with the fact that he demanded money from her way back when, must be why she is still so angry at him. She's even made excuses for Nicky Hilton's abusiveness ("He was drunk"), but for Eddie, no excuses.

It's become accepted wisdom over the years that Eddie Fisher's career ended as a result of all of the adverse publicity concerning Elizabeth, Richard, and Debbie, but that's not really true. When he got back to the States after leaving Rome in 1962, he was more determined than ever to immerse himself in his work. To that end, he put together a dynamic and carefully considered new act, which opened to rave reviews in Los Angeles at the Cocoanut Grove on May 24, 1962. The tour took him to Las Vegas, Lake Tahoe, Chicago, and Philadelphia before he made his successful opening at the Winter Garden Theater on Broadway on October 2, 1962 (where he recorded a double live album that is still worth listening to). Though he made no direct mention of Elizabeth, the new act was nothing if not autobiographical, with songs such as the American classics "You Made Me Love You," "This Nearly Was Mine," and "What Kind of Fool Am I?" Perhaps Howard Taubman, in his *New York Times* review, best summarized the entertainer's performance at the Winter Garden: "Eddie Fisher pours it on. Showmanship, rhythm, fervor. A thorough professional. Belts tunes like a home-run slugger."

The Taylor-Burton Sexual Revolution

Though there was no way for them to recognize it at the time, looking back today, it's clear that the extramarital affair of Elizabeth Taylor and Richard Burton was a sign of the times. Society was seeing a change occurring in sexual mores, and the *Cleopatra* stars were nothing if not a reflection of those changes. They were, in effect, spearheading a sexual revolution.

Dr. George O'Neill, the anthropologist who, with his wife Nena, wrote the book *Open Marriage: A New Lifestyle for Couples*, noted, "Of course, the basic changes were already underway. The old morality was slipping away though many were unaware that the revolution had arrived. Had they [Burton and Taylor] done what they did a decade before, their popularity would almost surely have been severely damaged. The *Cleopatra* scandal came along when our institutions were altering; we were questioning old values and trying on new ones for size. Because they were so much in the public eye, and because it is still true that all the world loves a lover, they were not only able to ride over the turmoil but to help speed up the revolution in moral standards."

"Men and women have long engaged in society-frowned-upon activities like extramarital affairs, but were fearful of the consequences if they were discovered; loss of prestige and loss of job were certain to follow," observed Dr. Joyce Wike, professor of sociology and anthropology at Nebraska Wesleyan University. "Then along came Elizabeth Taylor and Richard Burton, who were not only found out but readily admitted it. They didn't change sexual standards overnight. However, they helped supply the needed impetus. Celebrity leaders—even those who don't profess to influence—are very necessary. We reason, 'if they can do it, why can't I?'"

"According to the code of ethics today, I *was*, I suppose, behaving wrongly because I broke the conventions," Elizabeth wrote in her 1965 memoir, *Elizabeth Taylor*. "But I didn't feel immoral then, though I knew what I was doing, loving Richard, was wrong. I never felt dirty, because it never was dirty. I felt terrible heartache because so many innocent people were involved. But I couldn't help loving Richard."

Meanwhile, in Rome, the Italians joined in a chorus of condemnation about the illicit relationship between the two married stars. Rome's afternoon paper, *Il Giornale d'Italia*, summed up public opinion when it stated, "Nobody can forget the fatuity of her heart, which left behind four husbands in the short span of a thirty-year life, and is perhaps about to destroy, to her exclusive personal benefit, the marriage of Richard Burton."

Even Pope John XXIII entered the fray: "We like to call Rome a Holy City. God forbid it becomes a city of perversion." The Vatican radio station lashed out at those who consider marriage "a game which they start and interrupt with the capricious make-believe of children."

However, the most damning blast of all came from *L'Osservatore della Domenica*, which was published weekly in Vatican City. It said, in part, "The trouble is, my dear lady, you are killing too many [marriages]. When will you finish? In erotic vagrancy? And your poor children, those who are your true children and the one who was taken from an honest situation. Don't these institutions think before handing children to somebody? Don't they request moral references? Was it not better to entrust this girl to an honest bricklayer and a modest housewife rather than you, my dear lady, and to your fourth husband? The housewife and the bricklayer would have worked harder and would have seriously made sacrifices for their child. You, instead, have other things to do."

Elizabeth finished reading that article and sat frozen. The paper slipped to the floor, but she didn't shift her gaze from her now empty hand. At this rare moment in her life, she was actually speechless. She couldn't believe that the Vatican had questioned her right to adopt Maria. One thing she could always say about MGM: As much as she hated the studio, it had protected her from this kind of publicity. Mayer would never have allowed the media, the world's press, to have such a poor perception of her. Even at its worst, her publicity always seemed to somehow enhance her image. Somehow—and even when at cross-purposes with her—Mayer would have found a way to protect her. Now, alone at 20th Century-Fox, she had even managed to tick off the Pope!

Elizabeth and Richard had plans that evening and, she decided, they were not going to cancel them just to please the Pontiff. They went to dinner at the Grand Hotel. At her arrival, she was the subject of whispers and much staring. She looked stunning in an elegant black gown that was formfitting at the bodice and erupted into a flare of silk at the hips. The couple dined on cheese soufflés and steak. Then they went to meet Mike Nichols in a Via Veneto club. On the way, Elizabeth was stunned to hear people on the street actually heckling her in Italian. "What are they saying?" she asked the driver.

"Don't tell her," snapped Richard.

Elizabeth swatted him lightly. "Quiet." She leaned close to the chauffeur. "*Favore.* Tell me what they're saying."

The driver looked toward the backseat through his rearview mirror. "Homewrecker. Whore. Unfit mother."

Elizabeth sat back, and gazed out at the citizens of Rome. Richard leaned in to her for a gentle kiss on the cheek.

"Let's never come back here," she whispered.

Cleopatra Arrives

The day after the Vatican's vicious attack on her, Elizabeth Taylor had to film one of the most memorable scenes in *Cleopatra*. In it, the Queen, holding her son, Caesarion, makes her triumphant entrance into ancient Rome. If she is accepted by the Romans and they acknowledge Caesarion as Julius Caesar's only child and heir, the Roman and Egyptian empires will merge and she will then be the most powerful woman in the world. Otherwise, she will be banished and, humiliated, her life will lie in ruins. A throng of Romans would be portrayed by thousands of Italian Catholic extras. Grand in scope, this scene would become one of the most expensive ever filmed.

It was ironic that Elizabeth found herself in much the same situation as her royal character, due to all the negative press of late. Would the army of Italian extras accept her and go about the business of creating the scene at hand? Or would they, antagonized by the Vatican's position, jeer at her, rather than cheer for Cleopatra?

So far, it had not been a good day. On the way to Cinecitta, Elizabeth was subjected to taunts from passersby. Then, when she got to the studio, she was informed that there'd been a bomb threat placed against the production. The presence of security guards on the set, disguised in togas, only served to heighten the suspense. Elizabeth feared the possibility that one of the thousands of extras in that scene might have a gun and shoot her. "I don't think I can do it," she told Richard. "I am truly afraid."

In costume as Mark Antony, Burton said, "Don't worry about it. I'm here, luv. The police are here. It will be fine." He had a knife in his pocket, which probably made him feel he had some control over the situation. Realistically, though, what was he going to do with it? There was no way to actually protect Elizabeth if someone wanted to take a shot at her.

The wardrobe Elizabeth had to wear for the scene was impossibly heavy; the fifteen-pound headdress, made of twenty-four-carat gold thread, was two and a half feet high and practically impossible for her to balance on her head. Years later, she would recall, "I thought, well, in front of the children and my mother and father, I mustn't look afraid. So I got into my costume, which seemed to weigh hundreds of pounds. I got the whole drag on and crawled up on the [three-story-high] Sphinx, feeling totally trembly."

According to the script, as she made her way beneath the Arch of Titus, Cleopatra was to be greeted by the chants of her constituency. The extras were told to wave and shout at her, and scream, "Cleopatra! Cleopatra! Cleopatra!"

"She was terrified," said Chris Mankiewicz. "Not just because of threats, but the whole thing was supposed to tilt at one point, and she was deathly afraid of falling off of it."

"Richard was out of the shot," Elizabeth recalled, "but I was supposed to look at him. Mother and Dad and the kids were standing right next to him. Richard had his hand on his dagger—he'd had it sharpened. I don't know what he thought he could do, but he looked ready to sell his life dearly."

At the precise moment that Joseph Mankiewicz yelled, "Action!" the fifty-foot-high Sphinx, with Elizabeth and the youngster atop it and carried by three hundred Nubian slaves, began to slowly lurch forward. It was preceded by a company of dancing girls, charioteers with black horses, and trumpeters on white ones. As instructed, as she sat atop the monstrosity, she did not move a muscle. A frozen and regal glare played on her face and she stared ahead at Caesar, her arms folded and holding the emblems of Isis.

As Elizabeth made her way through the crowd, the extras did as they were told: "Cleopatra! Cleopatra! Cleopatra!"

However, as the scene continued, Elizabeth noticed that the chanting slowly began to change: *"Leez! Leez! Leez!"*

Caught up in the thrill of the moment, the thousands of extras seemed to forget they were in a movie. Now, in their eyes, atop that Sphinx sat not Cleopatra but Elizabeth Taylor.

The sound echoed throughout the cavernous set as the extras screamed and shouted and applauded and blew kisses at her. *"Baci! Baci! Baci!"* they shouted, which means "kisses" in Italian.

For Elizabeth, this was not only a moment on the set of a movie unlike any other in her long career, it was a moment in her life like no other as well. Obviously these Italians did not agree with the Vatican's position on Elizabeth—their sympathies were with her. "The tears were pouring down my face," she recalled. Joseph

Mankiewicz had to stop the scene as Richard and everyone else present—her parents, her children—came forward to surround Elizabeth, all crying. Mankiewicz handed her a bullhorn. *"Grazie! Grazie!"* she said to the crowds.

Sara couldn't believe what she'd just seen take place. She and Francis had come to be with Elizabeth during this difficult time, and she was glad that they had decided to do it. She would tell the story for years; it would become one of her best tales. She didn't even have to exaggerate this one, since it was already pretty fantastic. To say that she was proud of her daughter would be an understatement. Of course, Francis felt the same way. He sent a letter to his friend Stefan Verkaufen from Rome that said in part, "When I think about my beloved Elizabeth and what her life is like these days, it makes me cry . . . tears of both joy and sadness. This is her greatest role, Cleopatra, there is no doubt about it. But I am afraid she is paying a steep price for such glory. Of course, as well expected, she doesn't listen to me about any of it. God love her, though, she is her own woman, exactly like her mother."

The filming of that pivotal scene in *Cleopatra* impacted everyone who witnessed it, including Richard Burton. Never before had he ever witnessed such reverence toward a person. Never before had he known of a woman who could command such adoration. He simply couldn't get past it and would talk about it to others for weeks to come, as if he'd borne witness to some kind of divine event. Indeed, his presence at such a jaw-dropping display of adulation would be the catalyst for Richard Burton's new commitment to a life with Elizabeth Taylor. When he stood at her side for the next few scenes, he was consumed by one desire: Now she had to be his . . . and he would do whatever necessary to have her.

Elizabeth as a Mother

It was still—unbelievably enough, considering all that had transpired—April of 1962, Easter weekend. With their spouses now gone from them, Elizabeth and Richard were finally free to be together. Of course, Elizabeth was happy about that, but had another matter on her mind. She was stung by the position the Vatican had taken against her, and concerned that the natural mother of Maria might hear about the controversy and have second thoughts about having given over her daughter to Elizabeth. Though it was of course too late for this woman to reconsider her choice in giving up Maria, Elizabeth couldn't bear the thought that she might now regret it. She sent her a telegram. "She cabled her assurances that her love for Petra was as strong as ever," recalled the woman, "and that she would do her utmost to continue to provide the best for the child. She was so worried about my reaction to recent news about her, she later wrote me a letter to say that if I wanted, she would fly immediately to Mering to talk with me personally and reassure me of her devotion to Petra. It was not necessary. Her heart spoke for her."

Maria's natural mother might have been satisfied, but the press couldn't help but criticize Elizabeth's mothering skills. She was an easy target and, of course, she'd now given the media a big bull's-eye at which to aim. Speaking of Elizabeth's experience as a mother, Mike Todd had given an interview the afternoon before he died. "I've been around longer than Liz and I've learned a few things," he said. "Like when she makes mistakes that are not that important, I can tell her right off. But if they matter a lot, a guy has to have patience. Being a mother is a woman's most important job, and you can't tell her she's being a poor mother because then she gets hurt, real hurt. I can't say, 'Don't compete with the nurse, you're the mother.' I've got to keep quiet because Liz has to learn these things for herself." Todd recalled that near the beginning of Elizabeth's career, when her earning capacity was staggering, she took a studio suspension to have her firstborn (from second husband Mike Wilding). "Do you realize that this baby is costing you $150,000?" a friend asked her. "I wouldn't care if it cost a million," she said, "and I'm going to have another baby and another baby and another."

To be fair, Elizabeth faced challenges as a mother that most women of her time could never relate to, largely as a consequence of her career. However, she continued to dedicate as much of herself as possible to her children, and it wasn't easy for her to have the children she did bear.

"When I was pregnant with Liza, it was only a few months after my back operation," she has recalled, "and the doctors thought the pressure from the embryo would push the newly formed bone [in her back] right out and cripple me. They had a meeting and decided the baby should be aborted. I said, 'Not on your nelly.' And they explained why it must happen. And I explained why it was not going to happen. So they fixed my back brace with elastic gussets over my stomach to make room for Liza. I almost lost her three times." The back brace pushed the baby up into Elizabeth's ribs and even moved her heart a couple of inches, causing her to lose consciousness from time to time. Therefore, she was put on digitalis. In time, though, the medicine began affecting the baby's heartbeat. But, ironically, the baby now needed it to live; if they took the mother off the medication the child would die. It was decided to take Elizabeth off the medicine for twenty-four hours, risk her going into a coma, and then deliver the baby, if possible. The baby was born by cesarian section, and, they thought, stillborn. She didn't breathe for fourteen long minutes. They told Todd that the baby was gone, though Elizabeth would be fine. This was when the doctors suggested that Elizabeth not have any more children and asked if they could perform a tubal ligation, and Todd agreed to it. While all of this was going on, the baby began to breathe. She would live—and thank goodness for it, Elizabeth would say, because Liza was a part of Mike that continued in his stead.

Still, as much as she cared for Michael and Christopher Wilding, Liza Todd Fisher, and Maria Taylor, they were obviously affected by their mother's indiscretions and bad publicity; there was little Elizabeth could do to protect them from gossip and innuendo. It's not as if she were unaware of the ramifications. "I've been married too many times," she admitted in 1965 when speaking of the life she had given her children. "How terrible to change children's affiliations, their affections—to give them the insecurity of placing their trust in someone when maybe that someone won't be there next year. I was terrified that they would stop giving themselves to any [partner]."

Indeed, one day, Eddie Fisher was present in their lives. The next day, he was gone, replaced by someone the children had just met, and who they now knew as "Uncle Dick." Little Liza, who was about five, once asked one of Elizabeth's friends, "Did you see *Around the World in 80 Days?* My first daddy made that. My second daddy made a movie, also. And Richard, maybe my next daddy, makes movies too, lots of them, as does my only mommy." Richard never wanted Liza to call him Daddy, even after he and Elizabeth married. He wanted her to know that her father was Michael Todd, "and he was a very wonderful man, and don't you ever forget it." As youngsters, the Taylor children were well-adjusted and, for the most part, had fun, considering their circumstances. In the end, though, all of them seem to find it hard to trust the people in their lives, perhaps afraid that their stability could be rocked by the abandonment of someone important to them.

"My children are remarkable people," Elizabeth once said. "My life should have been murder for them. We lived like gypsies and, well, there's the obvious fact that I've been married too many times. They loved Mike. They loved Eddie as a friend, but when Eddie left they didn't even ask where he'd gone."

On the day the youngsters first met Richard, he was followed to the villa by excited men with cameras. They watched as Burton's chauffeur grabbed a broom and chased them away. Later, Elizabeth rushed the three children out of the villa—the baby, Maria, stayed behind with a governess—and all of them then climbed into a car with Richard and sped off into the dark night. The paparazzi, some on motor scooters and others in cars, chased after them. For the kids, it was probably like a game of cops and robbers, with the chauffeur driving at a dangerously high speed, trying to evade the photographers, and with the added attraction of their mother screaming, hollering, and cursing all the way.

Once they reached their destination, Torvainica, they ate at a restaurant called Corsetti's—seafood cocktail, lobster, salad, potatoes, and an ice-cream dessert, all under the watchful eye of the paparazzi. Before the children could finish their dessert, Elizabeth gathered them up and rushed them out a back door into a small decoy car, while Richard took the other back to the villa. The diversion did not work. The photographers just split into two camps, one to follow each car back to the villa.

When not on the road traveling to or from work on a film, Elizabeth would spend her days acting in front of the camera, doing press interviews, or having meetings about her career. At night, the children would usually be able to catch a quick glimpse of her as she got dressed to go out, usually to a club. When she was home for a longer period of time, she couldn't help but be distracted by the ongoing drama of her personal life, jumping up to answer the ringing phone, speaking in anxious tones, slamming the phone back down with a *"How dare you"* . . . and then, after a moment of furious reflection, calling back to give someone a piece of her mind.

Sometimes Elizabeth's children would meet her for lunch at the studio; she loved those times most of all. They watched wide-eyed as she filmed some of her scenes in the colorful Cleopatra garb. A break in filming gave them an hour together. They would have a light meal and, as they ate, laugh and talk about whatever interested them at the time. Then Michael, Chris, and Liza would return to the villa with their governess, while Elizabeth went back to work in front of the cameras. "I try to get as much time with them as I can," Elizabeth has explained in an interview. "I know I am doing a lousy job, but as God is my witness, I am trying to be as good a mother as Elizabeth Taylor can be."

Elizabeth's world presented so many challenges to her, there wasn't much time for her to do anything but battle her way through them one at a time, as best she could. There always seemed to be another problem just around the bend from the last one. In the end, as much as she loved them, her children—like the offspring of many celebrities—would have to learn to fend for themselves, and find attributes of their mother to be proud of wherever they could, such as in her work ethic and in the tenacity and determination she daily demonstrated in her life and career. Also, it's interesting that Elizabeth did not end up treating her children the way that her mother, Sara, had treated her in terms of being critical and judgmental. It was as if she'd made a firm decision to be much more accepting of their faults than Sara had ever been of hers. In fact, many people in her life felt that she might have been a little too permissive. However, no one has ever heard of any of Elizabeth's children complaining about her treatment of them; there have been no *Mommie Dearest* or *My Mother's Keeper* stories to tell, so far. Perhaps she didn't do as poor a job at mothering as it may have seemed—or maybe her children learned to look to her life as an example of the strength and perseverance it would take to get through their own.

Nightmare in Porto Santo Stefano

It was during their Easter break in 1962 that Elizabeth Taylor learned about a side of Richard Burton she'd hadn't seen in a man since her first marriage to Nicky Hilton: his violent side. (There have been many stories over the years about Mike Todd having roughed up Elizabeth, but she certainly has not confirmed that Todd was violent with her as she has Hilton.) During a three-day break, Elizabeth and Richard decided to drive to Porto Santo Stefano, about a hundred miles north of Rome. Though the weekend started off pleasant enough, it soon took a tragic turn.

According to Richard Burton's diary entry, he rented a small, two-seat Fiat sports car so that he and Elizabeth could make the drive. Once in Porto Santo Stefano, they stumbled upon a small piano bar and thought they had finally escaped public scrutiny. Richard recalled there being only "a couple of people" present in the establishment, "a boy and a dog and a waiter." However, one of the gentlemen present happened to be a newspaperman who, when he spotted the world's "hottest and most scandalous couple," as Richard put it, phoned the tip in to his paper. Within minutes, they were under siege from the media.

Undaunted, Burton and Taylor left the bar and continued on to their small villa on the beach, completely isolated—or so they thought. Once there, they frolicked on the beach, drinking and having fun, thinking that they had ducked the photographers and were alone. Or so they later claimed. It's difficult to believe they didn't know there were photographers present as they ate oranges and gazed out over the lovely Tyrrhenian Sea. However, as Richard recalled it, "We found out soon enough that every bush— and there were hundreds of them—contained a paparazzo. "We were well and thoroughly trapped."

He wrote that, at that point, the weekend was ruined for them. Feeling like caged animals, they took out their frustration by drinking "to the point of stupefaction and idiocy." The more they drank, the more paranoid they began to feel about their isolation. They tried to read, but couldn't focus. Instead, they had wild sex, or as Richard put it, "made a desperate kind of love." Afterward they played gin rummy; the competitive Elizabeth won game after game, much to Richard's consternation.

Somehow, Richard could not recall exactly how or why, the two began talking about love and death, and Elizabeth, in a dramatic moment, said that she was prepared to kill herself for him. "Here and now," she said, slurring her words, "I'll do it, Richard. That is how deeply I love you." They were both lightheaded from the finest brandies, vodkas, and champagnes available, and who knows what was going on in her mind when she made the veiled threat, but it's possible that she really was just trying to prove her love for him and to what extent she would risk herself for him. Richard laughed. It made no sense, yet in their mutual haze it somehow made all the sense in the world.

Elizabeth left the room and appeared a moment later with a bottle of sleeping pills. "I'll do it," she said. "I'll do it now, for you." Again, Richard laughed her off, thinking, he would later say, that she was threatening to off herself with vitamin C pills. By now, he knew that she had a flair for the dramatic. "The sad truth is that I can't live without you anyway," she said, "so if it's as over between us, as you said it was back in Rome, then I may as well do myself in."

"Don't be ridiculous! Good Lord," Richard flamed, "I left a perfectly good woman to be with a lunatic!" With that statement Elizabeth's almost Shakespearean threat turned from melodrama to deadly serious. She had known he was tormented by his decision to end it with "Syb." He felt tremendous guilt about breaking up his family, especially about his youngest child with autism. He couldn't escape what he called his homeland's inescapable truth: "The Welsh do not divorce easily." Though he said he was now in love with Elizabeth, he felt a strong loyalty to Sybil. He continued to telephone her after she returned to London, trying in some way to hang on, seeming to want to prolong everyone's torture. Now that he was free to have Elizabeth, it was as if he wanted to punish her for ruining his marriage.

Yet now, in this foggy hotel room, the echoes of that word, "lunatic," were met with Elizabeth's silent desperation. With it, he seemed to dare her to prove the trade he had made was worth it. She reached to open the bottle of pills. Richard swatted the container from her hand, sending it flying across the room. When she went to retrieve it, he lost control. "It didn't begin as a barroom brawl, but it certainly ended as one," he later told a friend. That night Richard's fury overtook him. A brutal altercation fueled by his seemingly bottomless rage took place; yet the last he seemed to recall of the event itself was that it began.

His hazy memory of that night resumes hours later, when he came to and staggered into the bedroom. There he found Elizabeth sprawled on the bed, her head hanging off the side of the mattress, her mouth agape. She was out cold. He shook her repeatedly, but couldn't awaken her. The sight of the empty pill bottle from earlier that night sobered him up quickly. "I wasn't even sure she had taken them at the time," he shared later. "It would have been just like her to flush them down the loo and wait for me to find her." He couldn't take that chance, though. He loaded her into a car for a hair-raising drive to Rome and back to Salvatore Mundi Hospital. The doctors, after pumping her stomach, told him she had taken a large dose of sedatives. For the second time in four months, Elizabeth Taylor had apparently decided that life was not worth living. "By God, what if she had died?" Burton asked in his writings. "Worse, what if she'd lived with an impaired brain?"

When she awakened, Elizabeth had two black eyes. Her face was swollen almost beyond recognition. Three weeks would pass before it would finally return to its natural beauty. During that time, she was unable to work on *Cleopatra*. Even heavy makeup was not concealing enough when it came to the results of Burton's temper. The studio said she was injured when the chauffeur had to stop her limousine unexpectedly.

While doctors advised her not to look in a mirror, she convinced Richard that she had to see herself. He retrieved a heavy wooden hand mirror from her satchel and handed it to her. When she got up the courage to view her lover's handiwork, she was stunned. "Well, now at least I look exactly the way I feel." She stared at him. "I suppose I should thank you for that."

Finishing Cleopatra

Finally, it was over. On June 23, 1962, Elizabeth Taylor filmed her final moments in *Cleopatra* on the stunningly beautiful island of Ischia, in the Bay of Naples. In the last scene, Cleopatra stands in all of her regal glory on a gold barge as it sails in front of thousands of admirers and arrives at Tarsus (which was actually Ischia Ponte). It's an elaborate scene; thirty-five handmaidens on the barge toss coins to swimmers in the river. Forty others scatter flowers into the water. Clouds of smoke create an ethereal atmosphere. The rigging of the barge is festooned with exotic flowers. The entire scene cost half a million dollars to film. The production had seemed to drag on endlessly: 632 days had passed since it began at Pinewood.

It's been famously reported that in order for 20th Century-Fox to be able to afford to make *Cleopatra*—with so many delays due, at least in part, to Elizabeth's debilitating illnesses—Darryl F.

Zanuck sold off most of the studio's back lot to a real estate developer.*

Though it was obviously costly and epic in size (and, at more than four hours, in length as well), the general consensus about *Cleopatra*, when it was finally released a year later, on June 12, 1963, in New York, was that it's not a very good movie. While it's photographed beautifully, it's a big brute of a film that in the end topples over under its own weight. Still, as much as some hate it, that's how much others love it. Brad Geagley says, "People call it the Eisenhower of movies for a reason; the farther away you get from it, the better it looks."

Part of the problem is that the movie wasn't well-written, which is understandable because the script was being constructed by Joseph Mankiewicz at the same time it was being filmed. At one point it was even suggested that the studio issue it in two parts—part one with Caesar and part two with Antony—at a suggested seven hours! (But, then, did that mean everyone had to be paid again? The answer being yes put an end to that folly.) The studio did the best it could in editing, but important moments were ultimately left on the cutting-room floor, scenes that might have explained certain of the characters' motivations. As it stands, there seems to be no reason for some of the choices that remain in the film's final cut.

Ultimately, the only reason to watch *Cleopatra* is to see just how stunning Elizabeth looks in it in her many lavish costumes. She's a regal vision, her eyes heavily made up, her complexion flawless. From this point on in her career, the Elizabeth Taylor the

---

* This is only partly true; the deal was already in place by the time *Cleopatra* was in production because the studio had lost so much on previous films. However, the losses of *Cleopatra* coaxed Zanuck into finalizing matters. That property is, today, Century City: 176 acres of high-rise office buildings, a sprawling shopping mall, and residential condominiums, just west of Beverly Hills and about ten miles from Hollywood. Century City remains an important business center in the entertainment community; many law firms and executives, particularly those with ties to the film and television industries, have offices there. Twentieth Century-Fox is also still headquartered in the area.

public saw was exactly the one she wanted them to see. She had final authority over all of her costumes, hairstyles, and makeup. She also had final say-so over all publicity stills that were released to the media. She had a keen sense of her image in photographs, and she wanted to make certain that her public only saw her best side, at least in pictures. Also, no doubt as a result of her mass popularity at this time, she was now guaranteed certain other important perks. Never again, for instance, would she have to fight over directors and scripts. She would for the remainder of her career have absolute authority over the director chosen by the film's producer, as well as the right to veto the script if she didn't like it.

However, her acting in *Cleopatra* seems inexpressive and dull, especially in comparison to the brilliance of some of her performances up until this time. For *Cleopatra*, she received the worst reviews of her career, so vicious that they are not even worth memorializing here. "When Elizabeth read them [the reviews], she had an attack of the vapors and retired to her bed at the Dorchester [where she was staying at the time, in London], for an indefinite period," recalled Hal Wallis, producer of Richard Burton's film *Becket*. "Her phone calls from bed to [the *Becket*] set were many, and interfered with Richard's work. He told me one morning, 'If you've got a picture for Elizabeth, I think you could get her today for $25,000.'"

Another reason to watch the movie is to see Elizabeth and Richard work together for the first time, in hopes of perhaps discerning some sense of magic between them. Surprisingly enough, considering what was going on in their private lives and the intensity of their first scenes together, they actually have little chemistry on the screen. In fact, the two act as if they've never even met; their characters' scenes of passion fall terribly flat. Perhaps because there was such sexual tension between them offstage, they had to work to suppress their true emotions at work and in doing so ended up muting their performances. Also, in all fairness to Richard, some of his best scenes failed to make the final cut, much to his and Elizabeth's dismay, and Mankiewicz's also, who felt that Richard was done a great injustice by the studio.

In the end, *Cleopatra*—which had been budgeted at $2 million—would cost almost $50 million to make (about $150 million in today's currency). It is still considered the most expensive movie ever made. However, it has had a long life, and it did manage to break even in 1966. With $430 million in earnings in today's money, *Cleopatra* now rests at an impressive number 37 in the list of all-time box-office moneymakers, a position that was aided by the film's sale to television and its release, first on VHS, then a special fortieth anniversary DVD edition in 2003.

The movie was nominated for nine Academy Awards, including Best Picture and Best Actor (Rex Harrison)—but not Best Actress. It would go on to win four Oscars, for Costume Design (Color), Cinematography (Color), Art Direction/Set Decoration (Color), and Special Visual Effects.

It was a huge frustration for Elizabeth that she'd spent so much time on this project, only to have it end the way it did—with her total dissatisfaction in it. She best summed up her feelings about it in her autobiography *Elizabeth Taylor* in 1965: "I was involved with *Cleopatra* for five years on and off and surely that film must be the most bizarre piece of entertainment ever to be perpetrated—the circumstances, the people involved, the money spent. Everything was such a nightmare that it is difficult to even know where to start. It had some curious effect on just about every person who worked on it.

"The final humiliation was to have to see it," she concluded. "The British Embassy trapped me into it. They requested me to take the Bolshoi Ballet as my guests to a screening of *Cleopatra*. I couldn't very well say no. When it was over, I raced back to the Dorchester Hotel and just made it into the downstairs lavatory before I vomited."

A Turning Point in Gstaad

By August 1962, Elizabeth Taylor and her new lover, Richard Burton, were at her home, Chalet Ariel, in Gstaad—Swiss playground for notables such as the Aga Khan and the Duchess of Luxembourg, Joan Crawford, Charlie Chaplin, Douglas Fairbanks, Brigitte Bardot, and many others. Given its glittery reputation, it's surprising when one goes there to find that Gstaad is basically just a lovely one-street village, a charming, attractively located place full of restored weathered-wood chalets. There are shops where a woman can purchase the finest designer wardrobe. Hairdressers have been trained in Paris and London. In the center of the village, which is free of traffic by law, there are expensive restaurants, shops, hotels, and bars. The surrounding ski areas and hiking trails are joined by three groups of mountain lifts. It feels like a magical place, especially in the winter months when the town is blanketed by rolling drifts of snow. Glossy magazines may advertise the town as a winter paradise, but St. Moritz steals its thunder in that regard. Gstaad is really more of a place to spend the odd ten grand renting a hillside chalet and sipping champagne than it is for skiing. In the summer, though, the weather is pleasant and hiking is the favorite pastime. The town's four helicopters had seats covered in fur to take skiers up the slopes, lest their wealthy bums get cold. In one hotel the Queen of Holland usually stayed, and another was favored by the King and Queen of Thailand. Louis Armstrong would perform there one weekend, Ella Fitzgerald the next.

Elizabeth paid half a million dollars, sight unseen (Eddie found it), for her sumptuous sixteen-room chalet in Gstaad with its acres of unfussy land, its sandboxes and newly installed bright red slide for the children. Built mostly of deep and warm oak, Ariel sat on a crest overlooking the majestic scenery and, off in the distance, Céligny, where the Burtons lived. Elizabeth's chalet was the only one in Gstaad with a fence around its property's perimeter. But it wasn't for security; it was a picket fence, decorative in intention. Elizabeth still owns the chalet today.

With the production of *Cleopatra* now over, she finally had time to consider the past few months of her life. However, in their first week there, she and Richard had one of their blazing rows, and it was only ten in the morning. It's unknown exactly what the disagreement was about, but it must have been a big one because it caused Elizabeth to reconsider some of her recent choices where Richard was concerned. "I wrote Richard a letter which said that we were destroying too many lives," she recalled. "We should part." She left the note for him on his pillow. Hours later, without any kind of emotional display, he left. Before he left, he told her, "I just wanted to take care of you."

"I can take care of myself," she said through her tears, only half believing it.

Despite her unhappiness, her mind was set and she would not contact him. As the days turned into weeks, she became morbidly sad. "I'd never seen her like that," said a woman who knew Elizabeth very well in Gstaad at this time. The two had lunch at Elizabeth's chalet the day after Burton left.

"The only thing I can do now is divorce Eddie and go on with my life," said Elizabeth. She was sitting on the veranda overlooking the Swiss mountains, wearing—judging from photos taken that day—a diaphanous yellow-and-red-striped blouse with white slacks. Her hair cascaded to her shoulders, her eyes shielded by ever-present sunglasses. A maid served large plates of spaghetti to Elizabeth and her guest, glasses of red wine, and a pot of coffee. "I don't know what I got from any of it," she said, referring to the affair with Richard.

"I found her to be in a contemplative place," said her friend. "I think she had made up her mind that Richard was out of her life. She said she doubted that she would ever see him again, and she said she knew it was for the best. But it had happened so fast—without much warning, she said—she was left off kilter by it."

When Richard Burton left Elizabeth's chalet, he drove off to his own home, a much more modest one, in the quaint town of Céligny, eighty-five miles away. With a population of just 520, mostly farmers, Céligny was a far cry from anything that could be considered a cosmopolitan town like Gstaad, and the much simpler lifestyle there brought into clear focus the true differences between Burton and Taylor. Simply put, she could never live anywhere where they had one store for groceries and vegetables, another for cheese, a church, a small restaurant—and a police force of one. There, Burton would join Sybil and his daughters in an easygoing existence, one in which everyone knew them and no one bothered them. Their quaint chalet had just six rooms, three of them bedrooms. A line of tall spruces stood immediately behind the structure. Through its green could be seen the heavy mist of Lake Geneva, a few yards away. It was a lovely place to live.

Meanwhile, just one mountain range away, Elizabeth was still just trying to get through the days. "I was dying inside and trying to hide it from the children with all kinds of frenzied activity— games, picnics," she recalled of the time after Burton left. "But they knew—not that I would unburden my problems on their small but steady shoulders. Michael wrote notes—'I know it's going to be all right, Mama.' Christopher once said, 'I prayed to God last night that you and Richard would be married.' That made me cry.

"Their sense of loss was almost as great as mine," she said of her children. "It was wonderful that they felt that way, but at the time I didn't know what to do about it. I tried to explain to them that Richard had little girls that he loved—that he loved my kids as well, but his obligation was to his family. They were very sweet about it, but couldn't figure out why he couldn't love us all."

Matissa Hart, a Norwegian who lived in Gstaad at this time, was befriended by Elizabeth Taylor in an unusual way. She recalled, "There was a little tea house in Gstaad called Charley's, down near the town's tennis courts. I frequented it often, and one day I walked in and there was Elizabeth, sitting alone having a cup of tea and looking sad. I decided not to approach her. However, the next day, again, there she was, alone with her tea. I thought it so odd. I went to her and asked if I could join her, telling her I was lonely and could use a little chat. She looked up at me with those eyes, blue as two pools of water. I was taken aback by them, and by the moment. I thought, 'My God, this is Elizabeth Taylor and I am standing here talking to her.' However, in no time, she had just become another woman, a very sad woman, someone who needed a shoulder to cry on. We sat there for two hours and, much to my astonishment since I was a total stranger, she told me about her sadness."

Elizabeth was wearing a simple paisley dress, rather common-looking, with sensible shoes. She had her hair in curlers—a bit of a surprise—and covered with a checkered scarf. ("Checkers and paisley, I thought . . . so odd a combination for a fashion plate.") Her hands trembled as she raised her cup of tea to her mouth, heavily lipsticked.

"I am famous the world over," she told Matissa, "yet I have so few friends."

"Oh, I'm sure you have many, many wonderful friends," Matissa told her.

Elizabeth sighed. "I do. But, really, how much can people take? People have their own problems, you know?"

"She said that other than her mother, she had no one to talk to. She said that her friend Roddy [McDowall] was visiting her, 'but he is quite through hearing about my miseries.' She added, 'I'm afraid I've been rather the bad girl,' and told me a little about the story of Eddie and Debbie. As for Debbie, she said, 'I sit here sometimes and think of her and wish that she and I could be friends again.' Then she laughed and said, 'She's such a Girl Scout, she could use someone like me in her life to shake things up.'"

Matissa Hart and Elizabeth Taylor met several more times before Matissa moved to New York with her new husband. "I have often thought of those times with her in Gstaad, and wondered how she was faring. When I would see her films, I would never be able to reconcile that she was the same woman I met at Charley's."

"Those months there in Switzerland were so full of pain and guilt that they zoom in and out and become all out of shape in my mind," Elizabeth would later recall. "I can remember moments of such horror."

Then, one day, the call came. It was Richard. He wondered how she was doing, he said. He missed her and wanted to have lunch with her. If she had only slammed the phone down with an indignant, *"How dare you interrupt my solitude,"* her life from this point onward would be a very different story. However, it wasn't meant to be that way. "Yes," she said, she would love to see him again.

The two arranged to meet that afternoon at the stunning, thirteenth-century Château de Chillon, an impressive turreted medieval castle where lucky tourists dine while taking in the breathtaking view of Lake Geneva. Elizabeth and her parents, who had a small chalet nearby, sat in the backseat of the car as their driver took them to the lake. They arrived at exactly the same moment as Richard, who pulled up in a red sports car. He looked tanned and rested, sober but a bit nervous with a dashing short haircut. His blue eyes danced when he saw Elizabeth.

One would have thought Elizabeth's parents, Sara and Francis, would have been hesitant about the prospects of their daughter once again seeing a man who had been nothing but trouble for her. But by this time, they had *both* abandoned the notion that they would have any influence on her. Marshall Baldrige recalled, "To be frank, those two poor people had been all but beaten down by bearing witness to Elizabeth's very difficult and troubling world. They were both worn to the bone. Francis told me that Sara was a different person—just worn out by it all. In the end, they just wanted her to be happy—and she clearly was *not* happy alone. Though Francis was certainly no big fan of Richard's—he felt that he would only end up hurting Elizabeth—he knew that Elizabeth wanted him, and only him." The Taylor parents encouraged Elizabeth on her way, telling her to have a wonderful day with

Richard. As Elizabeth and Richard stood with their arms around each other, Elizabeth's parents were driven off.

Elizabeth and Richard pulled away from one another, and then took each other in. In unison they chirped, "Well, you look marvelous," before bursting into laughter. They then enjoyed a quiet, if sometimes awkward, luncheon. However, it was a meal that would not be easily forgotten by Elizabeth. With many people, the truth of how they feel comes forth when they have had too much alcohol. Not so Richard. With him, his greatest truth was revealed when he was sober, when he could think straight and dig deep within to bare his soul, as he did during his luncheon with Elizabeth. "I love you," he told her, according to his later recollection. "But what scares me about you is that I think you are too selfish to be in a real marriage."

Elizabeth was stung by his observation. For once, Richard didn't mean to hurt her, he was simply being honest. He explained that he'd been so reliant on Sybil for so many years, she'd become his rock. She put aside her career for him and their children. She would do anything for him, he explained. "She put up with bloody hell from me," he said.

At last, the truth of why Richard was so reluctant to leave Sybil had come forth, and it actually made sense. He'd never had support and affirmation in his youth at home, and had turned to his mentor, Philip Burton, for it. Philip had been his greatest teacher, giving him the confidence to become an actor, to walk onto a stage and take a chance on failing—and instead prove himself a marvel at his craft. Then he had turned to Sybil. She had been his greatest salvation, the woman upon whom he could most depend. She'd always been there for him, even when he didn't deserve it. He couldn't bear to lose her because, in doing so, he would sacrifice one of his most beloved supporters. Actually, though, Richard was just as selfish as he had accused Elizabeth of being, since, in truth, the primary reason he was with Sybil was because he needed her. He never gave much thought to what *she* needed; if he had, he wouldn't have repeatedly betrayed her over the years. The irony of it all didn't escape Richard. "I know you, Elizabeth, because I am you," he told her. "I'm a selfish bastard. I have always been my own greatest concern, and I have never been able to abandon that notion, and neither can you, dear. Neither can you."

"But I would do it for you, Richard," Elizabeth said, according to her later recollection.

Would she, though? It was a stretch, she would later admit, to think that she could put aside her own best interests for another person. Had she ever done so in the past? Perhaps when she adopted Maria, but was that comparable to being a giving person in a marriage?

"I'm not certain you could do it for me, luv," Richard told her. "Tolstoy put it best: 'Everyone wants to change humanity, but no one is willing to change themselves.'"

"I *would* do it for you, Richard," she repeated.

The subject was changed. However, Elizabeth would not be able to forget Richard's summation of her. Was he correct? Was she so selfish that she couldn't survive in a loving marriage? On one hand, it bothered her that he felt this way about her. No one wants to be thought of as being a selfish person, after all. But on the other, she had to be realistic. She had to admit that his assessment of her was probably accurate. Of course she was selfish. She was accustomed to having the world spin around her desires. However, she truly felt that she had tried with her marriages to be a good wife. But then, upon closer reflection, she had to know that after the first one, the rest were arranged to fill a void in her life, a vacuum of loneliness. There was something about Richard, though, that made her want to . . . dare she? . . . *change.* "I felt that, yes, I could be more for Richard," she would later recall. "I suddenly realized that I wanted to be more. I wanted to change."

After their meal, he drove her home. They didn't even kiss. They would see each other a couple of times a week for the next few weeks before Elizabeth made what she would recall as "the most alone, mature, and unpopular decision of my life." She would be there for Richard, whenever he called, and for whatever reason.

If he wanted to talk in person, she would be there. If he just wanted to speak on the telephone, that was fine, too. If he wanted to have sex with her, she would be there for that as well. In return, she would require nothing from him—absolutely nothing. "If that's the way it's going to be," she decided, "that is the role I will accept."

Elizabeth believed that her decision was a mature one born out of what she felt was "an unselfish love for Richard." She just wanted him to be happy, she said, and if that happiness was with her, fine. If it was with Sybil? She would live with that as well—or so she said.

She was trying to prove that she would change, that she could be there for him. In her view, allowing him to not have any requirements of her was a first step in her quest to at least *try* to be a giving partner. It was obviously a misguided effort, or as one Taylor observer put it, "a big load of crap. Richard would never have allowed it, and she probably knew it. He was in too deep with Elizabeth to think of her as one of his floozies. She was too famous, too volatile, too . . . *Elizabeth* . . . to be the kind of woman he could just hide away and have sex with when he felt the time was right for it. It was a manipulation, no doubt about it." Elizabeth didn't see it that way at all. "By making myself so readily available, I lowered my stature in everybody's eyes," she would later conclude, "but mine—and, as it turned out, Richard's."

Richard Chooses

It was no surprise that, as a nod to the public spectacle of their lives together, Elizabeth Taylor would be paired with Richard Burton for another film. While 20th Century-Fox may have thought that the publicity that surrounded their personal shenanigans was to the detriment of *Cleopatra* (more likely, the movie's script and its editing could reasonably be considered, at least partially, to blame), MGM held no such reservations. Richard Burton was scheduled to make a film for the studio with Sophia Loren called *The V.I.P.s*. What's more interesting than the resulting movie, perhaps, is the fact that it was inspired by the true story of what happened when Vivien Leigh tried to leave her husband, Laurence Olivier, for her lover, Peter Finch. She and Finch intended to run off together and ended up in the VIP lounge at Heathrow Airport in London waiting for their flight, which was delayed because of the fog. After the two sat together for hours, she changed her mind about ending her marriage for him.

Without even knowing what it was about, or seeing a script, Elizabeth said that she would like to be in the film with Burton, instead of Sophia Loren. Of course, no studio was going to resist, and it was ironic that Elizabeth ended up at MGM again, considering all the bad blood between her and the studio. Perhaps the Academy Award she won for her last film at Metro, *Butterfield 8*, had helped to ameliorate her bad memory of that experience.

The V.I.P.s is an inconsequential trifle in which Elizabeth plays a wealthy and bored socialite who wants to leave her drunken husband, Richard, for a gigolo (played by Louis Jourdan). Chaos ensues when their lives and the lives of other characters intersect at Heathrow Airport, where everyone gets stranded during a heavy London fog. Despite the fact that the performances by Burton and Taylor weren't exactly Oscar-worthy, the film is an interesting ensemble piece, with several overlapping stories. Some critics enjoyed the efficient yet lovestruck secretary Maggie Smith played opposite Rod Taylor, who portrayed her boss. Others enjoyed the Orson Welles–Elsa Martinelli duo, as a money-obsessed producer and a scatterbrained starlet; these two definitely had the best lines in the film. Some felt that Margaret Rutherford deserved her Oscar as the eccentric Duchess of Brighton. Also, it was surprising that the music didn't get an Oscar nod too—it's a wonderfully evocative score. Still, while surrounded by excellence, Elizabeth and Richard could not have appeared less invested in this venture. So why would they make the film? Besides affording Elizabeth an opportunity to be with Richard, money was a motivating factor. Elizabeth got $500,000 for it, Richard about half that much.

It speaks to the power of this couple as film stars that, when it was released in the next year, *The V.I.P.s* was a hit, even out-grossing *Cleopatra*. Its two stars received 20 percent of the gross receipts, which would come to about $14 million—giving them another $4 million—especially amazing since the movie cost barely $3 million to make.

Financial considerations aside, it was obvious that Elizabeth really just wanted to be with Richard, and she said as much in her memoirs: "It was just an excuse for us to be together."

For Elizabeth, though, *The V.I.P.s* was a comedown. She hadn't made a movie this bad since . . . well, it's possible that she *never* made a movie this bad. British character actress Margaret Rutherford's memory of the movie was quite likely very different. She won a Best Supporting Actress Oscar for her role in the film, its only nomination.

In December 1962, Elizabeth and Richard checked into adjoining roof-garden suites at the Dorchester Hotel in London, where the movie was to be filmed. While making *The V.I.P.s*, the couple also spent a great deal of time at Richard's favorite pubs in London. They would start the morning with Bloody Marys, continue with a few bottles of champagne, then their brandies . . . and by that time it was just noon. One day, a reporter accompanied them to a pub. It was clear that they felt no compunction about sharing their habits with him, and by extension the world. "Hey, you shit-faced bastard," Elizabeth said to Richard, "give me a drink."

Burton spent weekends with Sybil and their daughters, while Elizabeth stayed back at the Dorchester counting the hours until his return. He told more than one reporter that he had no intention of leaving his wife and marrying Elizabeth. "You mustn't use sex alone as a lever, as a kind of moral, intellectual, psychic crutch to get away from your wife," he told critic Kenneth Tynan. "You can't say to her, 'I'm terribly sorry but I can't sleep in the same bed with you anymore because I simply have to run off with this infinitely fascinating girl.'"

What's more interesting than his comment is the fact that Richard would discuss such matters with a reporter for publication. It was as if he were using the press to pass on messages to Elizabeth. Or was he purposely fanning the flames of the publicity bonfire that had all but enveloped him and Elizabeth in recent months? Why Elizabeth would have tolerated such indiscretion from him is the real mystery, but tolerate it she did. After all, this was the *new* Elizabeth, and she wasn't going to push Richard, or question him, or make demands of him. Though her hands would shake with anxiety when she would read such reports, she was determined to keep her promise to herself and try to be as selfless as possible where he was concerned. When he would return from visiting his family, Richard would be very upset, and often in tears. "He's more miserable when he's with them than he is when he's with me," Elizabeth reasoned to Roddy McDowall. "But this is what he wants, I suppose."

On some days, Sybil would show up on the set and act as if she and Richard were happy, helping to make decisions about wardrobe. On other days, Elizabeth would be the one making the decisions, and she would veto all of Sybil's. It was a difficult and confusing time for everyone.

Finally in the spring of 1963, Richard Burton came to a difficult decision. He would leave Sybil. Their marriage was over. Of course, Elizabeth was elated. He had made his choice, and it was to be with her. The question, as she now saw it, was whether or not the two of them could make their relationship work without the heartache and angst that had been its hallmark from the very beginning, almost a year and a half earlier. Of course, what she couldn't have known at the time was that her drama with Richard Burton had only just begun . . .

True Love in Mexico

Through the summer and into the fall of 1963, Elizabeth and Richard remained in London and busied themselves with a variety of projects while, as Elizabeth put it, "we got to know one another away from the constant anxiety of making a movie together." Richard starred opposite Peter O'Toole in *Becket*, which was filmed at Shepperton Studios in Middlesex. Meanwhile, Elizabeth narrated and appeared in a TV special for CBS called *Elizabeth Taylor in London* (broadcast in October 1963), for which she was paid $250,000, the most anyone had ever received for doing a television program. "It's fine," she said. "I'm not interested in making movies right now. I just want to help Richard, do what I can for Richard."

Then, in September 1963, Richard and Elizabeth arrived in Mexico, where Burton was scheduled to go before the cameras in John Huston's film of Tennessee Williams's play *The Night of the Iguana*. When they arrived at Mexico City's airport, there was such a mad crush awaiting them that Elizabeth refused to get off the plane until security dispersed the crowd. "Don't be bloody ridiculous," Richard told her. "We will exit this plane and get through the crowd as best we can. This is our life, so get used to it."

"Get used to it?" Elizabeth said, her voice raised to a screech. "I've been doing this for twenty-five years, buster!"

In fact, Richard wanted to feel the adoration of the awaiting crowd. For him this was a new experience. The two exited the plane cursing and hollering at each other—followed by seventy-five pieces of luggage carried by airport personnel, most of which contained Elizabeth's tropical outfits for her trip. It was the perfect scene for the paparazzi. The next day, "Liz and Dick" (as they were usually called by the media, but not by anyone who actually knew them, though Liz did sometimes call him "Dickie") were on the front page of every newspaper, smiling, scowling, cursing, and posing. "We always give the people exactly what they want, don't we?" Elizabeth later joked with Burton. Then, to a writer, she said, "My best feature is my gray hairs. I have them all named. They're all called Burton."

"They were both very funny, and I think this is something people really have missed about them," said their friend the columnist Liz Smith. (Liz would later meet the Burtons on the set of their movie *The Sandpiper*.) "You didn't have that kind of ribald humor coming from a Hollywood couple at that time, and I don't think you've seen it since. I'll never forget, I was with them in Rome or somewhere, and he was spouting off about Dylan Thomas, and just being Richard Burton, talking endlessly. And after he finished, she looked at him and asked, very matter-of-factly, 'Do you ever give yourself the creeps, luv?'"

The Night of the Iguana would be filmed in Mexico City, Puerto Vallarta, and Mismaloya. It was a tough shoot; everyone was miserable from the heat and the awful, crawling creatures, though the cast was a good one that included three leading ladies for Richard: Ava Gardner, Deborah Kerr, and the then seventeen-year-old Sue Lyon, who had just recently appeared as the nubile temptress Lolita in Stanley Kubrick's film version of the popular Vladimir Nabokov novel of the same name. While in Mexico, Elizabeth had six-year-old Liza with her. Maria was in a clinic in Europe at this time, recovering from surgery on her hip. The boys, Michael, eleven, and Christopher, nine, were with their father, Michael Wilding, in Los Angeles, where they were going to start school. Elizabeth was readily available to Richard to help him with his script, really abandoning at this time any career plans she may have had just to be at his side.

Elizabeth and Richard were ensconced in a lovely tiled, four-story compound called Casa Kimberly in Puerto Vallarta. Spread out over 22,000 square feet, it had ten bedrooms, eleven baths, three kitchens, and a huge swimming pool. Mexican architect Guillermo Wulff later built another house across the street—adding four more bedrooms to the home—and the two structures were joined by a pink bridge that is an exact replica of Venice's Bridge of Sighs. Richard eventually bought the estate for just $40,000, and it would remain one of the Burtons' homes for the next decade.

Today, Casa Kimberly is a bed-and-breakfast (address: 518 Calle Madera), a tourist attraction not to be missed when visiting Puerto Vallarta. One doesn't even have to make an appointment. Simply ring the bell and, after a maid allows access, the tour begins, with guide Maurice Mintzer, who bought the estate from Elizabeth in 1990. "She took two paintings off the wall and left everything else to us," he says. "Richard was dead. She couldn't chase him anymore. It was the end of an era." Mintzer tells all sorts of stories about Elizabeth, such as her locking Richard in certain rooms when he was being difficult and also having the bridge built so that she could banish him all the way to the other house when he was really being unmanageable. Who knows if these stories are true, but they're fun tales for tourists to take home.

The couple's relationship only intensified during their time at Casa Kimberly. It was there that they first spent happy times together in a place that they considered their own. On November 10, 1963, Richard celebrated his thirty-eighth birthday. Elizabeth presented him with the complete Everyman Library of Classics— five hundred volumes, each bound in calfskin.

Lucille Wellman was a close friend of Ava Gardner's who, at Ava's invitation, came to visit her in Puerto Vallarta. "My first night there, Ava and I went to dinner with [noted screenwriter] Meade Roberts, and Richard and Elizabeth Taylor. Elizabeth looked marvelous in a white, flowing caftan and matching turban, with the longest, dangling diamond earrings I had ever seen. 'Careful, love,' Richard told her as she ate, 'your earrings are in your soup.' Elizabeth laughed and said, 'Jesus Christ, these goddamn earrings!' and she took them off and handed them to the waiter and said, 'Would you be a dear and keep these in the kitchen for me?' The waiter was absolutely floored. He took the earrings. Richard said, 'Luv, those earrings are worth $300,000 and you just gave them to the waiter?' She said, 'Only for safekeeping, dear. I'm sure he'll take very good care of them.' Of course, she could have just put them in her purse, but she had a flair for the dramatic, for just having a moment, or giving someone else—like the waiter—a moment.

"After the meal, she went to the kitchen to retrieve her earrings, and when she came back she told us that they had put them in the freezer for safekeeping. She just thought that was hysterical. 'Ice on ice,' she said. 'Here, try them on,' she told me, handing them to me. 'Oh, no, I couldn't,' I told her. 'No, I insist,' she said. 'They become you,' she told me when I finally put them on. 'You are absolutely beautiful in them. And they're freezing cold, too, aren't they? See,' she said with a laugh, 'I told you so!'

"Later during that trip, she showed me a beautiful diamond pin of an iguana, which Richard had given her in commemoration of the movie. It was designed by Schlumberger of Tiffany and Company, and Elizabeth loved it, as she did all of her jewels. She insisted that I try it on. She loved seeing her jewelry on other people. It gave her a chance, she said, to see what the pieces looked like from the vantage point of the admirer. Plus, she loved the expression on people's faces when they got to try on these exquisite pieces.

"I found her to be completely charming and guileless. She was well aware of the effect she had on people, I think, and she did whatever she could to dispense of it quickly. Richard was the same way. In public, they had a glow about them that said stardom. Privately, they were as 'normal' as they could be, I mean, given who they were. They seemed to get along well; they were very happy, at least that was my perception."

According to Wellman, Elizabeth put her head on Richard's shoulder and said, "I wonder if this man will one day be my husband."

"If we don't kill each other first," Richard said with a warm smile.

Elizabeth looked at him lovingly. "But what a way to go, darling," she said. "What a way to go."

He kissed her on the lips.

In December 1963, Elizabeth's family came to visit for Christmas: her parents, Sara and Francis; her brother, Howard, and his wife, Mara, and their five children; the Wilding boys; and even Maria, who was now out of the clinic where she'd been recovering after surgery. She was now walking without crutches, so it was an even more joyous holiday for everyone. The occasion marked a turning point in Elizabeth's relationship with Richard. She had never been more content. She also knew that Richard now felt as if he had a real place in her life, and his love for her seemed to grow with each passing day. Indeed, she had devoted herself to him, and he knew it. "He began to fall for her in a way that he hadn't before, and she for him," said his brother Graham Jenkins. "I think it was at Casa Kimberly that their true love was born. Before that, it was just a tumultuous romance. But in Mexico, I think she saw another side to him, and he of her. Now they were one."

Part Four

"LIZ AND DICK"

Elizabeth and Richard: "We Will Have No More Marriages"

By the beginning of 1964, Sybil Burton had filed for divorce from Richard, citing abandonment and cruelty. When her attorney noted in the paperwork that Burton had "been in the constant company of another woman," *Newsweek* called it "the throwaway line of the decade." The million-dollar settlement Richard gave her nearly bankrupted him—and he had to give her another half a million after that over a period of years, as well as the home in Switzerland—but he agreed to it because he felt so guilty about leaving her. It would be five years before he would speak to her again, and then just briefly over the telephone. Sybil, though, went on with her life, and in a grand style. She opened Arthur, a disco in New York, which quickly became the hottest celebrity nightspot in the city. She took a young lover, just twenty-four.

Elizabeth felt that Sybil's decision to divorce Richard was the best way to start 1964. She was proud that she'd spent the entire last year taking care of him, proving to herself and to him that she could, if called upon to do so, put her career and her needs aside for his. Then she got her divorce from Eddie. "I wouldn't stand in the way of this earth-shattering, world-shaking romance for anything in the world," Eddie said sarcastically.

By the time Elizabeth and Richard married on March 15, 1964, most of their friends and family were fairly exhausted by the specifics of their wild personal adventures and tempestuous romance. For those in the inner circle, it was almost anticlimactic when the couple decided to charter a plane and secretly marry in Montreal. For Elizabeth, though, this was a marriage she wanted more than anything else in her life. "I didn't have butterflies for this one," she said, "because I knew beyond all doubt that it was right." Richard, though, was nervous enough for the two of them. Ronald DeMann, Elizabeth's hairdresser at the time, recalled that Burton—who was by this time starring in *Hamlet* in Toronto en route to Broadway—was so nervous on the plane ride that "he drank himself silly." Elizabeth begged DeMann to convince Richard to eat, saying, "He's got to have some food in him. I don't know why he's so nervous. We've been sleeping together for two years."

Despite his nerves, it was clear that Richard truly loved Elizabeth. "I fell in love at once," he had said. "She was like a mirage of beauty of the ages, irresistible, like the pull of gravity. She has everything I want in a woman. She is quite unlike any woman I have ever known. She makes me not want to know any other woman, believe me, sincerely. I think of her morning, noon, and night. I dream of her. She will be my greatest happiness—forever, of course."

At the time, Elizabeth recalled, "The two of us act like we're seventeen-year-olds. My favorite time is when we're alone at night and for hours we giggle, and talk—about, maybe books, world events, poetry, the children, when we first met, problems, daydreams and dreams. We love to watch old movies on TV to regenerate our souls. Sometimes I wake up in the morning with my eyes absolutely swollen shut from crying at some wonderfully old movie the night before."

Elizabeth and Richard were married in the bridal suite on the eighth floor of the Ritz-Carlton Hotel in Montreal by a Unitarian minister (who was able to overlook Elizabeth's previous four marriages and conduct the ceremony anyway). It was Elizabeth's fifth wedding and she was only thirty-two. Richard was thirty-nine. Of course, Elizabeth was late for the ceremony, causing Richard to ask in his own inimitable fashion, "Isn't that fat little tart here yet? I swear to you she'll be late for the last bloody judgment."

When she did arrive, Elizabeth looked beautiful in a low-cut canary-yellow chiffon gown designed by Irene Sharaff—designer of the costumes in *Cleopatra*—that was patterned after the gown Elizabeth wore in her first scene with Richard in *Cleopatra*. At her neck was a $100,000 emerald brooch, which had been a gift from Richard during the filming of that movie. As a wedding gift, Richard presented her with a striking emerald-and-diamond brooch from Bulgari. He had given her earrings to match for her thirty-second birthday. A bracelet soon followed. Taken together, the jewels are sometimes referred to as the Grand Duchess Vladimir Suite.

Her natural hair was entwined with long and flowing wig pieces that fell in tendrils framing her face. The entire Ronald DeMann creation was decorated with Roman hyacinths. Burton was dressed in a dark suit and red tie and wore a sprig of freesia that Elizabeth plucked from her bridal bouquet and pinned to his lapel. Francis and Sara Taylor were present for the ceremony, though Elizabeth's children were not. Richard's valet, Bob Wilson, was the best man. Elizabeth was ebullient.

"You have both gone through great travail in your love for each other," the minister said in his remarks to them. They had to agree.

The ceremony took just ten minutes. Richard's agent, Hugh French, who attended the ceremony, recalled, "When the minister pronounced them man and wife, the loveliest of smiles appeared on both their faces. It was so very apparent that they were thrilled, that they took the vows very seriously."

"I truly believe in my heart that this marriage will last forever," said the now five-time bride. "I know I have said that before, but this time I really do think it is true."

Reflecting public opinion, there were a lot of jokes made at Elizabeth's expense, some of them pretty funny.

"If you're looking for a steady job, gals," quipped Bob Hope, "why not try out for flower girl at Liz Taylor's weddings?"

"Imagine! Marrying every husband you meet," quipped Walter Winchell.

However, Oscar Levant, who was a good friend of Elizabeth's, had the best line: "Always a bride. Never a bridesmaid."

More seriously, Elizabeth in 1964 recalled of the ceremony, "It was like coming home, a golden warmth. We knew then that there was only one way, indirectly, that we could make it up to all the ones who had suffered: by being good to each other and loving each other. But it has to be not just for now. In twenty-five years, fifty—then our marriage will have meaning; then all of the unhappiness will at least have been *for* something."

After their return to Toronto the night of the ceremony, Richard got back to the business of *Hamlet* and performed in the show that evening. He received six curtain calls. Finally, he stepped toward the front of the stage and said, "I would like to quote from the play—act three, scene one: 'We will have no more marriages.'" It brought the house down.

Prior to the marriage, Elizabeth had wanted to attend every performance she could, but her presence caused such an uproar during intermission that the theater couldn't raise the curtain for act two. With the public able to approach her while she was held captive in her seat, there was nothing she could do but smile and sign autographs. "It's best if you watch from the wings, luv," Richard suggested after they were wed. "Soon they'll be selling tickets to see you, and not me!"

For his part, Richard had been having some problems with the role. Perhaps he was distracted, or maybe he'd been off the stage for so long that he was rusty. Seeing that her husband needed help, Elizabeth dedicated herself to finding a solution for him. What could she do? She didn't feel equipped to help him with his characterization. "It's just so far beyond what I am as an actress," she said, in a moment of self-deprecating candor. "I wouldn't presume to tell Richard how to act on the stage." Still, she knew she had to do something.

Elizabeth decided to contact Richard's mentor and drama coach, Philip Burton, in New York, where he was a faculty member at the American Musical and Dramatic Academy of New York. Though she knew that Philip had been against her romance with Burton, she felt the bigger issue was that Burton now needed help, and she knew no one else who could give it. She begged Philip to come to Canada and work with Richard. "I think he just needs someone to tell him how truly brilliant he is," she said. "And he won't listen to me, his wife. But he would listen to you. Please," she implored, "do this for Richard, if not for me."

Philip wanted to assist his protégé, but felt torn by his allegiance to Sybil. When he asked her about it, though, she said, "Absolutely, yes. You must go to him. He needs you."

When Philip showed up in Toronto, no man had ever been happier to see him than Richard. He couldn't believe that Elizabeth had summoned his mentor, and he was elated.

Philip and Richard worked on Burton's characterization of the Prince of Denmark. The first night thereafter, Burton got the longest standing ovation he'd ever received from an audience. He was filled with a new confidence, now truly ready for Broadway. "Elizabeth was delighted," said Robert Burr, Richard's understudy. "That she could contribute to his well-being made her feel necessary in his life, and she would have done anything for him, really."

For Richard, it was further proof that Elizabeth really did care about him, did want to be there for him, and could do so if she set her mind to it. It hadn't been easy for him to let go of Sybil completely, but he had to admit that his new wife was proving herself to him with each passing day, and working hard at it.

"I owe this to you," he told her lovingly. "You did this for me, sending for Philip, and I owe my success in this show to you, my love."

Those were the words she'd wanted to hear. Elizabeth rushed into his arms.

On the final night in Toronto, Richard walked onto the stage of the O'Keefe Theatre and gave another stunning performance. At the last of several curtain calls, he said, "Some of you have come here to see Alfred Drake; some have come to see Eileen Herlie; some have come to see Hume Cronyn; and some have come to see Elizabeth Taylor," noting the fact that she was often in the audience for his shows. "Now, for the first time on any stage, Elizabeth Taylor has come to see you." With that, out walked his wife. The entire audience rose to its feet with a thunderous ovation. Richard Burton wanted to share his stage with her, and for him, it was quite the validation. There she stood, center stage, to accept their approval. No matter what she had done to antagonize the public with "Le Scandale," Elizabeth Taylor was still their beloved star. Richard put his arm around his wife proudly as the two walked offstage, applause echoing throughout the theater.

The Boston Brawl

After Toronto, the next stop for *Hamlet*, before it was to play Broadway, was Boston. It was in that city that Elizabeth and Richard truly realized how famous they had become . . . and what their lives would be like now that they had married. When they landed at the airport, there were about thirty-five hundred fans waiting for them. They managed to get through the crush and arrived at Boston's quiet Sheraton Plaza Hotel without incident. Though no crowd blocked the sidewalk in front of the hotel, the security detail guarding the entrance included one lieutenant, two sergeants, and twenty-four patrolmen. Hand in hand, the Burtons walked into the lobby, where they were greeted by the smiling hotel manager. Suddenly, from seemingly nowhere, a mob of people exploded into the lobby, entering like gangbusters through the back (and carelessly unprotected) entrance. The Burtons' entwined fingers were ripped apart as the crowd surged forward, lifting Elizabeth as if in a tidal wave and throwing her up against a wall like a rag doll. Some of the fans held roses, others photos of the Burtons that they wished to have signed. The riot became unmanageable, and Elizabeth began to scream, "Back off! Back away!" The fans tore at her clothes, yanked at her hair, clawed at her face. "I saw them grab her arms, and pull in opposite directions," one horrified eyewitness later recalled. "I thought she would just split in half. It was truly shocking, a terrifying scene. On the floor, getting kicked around by the crowd, was her alligator handbag with solid gold fittings. I just remember this bag being tossed about."

Elizabeth screamed for help. Somehow, Richard got to her. His clothes had been torn, some of his hair pulled out. Swatting away the fans like flies, he managed to get Elizabeth to the elevator. Finally, all of those police officers served some purpose when they blocked the elevator entrance and allowed the Burtons to sail to their ten-room suite on the eleventh floor.

Tom Gates recalls, "The caption on the back of a U.P.I. photo taken during the fracas states, 'Liz Taylor, hands to face, sobs as she is led down corridor to hotel suite by her husband, Richard Burton, after the newlyweds were mobbed as they arrived yesterday. Some 1,000 curious fans tore at their hair and clothing. Miss Taylor suffered back and arm injuries. She was treated by a doctor, given a sedative and put to bed.' [Elizabeth's publicist] John Springer told me that this was the scariest situation of his entire life. He also said that once he was reunited with the Burtons, nobody said a word as they were led to the hotel suite. However, once the three of them were safely inside, Elizabeth collapsed on the bed and, despite her injuries, began laughing uncontrollably at what had happened."

The following evening, when John Springer and his assistant Diane Stevens knocked on the Burtons' door, Elizabeth answered. She was wearing a black dress with pink shoes dotted with rhinestones. She also had on a silver mink coat. "I'm going to Richard's opening," she announced. "I'm all ready. I just have to touch up my makeup." As she said the words, though, she seemed to sway, as if still quite unwell.

"I don't think you can go," Diane said. "Elizabeth, you should go back to bed."

"That's what I tried to tell her," Richard said, entering the room. "But she won't listen to me."

"But for me to not be present opening night, it's just not right," Elizabeth said. "I simply must do it, Richard."

"But listen to me, Elizabeth, there are five thousand fans waiting at the theater's entrance," said Springer. "We just came from there. You can't do it. They'll kill you, for sure." Actually, there were just a few hundred fans at the theater. John was lying, but with good intentions.

"You see?" Richard said, reaching for Elizabeth. He held her closely. "Stay here, safe. You will be with me in spirit, my love," he told her. "That is all I need to carry me through."

She seemed to collapse into his arms. They kissed.

"That's when I really knew how much they loved each other," said Diane Stevens. "I had never seen such a connection between two people, so much caring. It made me melt inside."

Richard led his wife to the bedroom. As they walked off, Elizabeth turned to John and Diane. "The next time someone says how much they envy me, tell them about this night," she said, "when I couldn't even go to my husband's opening."

"Oh, please," Richard said. "Here she blows again," he added with a loaded smile. "Crying a river of tears because she can't have her way. Poor, poor Miss Taylor."

Elizabeth punched him playfully on the shoulder. "Oh, Jesus Christ," she exclaimed. "Just get me to the bedroom, before I pass out."

Richard's Hemophilia

After Boston, Richard made his Broadway star turn in *Hamlet* at the Lunt-Fontanne Theatre in April 1964. For the entire time he appeared in the show, there would be chaos in Times Square every time he and Elizabeth showed up at the theater, and then more pandemonium when they departed after the show. Gary Springer, son of the Burtons' publicist, John, was ten in 1964. "The crowds, the mobs that would be outside the theater every night, it was incredible," he recalled. "There was nothing like it in New York at the time, maybe in the country. They used to close 46th Street when the show let out, because there would be such a mob. I remember one time my dad and I were going to dinner with Richard. Elizabeth was meeting us at the restaurant. Richard had put me on his shoulders to fight through the crowd. Going from the stage door to the car, I lost both of my shoes, both of my socks, and my pants were being yanked down. The public couldn't get enough of them. Just a glimpse of the two of them was all most of the people needed, and that was about all they would get anyway, as the stars rushed in and out of the theater district in their chauffeur-driven Town Car."

Tom Gates recalls one memorable afternoon during the Broadway run of *Hamlet*. "One day, Elizabeth ducked out of the Regency and into the nearby Colony for lunch, and I was there, of course, wanting to photograph her. At this same time, a young man with a strong Texas accent named Van Zandt Ellis [the future concert pianist] happened by and asked if there was any way he could meet Elizabeth since she'd been the inspiration for a piano piece he'd written. We walked to the restaurant and I suggested he write her a note. He agreed, and as she exited dressed all in pink with a pink-flowered hat and clutching her little Yorkshire terrier, he handed her the note. She accepted it with a polite, 'Thank you.' She then started to cross the street without looking just as a speeding car approached. Luckily, the quick-thinking doorman grabbed her by the arm and [pulled her] back onto the sidewalk as the car whooshed by her. We were all nearly in shock by how close she had come to true disaster, but Elizabeth simply thanked the doorman as one would for opening a door. Just then, Philip Burton raced up, urgently asking if she were all right. 'I'm fine, really I am,' she said as she very nonchalantly opened the note. 'Philip, this is the sweetest thing,' she said as if her brush with death was ancient history, 'somebody has composed a sonata for me!' I then introduced her to Van Zandt and she thanked him profusely. Soon Richard's car pulled up and a huge crowd started forming as Richard got out of it. Before heading inside Elizabeth and Richard graciously posed with their little Yorkie in front of the Regency for what turned out to be one of my very favorite photos of them together."

During his Broadway run, Richard's reviews were stunning. Indeed, he was the toast of the town during this golden time, and no one was prouder of him than Elizabeth. She hosted many dinner parties in his honor at Sardi's, and happily basked in the glow of Richard's stardom. It was almost as if she didn't have a career herself—she never mentioned it, nor did she ever think of it—but that was exactly as she wanted it at the time. "I was totally devoted to Richard," she recalled, "and not for a second did I regret it. I was so proud of him, and I felt so much a part of things. I didn't need to make movies. I had made movies for years," she said, "and I was never as happy as I was during that early time in my marriage to Richard."

The Burtons were staying at the Regency, and their time there, with Elizabeth's children, was happy. The couple was more kind and loving to one another than ever in the past. "We were a real family," Elizabeth said dreamily. "It was picture perfect."

There were times, though, when Richard's drinking was a problem. After having as many as four martinis before going onstage, he would sometimes have trouble retaining his lines. Elizabeth, who'd previously had little problem with Richard's drinking while he worked, felt strongly that his work on Broadway was, as she put it, "much too important to just take a chance and muck it all up." She knew how hard he had worked at the role, and she didn't want to see him fail at it, even for one night. After a dozen shows, though, Richard didn't care as much as he had at the beginning of the run.

One night in May, Richard completely massacred the "Play's the thing" speech and was booed by someone in the audience. He was as infuriated as he was hurt. When he got back to the Regency, he found Elizabeth in the parlor, curled up on a couch, drinking a Vodka Collins and watching a Peter Sellers movie on television. "They booed, can you believe it?" he roared as soon as he walked into the suite. "How dare they, those sniveling bastards?"

"How dare *you*, Richard?" she said, looking up at her husband.

Burton walked over to the television and turned it off. "What do you mean?" he asked, his temper rising.

"How dare you allow those people to pay those high ticket prices, and then show up not able to perform?" Elizabeth said, now standing up and meeting him face-to-face.

"My drinking has never interfered with my work," he said.

"Well, we're all in denial about something, aren't we now, Richard?" she said, remaining calm. "Now, I'd like to get back to my movie. Please." It was an odd lecture coming from her, especially since she often used to stand in the wings and hand him glasses of champagne to sip on when he wasn't onstage. But to try to make sense of her mood that night, all these years later, is fruitless.

She turned her back to him to return to the couch.

Richard went into the bedroom and undressed. He returned a half hour later in his pajamas and robe, and in bare feet. "Are you still watching that goddamn silliness?" he asked her. He was clearly still angry.

"Oh, be quiet, Richard," Elizabeth said. "It's almost over."

"It *is* over," he declared. Then, with a thrust of his bare foot, he kicked in the television screen. In doing so, he cut himself so badly that it took Elizabeth more than an hour to stop the blood flow enough to get him to a hospital. It was then that Elizabeth discovered something about Richard that she hadn't known: He had hemophilia. A simple cut could bring on profuse bleeding and severe pain, even though his case was mild.

Richard had suffered from hemophilia since childhood.

Marie Bentkover, who was secretary to Richard's agent Hugh French, explained: "We worked hard to keep it from the press, just as a matter of privacy. As I understood it from Rich, it was first discovered in his two older brothers when he was eight years. They had to have their tonsils removed. They went to the hospital and nearly died from the operation. It was then that the hemophilia was discovered in the Jenkins family. Of his six brothers and sisters, four of the brothers were so-called bleeders. The other two brothers, and the girls, were not.

"We always knew that Rich's case could turn from mild to acute at any time, and it was always on our minds, if not his. Rich told me that it was known as the 'disease of kings' because of its common occurrence in the inbred royal families of Europe. 'So, of course, I would have such a disease,' he said, laughing."

By 1964, Richard Burton had not undergone any type of surgery that might provoke profuse bleeding. Even in barroom brawls, he usually escaped with only minor cuts. However, he did have a few close calls. He broke an arm as a youngster, and his nose was fractured in a fistfight. More recently, hoodlums had descended on him outside of Paddington Station to beat him up. He said it was a random attack. During that beating, Burton suffered a black eye. Worse, though, one of the assailants pinned him down and another stomped on his head with a sharp-pointed shoe. The cut was just half an inch long, but it took ten days for the blood to completely clot. It caused a ten-day delay in *The V.I.P.s*. He managed to keep it (the bleeding, not the beating) from Elizabeth. "When he was doing *Cleopatra*, he had to be careful not to nick himself while shaving. I bought him an electric razor for that film," said Marie Bentkover. "They didn't have them in Rome at the time. I brought one with me from America, and he was thrilled."

Though Richard was able to keep previous bleeding incidents from Elizabeth, the incident with the television set could not be hidden from her. She frantically took him to the emergency ward of a hospital. There, she demanded to know why he would not stop bleeding. Finally, Richard needed a dozen stitches and would have to limp through his performances for the next two weeks.

After learning of his medical condition, Elizabeth did her own research and learned that vitamin K is helpful in bringing on faster coagulation of the blood. From that time onward, she always made certain that a supply of vitamin K was on hand at all times.

"You cannot keep this a secret any longer," Elizabeth told Richard. "I've learned that there are more than a hundred thousand sufferers in the United States alone." At the time of this conversation, Elizabeth and Richard were dining with Hugh French and Marie Bentkover at Sardi's in New York. "I think you should go public with it."

Richard was hesitant. "I'm afraid it makes me look weak," he said.

She leaned over and touched his face. "It makes you look *human*, darling. We can help people. We should do something."

Dr. Richard Rosenfeld, who was a staffer at New York's Mt. Sinai Hospital at the time and was director of the Mt. Sinai Blood Bank, recalled, "Elizabeth and Richard learned that Mercedes McCambridge had the disease and had been very active in raising funds for it. In talking to her, they decided they had to do something, as well. In the sixties, it really was still an unmentionable disease. People had suffered through many centuries of misunderstanding and hiding of it. The Burtons wanted to drag it out of the closet and bring knowledge and understanding about it to the public."

As a foreshadowing of her very important work with AIDS in years to come, Elizabeth contacted the National Hemophilia Foundation and asked what she and Richard could do in terms of fund-raising for public awareness of hemophilia. Shortly there-after, they started the Richard Burton Hemophilia Fund. Dr. Rosenfeld served as chairman of the medical advisory board of the foundation's New York City chapter. Elizabeth was chairman of the fund, and very passionate about it. They raised hundreds of thousands of dollars through public appearances and different galas. They were even cited in the House of Representatives on June 17, 1964, for their work.

"Stars of the entertainment world have brought comfort to the handicapped, the sick and the lonely," said Congressman James G. O'Hara (D-MI) as he read his statement into the *Congressional Record*. "Hemophilia needs attention, and Mr. and Mrs. Burton are responding in the finest traditions of their profession when they associate themselves with the effort to conquer this terrible illness. Their efforts may help speed these developments and earn thereby the thanks of thousands of American families."

"Even Our Fights Are Fun"

In the summer of 1964, Elizabeth Taylor found herself working in a very different venue for her, the theater. Philip Burton had asked if she would participate with Richard in a literary evening at the Lunt-Fontanne to raise funds for his American Musical and Dramatic Academy of New York. The program, titled "World Enough and Time," involved the Burtons reading excerpts from the works of D. H. Lawrence, Shakespeare, Elizabeth Barrett Browning, Edwin Markham, and, oddly but maybe also appropriately, John Lennon of the Beatles. Elizabeth rehearsed for two weeks; she had a tough time with it. Some of the Burtons' friends felt that there was an ulterior motive to Elizabeth's work on the stage at this time. She was always very aware of the kind of education she had at MGM, and it never bothered her much . . . until she was with Burton. She then found herself in some ways feeling intellectually inferior. "I never mind being wrong with Richard because I learn from him and he never treats me like an idiot," she would later write. "He makes me feel an intellectual equal of his, which, of course, I am not."

"He was Higgins and she was Eliza," said Richard's good friend Joe Sirola. "In other words, here's a woman not terribly educated, not a great actress, didn't know the classics, any of that. And here she meets a guy, this theater star, who understood all the classics, could recite them back to you, this great actor. I always sensed that she didn't feel she was his match, intellectually. And the poetry and all of that was sort of trying to compensate, at least that's how I viewed it at the time."

It's also true that Elizabeth was often afraid of boring Richard. She and a tutor of the children's were walking on a beach in Puerto Vallarta once, and she was talking about her marriage to Richard and how much she loved him. She said, "But I'm afraid I'm going to lose him. I think I bore him. I don't think I'm smart enough." It was a stunning admission.

"It had to be tough on her," says Sirola. "I mean, to the world she was this great star. Privately, she had these insecurities about her value to Richard."

On the big night, she walked onto the stage swathed in pleated white silk, with emerald-and-diamond earrings and a delicate spray of white buds in her hair. It was a star-studded audience that included Carol Channing, Lauren Bacall, Montgomery Clift, and Beatrice Lilly. Elizabeth had barely started when she flubbed her lines. "Oh, I'll have to begin again," she said apologetically. "I screwed it all up." Richard quipped, "This is funnier than *Hamlet*"—which probably did little to assist her. Still, from then on, the audience was with Elizabeth as the underdog in the production. Her reviews the next day were generally positive.

Also at this time, Elizabeth was writing the second of her four books, *Elizabeth Taylor: An Informal Memoir*. (The first had been the children's book *Nibbles and Me*). "Even our fights are fun—nothing placidly bovine about us," she wrote of Burton. "Richard loses his temper with true enjoyment. It's beautiful to watch. Our fights are delightful screaming matches, and Richard is rather like a small atom bomb going off—sparks fly, walls shake, floors vibrate." When writing about the possibility of his cheating on her, she noted, "I would love him enough to love the hurt he might give me and be patient. I have learned that pride is very bad, the kind of pride that makes you say, 'I won't tolerate that.'"

At the end of the year, the Burtons filmed another movie together, their third, *The Sandpiper*. Elizabeth hadn't been in front of a camera in two years, having decided to devote that time to her husband and his career. Also, she would later explain, she could not obtain insurance from a studio due to her many health issues. "I didn't think I could get a job," she said, "so I grabbed *The Sandpiper* and let them pay their million dollars." She also noted that she never thought the film would be "an artistic masterpiece." Work of art or not, once Elizabeth was back in front of the cameras on a soundstage, she couldn't have been happier. The movie began filming in Big Sur, and ended in Paris. All of Elizabeth's children were there with her, including Maria (who had undergone a remarkable rehabilitation by this time, and who also had her own governess and nurse).

After a day of filming, Elizabeth and Richard would customarily have drinks together at the bar of the Lancaster Hotel. One evening, as the Burtons relaxed, three people rushed into the bar, two women and a man. The man began taking photographs and, before Elizabeth and Richard knew what was happening, rushed off. One of the women then began speaking in German, her words tumbling out quickly as she frantically motioned toward her friend. Suddenly, it hit Elizabeth: *The woman's friend was Maria's birth mother.* "Is this [she said the woman's name]?" Elizabeth asked. "Yes, this is her," admitted her friend. "I'm going to interpret for her." Elizabeth and Richard then realized that Maria's mother had been brought to them for a tabloid photo opportunity. Taylor was enraged. "You're no friend of hers," she screamed at the woman. "You're a journalist. And I'm going to kill you if you don't get out of here, now!"

"No. I *am* a friend of hers," the woman protested.

"Leave!" Richard bellowed. The woman ran from the room, leaving Maria's distressed natural mother with the Burtons. Elizabeth took her by the arm and urged her to sit.

Luckily, the Burtons' trusted attorney and good friend, Aaron Frosch—who spoke German—happened to be coming by the hotel to meet with them. Slowly the story unfolded. Apparently the editors of a gossip magazine in France had contacted Maria's natural mother in Germany and told her that the Taylors wanted to have a face-to-face meeting with her. She believed them, and that's why she was in France. Actually, it was all a ruse so that the publication could obtain photographs of Maria's poor natural mother in the same room with her rich adopted mother for a sensational story.

"Elizabeth felt awful about it," said Marie Bentkover. "She realized that these people's lives were forever changed by having an association with her. Elizabeth and Richard bought the woman a plane ticket so that she could return to Germany."

The next morning found the Burtons back on the set of *The Sandpiper*. Elizabeth had chosen Vincente Minnelli, who had guided her when she was still in her teens in two of her most successful early films, *Father of the Bride* and *Father's Little Dividend*, to direct the film, in which Elizabeth portrays an artist who has a complicated affair with an Episcopal minister, played by Richard. Elizabeth had wanted Sammy Davis Jr., whom she had recently befriended in New York, to essay the role of the man she leaves for the Burton character, but producer Martin Ransohoff felt the idea was "too ahead of its time, though it would surely have caused quite a sensation having Taylor and Davis involved in a romance on the screen in the 1960s." Future action star Charles Bronson ended up with the role.

When *The Sandpiper* was finally released in 1965, fans stormed Radio City Music Hall in New York for the premiere, to see Elizabeth on the screen for the first time in two years. The movie's theme, "The Shadow of Your Smile," became a hit record for Tony Bennett and remains a popular standard even today. The film was a box-office smash, bringing in more than $10 million. If nothing else, it validated the commerciality of its stars because, in truth, the movie suffered from a weak story that an even weaker script could not overcome. Despite brisk ticket sales, the Burtons knew they had made what Elizabeth later referred to as "a real turkey." When she received one lone good review for her performance in it, she quipped, "How dare that writer! I'm suing for libel."

Elizabeth Apologizes to Debbie

On the way to Paris on the *Queen Elizabeth 2* for filming of *The Sandpiper* there, Elizabeth was surprised to run into, of all people, Debbie Reynolds. It's a story Debbie loves to tell:

"Harry [Karl, whom she married after her divorce from Eddie Fisher] and I were about to leave for our vacation when we got a call from a columnist saying, 'Guess what? Elizabeth and Richard are going to be on the same cruise ship as you and Harry. How fabulous is that?' Well, I thought, we have to go by air, of course, or cancel the whole thing because, otherwise, it would be too much of a circus. Why, the media will eat us alive if Elizabeth and I are on the same ship. But, no, Harry said we should do it, and I had to agree. I really did not hold any animosity toward Elizabeth, though I hadn't spoken to her since, well, *before* the scandal happened, actually.

"So when we got onto the ship we found that there were six gigantic suites for, you know, big shots. Harry and I were in one of the suites, happy as clams, thinking, Goodness, this is big. The other five suites? Elizabeth and Richard, of course, and their entourage and their luggage and their animal cages and the birdcages and their . . . *lives*. I immediately sent a note to the Burtons' suite, one of them, anyway, and it said, 'Look, this is so silly. We should just meet and get it over with.' Our notes had crossed in the hallway! I no sooner sent mine when fifteen seconds later I got one from her saying the exact same thing.

"It was decided that we would meet in my and Harry's suite. That night, there was a knock on the door and I opened it and it was Elizabeth and Richard, she looking gorgeous and he looking rather amused by the whole thing. We talked a bit, and it was then that Elizabeth said to me, 'Listen, Debbie, I am so very sorry for the trouble I caused you. I don't know what I was thinking with Eddie Fisher. I mean, really? *Eddie Fisher?* I hate what I did to you. Truly.' I told her, 'Well, it's over now, Elizabeth. Let's just forget it and enjoy our cruise. I mean, you have five suites, we have one . . . how bad can things be? We laughed and got out the champagne and had a toast. 'Look how we lucked out,' Elizabeth said, clicking my glass. 'Who cares about Eddie Fisher anyway?'

"Then we went downstairs. Well, my God, you would have thought it was the Second Coming when we walked into that dining room, all those photographers hiding behind potted palms, patrons standing on their chairs for a good look at us. The four of us sat down and had a marvelous dinner despite it. Then Elizabeth had to go to the ladies' room and I went with her, as girls do. Fifty women rose from their tables and followed us. I was standing in line holding her purse with those women behind me. As soon as Elizabeth got into the stall, they started chattering at me, saying, 'How could you be here with her? I have never forgiven her for what she did to you. That homewrecker.' And I thought, well, I may have moved on but these women certainly haven't. I turned to one of them and said, 'My dear, there is no friendship so close as two women who detest the same man.' They all laughed. Then Elizabeth came out and took my purse, and I went into the stall. Who knows what they then said to her? All I know is that on our way back to the dining room, I whispered into Elizabeth's ear, 'Did those women talk about me?' and Elizabeth said, 'Oh, yes. I got an earful, all right. Apparently, they love me but aren't quite as fond of you.' We just had to laugh."

Who's Afraid of Virginia Woolf?

*A*rguably, the Burtons' greatest film achievement is their 1966 version of Edward Albee's *Who's Afraid of Virginia Woolf? The Sandpiper* hadn't done much good for the couple, other than financially, but it was responsible for their having met Ernest Lehman, writer of such films as *Sweet Smell of Success*, *North by Northwest*, and *Somebody Up There Likes Me*. Having recently completed the screenplay for *The Sound of Music*, Lehman had set his sights on the Tony Award–winning Edward Albee play. The four-character story involves the combative and often poisonous relationship between George, an associate professor of history, and Martha, his wife, the daughter of the president of the small New England college where George teaches. The film's action takes place over a single drunken and troubling night when the couple entertains campus newcomers Nick and Honey (played by George Segal and Sandy Dennis). When playwright Albee sold the film rights of the play to Warner Bros., he said the studio promised that the leads would be played by Bette Davis and James Mason, and, as he recently told Barbara Hoffman in the *New York Post*, "I was very surprised when it turned out to be Burton and Taylor."

The play is considered a black comedy, but there is tragedy lurking in practically every line. This is not so much a "battle of the sexes" as it is, as George rhetorically says to his wife late in the story, "Total war, Martha?" She spits at him, "Total!" *Virginia Woolf* today is almost painful to watch—a little like watching someone tear the wings off a butterfly—but oddly compelling, the viewer squirming in his seat in uneasy fascination, wondering what these two bitter, foul-mouthed dipsomaniacs will do or say next to humiliate each other (and their young guests, too, as it develops).

Elizabeth has said that she had a difficult time imagining herself as the character of Martha, not only because of the age difference between her and the character, but also because "I couldn't imagine myself dominating Richard." The script was so challenging, Elizabeth said, that her first read of it made her feel as if she had never acted before in her life. Neither she nor Richard had ever seen *Virginia Woolf* on the stage, so their interpretation of the roles would be uniquely them. The way Elizabeth explained her character sounded as if she were describing someone else—herself: "Her veneer is bawdy. It's sloppy. It's slouchy, it's snarly. But there are moments when the façade cracks and you see the vulnerability, the infinite pain of this woman inside whom, years ago, life almost died but is still flickering."

It seems that the Burtons' decision to bring Mike Nichols to Hollywood as the director of *Virginia Woolf* was a well-considered and, as it turned out, very shrewd one. By 1965, Nichols was *the* director in the Broadway theater. After a successful career as the partner of Elaine May writing and performing stand-up, he made his directing debut in 1963 in Neil Simon's monster hit *Barefoot in the Park*, which ran for nearly four years and earned Nichols his first Tony Award. He followed the next year with *Luv*, another huge success, and another Tony. *The Odd Couple* was his third show, his third hit, and his third Tony—all in three short years. With *Virginia Woolf*, Nichols would become as much a fixture and a presence in films as he had been and would continue to be in the New York theater.

Elizabeth would be paid $1.1 million for the film, Richard $750,000. She also received her now standard 10 percent of the profits. In the end, the Burtons cleared more than $6 million on this movie.

"Working together on the film was probably their best experience together in terms of their careers," says Diane Stevens, who worked for John Springer on the West Coast as a consultant to his growing public relations business. Springer, based in New York, was Elizabeth's very famous PR man who started working for them in early 1964. He'd represented luminaries like Judy Garland and Marilyn Monroe. "I spent many days on that set, and I can tell you that it was truly a collaborative effort between the Burtons, Nichols and writer-producer Ernest Lehman [who died in 2005]. It was Mike Nichols's and Rich Burton's idea, for instance, that [Elizabeth] lower the key of her speaking voice for greater effect. She was eager to take direction from Burton, never felt insulted or in any way demeaned by him when he offered direction to her. Rich, Elizabeth, and Ernest worked out the slow disintegration of the characters and modulated the performances so that they could get the most out of them in terms of pacing and storytelling. I would see the three of them huddled together in a corner, working on ideas.

"To see Rich and Elizabeth create together, focused on their chosen professions, was always a fascinating experience because I was so used to seeing them drinking or fighting or having fun. Richard told me that they felt they had the most freedom with those two roles, to do with them what they wanted, to really throw caution to the wind, as he said, and 'let 'er rip.'"

For Elizabeth, playing the role of the tormented Martha, a dowdy, blowzy character in her mid-forties, was a challenge unlike any other in her career. She gained twenty-five pounds for the part, which, she had to admit, was not difficult and, in fact, "rather delightful." The acerbic personality of the character, along with the combative relationship she had with her husband, probably wasn't as much of a stretch for Elizabeth to convey as she said it was in press interviews. It was very true that the Burtons had begun playing aspects of their relationship on the screen, first in *The Sandpiper*, then in *Virgina Woolf* and, in the following year, *The Taming of the Shrew*. Though they would say publicly that their roles as battling spouses were a caricature of who they were to each other offscreen, it really wasn't true. In fact, in their private lives the Burtons were not unaccustomed to the kinds of venomous exchanges in which George and Martha engaged on film.

Diane Stevens recalled, "I walked in on a major row during a break in filming the movie. Just as I entered Rich's dressing room, Elizabeth hurled a vase at him. He ducked, and it almost hit me. It crashed into pieces on the floor, and instead of apologizing, she reached for an empty pitcher and threw *that* at him, without even acknowledging that I had entered the room. 'You bastard,' she screamed at him. He ducked again. Then he picked up a fruit bowl and threw it at her. She ducked. I closed my eyes. I couldn't bear to look at the scene. Then I realized that I was standing in the middle of a war zone with dishes and glasses flying about, and me with my eyes closed. So I got the hell out of there. Fifteen minutes later, they emerged holding hands."

There are many memories of the Burtons during this time, some of which aren't very complimentary:

Diane Stevens: "Rich was becoming more miserable, I think, by all of the drama of being the costar of the Elizabeth Taylor story. Cognac in the morning. Vodka and tonic in the afternoon. Scotch and vodka at night."

James Bacon: "It was day and night, the drinking. It was bad. It brought out the worst in both of them, him more than her, I think."

Liz Smith: "I saw him misbehaving to her and even misbehaving to me. If you got him after lunch in the afternoon, he could really be quite mean."

Stefan Verkaufen, Francis Taylor's friend: "The family was concerned at this time that Elizabeth had found in Burton the alcoholic she had in her father, and they believed Burton's on-set drinking on *Virginia Woolf* was inspiring her to drink more to keep up with him."

Rose Marie Armocida, secretary to the Burtons' publicist, John Springer: "One of the reasons it was a closed set was because Elizabeth and Richard were having so many quarrels, and we just didn't want that out to the press. So they closed the set. It was just easier than taking a chance on the wrong people stumbling onto them in full fight mode."

It wasn't just alcohol that was a problem for Elizabeth, it was also her growing dependency on painkillers. She was in constant pain from her back problems, and there was no getting around it. She needed the drugs. Diane Stevens tells this story:

"I remember at one point sending a telegram at Elizabeth's direction to Doctors Carl Goldman and Victor Ratner in London. It just said, 'Urgent. Send pink pills at once. Elizabeth.' She didn't know the names of the pills she was taking, she only knew that she couldn't survive without them. Later, Dr. Goldman called me to say, 'Just for your information, the pink pills are Diconal, and they are on their way.' At the time, he told me it was one of the most powerful painkillers in the world. She was in agony during *Virginia Woolf*."

In the end, despite all of the melodrama that surrounded its making, *Who's Afraid of Virginia Woolf?* is considered a masterpiece by most film scholars. The film also proved a financial windfall for Warner Bros. It was nominated for thirteen Academy Awards, winning five, including a second one for Elizabeth Taylor. The film was also nominated, as was director Mike Nichols, writer Ernest Lehman, and Richard Burton, with all coming up empty. This slight to Nichols was rectified the following year when he took home the Best Director Oscar for *The Graduate*. Burton would turn in many Oscar-worthy performances for the remainder of his film career but would never win the statuette.

What little hope one gets from staying with the film for all of its two hours and nine minutes is saved for the very last minutes, when with the guests gone and the dawn breaking, George gently massages Martha's neck and shoulder, and beseeches her to come upstairs to bed. She touches his hand with hers as the camera moves in for a close-up of her hand on his and "The End" is superimposed on the shot. The relationship between the protagonists is never fully resolved and the viewer is left with a numbing sense of despair, almost certain that on some future Saturday night, George and Martha, and perhaps a couple of guests, will be going at it again tooth and nail.

Bad Movies, Great Riches, and Another Oscar

As the 1960s were drawing to a close and Elizabeth Taylor faced the relentless march of time, the inevitability of her approaching fourth decade suggested that her days as an ingénue were now a thing of the past. Leading-lady roles would give way to character parts, though *starring* character parts, to be sure. While she and Richard made movies together during these years, they also continued with their individual careers.

One of Richard's films was *Doctor Faustus*, an odd movie in which Elizabeth played Helen of Troy in a practically, if not completely, nonspeaking role. Also at this time, Elizabeth filmed *Reflections in a Golden Eye*, with Marlon Brando playing a part originally intended for Montgomery Clift. When the studio would not insure Clift because of his problems with drugs and alcohol, Elizabeth put up the insurance herself. However, Monty died at just forty-six from occlusive coronary artery disease before the movie went into production.

Elizabeth's roles in *Woolf*, *Shrew*, and *Reflections* were pretty much the same kind of harridan character, just placed in three different time periods. Elizabeth as "shrew" Katharina—"Kate"—in *The Taming of the Shrew* was a sight to behold in her teased-out wig and cinched bodice, bitterly spewing her lines and going up against Burton's Petruchio in much the way she would rail against the actor, her husband, in the privacy of their home. Not that they weren't entertaining. Franco Zeffirelli recalled the following exchange while the Burtons were rehearsing a scene in which Richard had Elizabeth pinned down. "Here I am, with six inches of fused spine," Elizabeth complained, "expected to push this baby elephant [Richard] off me."

Actor Michael York made his debut in *The Taming of the Shrew*. He recalls, "On my first day, I remember thinking, 'My God! These are the kings and queens of Hollywood, and at the top of their profession.' There was an overwhelming sense of glamour about them, intensified by the way they lived, you know, with their dressing rooms with dazzling white carpets and all of their butlers and maids, and so on . . . the Rolls-Royces, the jewels. They behaved like movie stars; old-fashioned movie stars. But I also found them to be enormously kind. There was also a sense of family. For instance, whenever her children were around, they were popped into costume, and then onto the set as extras."

In retrospect, none of the films the Burtons made during this time did them much justice. Most were bad choices, as if their excessively bad personal habits had caused them to also have poor judgment when it came to choosing scripts. Moreover, Elizabeth had other reasons behind her wrong-minded career decisions. As demonstrated earlier in her profession, she had little sense of her self-worth, no doubt due to her lost childhood. She rarely realized her value as an actress and was therefore always prone to making bad career choices. Now that she was not under the creative thumb of a studio, as she had been at MGM as a young woman, and could do what she pleased, her decisions were still not good ones. Richard, for his part, just went along with his wife. Together they were like the proverbial blind leading the blind, right into mediocrity.

It was probably with Tennessee Williams's *Boom!* that the Burtons hit their creative nadir. The plot concerned wealthy writer "Sissy Goforth" (Elizabeth), who lives with servants and nurses on a Mediterranean island. Her days consist of dictating her autobiography and begging for injections. Burton plays the "Angel of Death" and, as such, recites such deathless lines from Samuel Taylor Coleridge as, "In Xanadu did Kubla Khan/A stately pleasure-dome decree:/Where Alph, the sacred river, ran/Through caverns measureless to man/Down to a sunless sea." As any high school student of English literature knows, the poem came to Coleridge in an opium-induced dream. One interesting fact about *Boom!*, however, is that Elizabeth's brother, Howard, had a small walk-on role in it as the bearded skipper. As it happened, the actor who was supposed to play the role didn't show up for work. Howard, Mara, and the children were visiting Elizabeth and Richard on location, and Elizabeth prevailed upon him to take the part as a lark.

A few years later, in 1972, Elizabeth would make *X, Y & Zee*, a decidedly offbeat tragicomedy. The plot had something to do with a woman named Zee (Taylor) who finds out her husband (Michael Caine) is having an affair with a widow (Susannah York). When her husband leaves her, she attempts suicide. In the end, though, she somehow ends up in a lesbian complication with her husband's girlfriend.

Tom Gates happened to be in Rome just after the film was finished. He recalls, "John Springer had suggested that I try to say hello to Elizabeth, so I dropped off a letter at the Grand Hotel wishing her well. Later that afternoon there was a knock on my door by the old woman who ran the *pensione* telling me that "a

Mrs. Burton" was on the phone for me. I rushed to the phone and, amazingly enough, it was Elizabeth. She said that she had just received my note and wanted to invite me to a small private screening of *X, Y & Zee* that very evening. I went, and she couldn't have been nicer. The first thing she did was introduce me to the other people there—none of whom I knew except for Richard Burton—and then she mussed my hair and said, 'God, he has been such a pest in New York. He photographs my every move!' I ended up sitting in the same row as the Burtons for the screening and was fascinated watching Elizabeth watching herself on the screen. Very often she would howl with laughter—sometimes putting her hands up to her face or whispering something to Richard. I found it so amazing that she would extend an invitation to such a private affair to someone who was basically a fan, always with camera in hand. But I think it may have been a sort of reward for *not* taking her picture. You see, some time earlier, I had my little Brownie Starflash camera ready to capture her exit from her limo in front of the Regency Hotel. But, much to my surprise, she emerged crying . . . very unhappy about something. I put my camera down, not wanting to snap her picture while she was so upset. Her chauffeur walked her inside and then returned to say, 'Elizabeth asked me to thank you for not taking her picture when you saw how upset she was. She also said that it was awfully late for you to be out and asked me to drive you home.' Naturally, I thought I was dreaming. But that scenario repeated itself many times over the years, me taking 'good night' photos of her as she returned to whatever hotel she was staying at after an evening out and Joe, her chauffeur, then driving me home. In the backseat was usually some little treasure that I was convinced she left for me; a theater program or monogrammed handkerchief, or even a pack of cigarettes. *Wow*, I'd think, *Elizabeth Taylor smokes Salems*. It was all a very puppy-love, high-school-crush sort of thing."

The Burtons would also film an adaptation of Dylan Thomas's *Under Milk Wood* (with Taylor in another very small role), and *Hammersmith Is Out*, a farce in which Burton plays the devil, who, to prove his powers, makes Elizabeth—a waitress—a movie star. They both look fairly blitzed in every shot of *Hammersmith Is Out.* Elizabeth would seem a lot more coherent in *Ash Wednesday*— slim and beautiful, actually—but the plot, about an aging woman who has plastic surgery to hang on to her husband (played by Henry Fonda), is a bit hackneyed. However, despite the movie's shortcomings, her performance in it is admirable and reminded a lot of people that she could still act. By this time (1973), Richard was, apparently, annoyed by his wife's career and not willing to even be polite about it. "I sit here vulgarized by the idea that my wife is doing—violently against my taste—a fucking lousy nothing bloody film," he wrote to two of his employees about *Ash Wednesday.* "ET's singular acceptance of this film is because she wants to remain a famous film star. What the stupid [occasionally] maniac doesn't realize is that she is already immortalized [as a film person] forever."

These movies, no matter how bad, generally turned a profit. The Burtons put up their own money for *The Taming of the Shrew,* deferring their salaries and making a huge, multimillion-dollar profit on box-office and distribution receipts. The couple had to make these films, actually, just to keep up their lifestyle. Such good fortune afforded the Burtons the wherewithal to continue living the Good Life, which for her consisted of wild shopping sprees, especially for precious jewels. Her favorite is still the Krupp diamond. It had been owned by Vera Krupp of the famous munitions family, some of whom were charged at Nuremberg with the deportation of concentration camp inmates to be used as forced labour. "When it came up for auction in the late 1960s," she has explained, "I thought how perfect it would be if a nice Jewish girl like me were to own it."

To see the Krupp up close—33.19 carats, for which Richard paid $305,000 when he bought it for his wife on May 16, 1968, from Parke-Bernet Galleries in New York—is to behold probably the most amazing diamond in the world. It shimmers as if it's actually alive, with every color of the rainbow. It's still Elizabeth's most prized possession . . . her "baby," as she calls it. As much as she treasures it, though, people who know her well have to laugh at the number of times she's misplaced it. She's left it on the sinks of ladies' rooms all over the world. Luckily, she or someone else has always managed to retrieve it before it would be lost forever.

Of course, during her years with Richard, Elizabeth received a great deal of eye-popping jewelry from him. Among the most famous of the lot was the Taylor-Burton diamond, formerly the Cartier diamond (69.42 carats), for which Richard would pay $1.1 million). So large was this stone, which had been discovered in the South African Premiere mine in 1966, Elizabeth eventually decided to stop wearing it as a ring. Instead, she had Cartier design a V-shaped necklace of graduated pear-shaped diamonds, mounted in platinum, from which it would gracefully dangle. "Richard knew everything there was to know about jewelry," Elizabeth says. "The more he learned about the background and history of a piece, the more fascinated he became with it. He actually appreciated fine jewelry every bit as much as I did. It gave him such joy to see the expression on my face when he would present me with something he had spent hours selecting just for me."

Another of the fantastic gifts was the La Peregrina pearl, which Richard would acquire at an auction at Parke-Bernet Galleries for $37,000. It has a remarkable backstory. A slave discovered it in the Gulf of Panama in the 1500s and gave it to his master in exchange for his freedom. Eventually it somehow found itself a part of the Spanish royal jewels; Spain's Prince Philip II presented it to Mary Tudor of England as a gift to commemorate their engagement. It was later owned by Spanish queens Margaret and Isabella, and also belonged to the Bonaparte family in the early 1800s. Then, as was the case with many a rare gem, it ended up in Elizabeth's vast collection, courtesy of Richard's largesse. It's one of the world's best examples of a classic pear-shaped pearl; there truly is nothing quite like it. Tom Gates observes, "There have always been rumors that Elizabeth used the pearl as a dog toy, and that it actually has teeth marks on it! But when it was on exhibit at New

York's Museum of Natural History, I asked someone at the museum about the story and together we examined it and: no teeth marks. Another Taylor rumor put to rest!"

Later, for a birthday, Elizabeth would receive another generous gift from Richard: a Persian necklace made in 1627 for Nur Jahan, wife of the emperor Jahangir (who was the father of Shah Jahan). Richard said he'd wanted to buy her the Taj Mahal, but it was too big to squeeze into their chalet in Gstaad. The Burtons first saw the antique necklace during a layover at Kennedy Airport. Elizabeth says that in order to help them bide their time during the wait, "Cartier kindly managed to bring some jewelry out to the airport to show us while we waited for our connection."

Many decades later, Elizabeth Taylor would look back on this time with a sense of appreciation. "When I think about the sixties," she says, "I'm glad that I knew the wildness, glamour, and excitement when I was in my prime: the parties, the yachts, and the private jets and the jewelry. It was a great time to be young, alive and attractive and to have all those goodies. I enjoyed it."

Probably the biggest regret of this time for Elizabeth Taylor was the 1967 Oscar disappointment of *Who's Afraid of Virginia Woolf?*—and not that the Burtons both lost when nominated, because, as it happened, one of them won! Because of Richard's vast insecurity, however, neither he nor Elizabeth attended the awards ceremony.*

Elizabeth had been nominated four times in the past—*Raintree County*; *Cat on a Hot Tin Roof*; *Suddenly, Last Summer*; and *Butterfield 8*—and won once, for *Butterfield 8*. Richard had been nominated four times—*My Cousin Rachel*, *The Robe*, *Becket*, and *The Spy Who Came in from the Cold*—losing each time. When both were nominated for *Woolf*, he refused to attend the ceremony, he

---

* *Virginia Woolf* remains the only film in Academy history to be nominated in every eligible category: thirteen eligible categories/thirteen nominations: Picture, Actor, Actress, Supporting Actor, Supporting Actress, Director, Adapted Screenplay, Art Direction/Set Decoration (B&W), Cinematography (B&W), Sound, Costume Design (B&W), Music Score, and Film Editing.

said, because he couldn't bear to be passed up a fifth time. Elizabeth was ambivalent. She was of a mind not to attend. However, when her friends urged her to go, she relented. She had Dior design a gown for the occasion and she planned to attend alone.

Days before the ceremony, though, Burton began drinking heavily in London, where the couple was staying at the time, sinking ever deeper into depression. Finally, just hours before Elizabeth was scheduled to leave for Los Angeles, he asked her not to go. He said he'd had a nightmare that her plane crashed and she died. He was in such a desperate condition, she grudgingly agreed to stay with him. She then sent her regrets to the Academy of Motion Pictures Arts and Sciences. "We've almost never been separated," Elizabeth explained. "He gets into a terrible state when I'm away, especially when he gets tanked up. And he's my *husband*. How can I leave him if he wants me to stay?" Jack Warner sent her a cable back: "Do not burn the bridges you have built."

Warner's cable didn't mean much to Elizabeth, and in fact it annoyed her. She'd been in show business for many years and certainly didn't need his advice about "burning bridges." She was *Elizabeth Taylor*, after all—not some new starlet who needed to be concerned about studio politics. The more she thought about it, as she recalled it later, the more she realized she was right to not attend. Between herself and Burton, she was the bigger star, and she knew it. She didn't need to advertise it to the world by showing up alone. Besides, Richard became more distraught with each passing day about possibly being overlooked by the Academy. The more he dwelled on it, the deeper he fell into a state of depression, or, as Elizabeth once defined his dark moods, "like a whirlpool of black molasses, carrying him down, down, down."

"Look, there's no guarantee she will win anyway," Richard said, in a somewhat hollow justification for his behavior. "She could fly all the way, and then lose."

Of course, as fate would have it, Elizabeth *did* win the Oscar; Anne Bancroft accepted on her behalf. Richard lost; the Best Actor winner was Paul Scofield. No doubt, had the couple attended and the circumstances unfolded as they did, it would have been a dreadful night for Richard. Years earlier, he and Scofield had been friends in London. It was Scofield's first nomination, and the fact that he won would have most certainly sent Richard over the edge. Still, it was a shame that Elizabeth, who deserved much acclaim for her performance, could not be present to accept her second Academy Award just because her husband couldn't handle losing one. Instead, that evening the Burtons had a few friends over for dinner, never even mentioning the Oscars. In fact, Elizabeth didn't even know she had won until the next morning.

"Francis L. Taylor— All Our Love—1897–1968"

On November 20, 1968, Richard Burton took an emotional telephone call from Sara Taylor, telling him that Elizabeth's father, Francis, had died in his sleep. He was seventy-two. He'd not been in good health for some time; he had suffered a stroke in 1965 and another in 1967.

Though Francis had a difficult, challenging life, he had gotten through it with the greatest of dignity. He would leave very few people, if indeed any at all, who would have an unkind observation to make about him, and what greater legacy is there than that? True, he had not always been the ideal father. However, it wasn't because he didn't care, and it wasn't because he hadn't tried. On some level, Elizabeth and Howard seemed to understand, even if they'd both been disappointed in him from time to time. In more recent decades, however, Francis was always at his daughter's side when she most needed support: when she lost Mike Todd in the plane crash, when she had her tracheotomy, and, truly, in the midst of seemingly countless other times of melodrama. Though she felt neglected as a child, certainly as an adult she must have known that Francis tried to be a good father. Still, their communication was always strained and never quite what either of them truly wanted for each other. But there was always more time—or at least that's how it seemed. Shortly before her father's death, Elizabeth had planned a family reunion aboard the Burtons' yacht, *Kalizma*. Her plan was that everyone would be there to spend the Christmas holidays of 1968. It wasn't to be.

Elizabeth and Richard immediately made plans to fly to Hollywood for the funeral. At this time, Elizabeth was in a weakened state due to a recent operation that had been most difficult for her. She'd been forced to undergo a partial hysterectomy in September due to medical conditions that had developed after the birth of her last child, Liza. She already knew that she and Richard could not have children due to the tubal ligation she'd undergone after that birth, but still she couldn't help but hope, as she would tell it, that something might be able to be done for her. Now, with this new surgery, she was sure never again to have children, and this time she knew there was no chance of the situation ever being reversed. It was difficult for her to accept—she referred to the surgery as "the destruction of my womanhood." Since she was already so emotionally taxed from this event, Francis's death felt to her, as she would recall it, like more than she could bear. Though she had been prepared for his passing for some time, the news still took her by surprise. She had a complete breakdown, or, as Richard put it, "She was like a wild animal."

Still, Elizabeth showed surprising strength and composure during the flight to Los Angeles and then during the simple funeral service conducted by a Christian Science reader at Westwood Village Mortuary. With Richard beside her whispering that she must remain strong for her mother, Elizabeth was able to turn her attention to her deeply grieving parent.

On the short limousine ride to Francis's gravesite, Elizabeth and her mother sat mostly without speaking. At the service, they were pensive, until Elizabeth broke the silence, according to Marshall Baldrige, Francis's trusted friend from London, who was, of course, at the service.

"I should have spent more time with him," Elizabeth announced.

Sara said, "He would have liked that."

Those few words seemed to affect Elizabeth deeply; her strength and resolve began to crumble. She began to cry.

Her mother looked at her. "But I'm not crying, dear," Sara said plainly.

Elizabeth wasn't sure what she meant by her comment.

Sara continued, "If a man's widow isn't crying it isn't good form for others to do so. It makes me seem unfeeling."

"This late in Sara's life, she was still considering public opinion of paramount concern," observed Baldrige.

Francis was buried in the Sanctuary of Peace section of Westwood Memorial Park. The small golden plaque on the site reads: "Francis L. Taylor—All Our Love—1897–1968."

At the gravesite, Baldrige saw firsthand Sara's cool composure, and Elizabeth's attempts to keep her own in check. "I went to speak to Elizabeth, and she grabbed both of my hands very urgently and said, 'You knew him so well. Do you think he was happy? Do you think he lived a good life?' She seemed anxious to try to tie up loose ends where Francis was concerned. 'I know he loved you very much,' I told her. 'He always wanted the best for you.' Listening to this, she was emotional, very upset. 'Oh, how I wish we had more time,' she said.

"I wanted to say more to her, but Sara came and took her by the arm. 'There are a lot of people here you need to see,' she told Elizabeth, pulling her from me. It was there, for the first time in all of those years, I realized that Sara didn't much like me. She realized that I knew a lot about the inner workings of her family, and she didn't think that was appropriate.

" 'I'm so sorry about Francis,' I told Sara as she was walking away with Elizabeth. She turned to me and said, 'Yes, I'm sure you are.' It was chilly and upsetting. Then, as Elizabeth walked away on the arm of her mother, she turned to me and mouthed the words, 'Thank you.' "

"Learning from Each Other"

By the end of the 1960s, it was clear that Elizabeth and Richard had truly begun to plummet to the depths of alcoholism, even if they didn't recognize it at the time. Their drinking continued in a way that can only be described as out of control. Moreover, they continued to make career choices based on codependent decisions. For instance, in *The Comedians*, Elizabeth took a small role because Richard had told her that Sophia Loren might play the part. Elizabeth wasn't keen on the idea of Sophia having romantic scenes with her husband—plus, she just wanted to be with Richard. She also couldn't bear to be away from him when he filmed *Staircase* in Europe. She therefore asked that her movie *The Only Game in Town* (with Warren Beatty) be mostly filmed in Paris, despite its Las Vegas setting. The studio reluctantly agreed and, doing so, had to beef up the budget to re-create American streetscapes, casinos, apartments, and supermarkets in Paris. In the end (after eighty-six shooting days in Paris), the company moved to Las Vegas for ten final days of shooting at Caesar's Palace.

She managed to complete *The Only Game in Town*, but only while wrenched with unbearable back pain. Everything possible was being done to support her damaged spine—corset braces, tape bindings, therapy—but it seemed as if nothing worked. The pain was unrelenting and she would just have to learn to live with it.

In the third week of May 1969, the Burtons left Puerto Vallarta for London for the filming of *Anne of the Thousand Days*. For many weeks, Richard was supposed to have been preparing for this historical potboiler in which he was to play King Henry VIII. Every day in Puerto Vallarta, Elizabeth would retrieve the 144-page script, place it in front of him, and say, "Now read this, and learn it." He would spend ten minutes on it and toss it aside. Though he didn't want to do the movie, and regretted ever having signed on for it, Elizabeth didn't want to hear about it. "You signed a contract and we're going to England in one week," she had said. "I am going to stay on your ass until you learn this goddamn script." (Elizabeth took an uncredited bit part as a courtesan just to keep an eye on Richard, a part for which she was paid forty-seven dollars!)

Richard suffered from insomnia for the entire shoot and started taking sleeping pills ("Junkie Burton has finally arrived," he wrote in his diary on May 22). During some weeks, he drank to excess, staying up all night and then arriving late at the studio for work. In other weeks, he stopped and, during these times, couldn't even stand the smell of vodka. With Burton it was one extreme or the other. There was no moderation where he was concerned. It was always all . . . or nothing.

Richard explained that the reason he drank so much while making movies was "to burn up the flatness—the stale empty flat, dull, deadness one feels after a scene." If alcohol intake was key to a role's characterization, the more the better. For instance, in *The Spy Who Came in from the Cold*, he played Alec Leamas, a man with a drinking problem. He told a female reporter on the set, "I have lived the life of Alec Leamas most of my life and, I must say, it's very livable. I think I broke all of my own admirable records the other day on the set. I had to knock back a large whiskey, and we did forty-seven takes of that scene. Imagine it, luv, forty-seven whiskeys! Does it get better than that?" He joked that in Mexico, the local bartenders had a drink called the Richard Burton cocktail. "First, you take twenty-one shots of tequila," he joked in describing it. During filming of *The Comedians*, Richard followed the custom he had established on the set of *The Sandpiper*. He ordered sixteen bottles of champagne to be always on ice. If he drank a couple and later opened the refrigerator and saw a mere fourteen ready and waiting, he'd raise what he called a "bloody row."

On a more serious note, Richard remarked that the Burtons found their high-profile lifestyle troubling. "Elizabeth and I both suffer from feelings of insecurity," he noted. "We feel particularly unsure of ourselves when we are at a party because no one really wants to know us. They simply stare as if we are prize animals. What we do when we go to parties is drink to kill the icy isolation."

Still, despite the complexities of their private lives, there was a great advantage to the couple's working together at this time: They grew to truly appreciate each other's work. Richard clearly hated the Hollywood ethos that Elizabeth represented as one of its biggest stars. In turn, she wasn't thrilled about his snobbish attitude about it. Yet they still learned from each other.

From her, he learned about the technique of film acting. As he explained it, "She taught me subtleties in filmmaking that I never knew existed, such as the value of absolute stillness and also that my penetrating voice need not be pitched louder than a telephone conversation. But chiefly she taught me to regard the making of a film as exacting and as serious as playing Shakespeare on the stage. I suppose the major change in my film-acting technique has been affected by Elizabeth. She's the consummate cinematic technician."

He further observed, "Elizabeth is one of the most remarkably talented actresses I've ever worked with. She surprises the devil out of you. If you don't know her and you watch her rehearse, you say, 'Oh dear, here comes nothing.' She goes through rehearsals sort of like a sleepwalker. But when the camera starts whirring, she turns it on, the magic, and you simply can't believe your eyes. She has great power and an uncanny instinct for the right thing."

Elizabeth felt the same about Richard. "Working with Richard is working with the absolute pro," she said. "He gives you the feeling of antennae—a quivering, positive contact. He can turn emotion on and off in seconds, having it under complete control, yet you sense the latent power all the time, like a volcano about to erupt. Nerves are the nemesis of all actors and Richard will do anything at his own expense to put other actors at their ease, even to flubbing his own line or knocking something over—anything so the cut in the film will be his fault. Furthermore," she added, "I know of no other film actor who knows the whole script, everybody's lines, the day before he starts working. I think he's one of the greatest actors, without question, who has ever worked on the screen or in the theater. Unlike so many actors, he's not a stone wall. He gives so much. He has electricity. He speaks verse like prose and his prose sounds like poetry."

In another interview, Elizabeth said of him, "Richard is just like a well: There's no plumbing the depths. You can't describe a volcano erupting. You can't describe the sound of the wind in the trees when there is no wind." In somewhat less poetic words, what she may have been expressing was that he had a volatile temper, and, as anyone who knew them would attest, she was capable of matching it, and on a daily basis.

"I Sometimes Curse the Day . . ."

By the beginning of the 1970s, it had gotten worse between Elizabeth and Richard—the drinking, the insecurities, the fighting . . . all of it. Many of their more public arguments have been chronicled over the years in newspapers, magazines, and books. It would take a volume just to recount them all—and what a tedious volume it would be because, basically, the disagreements were always along the same lines: Both would have too much to drink. One would demand something of the other, not get it, and then throw a fit, maybe a fist, and, at the very least, a glass of liquor. As the months turned into years, the terrible and usually unpredictable temper tantrums between them would leave feelings of resentment that even the passing of time would not be able to erase. Elizabeth would lash out at him physically. Finally, he started hitting her back, at one point damaging her eardrum with a fist to the side of her head.

To be fair, despite their problems it's clear that the Burtons really did love each other and were committed to their relationship, such as it was. Sometimes they were able to see the light. In March 1970, for instance, they were having dinner with friends when the subject of their drinking came up, as it often did in conversation. The couple was not intoxicated . . . at least not yet. Richard pointed to Elizabeth and said, "Now, there's someone who could never give up a drink."

Who knows why his statement touched a nerve? Certainly Richard had said a lot worse about Elizabeth over the years. But for some reason, her temper boiled over. She snapped at him, "You know what? I hate your guts."

"Good God, woman," he said. "I can smell the liquor on your breath all the way over here." He was about six feet away. "You've had too much to drink, tubby," he said. "So bugger off."

Elizabeth turned to their friends and said, "You know what? I wish to Christ he'd just get out of my life."

From there, the scene got worse. By the time it ended, all of the guests at the party had gotten an earful, and it is doubtful they ever forgot a word of it.

Richard later said that he and Elizabeth had often said such things privately to each other when they'd had too much to drink. Never had he imagined it would come to this: "The eyes ablaze with genuine hatred," as he wrote in his diary, "her lovely face becoming ugly with loathing," and all of it in front of friends. The next day, she felt anguish over the breach.

"We're not very nice people, are we?" she asked Richard in front of Dick Hanley and other staff members.

"No, we're not," Richard agreed sadly.

Elizabeth approached him and embraced him tightly. "I only know that without you I would have been dead years ago," she said, now trying to soothe him. "I do love you, honey." She melted into his embrace; he kissed her fully on the lips.

In the midst of their mutual despair, the Burtons had to act cheerful for an appearance on Lucille Ball's sitcom *The Lucy Show*, taped in May 1970. At that time, of course, movie stars like Taylor and Burton did not normally show up on sitcoms like Ball's, but they hoped it would help in the latter's bid for an Oscar for *Anne of the Thousand Days*. Still, Richard made it clear in his diaries that he hated the experience. He was critical of Lucy, demeaning her nineteen years on television as a waste of time for her. He displayed a lack of understanding of the kind of discipline necessary to make a comedy show such as Ball's, in its many incarnations, for so long a time. He didn't understand it, so he ridiculed it. However, it's because of entries like the ones criticizing Lucy that one has to approach Richard's diaries with a certain amount of trepidation, because the truth is that it was actually Richard's idea to do the show. He and Elizabeth had met Lucy and her husband, Gary Morton, at a reception for David Frost at the British consulate. "I adore your show," Richard told the redheaded actress in front of witnesses, including Cecil Smith of the *Los Angeles Times*. "I want to do it." Lucy was speechless. "It's true," confirmed Elizabeth. "He keeps yelling that he wants to do it. Please let him. It's the only way to shut him up." That night, the Burtons hosted the Mortons in their Bungalow 3 at the Beverly Hills Hotel. When the Mortons arrived, the place was swarming with police officers. Lucy actually thought someone had stolen the Krupp diamond! In fact, one of the Burton dogs had gotten lost, and the hotel had called the police to find the mutt. Such was the Burtons' lifestyle. Six weeks later, they appeared on *The Lucy Show*—the numbskull plot being that Lucy tries on Elizabeth's Krupp diamond but then can't get it off her finger. (It was the real thing, too; it cost Ball $1,500 a day to insure the diamond.) Outwardly, Richard had nothing but praise for Lucy the entire time. "She's bloody marvelous," he told Cecil Smith, also present at the taping. So for him to be so critical of the experience in his diary—and he really was mean about it—seems a little disingenuous.

In truth, there were so many levels of psychological chaos at work within Richard Burton causing him to drink that he would have had to have been married to a psychiatrist, not a movie star, in order to have been fully understood. Or, as Elizabeth put it to *Look* magazine in 1963, he was "a snake pit of ramifications."

For instance, Richard still felt tremendous guilt about leaving Sybil and his daughters for Elizabeth, even after all this time. He was also torn about his career, angry about the way it had thus far unfolded for him. Though *Anne of the Thousand Days* had earned eight Oscar nominations, including Picture, Actor (Burton), and Actress (Geneviève Bujold), he was again overlooked on awards night. It had been his sixth nomination and his sixth loss. The movie won only for Costume Design. After Richard's loss, Elizabeth walked onto the stage to give the Best Picture award looking extremely unhappy. She was probably also despairing because she knew what it was going to be like back in their hotel suite later.

It would have meant a lot to Burton to have that one Oscar, especially since he was married to a woman who had two. He could have used the validation. People who knew him well think that he never felt he was as good as everyone else believed. He felt like a fraud and would never have been able to live up to *Olivier's* expectations, anyway. It's a common problem for celebrities to feel they are masquerading as pros when really they're amateurs, and this was one of Richard's issues. What a shame, too, especially considering that he gave some of his best performances while married to Elizabeth, yet he didn't seem to know it. Look at the list:

Becket, The Night of the Iguana, The Spy Who Came in from the Cold, Who's Afraid of Virginia Woolf?, Staircase, and *Anne of the Thousand Days.*

Some close to the couple also felt that it was really all over for Elizabeth, in terms of her marriage, when Richard lost the Oscar for *Anne of the Thousand Days.* It could be overstating it, but it's definitely true that the loss didn't make things any easier for them.

Of course, Richard had his hands full with Elizabeth, too. She was prone to selfishness. Her trenchant tongue could cut any man to size. Her tantrums were the stuff of legend. As is the habit of many child stars, she continued to abdicate all responsibility for her actions, instead blaming her behavior on her youthful fame and on never having had the opportunity to live a "real" life. Her drinking and pill-taking was a real problem, even for Richard.

Michelle Griffin, who was a close friend of Dick Hanley's, recalls what she remembers as "a rare but welcome moment of clarity" for Elizabeth. She was with the Burtons at Frank Sinatra's home in Palm Springs, in May 1970. "Elizabeth had to have a hemorrhoidectomy, which she decided to have at the Palm Springs Desert Hospital rather than in Los Angeles," says Griffin. "It was in an effort to keep it out of the news because she thought it was just too personal to have publicized. The pain was absolutely intolerable, both before and after the surgery. She was miserable. Frank Sinatra had been gracious enough to host the Burtons earlier in the year, and so they asked if they could stay at his compound while she recovered. He said yes, and also flew in her proctologist [Dr. Hyman Swerdlow] from Beverly Hills in the Sinatra private jet, and put him up at the estate as well. [Sinatra was in the Mediterranean at the time, vacationing.] It was me, Dick, Elizabeth, Richard, Dr. Swerdlow, and Elizabeth's mother, Sara."

The surgery was completed successfully—but, as was often the case after an invasive surgical procedure, Taylor spiraled into a deep depression. Her periods of healing were often difficult, both for her and for those around her. A pall fell over the sunny Palm

Springs estate, as all present waited for the day that Elizabeth would awaken renewed. Nearly a week passed with Elizabeth doing little more than summoning her mother for assistance: a request for medication to ease her pain, a plate of scrambled eggs, a bottle of ginger ale. Sara was there for her daughter, always with a smile, never allowing anyone to see how concerned she was about Elizabeth's condition—mainly her emotional state.

One morning, Elizabeth emerged from her room and attempted a lighthearted tone. "Come with me, dear," she told Michelle. "Let's have a spot of tea with my mother." Michelle, relieved that Elizabeth might finally be on the road to recovery, followed her into the kitchen and sat down with Sara, who was delighted that her daughter was up and about. Yet it was clear that Elizabeth wasn't truly out of the woods. While her physical healing may have been going well, she stared into her cup of tea and fell silent. "I am always so depressed during the springtime," she said. "The weather is beautiful, yet I feel so unhappy inside."

Griffin did not know how to respond. Her relationship with Elizabeth wasn't such that she felt she could be frank with her. Still, Elizabeth seemed to want to talk, so she responded, "You are doing the best you can," she said, taking a safe route.

"Oh, bullshit," Elizabeth said abruptly. "Richard and I have totally botched things up. And we know it. That's the maddening part." With that, her blue eyes filled with tears and she made a quick exit from the kitchen, leaving Michelle alone with Sara.

After Sara Taylor, who was now seventy-two, watched her daughter flee from the room, she turned to Michelle and said, "You know, I sometimes curse the day I brought my family to America." Her hands shook as she sipped her tea.

"But you are responsible for Elizabeth's success," an incredulous Michelle told the Taylor matriarch. "Just look at what you two have achieved. Why, she's *Elizabeth Taylor!*"

Sara sighed deeply, seemingly at a loss for words. After an uncomfortable silence, Michelle rose. She patted the elderly woman on the shoulder sympathetically, and then left her to her tea.

"Pray for Us"

When Elizabeth Taylor turned forty in February 1972, she tried to be optimistic about the future during star-studded birthday festivities in Budapest (where Burton was filming *Bluebeard*). "I love my life and everything is going so well," she told the press. A photo of her and Burton taken by Norman Parkinson in Hungary is quite haunting: Both are in luxurious black furs—she with a fur hood and wearing the magnificent Krupp diamond ring. He has his smoldering eyes fixed upon her because she is the only woman for him, no matter the cost to his ego or his emotional well-being. She returns his gaze with an equal measure of affection, but yet with a distant, faraway look that conveys both great love and tremendous sadness. By the time they began work on a two-part TV movie called *Divorce His, Divorce Hers*—their last film together—it was clear to anyone paying attention that the subject matter was more than a tad prophetic.

On July 4, 1973, she released the following statement:

"I am convinced that it would be a good and constructive idea if Richard and I are separated for a while. Maybe we loved each other too much—I never believed such a thing was possible." It's interesting to note that Elizabeth had a romantic view of why her marriage was in tatters: They had loved each other too much. If she viewed that relationship as loving, it certainly says a lot about her state of mind at that time, and about her criteria for a happy marriage.

"But we have been in each other's pockets constantly," the statement went on, "never being apart but for matters of life and death, and I believe it's caused a temporary breakdown of communication. I believe with all my heart that the separation will ultimately bring us back to where we should be—and that's together. I think in a few days' time I shall return to California, because my mother is there, and I have old and true friends there, too. Friends are there to help each other, aren't they? Isn't that what it's all supposed to be about? Wish us well during this difficult time." She ended her statement with a simple plea: "Pray for us."

And What of the Children?

Though the Burtons had their share of personal problems, they also had a brood of children to consider: her four, Michael, Christopher, Liza, and Maria; and Richard's daughter, Kate. His other daughter, Jessica, was still in a sanitarium. Somehow, they managed to give them as much of their time as possible. The children adored them, and the feeling was mutual. However, the fact of the matter was that Elizabeth and Richard were so consumed by their own lives and careers, their mutual depressions and assorted problems, is it any wonder they had trouble being good parents? Richard simply didn't have the patience or the selfless temperament it takes to raise children. Somehow, though, Elizabeth *did* have the ability to be a good, though perhaps not very strict—and certainly not always available—mother. There's no point in trying to paint her as the ideal mother. That's just not the way it was; however, she did try to make sure that any time spent with the children was quality time.

Elizabeth's firstborn, Michael—son of Michael Wilding—was a teenager now and having trouble with his grades in the boarding school he was attending. He kept getting kicked out of one after another, so much so that the Burtons seemed to be running out of educational options for him. Concerned about Michael's scholastic future, Richard spent hours lecturing the teenager about his future. However, Michael just wasn't interested in discussing his schooling with his stepfather. "Let's face it," Burton decided. "Our son is a hippie. His hair lies on his shoulders and we can't keep him in school. I tell Elizabeth that we should do either one of two things—ignore him or kick the living daylights out of him. It bothers Elizabeth, too, but she goes around sermonizing, 'He has the right to wear his hair any length he wants, it's his right as an individual.' We argue all the time and amazingly, the only one who sides with me is Mike Wilding [Michael's father]. He approves me taking stern measures."

Burton noted that the entire time Michael and Christopher were in Puerto Vallarta, the only reading they did was of comic books. "But they do have street smarts," he said at the time, "and that is important." He wasn't going to fret if they refused to read literature. However, he definitely did not approve of their smoking while away at school. Elizabeth was not much help. "They're only young once," she decided, repeating a favorite mantra. She said she wasn't going to ruin their spring vacation by "getting on their backs about stuff that they see us do here every day."

In October 1970, Michael—then seventeen—married nineteen-year-old Beth Clutter. Burton was unhappy about it. "The kid has no high school diploma," he raged. "He's got no job. What is he going to do, live off of us for the rest of his life?"

"He's our son," Elizabeth said. "We have to support him."

"For the rest of his life?" Richard said.

"I meant support his *decision*," Elizabeth countered. "But if he needs money, then, yes, we shall support him for the rest of his life. That's what parents do."

Burton was Michael's best man. The expression on his face when he saw what long-haired Michael was wearing to his wedding—a maroon caftan—must have been priceless.

Elizabeth gave the newlyweds a Jaguar and a $70,000 London townhouse as a wedding gift. She also arranged for the couple to receive a monthly stipend, which was fine with Burton, but he would just as soon have seen Michael get a good job.

One of the reasons the Burtons' marriage lasted as long as it did, at least to hear people who knew them well tell it, is that Elizabeth wanted some stability in the lives of their children. "He was definitely a stabilizing force," one Taylor aficionado said of Burton, "and as much as Elizabeth sometimes fought it, that's how much she appreciated it. I think it was important that the children saw a strong man in the household, especially the daughters. Burton was that kind of male influence—unforgettable and consistent. Maria and Liza knew no other man as their father, really. Just Richard Burton."

It was clear from his actions that Michael wanted to start his own life as soon as he possibly could, and be away from Elizabeth and Richard. The marriage, predictably, would not last long, though the couple would have a child in July, named Leyla, making Elizabeth a grandmother at the age of thirty-nine. She could not have been more thrilled about it. By that time, she and Beth had bonded; Elizabeth showed her nothing but kindness and warmth. To celebrate the birth, Richard bought Elizabeth a set of diamond earrings in gold and a matching choker in the center of which was a lion sculpted out of, again, diamonds and gold. In the lion's mouth hung two golden rings. Both stunning pieces were by Van Cleef & Arpels. "You look so amazing," Richard told her when she modeled the jewelry for him, "no one in his right mind would ever believe you were a grandmother."

At this time, Liza, the daughter of Elizabeth and Mike Todd, was having trouble with her studies, but she was a hard worker and determined to pull through. She and Richard were very close. They loved pulling pranks on Elizabeth. One Christmas, after all of the presents were opened, Liza approached her mother with a small box. "Daddy says that you forgot this box in your stocking," she said. "Well, what is it?" Elizabeth wondered. "You have to open it to find out," said the little girl, now beaming. When Elizabeth opened it, she found a beautiful ruby-and-diamond ring from Van Cleef & Arpels. Richard had promised that he would one day find her the most perfectly cut ruby in the world—his favorite gem because of its red color and its connection to Wales— and he had come through once again. Elizabeth scooped up her daughter and ran to Richard, whom she smothered with hugs and kisses.

Elizabeth's adopted daughter, Maria, still had a number of physical problems, with good days and bad days. Elizabeth, as always, took time to give special attention to her, as did Richard. Both were concerned at her timidity and hoped she would grow out of it.

Richard remained emotionally close to his daughter Kate—though at a distance due to the divorce from her mother. Because his other daughter, Jessica, was still in a mental hospital, it pained him to even think about her. "But you can't just exclude her from our lives," Elizabeth told him on more than one occasion. Still, whenever he thought of her, he couldn't deal with the anguish it brought him. All he could do, he reasoned, was to make enough money that she would never have financial worries. Anything else was more than he could handle.

Part Five

CONFUSION REIGNS

"What Makes Us Women"

Pray for us," Elizabeth had said in her statement to the press about her separation from Richard Burton. Rarely, if ever, had a star of Elizabeth's stature released a statement so personal about matters so private. Today, it happens all the time. Celebrities are anxious to talk about their personal lives if the venue feels safe, and they even find it cathartic to let the public in on their private anxieties. However, by 1973 Elizabeth had been such a constant fixture of the American culture—more than thirty years—that relationship she had with her public, her fans and foes alike, was real, not imagined, and she felt it should be cultivated. She loved being a star, rarely complained about it as do many celebrities—and felt compelled to explain her decision where Richard Burton was concerned. Of course, her surprising missive generated international headlines, right alongside President Richard Nixon's Watergate scandal. After she released the statement, she did as she said she would and flew to California. Meanwhile, Richard held a press conference in New York, while drinking from a bottle of vodka.

"It was jolly well bound to happen," he said, seeming in perfectly good nature. "You know, when two very volatile people keep hacking constantly at each other with fierce oratory, and then occasionally engage in a go of it with physical force, well, it's like I said: It's bound to happen."

Determined to get into shape both emotionally and physically for a new movie he was about to do with Sophia Loren called *The Voyage* (produced by her husband, Carlo Ponti), Burton saw a doctor and decided to stop drinking. On July 13, after about a week on the wagon, he left for Rome. So that he would not have to deal with the probing paparazzi constantly on his tail, Sophia and Carlo offered to put Richard up in the guesthouse of their sixteenth-century villa in the Alban Hills, about thirty minutes outside of Rome. Meanwhile, Burton told the couple's attorney, Aaron Frosch, to work out a divorce settlement with Elizabeth.

A couple of days later, Elizabeth, still in Los Angeles, got a telephone call from Richard. They had earlier organized their schedules so that they would both be making movies in Rome at the same time, and she was about to leave L.A to begin work on Muriel Spark's *The Driver's Seat* there. Richard felt that a faraway romantic setting might help diminish the tension between them. "We may as well be together here at the Pontis', luv," he told her. "It makes no sense for us to be apart."

Elizabeth was conflicted as to how to proceed, but since she did have to be in Italy for a film, she decided to take him up on his offer. On July 20, she arrived at Rome's Fiumicino Airport. She was met there by Richard in a Rolls-Royce. Wearing jeans, an orange T-shirt, and a huge diamond ring, she looked young and radiant as she worked her way through the mob of photographers to her husband. When the two finally met, they kissed passionately and embraced, gladly giving the gathered paparazzi an opportunity to snap pictures of their passionate reunion. Some of the reporters and photographers even applauded. It was as if they wanted the Burtons to be together again—and when one thinks of the great copy the couple had generated over the years, it's easy to understand why the media was so invested in their continued "happiness." Clinging to her man, Elizabeth made her way through the throng at the airport, and she and Burton then slipped into the waiting Rolls for the trip to the Ponti villa.

While their trip may have begun with seemingly enthusiastic adoration, the ride to their friends' home ended quite differently. Elizabeth bolted from the car and marched up a long stairway carved into the Italian hillside, leaving her husband to manage the luggage with their driver. Sophia, enjoying a book on a terrace, greeted Elizabeth as she approached her. "Amazing," Sophia declared. "Hours in an *aeroplane* and she still looks gorgeous."

Ellen Pallola, who was Loren's personal assistant at that time, recalled, "The Burtons started arguing the very day Elizabeth showed up at the villa. I heard her say, 'You *are* flirting with Sophia, and I won't have it. And you're doing it in Italian, so I can't understand a word! How dare you?'

"Burton took off with Mr. Ponti, enraged. I recall him saying, 'That woman came all the way from the United States just to make my life a living hell. And I'm the fool who invited her here.'

"Over the course of a week, the two of them caused so much turmoil at the villa that Mrs. Ponti finally pulled Mrs. Burton aside. She told her, 'Elizabeth, you must know that I do not have designs on Richard. Don't be ridiculous.'

"Miss Taylor said, 'Of course I know that. But he is such a flirt, and I'm sick of it. It's not just you, it's Annabella, too.' [She was referring to the twenty-nine-year-old Milanese actress Annabella Incontrera, who played Richard's mistress in *The Voyage*.]

"'Oh, please,' Mrs. Ponti said. "He's not having an affair with her, either. She's a friend of mine. I know her well.'

"'But they went to a musical together in Palermo,' Mrs. Burton protested.

"'I know,' said Mrs. Ponti. '*I was with them*. But, now that I see what your life is like, as much as I adore Richard, he is not the man for you. There is much too much suspicion. A marriage cannot survive suspicion. You must end this misery,' Mrs. Ponti told her.

"'I am,' said Mrs. Burton. 'It's over. Thank you for caring. It's over.'"

The next morning, Elizabeth left the Ponti villa, leaving Richard behind. Ellen Pallola recalled, "I helped carry her bags to the car. Before she got into the car, Mrs. Ponti grabbed her and embraced her tightly. 'I promise to stay in touch,' Elizabeth told her, 'and let you know how things go, though I'm sure you will read about it in the papers.' Before she let her go, Mrs. Ponti said, 'You know what makes us women, don't you? That we believe love comes before anything else, and that we would willingly give up everything for love. You must find your love.' Mrs. Burton, who was in tears by this time, got into the car and was driven off. I stood there with Mrs Ponti, waving good-bye to her. Mrs. Ponti then turned to me and said, 'Such a sad woman. So much love to give. But how she will ever trust any man enough to give it to him is the question. I'm afraid this marriage will be the one to ruin her for all time.' I was convinced that the two women had genuine affection for each other. It was obvious."

After leaving Sophia, Elizabeth checked into a seven-room suite at the Grand Hotel. Then she went to the studio. She had to begin work on the film, though she wasn't sure how she would ever be able to do it. The plot of *The Driver's Seat*, also known as *Identikit*, was so twisted, she didn't know how to relate to it. It had something to do with her character, a schizophrenic, looking for a suitor who would love her and then murder her. "How I ever get myself into these movies, I'll never know," she said at the time.

Elizabeth did not have a good night. Room service records are kept in strict confidence at the Grand, but many orders were delivered to Taylor's suite that evening. There's no telling what she was doing in that room alone, but a reasonable guess would be that she was drinking heavily. The next morning, she couldn't function. She was expected on the set that morning, yet didn't show up until 5 p.m.

"We waited all day for her," said the film's director, Giuseppe Patroni-Griffi. "When she arrived, she was in terrible shape. She said to me, 'I never thought I would ever have as bad a day as I am having today. I thought that when Mike Todd died, that would have been the worst day of my life. But, no, this is it. *This* is the worst day of my life.' I didn't even know how to respond. I suggested we put work off a few days. 'No,' she said. 'I must work. I must take my mind off of things.'

"So, we were ready to begin. Before we started, though, she asked that she be allowed to address the cast and crew. She stood before everyone and said, 'I am sorry I was late today. That is not like me at all. However, I am having a dreadful day, and I just hope that you will forgive me.' Everyone had been aware of the strain her roller-coaster marriage put on her personally. They had expected an aloof, yet professional actress that first day of shooting, but she revealed herself as something few of them expected. A human being. After her plea for forgiveness, the studio filled with applause. They gave her an ovation that must have lasted about three minutes. Some came up to her and hugged her. She returned their embraces fully and without hesitation. All of the barriers between star and the rest of the cast were, at that moment, completely brought down. We loved her and wanted the best for her. She was, at that moment and from then on, *our* Elizabeth.

"And we went to work."

Henry Wynberg

Earlier, in the summer of 1973, when Elizabeth Taylor was in a Los Angeles nightclub socializing with Peter and Chris Lawford, the elder Lawford introduced her to a tall, handsome man named Henry Wynberg. He was three years her junior, born in Holland to working-class parents. He was divorced and the father of a son (who was later killed in a car accident). He'd found work in California as a used car salesman.

Of the woman he refers to as "Elizabett," he recalls that the first thing he noticed about her was her great beauty, her silken yellow dress, and the fact that, indeed, she did wear real diamonds. The two barely spoke to one another, though, while at the club. Elizabeth was apparently enchanted by him. A half hour after he left, Henry got a telephone call from Peter Lawford asking if it would be all right with him if he brought Elizabeth over for a visit. It was an odd request, but how could he turn it down? If she wanted to see him, he certainly wanted to see her as well. Lawford brought her over to his home. "We looked at each other then, and we looked for quite a while," he recalled. "It wasn't love at first sight, but it was infatuation. There was only one place to go [he is, presumably, talking about his bedroom and, also presumably, Peter had left them alone]. We began dating openly. She started calling me at all hours, day and night, confiding in me about her marriage problems with Burton. Before I knew where I was, I was in deep."

He was an interesting guy, or at least that's how Elizabeth viewed him. He had nothing to do with show business, and perhaps it was precisely for that reason that she seemed fascinated by him. He was about as far removed from Richard Burton, in terms of life experience and temperament, as one could imagine. He had simpler tastes, was not abusive—at least not as far as she could tell, so far—and just seemed to be an easier personality. The two had an innocent flirtation, nothing more. But then, much to her surprise, Wynberg showed up in Rome when he heard she was having trouble with Burton, and checked in at the Grand Hotel. He called her room to see how she was faring, and she invited him up to her suite for a drink. The next thing everyone in her life knew, Elizabeth was romantically involved with Henry Wynberg.

Her secretary, Raymond Vignale, said, "Henry was more exciting, more fun, than Richard Burton. Richard had become a loner, he wanted to be at home, reading and writing. Elizabeth wanted to go out and dance. Henry loved dancing, loved socializing. It worked well with him."

As she filmed *The Driver's Seat*, the couple was photographed all over Rome—at dinners, while dancing. It was a very public romance, and that was the way Elizabeth wanted it. She did nothing to hide it. They were photographed on a cliff in Italy, the two of them embracing. Fully aware of the photographers with their long black lenses poking out from behind bushes and trees, she lifted her face to the breeze so that it would blow her jet-black hair back in serene undulation. She always knew how to be the perfect subject for a photo essay, even when she was supposed to be caught unaware. In the company of photographers, though, Elizabeth Taylor was *never* unaware.

Elizabeth took Henry with her to London to visit Laurence Harvey, who was dying of cancer and thus was reluctant to see her. She was such a drain on him, he had said, with her long and dramatic telephone calls over the years concerning her rocky relationships and many physical agonies, that he just didn't feel he could handle her in his weakened state. (The actress and Harvey had worked together in *Butterfield 8*.)

The visit was difficult. Elizabeth crawled into bed with the dying man and said she wished she could go with him to the great beyond, because that's how miserable she was in this world. She put her head to his chest and listened to his heartbeat. It was faint, she would later recall, with the spaces between the beats so far apart that she would hold her breath waiting for the next one. He was slipping away.

In November 1973, Laurence Harvey died of stomach cancer. He was just forty-five. Elizabeth was bereft at the funeral service, lamenting, "It should have been me. I have so little to live for, and he had so much."

"You have to stop thinking like that," Henry Wynberg told her, in response to her obvious grief over the loss of a good friend. "Something terrible is going to happen to you if you don't," he warned her.

"What else terrible can happen to me?" Elizabeth said sadly. "Every terrible thing in the world has happened to me already." Then she began to cry so hard that she couldn't breathe. It took her more than half an hour to compose herself.

Sure enough, the same month Harvey died, Elizabeth Taylor ended up hospitalized at the University of California complaining of severe stomach pains. With her Christian Science background at work, but in a twisted way, it was as if she could actually will herself to be sick, and with any ailment she chose, if she focused on the malady hard enough. It turned out she had an ovarian cyst. Her doctors didn't know whether it was malignant or not, and would have to operate. She was sure she had cancer, and had already begun accepting her fate. Henry Wynberg took a bed right next to Elizabeth's in her room and stayed with her. However, he wasn't long for that room, because as soon as Richard Burton, who was still in Italy filming *The Voyage* with Sophia Loren and Carlo Ponti, heard about the situation, he was on the telephone to Elizabeth.

At first, Elizabeth was determined not to return his call. That lasted for about a day. Soon she was on the phone begging him to visit her. She was sure she had cancer, she said, and she was scared. "I don't want to die alone," she said, crying. "Please, can I come home?" The time away from her had been, as Burton recalled in his diary, "six months of torture, agony." He told her that he had stopped drinking. He was a different man and he wanted—no, he *needed*—to see her as well. He knew about Wynberg but didn't care, he wrote, because he too had had what he called "cathartic infidelities." If she had heard any stories about him and Sophia, he said, she should ignore them because they weren't accurate.

The next day, Elizabeth had her surgery. The cyst was not malignant. There was great relief all around. Sophia and Carlo sent her a huge flower arrangement with a card that read (in Italian), "*Tutti scaturiscono che le estremità scaturiscono.*" ("All's well that ends well.")

Elizabeth checked out of the hospital and into the Scripps Clinic in La Jolla to recover. Wynberg got his extra bed in her room, and started tending to his girlfriend's recovery. "Three months from now, we may no longer be such good friends," he told the press at the time. "Or, perhaps we'll be something much more than that. Only God and Elizabeth knows."

The next weekend, though, Henry Wynberg was no longer in the picture. Richard Burton had taken his place in the extra bed in Elizabeth's room. He had flown in from Italy to claim his wife, and had no intention of leaving the States without her. "The next thing I knew," Elizabeth recalls, "he was by my bedside and we were squeezing the air out of each other and kissing each other and crying. 'Please come back with me,' he asked."

"It can all be over without warning," he said at the time, "and I can't bear the thought of losing the old girl." He was determined, he said, to live each day to the fullest with her and never let another petty squabble come between them. Of course, he had come bearing an impressive gift for her: He'd gone to Van Cleef & Arpels in Beverly Hills and bought her a thirty-eight-carat diamond heart-shaped pendant necklace. Richard had made quite a fortune on his movies with Elizabeth, even though most were not commercial successes. He had also invested well. Therefore, there was never a shortage of funds with which to buy his wife expensive gifts, and, it must be noted, some of his friends insist that he was using his and Elizabeth's joint funds for some of the more costly purchases. Of course, Elizabeth loved receiving the baubles, even if she had paid for a few of them out of her own account, either realizing as much or not. Her eyes lit up when she saw this latest one. As she admired the way it caught all of the light in the room, she quipped, "You sure know how to win over a sick woman."

Elizabeth Divorces Richard

As far as Elizabeth Taylor was concerned, with Richard Burton back in her life, Henry Wynberg was a thing of the past. She told Burton that she'd just been using Henry to get over their broken marriage—not that he even required an explanation.

"You've never seen anybody heal so fast," Elizabeth says of her time in the hospital after Richard showed up. "It was as if the Grand Maestro had placed a hand over my incision and healed me up."

As soon as Elizabeth was released from the clinic, she and Burton took off for Naples, seeming happier than ever. "Richard and I are back together again," said she, "and it will be the happiest Christmas of my life. I believe in Santa Claus again." Michael Jr. joined them in Gstaad for the holiday and was struck by how well his mother and stepfather were getting along. Perhaps they had actually found some peace with each other.

Elizabeth's recovery was, as always after any of her surgeries, difficult and longer than expected. Richard was at her side the entire time, showing great patience where perhaps there really wasn't much.

When Richard finally finished his film for Carlo Ponti, the couple took off for Puerto Vallarta, where they celebrated Elizabeth's forty-second birthday in February 1974. In front of photographers—of course—they had a "private" luncheon. After they ate their Mexican feast, he leaned across the table and took her lovely face in his large hands. He kissed her. She drew breath from him and kissed him back. The next day, the photos were in all of the papers.

After Puerto Vallarta, the two were off to Oroville, California, a small town about an hour's drive north of Sacramento, where Richard was scheduled to begin filming *The Klansman*, a story of racial discord in the South that costarred Lee Marvin.

Their marital bliss did not last long. The Burtons spent an unhappy tenth anniversary in Oroville, fighting and drinking. Unfortunately, whatever epiphany Richard had had when Elizabeth was in the hospital faded with the passing of a short time. Now he was looking at other women, giving them the "Welsh fish eye," as Elizabeth called it.

"It was brutal," veteran publicist Dale Olson, who worked on the set of *The Klansman*, recalled. "The final straw came when Burton presented an eighteen-year-old waitress with a ring and tried to act as if he was having an affair with her. I'm not sure he was, though. I think he was trying to be dramatic and make Elizabeth jealous."

The girl in question was from Oroville; her name was Kim Din-ucci. Beverly Wilcox was her best friend, also eighteen at the time. She recalls, "There was no romance with Kim. In fact, Richard gave us *both* rings. They were diamond-and-ruby rings worth only $450 each. He was this old guy—this movie star—coming on to us, and we were flattered, but there was no sex. We met him in the diner Kim worked in at the time. He was with Eliz-abeth Taylor, but very flirtatious. She was beautiful and very quiet. You could see the fury in her eyes as he was coming on to us, two eighteen-year-olds. Finally, she said, 'Richard, what are you trying to prove? You're acting like an old fool.' He said to me, 'As you can see, I have a bad case of Elizabethitis, and it will not go away.'

"He asked to meet with us that night at the Prospectors Village Motel, where he was staying. How could we resist? When we got there, he said he just wanted us to help him with his southern ac-cent for *The Klansman*, he was having trouble with it. So we sat up all night going over his script and working on his accent. The next day, he came back to the diner and that's when he gave us the rings. He slipped them on our fingers and said, 'Just a token to thank you for your help with the picture.' I thought it was a strange but sweet gesture. When I asked about Elizabeth, he said, ''Tis she who is the repository for my heart.'

"That night, he asked us to join him for dinner. So there we were, at a restaurant, the two of us local girls with Elizabeth Tay-lor, Richard Burton, and Lola Falana [one of the stars of the movie]. Burton started flirting with the waitress. He said, 'Now, there's a woman I would like to sleep with.' Elizabeth said, 'Why can't you stifle your little Welsh lusts until I'm out of the way? Do you have to parade it so openly?' It got very tense. Lola got up and left. 'I can't handle this,' she said. Then Elizabeth left. 'You'll not see the likes of me, again," she told us. 'I am leaving *Orville*'—that's how she pronounced it. *Orville*, instead of Oroville. After she was gone, Richard turned to the two of us and said, '*Orville*. Can you even fathom it? Anyway, would you two like a go of it back at the motel?' We said, no, absolutely not. It was pathetic and, really, very sad. I heard that Elizabeth left Oroville that very night. I remember thinking, these rich and famous movie stars are a lot more miserable than any of us living in the small town of *Orville*."

"That was it, as far as Elizabeth was concerned," confirmed Dale Olson. "I had a press reception scheduled for the two of them the next evening, a hundred reporters coming into town to interview them, but she was already gone. I called the media together and said, 'The bad news is that Elizabeth Taylor has left Richard Burton . . . again. The good news is that you now have a big scoop. And you also have Richard, who is still here and ready to talk to you.' So Richard did the interviews, but he was so sick, so out of it . . . I'm not sure it was such a good idea."

As soon as Elizabeth left town, Richard became deathly ill with a fever of 104, and was flat on his back at Saint John's hospital in Santa Monica. He tried to phone Elizabeth from the hospital, but she would not take his calls.

On April 26, 1974, the Burtons announced that their reconciliation attempt had failed. They were getting a divorce.

Two months later, on June 26, Elizabeth appeared in a courthouse in Saanen, near Gstaad, to finalize the divorce. Richard was not present, having sent a doctor's certificate from the United States saying he was too ill to appear.

The judge granted Elizabeth a divorce. She kept $5 million in jewels, even though they had been a joint investment for the couple. Richard, beaten down by the years, said, "Just let her have them. Who cares?" She also got Casa Kimberly ("Who cares?"), their yacht, *Kalizma* ("Who cares?"), lots of money, and other goods, such as a priceless art collection. She also was awarded custody of Maria, whom they had formally adopted as a couple in 1964.

Elizabeth Marries Richard . . . Again!

It wasn't over, yet. Indeed, if any of her friends sensed that Elizabeth Taylor's relationship with Richard Burton had not ended with their divorce, it was because they realized how attached she had become not only to him but also to the melodrama that had characterized their relationship for more than fifteen years. Also, despite her anger with him and disappointment with how their marriage had turned out, she was a determined woman who could not accept easily that she had invested so many years into a relationship only to have it fail. Indeed, within hours of the final decree, she was on the telephone with Richard asking him, "Do you think we did the right thing?" He was too ill to have an opinion.

For the next year and a half, Elizabeth would have one foot planted firmly in the past—she and Richard spoke on the telephone at least three times a week, without fail—and the other in the future—she and Henry Wynberg rented a home in Bel Air and began the next phase of their relationship.

In February 1975, Wynberg accompanied Elizabeth to Russia, where she would act in the first Soviet-American co-production, the third remake of the classic children's story by the 1911 Nobel laureate Maurice Maeterlinck, *The Blue Bird*, directed by George Cukor. It had received a silent film production in 1918, but it was the 1940 version with Shirley Temple that 20th Century-Fox had felt would compete head-to-head with MGM's *The Wizard of Oz*, something that the movie failed to do, despite its lavish production values. The 1975 version would also star Jane Fonda, Ava Gardner, and Cicely Tyson.

Shortly after filming began, Elizabeth ended up in bed with the flu, which was followed by a bout of amoebic dysentery. Her poor health helped to ruin the experience of making *The Blue Bird*.

Filming ended in August. In five months, she later noted, "I did about one week's work."

On August 11, the night of the movie's wrap party, she received a telegram from Richard Burton in Switzerland. Thinking it was a congratulatory message, she tossed it aside. Henry took a look at it and said, "Elizabeth, Richard wants to see you."

"What! You're kidding! Give me that," she said, grabbing it anxiously.

Three days later, on August 14, 1975, Elizabeth and Henry arrived in Switzerland. That night, Elizabeth met Richard at a friend's villa for dinner. As soon as she saw him, she rushed into his arms, her face awash in tears. She'd missed him desperately, she said. He told her that he shared her heartache, and that he wanted them to return to their romance.

The next day, the fifteenth, Henry was on a plane back to the United States, alone. In front of Richard, Elizabeth had told him earlier in the day that it was over between them. She gave him $50,000 and a gold watch, as if he'd been forced into retirement.

Richard would later recall, "Then for two days (16th and 17th), we [he and Elizabeth] circled each other—very wary, very polite.

"On the third day, we had a fight (18th). Then we knew we were ourselves, again."

Two days later, on August 20th, they announced their plans to remarry.

"I was upset," said Diane Stevens, who was an associate of their press agent, John Springer. "I called Elizabeth in Switzerland. 'What in the world are you doing?' I asked. 'I'm very worried about you, Elizabeth.'"

"'I know, I know,' she told me with a tone of resignation. 'But I love him and he loves me. Won't you please be happy for us?'

"What could I say? 'Of course, I am happy for you,' I told her. 'I just hope you know what you are doing.'

"She said, 'Honestly, he's changed. He's so different, so loving. He's not drinking as much. I think, this time, it can work.'"

Off Elizabeth went with Richard Burton—again—traveling

about the world in a dizzy haze, from Switzerland to Italy to Israel and then South Africa, battling each other every step along the way, and loving one another as was their way. Somehow, the conflicted lovers ended up in Botswana . . . and that's where, on October 10, 1975, they were again married. It would be Elizabeth's sixth marriage, to her fifth husband. They exchanged forty-dollar wedding bands. "Sturm has remarried Drang and all is right with the world," reported the *Boston Globe*.

Elizabeth loved this time in her life, even though it was so difficult. A lifelong animal lover, she was fascinated by African wildlife and had trained a team of monkeys to come into their camp every day by coaxing them with small bowls of fruit, which she handpicked from the trees.

In Johannesburg, she and Richard found a jewelry store in their hotel—naturally!—and discovered a pink diamond of ten carats, "very large for a pink diamond," Elizabeth notes. Burton bought it for her. However, after thinking about it for a few days, she decided that they should sell the diamond and use the proceeds to build three small hospitals in Botswana. "That pink diamond was huge," she says. "I think it was the biggest one I had ever seen in my life. You know how I am about jewelry, so for me to give it up . . . well, I really wanted those hospitals." The hospitals were built, she says, but then months later, "the jungles reclaimed them, and that still breaks my heart."

Ruining their time in Africa, Richard came down with malaria. The Burtons heard about an Italian-Egyptian pharmacist named Chenina Samin—always called Chen Sam—and asked her to fly to Johannesburg to care for Richard. She did such a good job with him that Elizabeth then hired her as—what else?—her publicist! And she remained in that position for twenty years. To anyone watching these events unfold, it seemed like sheer lunacy. In Elizabeth Taylor's world, however, it somehow made perfect sense.

In November 1975, Richard celebrated his fiftieth birthday. He was sober at that time but now truly looked as if he were dying. His skin was a terrible shade of off-yellow, and it seemed as if he were suffering from tuberculosis. Elizabeth was drinking enough for the two of them; not only was she was unhappy about Burton's failing health, she was already beginning to think that she had made a mistake in remarrying him. He wasn't the man she had married in 1964, eleven years earlier, that's for sure. But she also was not the same woman. "Can you ever go back . . . I mean, really?" she asked.

"I'm sorry. I am not a perfect person," she told Chen Sam, according to a later recollection. "I love him so much, I don't want to lose him. He's the best thing that has ever happened to me, the only man who had the power to change me for the better."

"I didn't think then that their second marriage would last ten minutes," recalled their personal bodyguard Brian Haynes. "But I could also see that they seemed to need each other. When he was there, she seemed to hate him. When he was away, she couldn't bear to be without him. They were often at each other's throats and there was plenty of hard-core swearing on both sides."

It was inevitable, perhaps, that Elizabeth would end up on the losing end of any bargain she had made with Richard to be happy "until death do we part." In Gstaad, during the Burtons' Christmas sojourn there, Richard met a tall blonde divorcee, Suzy Hunt, from England. She was only twenty-seven. He was drawn to her immediately, much to Elizabeth's dismay, and claimed that he could not help himself. He would pursue this younger woman, and he informed his wife of his plan.

Richard later said, "From the very beginning, she [Elizabeth] sensed a worthy adversary. Elizabeth is, by nature, a jealous woman, and like a good many women, she believes that where there is no jealousy there is no love. She didn't very much mind about the other women who popped up now and again when we were separated and divorced and all that. She didn't think they were any real competition. But now the chips were down." Would it have been any surprise to learn that, in fact, Richard liked the idea of making Elizabeth miserable by flaunting her new "adversary"? Such was the nature of their often poisonous relationship.

Hunt's involvement with Richard grew, though, beyond what Elizabeth had suspected, or at least hoped. Suzy wasn't merely a device to enrage her, thereby enlivening their humdrum marriage. Richard actually had feelings for this woman, or "girl," as Elizabeth described her.

One evening, when an argument over her husband's new assignation had reached its crescendo, Elizabeth pointed toward the front door and said, "That's it—I want you out!"

Richard, having expected the demand, said, "My bag has been packed since breakfast."

As he started off to gather his things, Elizabeth continued, "Out of our room. You'll stay in this house." Richard moved into a guest suite. Elizabeth knew that if he went out that front door, he might never come back. If their marriage had any chance of continuing, she decided, they would have to endure the awkward living situation until Richard's infatuation ended.

Elizabeth's plan to keep her husband close created at least one extremely uncomfortable moment, however. Whether orchestrated to irritate Elizabeth or not, Richard invited Suzy to his and Elizabeth's home. She was to pick him up to go to a dinner party, which would leave Taylor alone that night.

Elizabeth watched from the terrace outside the front door of their chalet as Hunt's limousine ground to a halt. Suzy emerged in a floor-length black gown and glided up the stairs, not noticing Taylor.

"Stunning," Elizabeth said, startling her. "I always loved that dress. I'm so glad it found a good home."

Suzy was speechless, seemingly awed by Elizabeth's presence. "You know, I'm sorry about this whole business," she told her, according to what she later recalled. "I never wanted to hurt you, of all people."

Elizabeth had heard this speech before, but in the past she hadn't been on the receiving end of it. She put up her hand to stop Suzy from continuing. "My dear," she said, in a world-weary tone, "you'll last only six months with Richard. That, I can guarantee." It wasn't so much a threat as a prediction, and one based on years of experience. She wasn't even particularly angry, as she would later tell it. She was too exhausted to be mad at a girl, all of twenty-seven, who didn't have a clue as to what she was getting herself into with a man old enough to be her father.

"Well, perhaps you are right," replied Suzy, "but my," she continued, "what a six months it shall be."

Elizabeth forced a smile. "Oh, certainly, dear," she responded, "for all of us."

A Diversion before Divorce

In January 1976, Robert Lantz, the agent representing Richard and Elizabeth, met with Burton in Switzerland to discuss future projects. After a year of doing *Equus* on Broadway, Anthony Hopkins had left the show, and Tony Perkins had taken the role. Now Perkins's involvement was coming to an end and Lantz went to London to see if he could motivate Richard into essaying the part. It would have been his first time on the stage since 1964 when he starred in *Hamlet*. "He was in terrible shape," said Lantz. "Tired, hungover, not well. He needed a project, something to get him back in the swing. He had a script already, and said he would read it over. The next morning, he came down the stairs and I could see immediately that he had not touched a drop of alcohol. He said, 'I'll do it. I think it's a wonderful idea. I love the play and I promise you, I will be all right.' And I said, 'Well, you know, it can change your life, if you can pull this off. You need this on every count.' And I said, 'Do me a favor? Don't let Elizabeth come. It will be a circus if you do, and this is a very serious moment in your life.' He said he would do his best."

Richard left Switzerland for New York to begin rehearsals for *Equus*, and he asked the willowy Suzy Hunt to join him. Of course, she flew to be at his side. He told friends that, now that he was sober (for the time being), he couldn't imagine what had gotten into him that he'd decided to remarry Elizabeth. "I don't know," he said, "don't even ask me. It's like a huge dream. I remember thinking, 'What am I doing here?' Odd place to be married, in the bush, by an African gentleman. It was very curious. An extraordinary adventure doomed from the start, of course."

Hurt by his remarks and by his assignation with Suzy Hunt, Elizabeth tried to exact revenge by seducing a thirty-seven-year-old Maltese named Peter Darmanin at a Swiss disco called the Cave. The two met on the dance floor, she the great movie goddess and he an advertising man with a regular nine-to-five, just blowing off some steam on a Friday night. She discovered him amid a swirl of colors and pounding noises, his agile limbs moving to the music, dancing alone. She sashayed over to him, swaying to the music, and apparently decided, "This one will do just fine." Then, without interrupting her dance of seduction, she cradled his jaw and tipped his face downward so that her lips could settle on his. They kissed, right there on the dance floor. It was quite a scene; everyone around them stopped to applaud. He later would recall that his head was spinning, and not just from the champagne, though he did consume a lot of it. In fact, they both were too tipsy to consummate their meeting that night. However, the next morning, Elizabeth telephoned Peter straight away and invited him to her chalet. There, they made love.

The next day, he moved into the house she and Burton had shared for many years.

"It was just about seven weeks out of my life," he now recalls, "but, really, it felt like seven years. She was obviously not over Richard Burton, on the phone with him constantly. She was trying to get him to take back that giant diamond ring he had given her. She was crying on the phone, saying, 'Just take it back, Richard. I don't want it. It means nothing to me now.'" (The jewel in question was the Burton-Taylor diamond, which had set Richard back more than a million dollars in 1969. He did not take it back.)

In February, Elizabeth received a telephone call from Richard. He said that he needed to see her immediately. He was in New York and having a difficult time in rehearsals for *Equus*.

"It was very painful for him, very difficult for him to learn the lines," said Robert Lantz. "Anthony Perkins generously gave up his last Saturday matinee before the Monday on which Burton was to make his debut. Peter Shaffer [the writer of the show, whom Lantz also represented], and I went to the theater and sat in the last row. The lights went out and the announcement came over the loudspeakers. 'At this performance Anthony Perkins will not appear.' There was a big groan. 'He will be replaced by Richard Burton.' And the house exploded like at a big ball game. Then Richard came on and I can truthfully say gave the worst performance any actor has ever given on the stage. He couldn't do the lines. He couldn't do anything. I was mortified for him. After it was mercifully over, I turned to Peter and said, 'What do we do? Do we go backstage? Or, what?' And he said, 'Of course we do . . . if only out of sympathy.' So, we went backstage.

"By the time we saw Richard he had already been given hell by the director, John Dexter. Now he was filled with new motivation. Nothing like failure to charge him up, I thought. He said, 'Robbie, I'm going back to the hotel. I'm going to cancel every appointment. I'm going to rearrange the furniture in the suite so that it resembles the stage, and I'm going to rehearse by myself all day Saturday, Sunday, and Monday, and I will appear Monday night as advertised.' He even put up a notice on the board backstage for the company to read. It said, 'I know I was terrible to all of you and to the public, on Saturday. I will never be like that again.' So, Monday night came and, of course, it was a totally sold-out house and big crowds in the street, you know, to await Mr. Burton's arrival.' He then gave a much, much better performance. Brilliant. I knew then he could do it if he put his mind to it. But this was a tough time for him, a lot of distractions."

Indeed, and one more was on her way, at Richard's behest.

"After Elizabeth got the call from Burton, her heart jumped into her throat," recalled Peter Darmanin. "She made plans to jump on a plane for New York. That was the last I saw of her."

Richard Asks for Another Divorce

Patrick McMahon, who worked for Richard Burton at this time as an assistant, recalled, "Richard came to the theater [the Plymouth] in a good mood one morning, which was rare in those days because he was nervous about the show and feeling inadequate in the role. But this particular morning he was ebullient. 'Guess what?' he said. 'Elizabeth is coming today for lunch.'

"Alarm bells went off in my head. Suzy [Hunt] had worked so hard to keep him off the bottle, and even though she hadn't been totally successful at it, he was drinking far less. We just wanted to get him through the Broadway run, that's all. It was always one day at a time with Richard, and he could afford no setbacks. The one thing, I felt, that could really throw him for a loop would be Elizabeth Taylor. He had already met her up at the airport the day before, and that was a huge mess with photographers and chaos, a big distraction. No one in the show really wanted her there, because they were afraid it would throw the star for a loop, but really, how could you keep her away—especially after he had apparently summoned her."

Morning came and went with no Elizabeth. Richard seemed disappointed, often peering out into the empty theater as if in anticipation of her imminent arrival.

Later in the afternoon, there was a bustling noise in the back of the Plymouth, a familiar female voice arguing with someone about something. After a moment of silence, the back door opened. From the stage, Richard looked into the empty expanse to see Elizabeth walking down the center aisle very carefully, both feet gingerly touching each and every step on her way down as if she was an old woman. She was wearing jeans with a lavender blouse that was dotted with beads and sequins and fake jewels and real gems mixed together, her hair in a big bouffant style. Patrick McMahon remembered thinking that she looked like "celebrated chaos in action."

"Oh, *dah-ling*," she said in a voice loud enough for Richard to hear on the stage. She stopped in the middle of the theater and threw her arms out toward him with a theatrical flourish. "I've arrived!" she exclaimed. "Have you missed me? Why, it's been *hours!*" She then continued down the steps, one at a time, with great deliberation. "But goddamn it," she said as she walked toward the orchestra section of the theater, "I don't have any money for the cab and no one in the lobby has a cent, not even in the bloody box office. How is that possible? Does anyone have any money in this goddamn place?"

Patrick McMahon ran out to the seating area and met Elizabeth halfway with a twenty-dollar bill. He handed it to her.

"What am I supposed to do with this?" she asked him.

"For the cab?" he offered.

"Well, I'm certainly not going to walk all the way back up those goddamn stairs and into the lobby and back outside to pay the cabbie," she said. "Be a dear and run up there, won't you?"

McMahon ran up to pay the cabbie as Elizabeth took a seat just outside the orchestra section, with all eyes of technicians and actors upon her. "Oh, don't mind me," she said with a dismissive hand wave. "Richard will tell you. I'm as quiet as a little lamb when I want to be. Just go on with your rehearsal."

After the cast completed the act it had been working on, Elizabeth applauded loudly. "Bravo!" she exclaimed. "Oh, yes! Bravo!"

"Good Lord! I think the old girl's had a bit too much to drink," Richard said. He still hadn't even come down from the stage to greet her.

"I heard that, buster," she said good-naturedly. "And I'm not. Not yet, anyway. But the day is still young."

At that, Richard walked down the steps of the stage and to her seat. She rose, seeming unsteady, and the two embraced.

Patrick McMahon, who had by now returned from his duty with the cabbie, recalled, "The sight of them together, 'The Liz and Dick Show,' well, it was something to see. The rest of the rehearsal was filled with her comments back up to the stage—all complimentary and exuberant, such as 'Oh, my! *Yes!*' or '*Mahvelous!*' or 'Perfection! Sheer *perfection!*' and Richard trying to hush her up from the stage the whole time. After they finished for the day, Richard walked off the stage and straight to her. He took her by the hand and the two walked up the steps, very gingerly— I mean, you would have thought they were in their nineties—and then out of the theater, talking to one another in an animated fashion and seeming as happy as they could be."

Alas, their postmarital bliss did not last long, as expected. They returned two hours later in the midst of an argument.

"You know that I hate to drink alone," Elizabeth said, now seeming in a fury.

"Well, you know better than to encourage me to drink," he said.

"What the hell has *happened* to you?" she said. "You are no fun anymore, Richard."

"The fight was loud but also comical, and everyone present enjoyed their banter," says Patrick McMahon. "It was almost as if they were performing for the technicians and other actors. But by this time, I was very nervous, though. I wanted her out of there. If Suzy showed up and heard that Elizabeth had been trying to get Richard to drink with her in the middle of a rehearsal day, it would have been a horrible scene. As it was, the rest of the day was shot. Richard was no good. It was over. He was disturbed and distracted. I just prayed she would not be back the next day."

The next day, rather than meet him at the theater, Elizabeth met Richard at the Lombardy Hotel on East 56th Street. When she showed up, he was waiting for her, with Suzy Hunt at his side, at the hotel's bar. He seemed nervous and not as well as he had been the day before, as if he'd had a setback. The truth was that he knew he could not do the show, already tough on him, until he took care of some unfinished business with Elizabeth. It was draining enough, and he couldn't have loose ends with her. "What's wrong with you, luv?" Elizabeth asked, now concerned.

"I want a divorce, luv," he said meekly. One hand rose to touch Elizabeth's face. She backed away from it, staring at him for a moment and seeming at a loss for words. Of course, that condition did not last long. "Why, you sonofabitch," she finally said, her temper rising from zero to one hundred in no time. "You dragged me all the way from Switzerland to tell me *that*?"

"I'm sorry, luv," he said. Then he and Suzy walked away from her, leaving her standing alone in the bar.

She was upset, but not so much that she didn't go to one of his preview performances anyway. She loved him, and she was used to being disappointed by him . . . and she wasn't going to miss his show, no matter what. After the performance, it was chilly backstage between them, as one might expect. The next day, when Richard got back to the theater, he went to his dressing room and, in a scene right out of *Butterfield 8*, saw a message from Elizabeth written in lipstick on the mirror. It said, simply, "You are fantastic, Luv." Richard didn't erase it for the entire run of the play.

On July 29, 1976, less than ten months after they were wed for a second time, Elizabeth Taylor and Richard Burton were granted their second divorce. Finally, she said, she wanted some jurisdiction over her own life, and the only way to obtain it was to let Richard go. "I love Richard with every fiber of my soul," she said before delivering what had to have been one of the greatest understatements of her life. "But we can't be together. We're too mutually self-destructive."

Part Six

COMING TO TERMS

John Warner

In the summer of 1976, as the paperwork was being finalized for Elizabeth Taylor's second divorce from Richard Burton, she was invited to a Washington bicentennial reception commemorating the two hundredth anniversary of the United States, and honoring Queen Elizabeth II of England. The invitation came about because Henry Kissinger had met Elizabeth Taylor and Richard a year earlier in Israel and was enchanted by them. When he heard how terribly unhappy she was at her separation from Burton, he invited her to Washington, where she began attending social and political functions on almost a daily basis. "She swept into Washington like Cleopatra into Rome," wrote one reporter at the time. Her escort to most of the functions was Halston, her fashion designer.

When she began to consider her appearance at the bicentennial reception honoring the President and the Queen, Elizabeth had thought she'd attend with either Halston or her hairdresser. She didn't want to go to the gala alone, she said, that much was certain. British ambassador Sir Peter Ramsbotham suggested that she go to the party with the chairman of the Bicentennial Commission, John Warner. Though she'd met him casually on several occasions, Elizabeth didn't remember him. However, after her date with him at the reception, she'd never forget him.

On the surface, it seemed that the Republican politician John William Warner Jr. was a different kind of man for Elizabeth, a complete contrast to anyone she'd ever dated before, let alone married. Six feet tall and silver-haired, Warner was born on February 18, 1927, to a family that was well-off, though not affluent. A Navy man, he served during the last two years of World War II and was then with the Marines in Korea. He got his law degree from the University of Virginia in 1956. A year later, he became an assistant U.S. attorney in Washington. That same year, 1957, he married heiress Catherine Mellon of the Pittsburgh Mellons, whose wealth of more than a billion dollars was derived from oil and banking. (Carnegie-Mellon University in Pittsburgh and Washington's Andrew Mellon National Gallery of Art of the Smithsonian complex are but two of the institutions that have benefited from the family's largesse.)

In 1972, Warner became Richard M. Nixon's Secretary of the Navy. Shortly thereafter, in 1973, his marriage ended, he says, over the couple's disagreement about the Vietnam War—he for it, she against. With his divorce from Mellon netting him a settlement of almost $8 million, he was living quite comfortably at Atoka Farms, a 2,200-acre estate in Middleburg, Virginia, when he met Elizabeth.

Three years later, in 1976, he took his position with the Bicentennial Commission. He was a distinguished man at the age of fifty, thought of as one of the most eligible bachelors in Washington. He was also a tad . . . *dull.* "You never thought of him as being funny or charismatic," said one person who knew him and his family well at the time. "He wasn't particularly witty, either. He was just a very nice, even-tempered man with simple tastes. A nice way of putting it? He was earthy."

In some ways, John seemed perfect for Elizabeth, a woman who needed a break in her life from the fast-paced, excessive lifestyle she'd lived as Richard Burton's wife for more than a decade. She was, at forty-four, no longer getting offers for plum roles, which didn't bother her. She felt that she needed time away from Hollywood anyway. Simply put, she was tired. Being half of "Liz and Dick" had nearly killed her—many times over, actually.

Diane Stevens no longer worked for John Springer but had stayed in touch with Elizabeth over the years. She says, "The romance with John happened very quickly. She went to his estate in Virginia, took a breath of fresh country air and absolutely loved it. There were farm animals and tractors, and horses and motorcycles which she and John rode. He has three children and they were teenagers, but not like her own in the sense that they were completely unselfish, not spoiled in the least. They were a delight to be around. 'You would not believe the life John has,' she told me on the phone that August. 'It's so tranquil, so beautiful with the most lovely rolling hills and the smells of healthy living. If I never make another movie again and could live here forever with no stress, I would be very happy.' As she spoke to me, she cursed and dropped the phone. 'What's going on?' I asked when she returned. 'Oh, I was cooking hot dogs on the grill for the kids and the damn little things slipped into the charcoal. Now I have to start all over.' This was a switch: Elizabeth Taylor grilling hot dogs! I told her that I thought she would miss the pace of not only Hollywood, but her jet-setting life. 'How will you exist without Rome, Paris, New York?' 'Oh, please,' she said. 'I've been all over the world and, frankly, I'm exhausted. I am absolutely sick of being *Elizabeth Taylor*. I'm sick of being the main attraction in a three-ring circus. Is that so wrong?' Then she had to go, she said, because she had to feed the chickens. So, I completely understood the connection she had with John Warner's life. It was as if Velvet Brown had grown up and was having a good life on the farm, riding her horse and feeding the farm animals.

"But I was concerned about Warner himself. When I finally met him a couple months later, I thought he was quite nice but not very challenging. Elizabeth needs a good challenge in romance to keep it interesting for her. Look at her husbands before him: Todd and Burton, the loves of her life, were very unpredictable and she loved that about them. I felt John was a little staid. But she seemed happy, so what could I do but be happy for her? It happened too quickly, though. The ink wasn't even dry on her divorce papers from Burton."

Elizabeth had to leave her Velvet Brown world behind for a

while to go to Vienna late in the summer to film the movie version of Stephen Sondheim's Broadway hit *A Little Night Music*. She didn't really want to do it, but had committed to the part earlier and decided to just brave it out as best she could. Her heart wasn't in it, though. She had to sing "Send in the Clowns," which terrified her. "Every great singer has done it," she said, "and now, here comes Chunko." She gained fifteen pounds during this production.

While Elizabeth was in Vienna, she and John Warner had lengthy conversations about life and love and, in a sense, began forging their romantic relationship by long-distance telephone communication. This was certainly a different kind of "falling in love" experience for Elizabeth, if only because, at least at this early stage, it was a relationship built on a foundation of something other than melodrama and misery. For her and John, there were no acrimonious fights and horrible name-calling sessions followed by passionate lovemaking. But contrary to what people on the outside may have believed to be the case about him by first glance, Warner slowly revealed himself to be quite the chauvinist. He made it clear early on that if Elizabeth was to be in his life, she would have to give up aspects of her own. "That Hollywood stuff and all those jewels will have to go," he told her. As she got to know him, she realized that he was a lot like her ex-husbands, controlling and manipulative. Rather than run for her life, she did just the predictable opposite: She began to cling to him and become emotionally attached. Once again, she had found a man who would dominate her and force her to adhere to his ways.

Elizabeth and John spoke for hours about his political agenda and ideals. He genuinely seemed to want to contribute to mankind, or at least to the state of Virginia. His temperament and personality were very different from the men Elizabeth had known over the years. All of her husbands had been in show business, with the exception of Nicky Hilton—and Hilton rarely crossed her mind. John Warner seemed the least self-involved man Elizabeth had ever known, next to her own father, Francis. She suspected that he might even be able to influence her out of her own self-interests

On October 1, 1976, John Warner stepped down from his position as director of the Bicentennial Commission and flew to Vienna to be with Elizabeth. He asked her to marry him and presented her with a dazzling ring made of rubies, diamonds, and sapphires. It was almost as if he couldn't decide which gem to give her so he gave her three of the best just to cover his bases. It was understandable; she *was* Elizabeth Taylor, after all. Imagine his predicament in trying to find an engagement ring that might impress her.

Elizabeth eagerly accepted the ring, and his proposal. True to her nature and pattern over the years, she was a woman who simply could not be alone . . . even for a few months. It had only been one year since she and Richard Burton had married the second time, and just three months since their second divorce was finalized. Between Burton and Warner, she'd almost ended up with Henry Wynberg. Considering the dire consequences she'd suffered in recent years as a result of her choices where, for instance, Richard was concerned, it might have made sense for her to at least come to terms with those two marriages (and divorces) before leaping headfirst into the next one. Only Elizabeth knows what was in her heart and mind at the time. However, in reading between the lines in interviews she's given and in what she's written in her books and articles, it becomes evident that she simply was not capable of reviewing her life without becoming so emotionally devastated that she would soon find herself in a dark state. Out of despair, she would turn to alcohol . . . and that would lay ruin to any kind of self-examination. She was strong in many ways, but not in one important way: It takes resolve and self-discipline to look back critically over one's experiences and vow not to repeat the same mistakes, and Elizabeth wasn't capable of doing it. In her defense, her life had been so charged with emotion for so many years, it's understandable that she would not want to relive much of it. However, in constantly moving forward without giving any real thought to the past, she would be doomed to a life of utter despair . . . and not fully understand the reasons for it.

If Elizabeth didn't know exactly what to expect from John Warner, she found out in the fall of 1976 when he gave a speech supporting Gerald Ford's bid for the presidency at a stock car race, in front of an audience of 35,000. He introduced Elizabeth as his fiancée and said that he wanted to make her a "citizen of the state." It was about all he could do for her, and unofficially, because she wasn't even a citizen of the United States! "I lean a little to the right and Elizabeth leans a little to the left," he told the roaring crowd, "and we both consider ourselves progressive-thinking people." Soon after, in November, he spoke at a function to commemorate the Virginia Military Institute's Founder's Day. Later that month, she flew to Los Angeles to do a small role in the television movie *Victory at Entebbe*, a three-hour made-for-television movie that wasn't a highlight in Elizabeth's career.

Elizabeth Marries John

On Saturday, December 4, 1976, Elizabeth married John Warner in an intimate sunset service at his Atoka Farms estate. The fifteen-minute Episcopalian ceremony was attended only by a few close friends and employees of the couple. At this same time, the incumbent Virginia Senator William Scott announced that he would not seek reelection. The Warners would spend early 1977 testing the political waters for his own possible senatorial candidacy.

Since much of John Warner's Republican constituency was

conservative, the question at hand was whether or not the "wow factor" of Elizabeth Taylor's presence on his arm and behind his podium would outweigh the controversial image of a Hollywood actress who'd been married seven times. Some of John's comments about Elizabeth seemed particularly egregious. He liked to call her his "little heifer," for instance. Often he referred to her as his "little woman." As insulting as this might have been to many women at this time—particularly given the burgeoning feminist movement of the 1970s—Elizabeth took no issue with such remarks. Every time she married, she'd made it clear that her greatest desire was to be totally engulfed by her husband. She had repeatedly said over the years that, if possible, she would gladly abandon her career to be the wife of . . . (fill in the blank). Now that she was Warner's wife, she would repeat similar refrains, but with new themes having to do with finding her true home: "I am so happy to just be John's wife. I finally feel that I have a home. My search for roots is finally over."

In February 1977, Elizabeth and John took off for Los Angeles where she had a cameo in a political thriller called *Winter Kills*. They'd made a vow that they would never be apart—the same promise Elizabeth had made with her other husbands. In the film, which starred Jeff Bridges and Anthony Perkins, Elizabeth was on-screen for about thirty seconds and mouthed four words: "Son of a bitch." John Warner even made his motion picture debut in that brief scene—or at least his right arm did. Elizabeth played a madam who was blackmailing the President of the United States. Warner played the President, unseen except for the arm. He had no lines. Some who knew Elizabeth joke that it was the first time he'd been quiet since meeting her.

The rest of 1977 found Elizabeth playing perhaps the oddest and most incongruous role of her life: the wife of a senatorial candidate.

It may be an affront to Elizabeth to note here that she had spent a good deal of her life up until this time as a self-possessed and, sometimes, selfish woman. It's difficult to believe that she would disagree with this harsh assessment. Elizabeth is not like a lot of celebrities of her stature who refuse to recognize their faults and instead live in constant denial of them. However, this is not to say that she could not be a supportive wife when she wanted to. She prides herself on what she has called her "old-fashioned sense of a wife's obligations and [I] always have been the malleable one in marital situations. I adapt one hundred percent to my husband's life, willingly and happily." It's true. Don't forget that she was the wife who traveled the world with Mike Todd helping to promote his *Around the World in 80 Days*. She was also the one sitting ringside at all of those Eddie Fisher performances, and how much fun could that have been? She put her career aside for Richard Burton's on several occasions, and were it not for her there were many performances Richard never would have been able to complete.

As John Warner's wife, though, her loyalty would be pushed to the extreme on the campaign trail. Could she survive without a limousine at her beck and call, and instead travel on a Greyhound bus? Would she be able to be punctual? (Had she ever been on time for anything in her life, *ever*?) Could she survive without her hairdresser, her makeup woman? More important, could she give of herself in a totally unselfish manner to someone else's cause, a venture that really had nothing to do with her own career, her own personal desires, or even her own interests? With her other husbands, she had been available to support them, but it was easier for her to do since their ventures were show business—related and she had been comfortable and at home with that. It's also true that she had given money to hospitals and charities in the past, but writing a check or making a quick speech was never much of an investment for her. It certainly wasn't the same as spending day after day on the campaign trail.

As Elizabeth and John traveled the state to win support from his party for his possible candidacy, she met at a grassroots level with the very people who had supported her movie career for so many years: her so-called "public." Shaking hands with people in the "real world," kissing their babies and making conversation with them, all the while smiling cheerfully, was a new version of Elizabeth Taylor Warner, one that completely captivated her public in part because of its accessibility factor. Her fans were used to Elizabeth running *from* them, not *toward* them. And, for her part, she had to recalibrate the way she thought about the public, thinking now of it as consisting of allies, not foes. Paparazzi had for years been the bane of her existence. Now she had to accommodate them and smile gamely in their direction rather than risk the wrong kind of picture being published in the press.

The routine was the same, day after day: As the Warners would pull up to a political rally in their Greyhound bus, John would squeeze his wife's hand and whisper, "Game time," in her ear. She would spray perfume on her wrists, and gently rub them together. "Okay, let's do it," she would say as the driver opened the door. "You'll be great," he would tell her. Then they would be off, into the crowd for another day of baby-kissing and handshaking— 2,000 hands a day, Elizabeth estimated. Later, John would stand at a lectern and give a well-executed speech, Elizabeth all the while gazing up at him with admiration . . . the perfect politician's wife.

There were, of course, some comical moments on the campaign trail, as one would expect from Elizabeth Taylor. For instance, she and John were in a private airplane flying over Virginia when she suddenly had to go to the bathroom. The plane's facilities were in disrepair, but she had to go, and she couldn't wait another second. John instructed the pilot to make an emergency landing in an open field. When it landed, Elizabeth had a choice of either going in the field or running to a nearby home. She chose the house, which, as she looked around, truly seemed to be in the middle of nowhere. Imagine the surprise of the woman who answered the door to find Elizabeth Taylor standing there asking if she could use her bathroom! "I'll never forget the expression on that poor lady's face," Elizabeth said, laughing.

Elizabeth would later observe that the discipline and perseverance she'd depended on for years as an actress in Hollywood would be key to her success on the campaign trail. She would also have to admit that the work of a politician makes that of the actor look like child's play. She was taken aback by the obvious: that what comes out of the mouth of a politician or his wife has to be "golden" because there are no retakes, no "director's cuts." A politician has to think on his feet, not depend on a script. For Elizabeth, a woman who has always had a script before her when performing, either onstage or, much more often, before a camera, this was not easy. Still, she welcomed the challenge. When it came to giving speeches or answering questions, she would not have memorized a script but she would do her best to remember the one thing that would always be true: She was still Elizabeth Taylor, no matter the venue, a smart and savvy woman. If she gave sincere thought to what she was saying and spoke from the heart, she could speak extemporaneously and not go wrong.

Day after day, week after week . . . it was the same grind. Just dealing with the public in such close proximity was a challenge. "You're a lot bigger in person than I thought you'd be," a housewife told her at one rally. "How nice," Elizabeth said with a frozen smile. John walked over and pulled her away. "Thank you for rescuing me," Elizabeth told him. "Funny," he said, "I never thought of you as the kind of woman who needs rescuing, Pooters." She put her head on his shoulder as they walked into the crowd. (Warner's nickname for Taylor was "Pooters.")

Still, despite any difficulties she may have experienced, there was something redemptive about this time in Elizabeth's life. She was spending all of her time devoted to something other than herself, or her career. Most of her life had been consumed by her own very dramatic history, so for her to now place as top priority John's political career and, by extension, maybe even the well-being of his broad constituency was a good lesson for her. "The campaign was harder than anything I'd done in my own career," she would later say, "but I have to admit that there was something exhilarating about it." Indeed, she had to admit that giving of herself in this way felt good and made her feel that she was contributing to something important, something that really mattered. Still, it ate away at her that she wasn't being true to who she was as a woman, as a movie star. She enjoyed what she was doing with John Warner, but still, on a deep level—as she would later explain— she wished that she could experience that sense of generosity and also preserve her identity as a star, the person she'd been since childhood.

Not that there wasn't the occasional show business work. For instance, in the summer of 1978, Elizabeth went to Los Angeles to tape a TV movie of the week called *Return Engagement*. It was a Hallmark Hall of Fame television movie in which Taylor portrays Emily Loomis, a professor of ancient history at a small California college. She reluctantly rents a room in her house to a new student, played by Joseph Bottoms. Both happen to be loners—she with a secret past—and after an initial shaky start, they eventually develop a rapport in which they help one another emerge from their emotional shells. Strange as it always was to see the great screen legend Elizabeth Taylor in a TV movie, once the viewer got past that distraction the film was actually quite enjoyable. Elizabeth was heavier in it than perhaps she'd ever been on film. Though she was unhappy with her appearance, the extra weight did somehow underscore her character's sense of loneliness and desperation. In that sense, her physical appearance was an asset to her characterization.

In the end, at the GOP convention, John lost his party's vote to run for the Senate. The victory went to his opponent Richard Obenshain, former chairman of the state Republican Party. He would be running against Democratic candidate Andrew P. Miller, a former state attorney general.

Elizabeth returned to Virginia in July, determined to help John find a new place in politics. But then, in a twist as sudden and tragic as any of Elizabeth's true-life plotlines, Richard Obenshain was killed on August 2 in a light plane crash. The task of picking a new GOP nominee fell to the seventy-eight-member Republican State Central Committee. They chose John Warner, although he was regarded as less conservative than Obenshain; there was no one else in the running. At a press conference, Warner said that his wife "will join very actively in my campaign." He also said she was hit "very severely by Obenshain's death because one of her previous husbands, film producer Mike Todd, was killed in a plane crash." Obenshain "was a good friend, he waged a good fight and gave all he had," Warner said. "Fate has dictated that someone must step up and assume that responsibility."

John Warner received encouragement and offers of support from political leaders throughout the state. He portrayed himself as a strong candidate who could lead, who cared about people, and who "doesn't need on-the-job training. I pledge every ounce of strength and wisdom I have in this race," he said.

For the next three months, Warner would campaign tirelessly, spending more than a million dollars in his bid to convince voters that he would do them proud as their Senator. Everywhere he went, Elizabeth was at his side, shaking hands, posing for photographs, giving brief speeches. The days were long—twelve, sometimes fifteen hours—and the work grueling, but with no pretense and no star attitude, Elizabeth was determined that she would see it through, and do so without betraying that she was beginning to lose her identity in the process. An interesting metaphor for what she was going through at this time comes in the form of an anecdote about her favorite color, purple. A delegation from the Republican Party came to her one day with the request that she not wear the color. Elizabeth Taylor not swathed in purple fabric? Never! However, she was told that the color denotes passion . . . "and we mustn't have passion," . . . and also royalty . . . "and we mustn't have royalty." Elizabeth would later joke that she wasn't sure if they were trying to prevent her from looking like a whore, or the Queen . . . but at the time it wasn't funny to her. Rather, it felt like evidence of what she was losing in her marriage: her very identity. She stopped wearing purple.

The campaign went onward without incident except for one potentially fatal event that happened at the end of October. While at a political buffet in Big Stone Gap, Virginia, Elizabeth went into the kitchen with John. "Have a piece of chicken, Pooters," he suggested. "Who knows when we will have the time to eat again." Elizabeth reached for a breast, took a huge bite, and swallowed. She then began to choke on a bone she later estimated was about two and half inches long. In an attempt to dislodge it from her throat, she swallowed some bread, which only made matters worse. It was clear to everyone that she was choking to death. She was rushed to Lonesome Pine Hospital, where the bone had to be removed by a surgeon. Later, John Belushi's popular portrayal of a zaftig Elizabeth choking on a chicken bone on a *Saturday Night Live* sketch was horrifyingly funny. But Elizabeth did have the last word in her *Elizabeth Takes Off* book: "How ironic and sad that that gifted young man satirized my excesses and then died of his own." (Belushi died of a drug overdose in Hollywood on March 5, 1982.)

Finally, on November 7, 1978, John Warner was elected to the United States Senate, by less than a 1 percent margin. Out of 1.2 million votes, he won by just 4,271. Without Elizabeth, there's little doubt he would have lost. "I have to have at least 4,271 fans in Virginia," she joked afterward, "so at least I know I pulled my own weight." She couldn't say much, though, during the election-night festivities at the Jefferson Hotel in Richmond. Hardly able to speak, she'd just been released from the hospital and had been told not to strain her vocal cords. "I'm just so thrilled because I know you did the right thing," she said from the lectern, her voice barely a whisper.

"I cannot tell you how happy and proud I was of him," she said of John Warner when remembering the day he was sworn into office, "and, yes, of myself, too. The ceremony marked one of the happiest moments of my life. I had no idea," she concluded, "that it also marked the beginning of the end of my marriage."

An Important Transition

When people who have followed Elizabeth Taylor's life and times think of her marriage to Senator John Warner, they usually view those years as little more than just transitional between her fifth and sixth husband, Richard Burton, and her eighth husband, Larry Fortensky. It's true that the six years Elizabeth spent as Warner's wife were the most uneventful in her career. There were a couple of mediocre movies and a theater venture, as we shall see, but the glory days of her legendary career were pretty much behind her. It happens to the best of film stars as they mature. Elizabeth has said that she understood as much and wasn't overly concerned about it. However, people who know her well have said that this was a much more difficult transition for her than she has let on. "The pressure on her to stay youthful and beautiful had been one she'd lived with all of her life," said one good friend of hers. "With the passing of time, it was clear that she could not defy Mother Nature. She was getting older, and Hollywood was losing interest. It was a hard thing for her to accept. I know she was depressed about it, drinking a lot because of it. It just added to the general malaise of this time frame."

Even though the years as Mrs. John Warner would not yield much in terms of her film career, it would prove significant in the bigger picture of her life. It was during these years, after all, that Elizabeth would undergo a slow yet dramatic personal transformation of body and spirit that would begin to define her future character and personality.

One of the biggest problems in Elizabeth's life up until she married the Senator had to do with time: She never had any . . . to think, to review, to assess where she'd been, to contemplate where she was headed and how she felt about it. As for having any kind of inner life, of coming to terms with her mistakes and resolving to move forward and never make those choices again . . . it just was never Elizabeth's way. Not only had she constantly been on a professional schedule of making movies, she had also been living a tumultuous personal life with her many illnesses and many husbands.

The first time Elizabeth actually *did* take the time to consider her life was during her marriage to Senator John Warner. It was then that she began to review some—though certainly not all— aspects of her past, and come to certain conclusions. Ironically, there was little else to do in those rolling hills of Virginia for a movie icon in her fifties no longer the toast of the town. Her unintended and self-imposed exile was exactly what she needed at this time in her life. In 1987, Elizabeth would write a self-help weight-loss book about her experiences during this time, *Elizabeth Takes Off*. Certainly, if she hadn't married Warner and then taken the time to finally assess her personal needs, she might not have become the Elizabeth Taylor we all know and associate today with AIDS research and charities.

Elizabeth was bored to tears, as she would tell it, during the years she was married to John Warner. After the constant adrenaline rush of the campaign trail, to suddenly find herself alone on a giant farming estate in Virginia was a shock, definitely something for which she was ill-prepared. After all, she was a woman accustomed to a busy schedule and constant activity, and her social schedule had almost been the death of her on several occasions. Now she had little more to do than tend to the gardens of melons, peppers, and tomatoes, her previous life in Hollywood seeming worlds away. It was peaceful, yes, but also incredibly dull.

Once Warner's senatorial campaign was over he then left her to her own devices for the rest of their marriage. Elizabeth will say today that she and John had shared everything during the early days of their courtship and marriage and that when he was elected she found herself "in a kind of domestic Siberia." In fact, they shared everything . . . that mattered to John. Elizabeth later tried to play down the situation by saying he "turned to his senatorial tasks with passionate devotion." When he became a Senator, Elizabeth had to admit, "I had no function anymore, not even as an ornament."

It wasn't totally Warner's fault, though. He *was* a hardworking man, and no doubt viewed Elizabeth as a resourceful woman who had made her life work in the past—at least that's how it must have seemed to outsiders—and would certainly find a way to make it work in the present. He probably thought she could take care of herself. In truth, there was probably nothing keeping her from a full and exciting life as Mrs. John Warner. After all, she was Elizabeth Taylor. *She* made the rules. Years later when she was promoting *Elizabeth Takes Off*, she was interviewed about this time by Jane Pauley. Elizabeth was talking about her life as a Senator's wife and making many excuses as to why it didn't work for her. Pauley gave her a look of skepticism. Elizabeth then backtracked: "Oh, but it's not that I couldn't have tried harder . . ." In fact, she simply could not cope and had lost interest in life, in trying to find a way to make it worthwhile for herself.

It must also be noted that, traditionally, Senators' wives serve little purpose in their husbands' careers, other than as partners on the campaign trail. Most don't even move to Washington from their home states, preferring to stay behind and raise their children and continue with their domestic duties. However, not only were Elizabeth's children grown, but she had never been a housewife and wasn't about to become one at the age of forty-nine. John would leave the estate in the morning after a rushed breakfast. Elizabeth wouldn't even bother getting out of bed. Eventually she would rise, and then spend the day watching soap operas on television and talking to friends on the telephone. Sometimes she would visit hospitals, particularly the mental health wards, where she formed relationships with several of the young patients. She also gave acting seminars—forty-five of them in a five-year period—which, for the most part, only served to further depress her. She was a film star, not an acting teacher. She didn't even recognize her own life anymore. Her nights were worse. Warner would show up at home with stacks of paperwork and involve himself in his work while Elizabeth tried to figure out ways to get his attention. There was the occasional cocktail party, but for the most part nothing much for her to do.

On some weekends, she would flee to her friend Halston's East 68th Street digs in Manhattan. During these sojourns, she would hang out with Andy Warhol and Truman Capote at Studio 54 and party with the Liza Minnelli crowd. The tabloid press had a field day, photographing and publishing unflattering pictures of an overweight, boozy, obviously miserable Taylor that took her Martha character in *Virginia Woolf* to a whole new level. It was reported that her weight had ballooned to nearly two hundred pounds. The seventy tent dresses, muumuus, and caftans she had ordered from Halston before her marriage to Warner could scarcely conceal her growing girth. The photo of her struggling to exit the backseat of a car during this period was famously selected for the cover of Kenneth Anger's *Hollywood Babylon II*.

As she tried to come to terms with her new identity as a politician's wife, Elizabeth faced a crisis of self-esteem. It may seem strange to those who don't know Elizabeth Taylor personally to think that she would grapple with issues of self-esteem, since she has always seemed confident and secure. But of course, like most of us, she has had those times in her life when she was unsure of herself and her place in the world, rare as they were and never did she feel more like that than when she was married to John Warner. During this time, she became more depressed than she'd ever been before, and that was saying a lot considering some of the dark moments she'd experienced in her life. "It was there," she says, in Virginia, "that I first lost confidence in Elizabeth Taylor the person."

Her only outlet was to eat and drink and take pills to escape her unhappiness. Actually the pattern of abuse had started earlier, on the campaign trail and, obviously, even before that. As we've seen, excessive living had always been a problem for Elizabeth: too much liquor, too many pills . . . too much food. As her weight soared, Halston kept making her caftans bigger, and she just continued to eat to dull her pain.

By the end of 1979, Elizabeth was in real trouble. Her marriage was just about over—they were living separate lives, his outside the house and hers in it—and her health had seriously deteriorated. "I was falling apart in every direction," she recalled. "And for the first time in my life, I had lost an essential ingredient of self-esteem. My pride." The constant barrage of fat jokes by popular comics during this time only served to further whittle away at her. She had never much cared what people thought about her in the past. But to be made fun of, to now suddenly be the butt of jokes, was more than she could bear. It hurt her deeply, probably more than the comedians ever imagined, if they even cared (which, more than likely, they didn't).

The day that Elizabeth forced herself to look into a full-length mirror after getting out of the bathtub was one she would not soon, if ever, forget. As she gazed at her reflection she realized that she was no longer the most beautiful woman in the world, as had been thought of her in the past. It wasn't just her zaftig outward appearance, either. She might have been able to live with it if she'd been truly happy with herself. However, she obviously wasn't. When she looked into the mirror that day she saw not only an obese woman, but a person who had allowed the circumstances of her life to crush her. It was on that day that she knew she had to accept the truth about herself and deal with it . . . somehow.

Once Elizabeth decided that she had to lose weight, she was dedicated to doing it, even if meant having more than a few lapses in judgment along the way. She knew that her life would have to change before she would truly see a change in her physical body, but she wasn't ready to leave John Warner yet. That process would be a slow one. She wasn't in a mad rush to be on her own at this time, and since he was practically an absentee husband it wasn't as if they were fighting and she had no choice but to get out of a bad marriage. Instead, she decided to recapture some of her career, thinking that if she were motivated to lose weight because of an impending role, she might be more likely to stick to a diet.

In May 1980, she accepted a role in the comic thriller *The Mirror Crack'd*, her first speaking part in a film in almost four years. The movie filmed in London and gave her an opportunity to get out of America and away from her husband for a time. When EMI Films decided to make this movie, based on the novel by Agatha Christie, it seemed like an excellent idea, especially with the cast of stars it eventually assembled: Taylor, Angela Lansbury, Kim Novak, Rock Hudson, and Tony Curtis. How could it go wrong? Well, it did . . . and very wrong. One critic said, "It plays like a TV movie of the week," a perhaps too harsh assessment. But despite the presence of five onetime important Hollywood stars, the film could not overcome the hoary plot and mediocre writing. It would fizzle at the box office.

In July, Elizabeth returned to America to attend the Republican convention in Detroit, sitting in the VIP box with her friend Nancy Reagan as Ronnie was nominated for President. The Reagans had recently purchased a home next to the Warners in Virginia, and Elizabeth had hosted a chicken barbecue for them (and 4,000 of their closest friends) at Atoka Farms. Though it was an exciting night at the GOP convention, the world of politics held less meaning to Elizabeth by this time. She had been saying that she felt that she wanted to do something on the legitimate stage, a real challenge for her because it truly was something she hadn't done before, save a few personal appearances and readings with Richard Burton. She needed a good challenge, though, and so she reached out to producer Zev Bufman, whom she had met about a year earlier in New York. The two chose to mount a production of *The Little Foxes*, for which she would be paid $50,000 a week—a pittance considering what she was used to earning, but still more than any other actress had ever been paid to do theater work.

The Little Foxes

When Lillian Hellman's gothic turn-of-the-century drama *The Little Foxes* was translated from stage to screen in 1941, four leading members from the Broadway cast were invited to re-create their roles in the William Wyler film version for RKO. Noticeably absent was Tallulah Bankhead, who had been a sensation on the Great White Way as Regina Giddens. Bette Davis, then at the very pinnacle of her star power, already with two Oscars on her mantel, went after and got the role onscreen of the greedy, murderous, beautiful Regina. Now, forty years later in 1981, Elizabeth, with a string of successful film roles in which she had played very strong, highly motivated Southern beauties—*Giant*, *Raintree County*, *Cat on a Hot Tin Roof*, and *Suddenly, Last Summer*—in what would be her Broadway debut, decided to add Regina Giddens to her portrait gallery of willful femmes fatales from the Deep South.

Her director, Austin Pendleton, remembers his first meeting with his leading lady. "My first reaction when she walked into the room was that she was just like a terrific kind of . . . *gal*," he said. "She was just so direct. She was also extraordinarily beautiful, but there is something about her beauty that includes you in, instead of excluding you. She is extremely generous as an actress, and also a person who has a great appetite for life, for living, for connecting with people . . . for finding the excitement in life. And I thought, what if Regina in *The Little Foxes* had some of those traits? I always thought that was true of Elizabeth anyway, even before I met her, when I was a kid going to her movies. I thought back then, wow. She wants love. She wants good times. She wants her life to be an exciting one. And part of the reason I knew she would have no trouble making the transition from film to stage is because so many of her movies were adaptations of theater pieces: *Cat on a Hot Tin Roof*, *Virginia Woolf*, *Suddenly, Last Summer*, where you had long sustained narrations with tremendous builds, hills and valleys, and I knew if she could do that in front of a camera, she could do it onstage, too."

To begin losing weight, Elizabeth went to a health spa, where she dropped a few pounds. Each time she went back, she would lose a little more. It was a tough process. "I wanted to eat, to be frank," she would recall. "I learned that the only way to lose weight is . . . guess what? *Watch what you eat and exercise.* There is no shortcut."

Elizabeth tells a story that happened one day at the Palm Aire Spa in Pompano Beach, Florida. A young woman, maybe twenty-one, was in the swimming pool exercising and appearing to be quite frustrated. She was terribly overweight. Elizabeth could see the anxiety written all over her face as she attempted to do some water exercises and failed repeatedly at them. Elizabeth, who had just gotten out of the pool herself, went to its side and knelt down. "Don't push yourself so hard, honey," she told the stranger. "You'll get there, I know it. You have to be patient."

"But it's so hard," said the woman, now with tears in her eyes. "I can't do it. I'm a failure at this."

"Nonsense," Elizabeth said as she got back into the pool herself. "Here, let's do those exercises together," she told the surprised young woman. Soon, the two were exercising together, Elizabeth helping the woman with her coordination and posture during the movements. At that moment, it wasn't Elizabeth Taylor, film icon, with some overweight stranger in a swimming pool. Class, status, celebrity . . . none of it meant anything when two flesh-and-blood women were working together to obtain optimum health. "It seems like a nothing moment in the telling of it," Elizabeth would later tell the present author, "but when it happened, it was a real moment. I heard later that I had inspired that young woman, that she was about to give up before that day. Maybe that was true. But she had given me so much in that short time because her presence in that pool, and her exasperation, really crystallized for me that I was not alone in that battle, that it's a struggle for many of us and on a daily basis. You never know," she concluded, "when the golden moments will happen that will change the way you think about things."

Over a period of months, she eventually lost forty pounds, but only by truly dedicating herself to the process because she had a goal: to get on stage and not look heavy in her costumes. She felt a responsibility not only to herself, but to the audience that would be paying money to see her. She wanted to look her best for them. It inspired her to continue to move forward with her dieting and exercise programs. By the end of 1980, it was clear that her marriage was in trouble, but she wasn't as concerned about it as she was about her health and the possibility of rejuvenating her career.

The Little Foxes' pre-Broadway tour had its premiere on February 27, 1981, Elizabeth's forty-ninth birthday, at the Parker Playhouse in Fort Lauderdale, Florida, reportedly chosen by the producers because of its proximity to the spa that Elizabeth had frequented in order to slim down and shape up for what promised to be a grueling eighteen months. The spa worked. At a svelte forty pounds lighter, Elizabeth's next stop was the Eisenhower Theatre at the Kennedy Center in Washington, where President and Mrs. Ronald Reagan occupied a box on opening night. John Warner had arranged for almost half of the United States Senate to be in attendance. Afterward backstage, Elizabeth was chilly to Warner, the strain between them evident.

After Washington, the show was off to New York, where it opened at the Martin Beck Theatre (since renamed the Al Hirschfeld Theatre) on May 7, 1981. The reviews would be mixed, but the audience reception was strong—and Elizabeth had achieved what she'd set out to do by taking the job. She looked like her old self, that much was certain. An hour after the final curtain, when she strode into Sardi's on the arm of John Warner everyone in the restaurant stood up and began applauding. Upon seeing Rock Hudson at a table, she went to embrace him. The cheers grew even stronger.

In New York, Elizabeth appeared for 123 sold-out performances, until September 6. She missed only two weeks when the play was shut down after she became sick with recurring bronchitis. The play was a personal success for her, and for it she was nominated for a Tony, although the play failed to win any of the six for which it had been nominated. Elizabeth was, however, honored with a Theatre World Award as well as a special Outer Critics Circle Award.

After New York, the show moved on to New Orleans and then Los Angeles. While on the West Coast, Elizabeth spent the day taping scenes for a five-day run on her favorite daytime drama, *General Hospital*.

Throughout the run of *The Little Foxes*, John Warner was not really in Elizabeth's life, though they were still married. It was clear to them both that the marriage was over. It became even clearer to Elizabeth when he called her in London and told her that he had sold the estate and bought an apartment at the Watergate Hotel. She would have to find a place for all of her animals, he said. She had horses and dogs and cats, and nowhere to put them. Certainly she deserved more consideration! She noted that she had even sold the famous Burton-Taylor diamond to New York jeweler Henry Lambert for $3 million (three times what Burton paid for it) in order to help defray the costs of Warner's political campaigns. (Lambert, in turn, sold it to internationally known diamond merchant Robert Mouawad.) She said she was "sick" about having parted with the piece.

Still, she wasn't as angry at Warner as one might have expected, which was remarkable. Lucky for him that she had so many other pressing matters on her mind and there wasn't much time for her to feel animosity toward him. She was just over him, finished with the marriage. He felt the same way. The official announcement came on December 21, 1981: They were separating. By the beginning of 1982, Elizabeth had moved back to Los Angeles, purchasing the home of Nancy Sinatra, Frank's first wife, on top of a steep hill at 700 Nimes Road in a heavily wooded section of Bel Air, for about $2 million. Again, as in Virginia, her neighbors here would be the Reagans. This beautiful estate, behind stone walls and iron gates, complete with swimming pool and amazing view of L.A.'s wide vista, remains her comfortable home to this day. It's not an opulent place. It's three stories, but much smaller than one would expect as living quarters for a star of her magnitude.

She was a single woman, again . . . and happy to be "home," back on the West Coast where her career had begun so many years earlier. However, no matter where she ended up in her life, she could never escape the truth: She was a very sick woman, emotionally as well as physically. Though it might have seemed difficult to imagine considering her life up until this time, Elizabeth had not done the one thing she'd need to do to in order to balance the scales of her life, to finally move forward and leave the past behind: She'd have to hit rock bottom, and she was about to do just that.

Sifting Through the Wreckage

Elizabeth Taylor arrived in London on February 23, 1982, to begin rehearsals for *The Little Foxes* there (which was scheduled to open at the Victoria Palace on March 11). Her first order of business was to visit Richard Burton. She hadn't seen him since 1976, when he'd asked her for a divorce in a New York hotel. Since that time, they had both married other people. Still, she'd spent so much time in Virginia with nothing to do as John Warner's wife but wonder about Richard, worry about Richard, obsess over Richard, and try to put her relationship with him into some perspective. What could she take from her two marriages and divorces from him? So much of it made no sense. When she was taken to the hospital on Christmas Eve 1981, complaining of chest pains, who was the first person she called on the telephone? Richard. The two then commiserated about their ruined marriages, hers to Warner and his to Susan Hunt, from whom he was now separated. They promised to see each other in February when Elizabeth would be in London for the opening of *The Little Foxes* there and her fiftieth birthday party. That time was now upon her.

There had been a dark flip side in coming to terms with the past for Elizabeth, one that, in retrospect was perhaps not surprising considering her history. The more she thought about days gone by, the more she drank to escape the pain of so many memories. In recent years, her drinking had become more out of control than ever. She was sinking deeper into a dark abyss, unhappy with the way her life had turned out, wondering if she could have done anything to change it.

As she drank, she also took pills, Percodan being her drug of choice to numb the pain, not only in her body but also in her heart. It was as if dealing with her past life was making things worse for her in the present. "Drugs had become a crutch," she would later admit. "I wouldn't take them just when I was in pain. I needed oblivion, escape . . . I was hooked on Percodan."

It wasn't a new problem, obviously. "There was a doctor, an infamous guy named Max Jacobson," Debbie Reynolds recalls, "who had everyone in Hollywood and Washington and New York hooked on drugs. This is the evil guy who turned Eddie [Fisher] into a speed freak. I used to call him Dr. Needles. I hated him, wouldn't let him come near me. Others called him Dr. Feelgood. He's the one, I think, who got Elizabeth really hooked on drugs. He had vials of bottles in his pocket and he'd give you a shot for anything. If you said, oh, my ear aches, he'd shoot you in the ear. Oh, I have a noseache, he'd shoot you in the nose. He ruined Elizabeth, if you ask me."

The late Sydney Guilaroff once agreed. Of Jacobson he also told his biographer, Cathy Griffin, "I despised him ever since he treated Elizabeth. He's the one that started her on drugs because of her back pain. There were times when I would forget and go to see her and hug her or squeeze her too tight, and she would go, '*uh-oh.*' In other words, 'I'm in pain.' There were a lot of other doctors, but I believe he got her into the drugs to start with and always made himself available to her, just to make sure he had her as a patient."

To fully comprehend the scope of Elizabeth's drug problem, consider this: In the five-year period between 1980 to 1985, she was given more than a thousand prescriptions for different drugs ranging from sleeping pills to painkillers to tranquilizers. *More than a thousand.* On one particular day in the mid-1980s she was prescribed massive amounts of Demerol, Percocet, Xanax, and Ativan.

On the one hand, Elizabeth's situation demonstrates the lax attitude of the medical profession when it comes to celebrities. It is hard to forget the death of Elvis Presley in 1977 from a heart attack following an all-night binge of prescription drugs. People often have a hard time saying no to stars, and not just doctors. It's one of the reasons the rich and famous have so much trouble in their lives. It's corruptive for an emotionally unstable person to be able to have all of her dangerous desires instantly granted, no matter what it may be that the patient believes will get her through a stormy time. For Elizabeth, it was prescription drugs, and she had no trouble getting them.

On the other hand, consider this: *She needed them.* She was in chronic pain and these drugs were prescribed to her for good reasons, even if they were overprescribed.

It was in this treacherous environment of alcohol and drug usage that Elizabeth attempted the monumental task of sorting out her past with Richard Burton. Even under the best and most sober of times, it would have been a challenge to sift through the wreckage of their two marriages and divorces. In the end, the conclusion she finally came to, doing the best she could on her own without a therapist to guide her, could not have been more depressing: She loved him for no reason other than that she'd always been compelled to do so. That was it. After months of deliberation about it, the only thing she was able to come to was as simple and as unsatisfying—and as superficial—as digging her heels into the ground and saying that she had no choice in the matter, fate had decreed it. And, worse, she had to admit that she still felt the same way about him. It certainly wasn't much, in terms of trying to reconcile the past.

As soon as she got to London, Elizabeth felt compelled to make a pilgrimage to the Hampstead Heath home, one of the houses in which she and Howard were raised by Francis and Sara. The old homestead had been owned since 1981 by socialite Susan Licht and her husband, a banker. Elizabeth, feeling confused about her present and hopeless about her future, needed to go back to a time when life had been simpler. She missed her father, she would say, and lately could not get him off her mind.

Sara was still alive, of course, but she was elderly and not well. Elizabeth still had ambivalent feelings about the way she had been long ago pushed into show business by her mother, but she was working her way through them. What else could she do but just go on with her life? It hadn't been so bad, after all. Perhaps Sara had done her no favors by encouraging her along the road to stardom, and certainly Francis had felt that way. However, Elizabeth's life had been filled with as many blessings as curses, and she couldn't spend the duration blaming her mother for the bad and not at least crediting her for *some* of the good. Sara Taylor would be present in the audience for the London opening of *The Little Foxes*, which actually helped make the evening complete for Elizabeth. Still, Elizabeth wouldn't think to burden her with the details of her present miseries.

One afternoon at 4 p.m., Elizabeth showed up at the Lichts' door with actor Nicolas Costa, a costar of hers in *The Little Foxes* (who was born in Hampstead). "We're taking a stroll down memory lane," she told Susan, after apologizing for not calling first. "We've never met and I didn't have your phone number," she explained. "I hope you don't mind." After a stunned Susan let Elizabeth into the house, Taylor walked about with Nicolas, reliving some of her fondest memories. "The nursery was there," she said, "and there," she added, her voice quivering as she pointed to a closet underneath the staircase, "why, that's the walk-in closet where the awful maid used to stick Howard when he was a bad boy." Susan and Nicolas were stunned by Elizabeth's recollection of what had to have been an awful punishment for her brother. She also remembered that Sara had wanted to coax Howard into show business and arranged for him to have an audition with Universal. However, the youngster was so determined to stay *out* of show business that he shaved his head before the audition so that he would not be accepted! The matter-of-fact manner in which Elizabeth rattled off these memories was a little disturbing. It made the others wonder just what kinds of domestic problems the Taylor children had dealt with, situations that no one other than they and their parents would ever know about—or talk about. It was the first time, Elizabeth quickly said, that she had thought about those stories in years. In fact, she'd forgotten all about them. The actress shook her head sadly. "You know, I came here to feel better, and, oddly, I feel worse. But you have done a marvelous job of redecorating the house," she told Susan, trying to perk up. "It's just lovely. Maybe one day I will buy this house from you and live here again," she concluded, her voice tinged with sadness.

When Elizabeth Taylor aficionados hear this story, they think of another time Elizabeth blurted something surprising about her childhood, during an appearance she made at an interview Michael Jackson did with Oprah Winfrey in 1993. Elizabeth said a few words, and she mentioned, out of the blue, that she had also been abused, like Michael, as a child. Jackson had been physically abused by his father: Was Elizabeth saying that the same thing had happened to her at Francis's hands? There was no other frame of reference for it; she never mentioned it before, or since. It's just as likely that she was talking about emotional abuse, referencing her father's lack of involvement in her life. Though there are no other sources to support that Francis had hit Elizabeth, Stefan Verkaufen, who knew Francis, said, "I can see it. He was frustrated. He drank. Sometimes, when he was drinking, he would lash out. I never asked him if he hit his children, but as much as I truly loved Francis, I can't say I would be surprised if he did." If it's true that she was abused by Francis, it does provide another puzzle piece to her life. Certainly some of the men in her life had beaten her, drank, abused her in some fashion. One way or another, it always seemed as if she were reliving her childhood trauma. Maybe this is why whenever she would think of Richard, who was sometimes abusive, she thought of Francis.

Later that day, Richard Burton was to arrive in London. As it happened, he was flying into London for a charity performance of fellow Welshman Dylan Thomas's *Under Milk Wood*, at the same time as Elizabeth's rehearsal schedule for *The Little Foxes*. She called him and reminded him that they'd agreed to see each other. He remembered and said he couldn't wait to see her as well. Her mood was lifted just hearing his dulcet tones on the telephone.

A Birthday Reunion with Richard

Elizabeth sent a car to collect Richard at the airport and bring him straight to her Chelsea townhouse at 22 Cheyne Walk, which had been leased for the run of the play. When he showed up at her doorstep, she was stunned by how he had aged. He was fifty-six now, but he looked a good fifteen years older. He'd always liked to say, "Forty is enough for Dylan, and it's enough for me" (speaking of his hero, Dylan Thomas, who died at forty). He had now surpassed Thomas by sixteen years, but was the worse for wear. He was thin—down from his ideal weight of 175 pounds to about 140—and weak. Not only had all of the drink definitely caught up with him, he was in unremitting pain from a damaged nerve in his hip that had made his right arm almost useless. He'd also had a serious back surgery almost a year earlier and had not fully recovered from it. Finally, he was suffering from ulcers. She thought he looked terrible; her heart went out to him. She suspected that he felt the same way about her—after all, she was terribly overweight and seemed out of breath just in running to the car to greet him. She had been on the road with *The Little Foxes* for eighteen months and had gained back all the weight she'd lost, and then some.

For a few moments, Elizabeth and Richard took each other in with stunned silence, probably wondering how they—two of the most beautiful and sexy figures of the 1960s—had turned out as they had in the 1980s. They couldn't even joke about it as might have been their inclination; it was just that bad. They ignored the obvious about one another and made small talk. Elizabeth then gave Richard a guest room and invited him to a $50,000 birthday party being tossed for her by Zev Bufman at a discotheque called Legends.

The birthday party for Elizabeth's fiftieth was difficult. She wore a silver-and-purple harem pants outfit, in which, given her weight, she did not look her best. "I recently came across one picture taken at my fiftieth birthday party," she once recalled. "It made me shiver. My eyes had disappeared into suet. I'm wearing stage makeup and I look for all the world like a drag queen. I did my best to deny the truth," she said, "but my self-image suffered badly."

Richard wore some sort of a mink jacket, with slacks. His shoulders were stooped, his posture that of a much older man.

Guests at the party included Tony Bennett, Ringo Starr, and Elizabeth's children, including the pregnant Maria. Speaking of her mother and Richard, Maria said, "It was they who taught us how precious love is." In the background, the former lovers danced cheek to cheek, seeming lost in their own reverie.

Richard did not drink much at first, but Elizabeth, no doubt feeling the pressure of the evening, did not know when to stop. She would later admit that during this time she could not leave the house without taking at least two Percodans mixed with Jack Daniel's. She felt that the combination of the drug and alcohol made her somehow more talkative and social, more engaging. "It gave me false courage," she would say. "Then, during the course of an evening—like every four hours—I'd take another two Percodans. And of course I had a hollow leg. I could drink anybody under the table. My capacity to consume was terrifying."

One of Richard's attorneys, Aaron Hill, was present at the party. He recalled that at one point in the evening, Elizabeth approached Richard, a glass of champagne in each hand. She handed one to him. "Here, darling, a toast," she said. "To us."

Richard took the glass. "Perhaps you shouldn't, luv," he said, taking her glass from her as well. She quickly took it back, as if she were somehow seizing power from him. "I *said* . . . a toast," she insisted. Some of the party guests sheepishly gathered around her, seeming embarrassed. "To us," she began in a loud voice. "The greatest goddamned couple of all time. *Liz and Dick*," she continued, slurring her words, using the "Liz" appellation she so loathed. "The toast of the whole goddamn world. Long may we live . . . to love and torture each other . . . until death do we part . . . *and even then!*"

"Hear! Hear!" someone said as people raised their glasses.

"That was quite a toast, my luv," Richard remarked.

"You bet your ass it was," Elizabeth said, clinking his glass. Then, with a loud cackle, she grabbed him by the arm and dragged him back out onto the dance floor. Kicking off her high heels, she danced in a seductive circle in her harem outfit all around Richard to the pounding disco rhythm of Donna Summer's "Love to Love You Baby." Richard just stood frozen in the middle of the floor, stiffly wagging nothing more than his head from left to right. It was an odd sight.

At 1:30 in the morning, Elizabeth took Richard back to her townhouse. They were both intoxicated. She put him to bed and lay next to him, running her fingers through his hair, as she would later recall it, until she knew he was asleep. She spent the night staring at his face, she would tell confidantes years later, trying to divine just what it was about him that had held her captive for so many years. He wasn't much to look at any longer, but still . . . there was something about him. Was it just a matter of shared history? They had always been there for one another . . . or had they? She still loved him, that much she knew. She fell asleep with her head on his chest. In the morning she awakened with a pounding headache, her head now on a pillow. He was already gone. There was no sign that he had ever been in the bed. It was as if he'd never even been in the townhouse at all and she had dreamt the entire birthday evening with him.

That night, Elizabeth felt that she had to see Richard. She knew that he was performing *Under Milk Wood* at the Duke of York Theatre and decided that she would attend the performance.

While Richard was onstage working, Elizabeth, in jeans and a sweater, suddenly walked out from the curtain behind him. The audience erupted into applause, but Burton didn't know why until he turned around and saw his ex-wife standing there. It was a very strange thing for her to do, to interrupt his performance as she had, and he didn't quite know what to make of it. Had she intended to sabotage his performance? Had she been drinking? On some level, he later decided, that's exactly what she had in mind, and exactly what she'd been doing. He looked startled and upset. As the crowd cheered wildly, Elizabeth took a deep bow. "Oh, thank you all, so very much," she said, as if finishing a performance. She then blew kisses at the audience with wide, dramatic arm gestures. After the crowd simmered down, she turned to Richard and, in Welsh, said very sweetly, "I love you."

"Say it again, my petal," Richard said, now having collected himself. "And say it louder."

"I love you!" she exclaimed, again in Welsh. Again, the audience cheered, this time on its feet.

Before she walked offstage, Richard kissed her on the cheek. He then tried to resume his performance, but he had lost his place in the script. "I've got the wrong page," he said, apologizing. "Excuse me. I'm a tad distracted."

After the performance, Elizabeth and Richard left the theater together and went back to her townhouse. He stayed for a couple of hours, during which they had a few drinks and a few laughs, and then he went home. Elizabeth felt happier than she'd been in some time and, as she would later tell it, went to bed and slept soundly for the first time in months.

The next morning, though, she woke up to a huge disappointment. Apparently, when Richard showed up at his hotel the morning after he'd spent the night at her home, after her birthday party, the press was lying in wait for him. The reporters pounced on him for clarification of his relationship with Elizabeth. Now those comments were all over the papers. His version of what happened the night of her birthday was not truthful: "When Elizabeth and I went back to her house after her party, they were all there—the homos and the hangers on. I ordered them all out of the room. I just said 'Get out!' and they all melted away. Then Elizabeth looked at me and said, 'Hey buster, aren't you going to kiss me?' I took her in my arms and kissed her. After we kissed, I pulled her down on the couch . . . just like that. For old times' sake."

After that comment, which suggested that he and Elizabeth had made love, Richard was on a roll. His appearance with Elizabeth had generated interest in him and in *Under Milk Wood*, and he obviously liked the attention. He told the reporters that he had once met John Warner and the first thing he noticed was that "he's smaller than me. He took me to the side and said, 'Well, I've got your Liz now. You were a fool to let her go, weren't you?' What a remarkably objectionable thing to say." He further stated that

Elizabeth had to sell the Burton-Taylor diamond "to support him." He seemed miffed that she got $3 million for it, and asked, "Why didn't the little bitch sell it back to me?" He said that Elizabeth wanted nothing more than to marry him again, but that he refused to do so. "She's an erotic legend—a black-haired dwarf with a big stomach and overflowing breasts. I love her. She's a dear, sweet wonderful legend, and a little bitch." As for her try on the London stage in *The Little Foxes*, he took the opportunity to interfere with her chances with the critics, saying, "I firmly believe she cannot act onstage. In fact, when it comes to the stage, I always tell Elizabeth that she is a divine joke. She normally hits me on the head when I say this."

When Elizabeth read Richard's account of the evening and then his subsequent comments about her, she was truly crushed. She called his brother, Graham, and asked how Richard could have said such things about her. They most certainly did *not* make love on the night of her birthday party, she said. Her publicist, Chen Sam, as well as her bodyguard, her hairdresser, and dresser were all staying at the townhouse, she explained, and she would never have felt comfortable making love to Richard with so many people in the home. How could he take an evening that had been so sweet in so many ways, at least in her memory of it, and turn it into a sordid one-night stand? And furthermore, she had no memory of his ever meeting John Warner, or so she said. In fact, everything Richard had told the press was full of lies. Graham didn't know who to believe, and, no doubt, after so many years of drama between his brother and ex-wife, he didn't much care.

To the hounding press, Elizabeth said of Richard's commentary about her, "I simply don't believe any of it was ever said. Yellow journalism, that's all. I know Richard and I also know he has more class than to say things like this."

Aaron Hill, Richard's attorney (not Aaron Frosch, another of his attorneys) recalled, "Elizabeth called me in tears at about eight in the morning. She said that she couldn't believe the things coming out of Richard's mouth. She didn't even want to speak to him about it, she said, she was too bereft about it.

"I told her, 'Elizabeth, look, he's obviously trying to push you away. Can't you see that? He loves you but he knows that you are poison together. You know how he is. He didn't mean those things.' I didn't want to tell her that he'd met someone else in Vienna [Sally Hay, thirty-four years old and the production assistant of director Tony Palmer on the movie he was working on at the time, *Wagner*]. I wasn't sure if she knew or not. [She apparently didn't. Not yet, anyway.] But I knew that Richard had become serious about this other woman very quickly.

"'But if he would just give us a chance,' she said. 'We're older and wiser now.' I told her, I begged her, in fact, to leave him alone. I told her that he would continue to torture her with his words and actions until she was either gone from him forever or she hated him. She said that they had been beating each other up for so long, she didn't know what to think about any of it. She then asked me to meet her in person at her home. I tried to get out of it, but she was persistent and adamant. 'We must discuss this matter in person,' she insisted. So I agreed to meet her that morning, though very reluctantly."

When Aaron Hill showed up at Elizabeth's door, she greeted him in a flowing white caftan, her hair wrapped in a silk matching scarf. She wore no makeup, her eyes red from crying. He sat down in the parlor, she across from him.

"So, have you talked to Richard about me?" Elizabeth asked, according to Aaron's memory. Her voice was flat and devoid of expression, as if she were exhausted. She fixed him a drink, Jack Daniel's with six cubes of ice. "My lucky number," she said as she dropped each cube in the glass after having poured the liquor, thereby splashing it messily all over the bar.

"Yes, I have," Aaron said, lying. He took the drink but discreetly put it down. It was only 10 a.m. "Elizabeth, he's so very sorry he hurt you with the press. He said that the reporters just wouldn't leave him alone and he only wanted to give them good copy. He didn't mean a single word of it. He's surprised you are hurt, says you know better than to take him seriously."

"But you told me earlier that he was trying to push me away," Elizabeth said, her tone accusatory. "Which is it? Is he sorry, or is he trying to get rid of me?"

"It's *both*, Elizabeth. You have to protect yourself. You have to leave him alone."

"But he looks so sick," Elizabeth said. She reached out and took the attorney's hands in her own. "Please. You must help *me* so that I can help *him*," she said. "He needs me now more than ever. As you well know, I have always been there for him," she said, "and I'll be damned if I am going to stop now."

Aaron had no comment. He would later say he was struck by her devotion, especially in light of Richard's very cruel public comments about her.

"So, listen, I have an idea," Elizabeth continued, suddenly speaking with confidence. It was about to become clear why she had asked to see the attorney in person. "Zev [Bufman] and I were talking and we thought it would be just *fabulous* if Richard and I were to do a show together, a play . . . so, look, we're thinking of Noël Coward's *Private Lives*." She seemed elated. "Just think of the *money* we could make. Liz and Dick onstage, for all of their fans to see, up close and *personal*. And throughout it all, I would have a chance to keep an eye on him," she continued. "And we would be together, and . . . who knows what can happen? Maybe a *third* marriage," she said with a laugh, but probably not kidding. "Isn't this a just a *grand* idea? Tell me you will help me," she said, pushing. "Tell me you will talk to Richard and convince him that this is a good idea. Promise me."

Aaron Hill promised to talk to Richard about Elizabeth's proposition.

"God Has Kept an Eye on My Children"

As 1982 came to a close, for Elizabeth Taylor the happiest memories of the year probably involved her children. Earlier in the year, in February, she had married off her adopted daughter, Maria—now twenty-one—to entertainment agent Steve Carson. Maria had grown into a beautiful woman, and with her bluish green eyes, dark hair, and full face, she actually looked as if she could be Elizabeth's natural daughter. Now she was working as a model and her previous handicaps were all but forgotten; she had no limp whatsoever. Brian O'Neal, a good friend of Steve's and Maria's (he worked in the same talent agency as Steve, the Fifi Oscard Agency), recalled that Steve nearly got off on the wrong foot with Elizabeth when the announcement of their marriage was made in the press before she'd had an opportunity to make it herself. "He had not yet met Elizabeth, and definitely didn't want her to have the wrong impression of him," says O'Neal. "He got her on the phone as soon as he could. They had a tense conversation, during which he asked her, 'Are you going to be mad at us forever?' His face softened at her answer. When he hung up, I asked what she had said. She told him, 'Steve, know this about me. I'm never mad at anyone forever.'"

Maria would introduce her friend Brian to Elizabeth at the rehearsal dinner, which took place at the Tavern on the Green. "She looked terrific in a dark blue satin dress, diamonds on her ears that were the size of golf balls, a jeweled necklace, and gold slingback shoes. I was nervous. 'What should I call her?' I asked Maria. 'Well, there's no need to call her Miss Taylor. And definitely do not call her Liz. Just call her Elizabeth.' When we met, she was perfectly charming. The next day was the wedding ceremony in a suite at the Helmsley Palace Hotel. My position was directly next to Princess Grace of Monaco." In the middle of the ceremony, during a quiet moment between the newlyweds, a clock radio went off somewhere in the suite with loud, blaring music. Princess Grace looked at Brian, a horrified expression playing on her face. She then started searching for the source of the intrusion, trying to be discreet as she looked under pillows and behind couches. Finally, Elizabeth's trusty publicist, Chen Sam, appeared, holding the offending radio in one hand and the plug in the other; she had saved the day. Elizabeth mouthed her thanks to Chen, seeming quite relieved. The rest of the wedding went off without a hitch. (Maria would have a baby in November 1983, naming the child after her beloved mother.)

Later in the year, Michael would marry Brooke Palance, daughter of the actor Jack Palance. His relationship with Elizabeth had gotten so much better with the passing of time. An actor himself, though one for whom commercial success had always been elusive, he was heartened by his mother's unwavering support of his career, with always trying her best to make his opening nights in theater productions. He'd turned out to be a levelheaded, respectable person, getting past his hippie phase with apparent ease. A year earlier, in 1981, his brother, Christopher, had married Aileen Getty, an oil heiress and one of fifteen grandchildren of billionaire John Paul Getty. They would have two children, Caleb and Andrew, and move to Pebble Beach, Florida, where Christopher would become a stained-glass artist. Then, in 1984, Liza would marry artist Hap Tivey. Over the years, Elizabeth had done the best she could with her children, despite her own problems and complications, and apparently it was enough, because her children did seem to turn out quite well. As she put it at Maria's wedding, "God has kept an eye on my children, I think, even during the times when I wasn't able to do so."

Elizabeth Gets Her Way

*A*fter having seen Richard Burton in London, Elizabeth Taylor couldn't help but spend the rest of the year obsessing over him. Earlier, in July and at the end of the run of *The Little Foxes* in London, he'd had the audacity to show up backstage with his new girlfriend, Sally Hay. Elizabeth tried to be cordial, but it was difficult. She was heartsick. Richard had, obviously, moved on . . . again. She would not give up hope, though, that maybe they would be together again, somehow. The good news for her was that he had agreed to star with her in *Private Lives*, which would begin its run on Broadway in the spring of 1983, and that entry in her calendar definitely made her feel optimistic about the future. It would be produced by her newly formed Elizabeth Taylor Theater Company, a venture in which she partnered with Zev Bufman. She would tell anyone who asked that she had no designs on Richard whatsoever, that she had come up with the idea for *Private Lives* strictly as a business venture for the company . . . but even people who didn't know her well knew better, including Sally Hay. "It all seemed accidental but now I'm inclined to think it was very clever on Elizabeth's part, unconsciously perhaps," she says. "The original idea had just been to tape it. And then it was decided to stage it first. Then it was suggested that it be the lead play in Elizabeth's instant new theater company. Had the deal been, 'Do you want seven months on tour with *Private Lives*,' Richard would have fled. But it only came to that when he was too far in."

In the fall of 1982, Elizabeth and Richard summoned their agent, Robert Lantz, to a home she was renting in Bel Air. When he showed up, Zev Bufman was there with Taylor and Burton. Lantz recalls, "I walked into the room and Elizabeth very excitedly said, 'Robbie, we have decided to move forward with the best idea, *ever*. Just wait until you hear it.' Then, after a big, dramatic pause: '*Elizabeth Taylor and Richard Burton in* Private Lives.'

"I made a face. 'No,' I said. 'I don't think it's a good idea at all.

In fact, I think it's a terrible idea.' Richard said, 'But Noël Coward always wanted us to play it.' I said, 'Oh yeah? When? Certainly not *now*.' They were both quickly peeved at me. I said, 'Elizabeth, come into another room with me.' And she did. Richard remained with Zev Bufman.

Once alone with Elizabeth, Lantz repeated his objections. "Elizabeth, this is a terrible mistake," he said. "Neither one of you is in any shape to do this kind of delicate drawing room comedy right now." He tried not to make eye contact with her. Long ago, Richard had warned him that, when in a disagreement with Elizabeth, never look at her, "because if you look into those eyes, it'll be all over. She will win."

"Are you mad?" Elizabeth asked. "Didn't Richard just tell you that Noël Coward always wanted us to do it? Of course it's right for us. And we'll just make oodles of money. I promise you, Robbie, this shall work."

It was clear to Robert Lantz that there was no talking Elizabeth out of the idea, and averting his eyes wasn't going to help either. It wasn't just the inappropriate nature of the play for the kinds of actors they were; it was the personal drama he knew would result if his two clients were to once again join forces. However, he had worked for Elizabeth long enough to know not to disparage her relationship with Richard. "Okay," he said, finally. "I will do everything you need me to do in terms of deal-making. But I won't take a commission."

"What?" she said. "Robbie, you're crazy! What in the world . . . ?"

"Because it's blood money," he said. "This can lead to nothing but misery for you and Richard, and, as your agent and more importantly your friend, I absolutely refuse to profit from it."

Elizabeth couldn't believe what she was hearing. She'd been represented by Lantz for many years and had never heard him come out so adamantly against one of her ideas. It made her take pause. "My God, you're serious, aren't you?" she asked, now seeming concerned that maybe he was right and she *was* making a mistake. It was a good tactic on his part.

Howard and Elizabeth on the set of *Boom*, in which Howard had a brief walk-on part, in October of 1967. By this time Howard, thirty-seven, was an oceanographer. (TOM GATES COLLECTION)

Elizabeth always enjoyed playing "dress up"—but never more than in the '60s as Mrs. Richard Burton. SHAROK HATAMI/REX PHOTOS)

This late 1960s picture says it all: Elizabeth is in costume for *Dr. Faustus*, in which she appeared as Helen of Troy, the face that launched a thousand ships. (TOM GATES COLLECTION)

After Francis Taylor died in 1968, the widowed Sara went on with her life, her loyal daughter, Elizabeth, always at her side. Here are mother and daughter in the early 1970s. (RETROPHOTO)

Following her second marriage and divorce from Richard Burton, Elizabeth took John Warner as her sixth husband (and seventh marriage), on December 4, 1976. Here they announce their engagement in Vienna, where Taylor was filming A Little Night Music. (PHOTOFEST)

On January 15, 1979, John Warner was sworn in as a senator of Virginia by Vice President Walter Mondale. Elizabeth, who had campaigned tirelessly for her husband, holds the family Bible; looking on is the senator's mother, Martha Warner. (CONSOLIDATED NEWS PICTURES/REX PHOTOS)

In May 1981, Elizabeth made her Broadway debut at the Martin Beck Theater in *The Little Foxes*. Over a period of months, she had lost 40 pounds in preparation for the role. She wanted to look her best—and, truly, she had achieved her goal.
(OPENING NIGHT PHOTO BY TOM GATES)

All decked out as an actress playing Mary, Queen of Scots for the 1980 Agatha Christie film *The Mirror Crack'd*. Elizabeth was joined on screen by Tony Curtis and Kim Novak as well as good friend Rock Hudson, whose tragic death from AIDS would give her life a meaningful new direction. (TOM GATES COLLECTION)

Richard truly was a king among men. His death in August of 1984 hit Elizabeth hard, and she would never really get over it. "Something was different the last time I saw him," she would later remark. "And I don't think I imagined it. I just knew that my sweet Richard was going to be okay. I knew it in my heart." (RICHARD YOUNG/REX PHOTOS)

In her old age, Elizabeth's mother, Sara, had the spirit of a passionate artist whose vision—her daughter's stardom—had been successfully realized. Here mother and daughter pose in New York where Elizabeth was honored by the Film Society of Lincoln Center in 1988. (DAVID McGOUGH/TIME-LIFE)

Elizabeth and her eighth husband, Larry Fortensky, in Gstaad in December 1994. Elizabeth would take a fall during this vacation, and despite painful hip replacement surgeries, things would never quite be the same for her. Still, she would, as always, persevere. (JAMES ANDANSON/ CORBIS SYGMA)

Elizabeth made the successful transition from child star to film icon—as well as from motherhood to fragrance mogul. (PHOTOFEST)

In the 1980s and beyond, Elizabeth reinvented herself as an activist for AIDS research. Over the years, she would raise millions of dollars, not to mention public awareness, in work that she considers the most important of her life. Here she is at a fundraiser for amfAR at Ellis Island on June 21, 2000. (PHOTO BY TOM GATES)

In May of 2000, at the age of sixty-four, Elizabeth was honored as Dame Commander of the Order of the British Empire—the female equivalent of a knighthood. Here Elizabeth poses with her children and their spouses at the Dorchester Hotel after the ceremony. Back row: Michael Wilding Jr. and wife, Brooke; Christopher Wilding and wife, Margie. Front: Maria [Fisher] Burton Carson McKeown, Elizabeth, and Liza [Todd] Tivey. (RICHARD YOUNG/REX PHOTOS)

Elizabeth in November 2005 at the BAFTA Awards (British Academy of Film and Television Arts) in Los Angeles, during which she was the year's recipient of the Britannia Award for Artistic Excellence in International Entertainment. These days, any public appearance by Elizabeth Taylor is rare . . . and welcomed. Mostly wheelchair bound, Elizabeth still commands the attention of the press and of her public. (MARIO ANZUONI/REUTERS/CORBIS)

Elizabeth Taylor: a timeless beauty. (Tom Gates Collection)

"I am quite serious," he said, holding his breath in anticipation of her next move.

"Well, then, fine," she decided, taking an abrupt turn. "We're doing the show anyway. Richard wants to do it, and so do I. I'm just going to take a chance and see what happens. I've been taking chances all of my life, Robbie, as you well know, and here's another one," she said, worked up once again. "I know our public. They will love it."

That was the end of the discussion.

Though she expressed confidence in the future, Elizabeth couldn't help but feel a certain amount of anxiety about anything that involved Richard. At around this time, she repeated an old habit, falling into the arms of a man she may have thought of as an intermediary lover. His name was Victor Gonzalez Luna, and he was a wealthy Mexican attorney, five years her senior. This new consort would be in her life for just a few months.

She and Victor Luna ended 1982 by traveling together to the war-torn Middle East on a bizarre "diplomatic mission" Elizabeth had decided to undertake without the cooperation of President Reagan or the White House. "All it takes is love and understanding," she declared on December 27, 1982, in a Tel Aviv press conference to explain how she might handle the strife between Israel and Lebanon. The less said about this venture the better. The trip was cut short after she was two hours late for a scheduled visit with several hundred wounded Arab and Israeli children.

Actually, Elizabeth was in no shape at this time to be making faux diplomatic missions, nor did she know what she was talking about in this regard. When she returned, she took a job in Canada in late January 1983, filming a television movie with Carol Burnett called *Between Friends*. In it, she plays someone who eats and drinks to excess and who befriends a woman, Carol, who has indiscreet sex with men who are all wrong for her. "I like a man to be the boss," Elizabeth said as her character in the movie. "Some of us just need a man, and I'm one of those." It was an eerie case of typecasting in a movie that came and went without much fanfare. The best thing about it was watching Taylor's easy rapport and camaraderie with her friend, the great Carol Burnett.

Private Lives and Private Miseries

Noël Coward's *Private Lives* is a comic gem that's served couples well for more than fifty years. One of those couples was the playwright himself, who teamed with Gertrude Lawrence, one of the theater's greatest stars, when the play debuted at the Times Square Theater in New York on January 27, 1931. (Coward and Lawrence were supported by Laurence Olivier and his then wife Jill Esmond.) A hit, it ran for 258 performances. Next up, in a revival in 1948 at the Plymouth, was Tallulah Bankhead and Donald Cook, who after 248 performances took the show on the road and played to packed houses all across the country. (Could Elizabeth have thought that since she'd made such an impact as Regina in *The Little Foxes*, a role originated by Bankhead, perhaps lightning would strike twice?) The play opens with two newly married couples, Elyot and Sybil and Amanda and Victor, who are honeymooning in the same hotel in Deauville, France. The problem is that Elyot and Amanda were once married and, through happenstance, are reunited when they share an adjoining terrace with their new spouses. It's a clever comedy that takes wit and subtlety to pull off. Elizabeth and Richard were a lot of things, but subtle wasn't one of them.

By the second week of March, Elizabeth and Richard were in New York to begin rehearsals for the play, which was to be directed by Milton Katselas. The show also starred John Cullum and Kathryn Walker. The durable Coward comedy of manners quickly became "The Liz and Dick Show" by advance publicity and was so overhyped that theater critics seemed to be rubbing their hands together, just waiting to pounce on it with all fours.

For her stay in New York, Elizabeth moved into Rock Hudson's castlelike apartment building in New York, the Beresford on 81st Street with its striking views of Central Park. The night before the first run-though, Elizabeth found herself in a restaurant with her date, Victor Luna, and Richard and Sally Hay, Richard's new girl-friend. It was a wretched evening. "I need a headache pill," Eliza-beth said at one point, according to the waiter who served them. "So be a dear and get me a drink. Jack Daniel's on ice." Then, ten minutes later, "I need a pill for my tummy. Another Jack Daniel's, please." Had it not been for the presence of her daughter Maria and her new granddaughter Elizabeth Diane, she might not have been able to get through the night. Her greatest frustration was that she couldn't get Richard's attention. He wouldn't allow a mo-ment's eye contact with her, as if he sensed that one look in her direction would start a fight he would never be able to finish. All of his focus was on the safe bet for him, which was Sally. He couldn't have been more solicitous toward her. Elizabeth hated the way he acted when he was with her. Even in her best times with Richard, he had never been so giddy. It was all an act, she de-cided. He was faking it, trying to make her jealous. As the night wore on, everything he did that made Sally giggle made Elizabeth want to smack him across the face.

The next day, at that first rehearsal, she showed up without so much as having read the play, let alone memorized any of her lines. As usual, Richard not only knew his lines, but hers as well. Once upon a time, that was a habit of his that she had found ap-pealing. Now she just found it irritating.

In his diaries of this time, Richard wrote about some of the re-hearsals for *Private Lives*, the first being on March 13. He noted that, in terms of her beauty, Elizabeth's face was "OK, but [her] figure, *splop!*" On the next day, the fourteenth, he said that she was in such bad shape she couldn't even read the script. He found her to be as "exciting as a flounder" as she rehearsed, but still had hope that she would soon rise to the occasion. However, he predicted "a long, long 7 months." He also wrote that Elizabeth had begun to bore him, which he never would have imagined possible so many years earlier when they'd first met. "How terrible a thing time is," he observed. Twice an hour, he wrote, she would complain to him about her abject loneliness. Though concerned about her, he admitted it would not have bothered him in the least if he had to be replaced in the role.

Private Lives previewed at the Shubert in Boston on April 7 for a limited run, then at the Lunt-Fontanne on Broadway (where Richard had appeared back in 1964 in *Hamlet*) on May 8, 1983. Opening night was a mess. The curtain went up thirty-five minutes late. Then the intermission between the first and second acts was longer than the first act! The next morning, Frank Rich in the *New York Times* wrote a raspberry of a review: "[It has] all the vitality of a Madame Tussaud exhibit." Other reviews were equally brutal, both in newspapers and on television. Only Joel Siegel of ABC seemed hopeful, stating that "more time might have improved the production." During the play's rehearsals, Elizabeth had asked the director, Milton Katselas, "Should we play it like the audience is looking into our bedroom window?" "Yes," he said. It didn't work. Burton, though sober at the time, suddenly refused to stick to the script despite having been the only one to know the show inside out by the first rehearsal. His ad-libs threw off the other cast members, who were expecting to be cued by his lines. "I think there is some fun in it for me," Burton said at one point early in the play's New York run. "Especially when I start inventing my own lines."

Though it was savaged by the critics, the public rushed the box office and the show made enough money in advance sales that it, quite literally, had to go on. Elizabeth and Richard downplayed the effect their poor notices had on them. In actuality, though, it was a stressful time. Richard was not used to being panned for his stage performances, and he felt that if Elizabeth hadn't been sharing the stage with him, the show would have been received quite differently. However, the simple mathematics of the box-office figures made it clear: Their fans wanted "Liz and Dick" together again. The opportunity to see the two stars up close and in person was too tantalizing to resist. If the public only knew what was going on backstage . . .

Obviously, Richard understood the unspoken—that Elizabeth had designs on him and a possible third marriage—and he was not interested. He was in a different phase of his life that Sally had brought him. He was trying to take care of himself, and the less emotional chaos around him, as Sally saw it, the better. Everyone knew only too well that melodrama had always been Elizabeth's forte, and even when there was none inherent to the day's events, she would find a way to create it.

Elizabeth was deeply upset over the critical reaction *Private Lives* received. It seemed to some present during the run as though she was also playing the victim for Richard's benefit, in the hope that he would try to rescue her from her misery. She would head directly to her dressing room and lock the door before performances. During table readings (where actors run their lines to refresh their memories) she would hang her head and mumble her speeches. "Richard got the distinct impression that Elizabeth was waiting for him to throw her a lifeline," said one of the production staff. If that was the case, however, Burton wasn't biting. In fact, the combination of the poor reviews and Elizabeth's unpredictable moods led him to want out.

Richard had heard that John Huston was directing the film adaptation of Malcolm Lowry's *Under the Volcano*, and he put in a call to the famous director, expressing his interest in the project. Huston's response was just what he had hoped—he offered Burton the role. The job would have to begin in August.

Of course, Richard knew he was under contract to *Private Lives*, but he believed that it wouldn't be a problem. Elizabeth was the show's producer; she had even formed a corporation, the Elizabeth Taylor Theater Company, to get the show produced. He had always managed to get his way with his ex-wife in the past, and he thought she could now be persuaded to release him from his contract, even though cutting short his participation would mean that someone else would have to be in his place in the very important city of Los Angeles, the final tour stop in October. After numerous attempts to speak to her about his upcoming scheduling conflict, though, it became clear that Elizabeth was avoiding him. Finally, Richard had to schedule a sit-down meeting with her. She, as producer of the show, was obliged to attend it.

Richard, Elizabeth, and two of their associates met at the Laurent Hotel in New York, where Richard was to plead his case. Elizabeth showed up at the meeting with her "producer hat" on, and appeared relaxed and businesslike. Richard explained to her that he had a wonderful opportunity to work with John Huston, his *Night of the Iguana* director, on a project about which he was extremely excited, *Under the Volcano*. He needed to be released from *Private Lives*. Elizabeth listened to her ex-husband's pitch, then took a few moments to deliberate.

If Elizabeth had ulterior romantic motives where Richard was concerned, they certainly had not been successful, had they? Here was this man she had felt such a deep connection with, once again wanting out. This time though, she had power. A piece of paper made him obligated to stay with the production—to stay with her. She made her decision.

"Richard, I think it would be very wrong to disappoint our fans," she told him. "So I have to say no." She was not going to let him out of his contract. Finally she held him in her grasp, and this time she wasn't letting go.

For a moment, Richard was speechless. "Very well, then," he announced as he rose to leave, his tone deep and theatrical.

Elizabeth must have sensed his building fury. "Now, Richard," she said, "please don't be cross with me."

"I'm fine, luv," he told her coolly. "Let's just move on now, shall we?"

Richard left the meeting without saying a word about his true feelings, rather than give Elizabeth the satisfaction of knowing how angry he was about the matter. Still, his attempts to leave the production had made it clear to Elizabeth that he didn't have the emotional attachment to this project that she did. It was business for him . . . so she would make it business for her as well. And what better way to clarify that her personal life didn't include him than to present her romantic interest in another man publicly? She certainly had not kept her relationship with Victor Luna a secret, but prior to Richard's attempt to flee *Private Lives*, she rarely mentioned Victor's name. Many crew members had even been unaware of his existence. Suddenly, though, Elizabeth's backstage conversations began revolving around Luna and her growing infatuation with him. She even canceled a few performances, announcing that she and Victor had to go off somewhere to "recuperate" from another one of her illnesses. This infuriated Richard, who said, "This has proved it. I can never get together with that woman again."

When Elizabeth did show up, she was often late, which Burton found completely unacceptable. Of Elizabeth, Brooke Williams—Richard's trusted friend—told his biographer Melvyn Bragg, "Her tardiness drove him crazy night after night. He would be there over an hour before—make up—chat—have a cup of tea. 'Where is she, Brooke? Is she here yet?' He would get tremendously agitated. She'd arrive, making up in the car, with a couple of minutes to spare—but then half of the audience was out on the streets waiting for her. So they had to be herded in. The curtain never went up on time—and this just drove him crazy."

On a few occasions during the run, Elizabeth had her understudy step in to perform. Audiences were horrified. Much to Richard's own horror, people would stand up during those performances and actually leave the theater. Without Elizabeth in the show, some felt it a waste of time. It was a humiliating experience for Richard, who was growing tired of his ex-wife's "antics."

"Wait a second. She won't let me out of my contract, yet *she* never shows up for work," he fumed, exaggerating his point but, in his mind, still making a good one. "And she's taking *him* with her. Enough is enough!"

Richard summoned his friends Bob Wilson (his secretary), and Ron Berkeley (his hairdresser) to his suite. "Sit down, fellows. I have an announcement to make," he said. "Sally and I are getting married."

Both men realized that Richard's sudden decision to wed was made out of anger. "You're only doing this to spite Elizabeth," Ron said. "Don't do it, Rich. Not right now."

"Maybe you're right," Richard said angrily. "But I don't care. I'm marrying Sally immediately. We're going to Las Vegas to do it. So don't try to stop me." His mind was made up. If Elizabeth had tied him to the production and was now attempting to flaunt her romance in his face, he would have the last laugh. There would be a new Mrs. Richard Burton—and, despite her apparent wishes, it would not be Elizabeth Taylor.

Richard Marries . . . Someone Else

Richard Burton and Sally Hay went to Las Vegas and were married on Sunday, July 3, 1983. Afterward, he telephoned his brother Graham Jenkins and told him the good news. Graham, not realizing that Burton had not yet told Elizabeth, called friends at the BBC to pass the news on to the media.

On Monday morning, the Fourth of July, Elizabeth opened her newspaper to find that Richard had officially declared his independence from her, again, by marrying someone else. That she had to read about it in the newspaper rather than hear about it from him was, for her, a dagger in the heart. She couldn't believe his cruelty. The fact that he was making about $75,000 a week because of something she had generated for him, whether he appreciated the work or not, made her feel that he should have had at least a modicum of consideration for her.

In many ways, Richard's sudden marriage to Sally was his final act of domination over Elizabeth. He had long known that she wanted him back, and he had refused to give in to her. So he had won that round, and even topped his win by introducing a new woman into the emotional hurricane—a younger one at that! Then he had wanted out of the play in order to do something he viewed as much more deserving of his time as an actor, and she had refused to allow it. Round two to Elizabeth. Now, in round three, he would prove himself the victor again. Just as all the eyes of the world were on him and Elizabeth because of *her* play, *Private Lives*, he would humiliate her by marrying Sally.

Patrick McMahon, who was still working for Burton at this time as an assistant, recalled of Elizabeth, "She called me and was very upset. For her to have called me meant she was telephoning everyone she knew because I was way down on the list of people she had anything to do with during *Private Lives*. Richard had his camp and she had hers. I was in Richard's. I don't think I'd had more than two conversations with her."

"Does he hate me so much that he wants to see me dead?" Elizabeth asked. "Doesn't he know how this would affect me? Doesn't he even care?"

"I'll tell Richard to call you, Elizabeth," McMahon said, not able to offer much more.

"Oh, don't bother!" she snapped. "He could have waited, you

know," she concluded. Then, in a voice that was hardly audible, she added, "He owed me at least that much." With that, she hung up.

The fact that Elizabeth was making the rounds with hurt and angry telephone calls soon got back to Richard. He called his brother and gave him a piece of his mind for having gone to the BBC. "How could you do that?" he asked angrily. "You gave me no time to call Elizabeth, and *she* should have been the first to know." Of course, Richard had had plenty of time to inform Elizabeth of his decision, if he had really wanted her to know about it. But apparently he felt the need to vent his ire on someone, Graham being the handiest.

To save face, Elizabeth issued a statement saying that she was "thrilled and delighted" for the newlyweds. Soon after, so as not to be outdone, she announced her own engagement to Victor Luna—though, in retrospect, it would seem that she had no real intention of marrying him.

During the course of the Broadway run, Elizabeth would be unable to appear more than a dozen times due to her "laryngitis." The play's audiences attended faithfully, though, and responded enthusiastically. But word gets around pretty quickly on Times Square and attendance soon dwindled. It closed on July 17 after sixty-three performances and twelve previews, almost a month earlier than it was scheduled to end. It hardly mattered: A four-week booking into the Forrest Theatre in Philadelphia began immediately, on July 20.

The couple's agent, Robert Lantz, recalls, "It was while we were in Philadelphia that a meal was planned for the newlyweds—Richard and Sally—and the newly engaged couple—Elizabeth and Victor. Chen Sam, Elizabeth's publicist, said, "After the show tonight, we shall all dine and get to know each other.' Good Lord, I knew *that* was not a good idea."

Lantz sat between Elizabeth and Richard, wisely keeping them separated. On Elizabeth's left was Luna. On Richard's right, Hay.

"Look at my ring, Robbie," Elizabeth said, holding out her

hand. "From my sweetheart, Victor. Oh, Robbie, we are just so happy," she added, really putting it on, obviously trying to vex Richard.

"Why, it's quite nice," Lantz said as Elizabeth extended her hand in front of him.

Richard inspected the ring as well. "Hmmm. One carat, I see," he said dryly. "You *are* on a diet, aren't you, luv?"

Everyone laughed nervously. Everyone, that is, but Elizabeth.

Robert Lantz recalls, "Actually, the show they were doing *off-stage* was much more entertaining, I thought, than the one they were doing onstage."

Elizabeth continued to have trouble during the run of *Private Lives* as she balanced the anxiety of working on a stage in front of a live audience with the stress of her private relationship with Burton—or what little there was left of it because he had set it up so that they were never alone together. His new wife was always present. Worse for Elizabeth—though undoubtedly best for Richard—he was not drinking. In her mind, he was never any fun sober, and his teetotalling only served to remind her that she was not doing the same, making her feel worse about herself. She also speculated that Sally was influencing him to stay sober for the run of the show. In Elizabeth's mind, how dare Sally take better care of him than she herself might have in the same situation? The frustration and unhappiness ate away at her.

Robert Lantz recalls, "On a couple of nights in Philadelphia, Elizabeth was ill and an understudy went on in her place. It didn't work. People wouldn't even come to the theater when they heard Elizabeth was not going to appear. They had tickets, but didn't show. Richard, who had not played to a half-empty house in living memory, was not happy to be put in this position, I can tell you that much. He was the theater star, not her. She was a movie star, yet she was the one they were coming to see in the theater . . . not him. It took a toll on him."

"She was clearly putting him in his place," says Patrick Mc-Mahon. "She was saying, 'Look, you can go off and marry anyone you want. You can humiliate me till the cows come home. But let it be known that I am still the bigger star . . . and if you aren't convinced, take a look out into the audience when I'm not standing next to you on that stage, and tell me just how many empty seats you count.' It was a psychodrama, all right."

After stops in Washington and Chicago (where Elizabeth missed the opening night), *Private Lives* arrived with a big fanfare at the Wilshire Theatre in Los Angeles, where it began a ten-week run in October. "The minute the curtain went down, Jack Daniel's was waiting in the wings," Elizabeth would later recall. "It didn't matter that we didn't get good reviews. We still played to packed houses. No one was coming to see the English drawing room comedy anyway. Everyone bought tickets to watch high-camp 'Liz and Dick.' And we gave them what they wanted. I wanted to stop, to put an end to this torture, but the contract had to be fulfilled."

The *Private Lives* tour finally ended in Los Angeles, in November 1983. The present author sat in the audience of their final performance. A memorable moment was one during which Elizabeth was to hit Richard with a pillow. She hit him so hard you could hear his grunt loud and clear, and it sounded painful. The audience laughed heartily, but there was something disquieting about it to anyone aware of Burton's physical frailty at this time. The show went off without a hitch until the third act, when Elizabeth began throwing biscuits at someone in the first row, as if sharing a private joke with that person. From that point on, it seemed as if all bets were off as Elizabeth followed Richard's lead of not sticking to the script. The two started making up dialogue as they went along. One would have thought they were doing a sketch for *The Carol Burnett Show*. It was as if they'd decided they'd had enough of Noël Coward's nonsense and wanted to toss it aside in order to have some fun for the first time in months. The audience ate up their antics, as if finally being given entrée to the private lives of two celebrities whose public fame and notoriety had kept them on tenterhooks for almost a quarter of a century. When the stars took their bows, the crowd seemed not to want to let them go. As Elizabeth and Richard stood at the edge of the stage clasping hands, there was a sense that this would be the last time they would ever be seen in public together. Elizabeth's face was inscrutable. Who knew what was going through her mind? Still, the moment felt nostalgic before it had even passed.

Backstage, after that final performance of *Private Lives*, there was no heartfelt farewell between old lovers, no significant moment that Elizabeth Taylor and Richard Burton might take with them and remember for the rest of their lives. As much as Elizabeth's life and times often seemed to reflect the pathos and melodrama of the best cinema, the truth of it was sometimes a bit less satisfying. In this situation, the reality was that after twenty-three years of loving one another while at the same time waging war on each other, she and Richard had simply worn themselves out. Earlier, she had given him a photograph of the two of them, set in a heart-shaped picture frame upon which had been engraved, "For Private Lives. To My Dearest Dickie. From 'your second time' in life." Now there was nothing more for either of them to say or do or give to the other. Though Elizabeth at fifty-one, and Richard, fifty-seven, had each made in excess of a million dollars during the play's run, both were left to wonder if it had been worth it.

After the final performance, Elizabeth went to her dressing room and greeted the usual smattering of VIPs, thanking them for coming to the performance. When they had all been shuttled out, a wardrobe assistant came to fetch her glittering stage costume. She knocked on the door, and Elizabeth called her into the dressing room. Taylor was sitting in the room staring into a mirror, occasionally tipping back a glass of whiskey. Still wearing her wardrobe, she said, "No need to have this cleaned. It will be burned in a few hours."

The assistant laughed awkwardly and told Elizabeth how honored she was to have worked with her. Taylor was gracious enough, but kept their exchange brief.

Before going, the wardrobe girl asked, "Is there anything I can do for you?"

Only the sound of clinking ice cubes was heard for a moment. Then, without moving, Elizabeth said, "I'm just going to stay here a while. Sometimes miracles happen."

No one knows if she was waiting for Richard to come say his good-byes, or whether she hoped for some other "miracle." However, as it would happen, after that final show, Richard immediately went his own way with his new wife, back to Europe where the two would, at least he hoped, live a good and long life together. After waiting for about an hour, Elizabeth had little choice but to go her way as well . . . only alone.

Intervention

By December 1983, Elizabeth Taylor's friends and family were truly afraid for her life. "You would be talking to her and suddenly you would realize that she had passed out with her eyes open," one intimate recalled. "She would appear to be dead, her breathing so light. You would call an ambulance. They would rush her to Cedars [hospital], sirens blazing. They would save her.

"The next day she would be released, drinking from a flask and taking pills in the car on the way home, thanks to all of her enablers, the kiss-asses who surrounded her and refused to tell her no. She'd spend hours on the phone, talking to anyone who would listen. It was always about Richard and how he had hurt her but how she would take him back again if he wanted her; about Victor, and why he meant nothing to her; and she would go all the way back to Eddie Fisher and what a jerk he had been to try to get money out of her when they divorced. Then, again, another scare and back to the hospital, sirens blazing."

Then, home the next day for more liquor, more pills—days and nights blending together in a haze of alcohol and drugs and misery. Watching her old movies on TV, passed out in front of the set, it was a slow descent into a Norma Desmond–like madness. She thought that she had come to terms with her life and her past when married to Senator John Warner and living in Virginia. However, what she'd actually done was something comparable to poking around at her deepest wounds and causing them to bleed profusely without then caring for them. Within just a few years, she was worse off than she'd been in Virginia. Now, as she would tell it, she was "awash with self-pity and self-disgust."

During one of her hospitalizations—this one for colitis—on Monday, December 5, she awakened to a room full of visitors. Her brother, Howard, was present, having just flown in from New Mexico, as were three of her children, Christopher and Michael Wilding and Liza Todd, who had come from New York. Also present was her good friend Roddy McDowall, and her doctor. At first she was surprised that they had all come to visit at the same time. "How nice," she thought. She was happy to see them. However, that feeling didn't last long. Each took a folding chair and put it at her bedside, encircling her. Each then began telling her that they couldn't bear to see what she was doing to herself. They wanted her to get help, they said, and they would not leave until she agreed to it. Then each of them read from a prepared paper, a litany of transgressions, how she had hurt them, how she had embarrassed them, how she had humiliated herself. She would later say that she didn't even remember half of the incidents they'd pointed out to her. They each ended by saying that if she didn't get off of drugs, they were certain that she would soon kill herself. Howard in particular was choked up and barely able to get the words out. It was clear that he hated seeing his sister, of whom he had been so proud, destroy herself.

Of course, this was a so-called intervention, and she knew it right away. When she looked up at them from her sickbed, all she could see was the pain in their eyes. It hit her hard that she was the cause of it. Howard said that they wanted to take her to a "clinic," as he called it, to help her reconcile not only her drinking and drug habits, but also her emotional problems. "Well, I need time to think about it," Elizabeth said, unsure how to proceed. "I need two hours," she decided.

"No, we have a car downstairs and we are going now," Liza said.

"Listen, stop being so bossy," Elizabeth told her, now being firm. "This has to be my decision."

After they left her room, she began to ruminate on what they'd just told her. She'd always thought of herself as the one to make decisions about her future, and now she was being told that she must do something she wasn't sure she wanted to do. However, she also couldn't imagine living another day in such despair and, worse yet, inflicting it upon her loved ones. She knew that the decision would have to be hers, though . . . or she would never follow through with it. She also knew, as she would later explain, that she must have really hit rock bottom or her friends and family would never have gone to such great lengths. When they were gone, she thought about every word her friends and family had said to her, and she knew that they were right. After all, she did have a bottle of Jack Daniel's in her hospital room, didn't she? And she was mixing the drink with Demerol. She *was* killing herself—only she was so high, she didn't realize it—and she didn't want to die, that much she knew. How many times had she willed herself back from the brink . . . only to now end up at a possible point of no return?

In two hours, everyone returned to her room. Elizabeth told them that she would go with them. They dressed her, checked her out of the hospital, put her into a car, and drove her two hours from Los Angeles to Rancho Mirage, a suburb of Palm Springs. There Elizabeth Taylor would check into the Betty Ford Center, where she would begin the next chapter of her life.

Betty Ford Center

Elizabeth Taylor didn't know what to expect of the Betty Ford Center when she was driven to its front entrance on Monday night, December 5, 1983. At that time, the Center was not as widely known as it would become in later years, having only recently been founded in October 1982 by former First Lady Betty Ford. Like Elizabeth's intervention conducted by her family in her hospital room, President Gerald Ford and the four Ford children had confronted Mrs. Ford with her own addiction to alcohol and prescription drugs. After Mrs. Ford was treated for her own alcohol and chemical dependency at the United States Naval Hospital in Long Beach, she sought to establish a treatment center that was, at first, to be targeted to women's needs. The Betty Ford Center is comprised of nine complexes alongside a man-made pond called Lake Hope in the middle of a desert oasis. Surrounded by rolling sand dunes and verdant hillsides, it soon became a facility for men and women, with half of its space devoted to each, the quarters always separate. Elizabeth put the Center in the news by being the first major celebrity to seek treatment there. After her highly publicized treatment, many dozens of celebrities would follow her example—Liza Minnelli (whose sister, Lorna Luft, would organize an intervention and bring Liza to the Betty Ford Center just a month after Elizabeth), Mary Tyler Moore, Johnny Cash, Robert Downey Jr., Tony Curtis, Don Johnson, and even Eddie Fisher. But in December 1983, Elizabeth was the first. (Her longtime friend and fellow MGM contract player Peter Lawford was there at the same time. Later Elizabeth said, sadly, "He didn't make it." He died of liver and kidney disease a year later.)

Her friend the columnist Liz Smith recalls, "It's hard to remember that the reaction to it was such shock. Now when stars go into the Betty Ford Center, it's a big yawn. But back then, it was really startling. It wasn't her style to be too secretive, though. She's very frank and up-front. I suppose she felt that if she had the courage to say she was an alcoholic we should all have the courage to accept it and treat it respectfully. It was an enormous sort of scandal at the time. Now it just seems like she did the right thing."

Elizabeth was dropped off at the front door of the Betty Ford Center, her friends and family not permitted to enter with her or spend a great deal of time saying good-bye. The coddling of a superstar was to end immediately. A nurse's aid met her at the door and walked her to a sparse room with two beds—which cost about $150 per night. She had no makeup and no clothes, except for those on her back. "I thought, well at least there'll be tea in the room," she later told Helen Gurley Brown. "Forget it, darling. Nothing!"

For the next seven weeks, Elizabeth would wear jeans and sweaters, or athletic wear. She would rise at 6:30 a.m. for breakfast at seven. She would keep a regimented schedule, eat in the cafeteria with the others, do daily chores, and attend meetings similar to those of Alcoholics Anonymous. Though there are no bars on the windows, no locks on the front doors ("It's your honor that keeps you there," she would later explain), on that first night she was scared, more terrified, she would admit, than she'd ever been in the past.

The first week was spent detoxifying. She went through terrible episodes of withdrawal, as one can imagine given the amount of time she'd depended upon alcohol and drugs. It didn't make matters any easier for her when she began to feel what she would call "an unauthorized presence at the clinic." She called Betty Ford—and it's probably a safe bet to say that none of the other patients were able to call Mrs. Ford personally, but Betty was Elizabeth's sponsor—to tell her that she had a feeling that she was being watched by paparazzi. After so many years of being scrutinized, she had a sixth sense about such things. Of course, she was right. Days later, pictures of her in her robe sitting on a patio, taken by a camera's telephoto lens, would find their way to the front pages of tabloids around the world. By that time, though,

Elizabeth and Betty had made an announcement about her treatment to beat the media to the punch with the story.

Four days into her treatment, she would begin to keep a journal about her treatment for alcoholism and drug addiction. All of the patients were instructed to do so; hers was in a blue notebook.

On Friday, December 9, she wrote:

"I've been here since Monday night, one of the strangest and most frightening nights of my life. Not to mention lonely. But I am not alone. There are people here just like me, who are suffering just like me, who hurt inside and out, just like me, people I've learned to love. It's an experience unlike any other I've known. Nobody wants anything from anybody else, except to share and help. It's probably the first time since I was nine that nobody's wanted to exploit me. Now, the bad news. I feel like hell. I'm going through withdrawal. My heart feels big and pounding. I can feel the blood rush through my body. I can almost see it, running like red water over the boulders in my pain filled neck and shoulders, then through my ears and into my pounding head. My eyelids flutter. Oh God, I am so, so tired."

It would take a week before she would be able to say the words that would mark her first step toward recovery: "Hello. My name is Elizabeth, and I'm an alcoholic and a drug addict."

It was in group therapy that Elizabeth was finally forced to face the truth about herself. It wasn't easy for her to speak about her personal problems in front of strangers. After all, she's not just a mere celebrity, she is one of the most famous women on the planet, arguably a cultural icon. Everyone knew they were in the presence of a so-called "living legend," and they knew all about her, or at least they thought they knew about her, based on what they'd read in the media. Therefore, it was difficult for her to be candid. She didn't have the cloak of anonymity that gave the others the freedom to be open about their lives and mistakes without having to worry about being harshly, and personally, judged. However, she had always been set apart from others, hadn't she? It had been her story since childhood. She'd married and divorced in the public eye. She'd had her children in the public eye. She'd mourned a husband and other friends in the public eye. If she'd done all of that with the world watching, surely, she figured, she could come to terms with it in the presence of just eleven strangers.

One woman who attended many sessions of group therapy with Elizabeth recalls, "She was completely without artifice, totally un-pretentious, so much so that when she would casually drop a sentence such as, 'You know, that reminds me of the time Eddie and I fought about Debbie,' or 'I just remembered a huge fight I had with Richard,' it was a little jarring because you knew exactly who she was talking about. These were people we had grown up with, seen as celebrities. But, to her, they were just people who'd passed through her life. If it took her a few beats to adjust, I can tell you that it took many of us equal time to do the same thing. It's not every day you sit in a room with Elizabeth Taylor and have her cleanse her soul about something she and Richard Burton fought about while making *Cleopatra*."

Another complication for Elizabeth had to do with accepting that she would be challenged by the others in her group. She had long been accustomed to people simply agreeing with her, never denying her anything. She certainly wasn't used to being contra-dicted, except, perhaps, by Richard Burton. Indeed, one of the reasons she'd been able to indulge herself with all of the alcohol and drugs she could consume was because she was an entitled per-son living an entitled life . . . no questions asked. "But in group therapy, you're up for grabs," she would later observe. "People call you on everything. You can tell when somebody is hiding behind lies. After a while, all of your gimmicks and tricks are stripped away. You're raw, defenseless. That's when it starts being con-structive."

"Again she was entirely able to adjust from being a grand diva to being just one of us," said the woman from her group therapy. "She actually appreciated being put in her place. Once, she told an emotional story about her father, the details of which I would never reveal. Anyway, when she finished I just thought she was full of it. 'That's a load of baloney,' I told her. Everyone held their breaths for her reaction, and she just laughed and said, 'Jesus Christ! You're right! It is! I'm so used to telling that story that way, I have almost forgotten what really happened. Now, here's what *really* happened . . .' And then she told the story again, and this time honestly.

"I thought she was an amazing woman, far more complex and thoughtful than I ever would have imagined based on her public persona. At first, everyone was pulling for her to get sober so she could continue living the fabulous life we all believed she'd been living up until that time. But after many weeks of getting to know her, we started wanting her to live a *new* life, a better life, because we grew to love and appreciate her. At that point, it was time for all of us, not just her, to let go of the fantasy of Elizabeth Taylor's world and begin to deal with the reality of it."

Of course, Elizabeth faced problems the others in her group could never truly understand, try as they might. She'd been a star since childhood, her life often mirroring and, just as often, contradicting the film roles in which she'd immersed herself. Her world was built on illusion, on pretense. Going back to her first marriage with the abusive Nicky Hilton, she didn't know anything about love and romance other than how it had been scripted for her in *Father of the Bride*. It was a rude awakening, then, when she discovered that there could be a dark and abusive side to marriage. Similar disappointments would follow as she and others around her endeavored to separate her *true* self and her *true* experiences from the mythology of who she played on the screen. It's easy for outsiders to judge a movie star's identity crisis by saying of her work, "Oh, please! That's just make-believe. Get over it." However, for a woman who's lived in a place of unreality for the better part of her years, it was often difficult for her to separate her personality from that of the characters she'd portrayed in front of a camera.

Also, the fact that Elizabeth never had a "real" childhood was something that had bothered her for years, but she said she didn't realize how much an issue it was for her until it came up during therapy at the Betty Ford Center.

"She had been working since the age of nine," said a friend of hers who has talked at length with her about her recovery. "Frankly, she felt cheated. She felt, somehow, wronged. But she didn't feel she could complain about it because, after all, who would listen? 'Who was going to feel sorry for Elizabeth Taylor?' she told me. 'I felt silly being upset about it, as if my feelings had to be suppressed.' In fact, she blamed her parents. Why couldn't her father have tempered her mother's ambition so that she could have had a more normal lifestyle? She had to work through it to come to terms with the fact that even though her life was not the norm, it was what it was . . . and she became who she was and had the privileged life she'd had partially as a result of her mother's persistence and determination. 'It certainly wasn't Mother's fault that I drank and ate and took pills once I became a star,' she told me. That was *her* choice. It was how she had decided to reconcile her fame, the pressures of her lifestyle and public image versus her private self. 'And, by God, I'm not going to spend another minute punishing my poor mother for my mistakes,' she told me."

As well as trying to discern her true identity as a woman, Elizabeth obviously had to come to terms with many years of self-abuse with alcohol and drugs—that was the primary reason, after all, why she was at the Betty Ford Center. She admitted that for the last thirty-five years she was not able to drop off into a good night's slumber unless she took at least two sleeping pills. When asked to sit down and actually count, she tallied at least twenty major operations over the recent years, so it was no wonder that drugs had become such a crutch to her. She confessed that she didn't only take medication when she was in pain, though. She would take pills to feel comfortable in social situations. Percodan had become her drug of choice, which she would always take with a couple of drinks.

Through therapy, she began to clarify in her mind that most of her actions regarding not only Richard but also her other husbands were made while either drinking or coming out of an alcoholic haze. Combined with all of the drugs she was taking, is it any wonder that her marriages were always filled with such confusion and hostility? It was difficult for her—as she would later tell it—to reconcile that she'd made so many life-altering decisions while under the influence of alcohol and drugs. However, it was the truth, and there was no escaping it. She'd apparently even tried to kill herself, and maybe even twice! Now it was impossible for her to fathom that she'd ever thought life was not worth living. The only thing she could do was forgive herself and everyone else, go forth with her life of sobriety . . . and pray for the best.

Perhaps the most important element of her treatment at the Betty Ford Center had to do with the cultivation of an inner life. Prior to being admitted to the Center, the most time Elizabeth Taylor had ever spent analyzing her years on this planet was when she was married to John Warner and found herself in self-imposed semiretirement as his wife. She'd come to certain significant decisions at that time, most having to do with her loss of identity and her need to lose weight in order to once again feel a sense of pride about herself. However, unguided by professional mental health care workers, any true dissection of her life and times usually led to heavy drinking and the taking of medications to dull the pain of bad memories as they came flooding back to her. At the Betty Ford Center, therapists were present to guide her through her tumultuous history and to assist her in coming to terms with it. It soon became clear to her that her unsupervised evaluations of the past were largely responsible for her having become so reattached and even obsessed with Richard Burton. In wondering if things could have been different with him, in trying to figure out why she was still so confused about her marriages to him, she felt compelled to revisit the past by bringing it into her present. Thus all of the unfortunate business with Burton during her fiftieth birthday party in London and then the subsequent nightmare with him in *Private Lives*.

Though it was a difficult seven weeks, the time would have a great impact on her and inform who she would now be as a woman who no longer depended on alcohol and drugs. Of course, it was less than two months. It had taken her probably more than thirty years to get to the point where she would finally admit that she needed help. During the next year, Elizabeth would return to the Center for periodic outpatient therapy sessions to gauge her progress. After all, the Betty Ford Center does not offer its patients a quick fix, but rather the tools to use to maintain their sobriety in the outside world. Still, it's just a few months, or even a few years in some cases, in a person's life, certainly not enough to guarantee any kind of results considering the complicated psychology of addiction. Indeed, when a sober Elizabeth Taylor was finally released from the Betty Ford Center on January 20, 1984, she realized that the real work of her lifetime was still ahead of her.

Richard Burton Dies

Elizabeth Taylor was at home with her daughter Maria in Bel Air, California, on August 6, 1984, when the call came from her publicist, Chen Sam. Richard Burton's longtime associate, Valerie Douglas, had just phoned Chen to give her the most dreadful news, and now she had the terrible task of passing it on to Elizabeth: Richard Burton was dead.

Chen tried to fill Elizabeth in on the details:

A day and a half earlier, on August 4, Richard had complained of a headache. His wife of thirteen months, Sally, thinking it nothing serious, gave him a couple of aspirins. Burton and John Hurt, with whom he'd just finished the movie *1984* (based on

George Orwell's book), had gone out drinking the night before, and Sally assumed that Richard simply had a hangover. That evening, he went to bed early in order to read and make some notes in his journal, as he often did before retiring. Sally joined him shortly thereafter. The next morning when she awoke, she found her husband's breathing labored and she had trouble awakening him. She called for an ambulance, which took him to a local hospital, where it was determined that the problem was serious. Apparently, he'd had a brain hemorrhage. Richard was transported to a hospital in Geneva. Once there, he underwent surgery. Sally went back to the Burton chalet in Céligny to make some calls, but she had no sooner gotten there than she was summoned back to the hospital. Richard had died. If he had pulled through the surgery, Sally was told, he probably would have been wheelchair-bound and unable to speak. All who knew Richard believed he wouldn't have wanted to live that way. Without the ability to communicate, life would have been torturous for him. So, in keeping with his no-nonsense approach to living, at fifty-eight, with no foreshadowing that his bombastic life was coming to a close, it had. His final entry in his journal: "Tomorrow and tomorrow and tomorrow . . . Our revels now are ended."

Richard and his brother Graham Jenkins had had a conversation about Elizabeth three weeks before Richard died. Richard had said that he missed Elizabeth "all the time," but he had come to the realization that he was too old and ill for her to be able to take care of him. His life with her certainly hadn't worked out as he'd hoped. He had imagined that they would grow old together and live in peace with one another, though he couldn't fathom why he felt that way since it had never been like that between them. In the end, he was glad that he'd found Sally. "She knows how to take care of an old man," he said wistfully. Before they parted, as he embraced his brother, his greatest love was still on his mind. "You know, Elizabeth and I never really split up," he told Graham. "And we never will." It reminded Graham of a recent visit to Elizabeth's home. In every room and in every hallway, he would recall, there were framed photographs of Richard. "He's where I can keep an eye on him," she explained with a smile. "And he'd better believe it."

Elizabeth was, as one would expect, crushed by the news of Richard's death, as was, of course, Maria—Burton was the only father she'd ever known. Elizabeth fainted. When revived, she called Victor Luna and asked him to be with her. He wasn't exactly helpful. "I knew she would be devastated, shattered," Luna said, "but I didn't expect her to become completely hysterical. I could not get her to stop crying. She was completely out of control. I realized then how deeply she was tied to this man, how vital a role he had played in her life. And I realized I could never have that special place in her heart she keeps for Burton. For me, the romance was over, and I told Elizabeth that." One can only hope that he waited to deliver that bit of news. In truth, she was over him anyway, and would not have put up much of a fight. He had given her a sixteen-and-a-half-carat sapphire-and-diamond engagement ring from Cartier, worth almost $300,000. It was one ring she happily returned.

For the next few days after Richard's death, Elizabeth sat in front of the television, numb and unaware of the passing of time. Diane Stevens called; the two hadn't spoken in some time since Stevens had moved to Paris to be with her ill mother. She said that when she called, Elizabeth told her she was looking through a scrapbook of photos of her and Richard. "I'm so sorry about Rich," Diane told her via long-distance telephone. "I know how much you loved him."

"You were there for so much of it so, yes, I think you do know how we felt about each other," Elizabeth said. "Most people, I'm afraid, don't get it."

"Would you like me to fly in and be with you?" Diane asked her.

"I'll be fine," Elizabeth said. "My God, the trouble we caused each other," she said with a small chuckle as she apparently thumbed through the photographs before her. She mentioned that she'd been afraid to feel anything at all for the last couple of days for fear that she would be totally engulfed by waves of sorrow, as she had been when Mike Todd died. However, when she started remembering Richard, she was surprised to find that she actually felt . . . good. "And right now, talking to you," she said, "I only remember the good times. It's as if all of the bad memories died with Richard, leaving only the good ones."

No doubt, Elizabeth's grief over Richard's sudden death was eased somewhat by the knowledge that they had finally set things straight with one another. Earlier, in the spring of 1984 when she and Victor Luna were on a vacation in London, they had met with Richard and Sally Burton at a London pub. The energy between Elizabeth and Richard was different, somehow not as charged as it had always been in the past. "You look wonderful, luv," he said to her. She told him about her experiences at the Betty Ford Center and, as she later recalled, said that she wished the two of them could have had such therapy back in the sixties when they were married to one another and living their lives in a style that was totally out of control. Richard had to smile. "Ah, but then we wouldn't be who we are now, then, would we?" he mused.

Somehow, the conversation turned to Elizabeth's relationship with Victor Luna. Victor mentioned that he hoped Elizabeth would soon settle down with him in Guadalajara where they would lead, as he put it, "a nice, simple life with wholesome, Catholic values." He also mentioned that he wasn't very approving of Elizabeth's jet-setting lifestyle, and sincerely looked forward to the time when such excessive living would be behind her. At that, Richard and Elizabeth shared a secret look as if to say, "This poor man doesn't have a clue, does he?"

For the rest of their time together that day, Richard had seemed happy, excited about a few projects on the horizon. Though he was still drinking, he didn't seem as weak and sickly as he had when he was onstage with Elizabeth in *Private Lives*. He looked fit and well. He had mellowed and it became him. Maybe the marriage to Sally had been the best thing that could have happened to him, Elizabeth posited. She wasn't sure what to think, actually, to hear her tell it. She would never really move on, though. She knew that much. She would say that she didn't wish to do so, anyway. She *wanted* to love Richard Burton, she just didn't want to feel so much pain about it. "Something was different the last time I saw him," she would later observe. "And I don't think I imagined it, given what would happen in a few months. I just knew that my sweet Richard was going to be okay. I knew it in my heart."

After they saw each other in London, she and Richard stayed in touch, communicating many times a month by telephone. Sally, who felt she had good reason to be suspicious, would later say that Elizabeth was "having another go" at winning Richard back, "making phone calls," she said, "making suggestions that they should work together." Nothing could have been further from the truth. In fact, Elizabeth just wanted to stay connected to Richard and see if, as per her ongoing therapy, it was possible to integrate him into her world in a way that would not be disruptive to either of their lives.

Now he was suddenly gone and Elizabeth had to make a decision about whether she should go to the memorial service in Wales. She asked Graham what she should do, but he didn't feel comfortable encouraging her to go, as much as he knew she wanted to be there for Richard. He later noted that Sally "resented the enduring love of the woman who gave Richard his happiest years, Elizabeth." At the time, though, he was more discreet. "I would want to encourage you," he told Elizabeth, "but I'm afraid we would have a riot on our hands." He was referring to the crowds who would come to see the grieving Elizabeth, but he also might have been speaking of a final square-off between Elizabeth and Sally.

"Well, then it has to be Sally's decision," Elizabeth finally decided. When she called Richard's widow, it was clear that Sally really didn't want her in Wales. She said that she feared her presence would cause a circuslike atmosphere at the service, and she wanted Richard to be remembered with more dignity on that day. Perhaps, then, Elizabeth said, she could go to the funeral, which was to be in Céligny. No, Sally said. That also would not be a good idea. It was clear that Sally did not want Elizabeth to be a part of any of Richard's services. Elizabeth was heartsick but, still, she understood. In the end she was determined to abide by Sally's wishes. Of course, Sally had only been in Richard's life for about two years, Elizabeth for almost twenty-five. It was difficult for Elizabeth to allow her to make these important decisions, especially when she realized that Sally was going to have Richard buried in Switzerland. Elizabeth could not begin to count all of the times Richard had told her that he wished to be buried in his hometown of Pontrhydyfen, Wales. "It's a good thing I'm not drinking, that's all I can say," Elizabeth told one friend, trying to stay optimistic.

At the last moment, Sally called to tell her she'd had a change of heart. Yes, she said, of all people, Elizabeth should be present at the memorial service. However, by that time there was no way Elizabeth could have gotten to Wales in time. Whether Sally was merely trying to be gracious or whether she actually wanted Elizabeth at the service is something only she would know. However, Elizabeth was determined not to think the worst of her. She knew that she was grieving deeply and perhaps not thinking in a completely rational way. "Richard would want me to hold my tongue, just this once," she told Graham. "So, for him, I will do that. Later," she said with a wicked smile, "we shall *really* talk." (Years later, Sally would say that she truly did regret telling Elizabeth not to attend the service, "and I wish now that I hadn't done that.")

On August 19, about a week after the Welsh memorial service at the Bethel Chapel, Elizabeth embarked on a pilgrimage to Pontrhydyfen. Graham Jenkins picked her up at Swansea airport in a Rolls-Royce. As she stepped out of her private jet, a crowd of about a hundred greeted her with cheers. She looked radiant, dressed in pink and wearing the Krupp diamond, the best of all of the jewels Richard had given her. However, it wasn't a time for good cheer. She'd come to visit Richard's family, after already having visited his grave in Céligny the previous weekend. While she ate dinner that night at the modest home of Burton's sister, Hilda

Owen, and her husband, Dai, a crowd of mourners stood outside their front door singing old Welsh songs like "We'll Keep a Welcome in the Hillside." Over a roast beef dinner, Elizabeth told the Jenkinses about her experience when she went to the gravesite, a comedy of errors she knew Richard would have enjoyed.

As it happened, when she showed up at the graveyard in Switzerland, Elizabeth and her daughter Liza—who had just married eight days before Richard's death, to artist Hap Tivey, and had attended Richard's funeral—were greeted by a rowdy group of paparazzi. They reasoned that she would eventually show up at the gravesite, and they got their wish when she finally appeared before them, and with blonde hair to boot. She was at a loss as to what to do, she said. Should she storm off in a huff? "Oh, how they would love that picture and be happy to send it everywhere: Elizabeth in a rage at Richard's grave," she said. Or should she just allow them to follow her to the grave? "But it seemed so wrong," she observed, "that I couldn't be alone with Richard in those moments. It wasn't fair." At a loss, she roamed the graveyard, as if she was looking for but couldn't find the gravesite. "But guess what?" she said, "I really *couldn't* find it!" There were two small cemeteries in Céligny, with 250 yards between them, and Elizabeth had gone to the wrong one! No doubt the photographers could have told her as much, but they clearly wanted to document the gaffe without interfering with the story. When Elizabeth and Liza finally figured it out, they walked with great purpose right out the front gates as if they'd always intended to take a stroll through that very cemetery and had just finished their little walk. "Can you believe it?" Elizabeth laughed. "And those bastards didn't say a word to me that I was in the wrong place!"

Elizabeth returned to her hotel sensing that wherever Richard was, he was probably howling with laughter at her and Liza's inept gravesite visit. She could almost hear his voice saying, "Well at least you had a fifty percent chance of getting it right, didn't you, luv?"

Very early the next morning, August 14, just as the sun was ris-

ing, as Elizabeth told the Jenkinses, she and Liza found their way to
the other cemetery—the right one. Of course, the photographers
were present there too. This time, Elizabeth thought to arrange to
have four bodyguards accompany her. As soon as they arrived,
mother and daughter went directly to Richard's grave, and as they
stood before it, each bodyguard popped open a multicolored um-
brella to shield the two women from the photographers' lenses. As
soon as Elizabeth knelt at the grave, she began to cry. She wept for
a good fifteen minutes with Liza trying to comfort her. When it was
time to go, the pair walked slowly out of the cemetery, Elizabeth
leaning heavily on Liza's arm. Elizabeth would describe her moments at Richard's grave as unusually intimate. "I couldn't help
thinking that it was one of the few occasions ever that Richard and
I were alone." It was as though she had decided to view the event
through a distorted lens, without the press hovering or the pappa-
razzi capturing as much as they could of her misery. When it came
to Richard, she craved moments that mattered—and that's just
how she would view her precious time with him at the end.

Before returning to the States, Elizabeth walked the grounds of
the chalet in Gstaad she and Richard had shared. "So many memories, some of them quite good," she told the groundskeeper who
worked there from 1980 to 1985. He was a kindly old man who,
with his wife, took care of the property when Elizabeth was not
there. He still lives in Gstaad today. He remembers Elizabeth's
time in Switzerland shortly after Burton's death as bittersweet.
She hadn't fallen into one of her deep chasms of misery but,
rather, seemed to be processing her loss. It was as if she was taking
stock of just who she was now, without Richard Burton out there
somewhere else on the planet. He had for so many years defined
her. Now she would have to define herself.

At one point, while the groundskeeper was trimming hedges,
Elizabeth summoned him with urgency. "I need you," she said,
waving him over. She then led him to a storage room that was so
dark a flashlight had to be located for them to enter it.

Many years earlier, Elizabeth had returned to the chalet after being on location with a movie only to find that Richard had re-placed a tremendous oriental carpet in the study with a bear rug, complete with head, teeth exposed in a ferocious manner. Elizabeth was horrified. After much shouting and acrimony, she had the "eye-sore" replaced by the classic, understated oriental that had originally been there—which, of course, led to more shouting and acrimony.

Elizabeth wiped away cobwebs in the dim cellar, leading the gardener to a corner of the musty room. She knelt down and slid a crate out from under the wine rack. Behind it, butcher paper, yellowed and aged, could be seen wrapped around a large object. Taylor ripped away a piece of the paper, revealing a set of fangs. "This was Mr. Burton's," she said. "It belongs in the study." The two then carried the rug, once banned from the chalet, back in-side—to the place it may have belonged all those years.

Elizabeth supervised as the rug was placed, deciding just the best way for it to be laid. After it was down, she inspected it. Then, in a moment that surprised the groundskeeper, she burst out laughing. "Why, it's awful," she said, amused. "It's simply grotesque."

"Shall I take it out?" asked the groundskeeper.

She didn't answer. Instead, she stood in the doorway, her arms crossed, studying the fur. "Well, it *is* awful," she said with a mis-chievous smile. Then she sobered a bit. "But leave it be," she de-cided. "Some awful things are perfect, just as they are."

Transition

What had followed Elizabeth Taylor's release from the Betty Ford Center was a metamorphosis—comparable to the transfor-mation that occurs when a caterpillar emerges from a chrysalis and becomes an indescribably beautiful butterfly. A cliché, perhaps, but true nonetheless. It was the perpetually tanned George Hamilton who took charge of her makeover, escorting her to a number of industry functions for about a year or so. On one such occasion, she entered on Hamilton's tuxedoed arm at a National Film Society awards dinner at the Sheraton Universal in Universal City, California, during which she presented a career achievement award to the longtime MGM hairdresser Sydney Guilaroff. She was in an all-white, off-the-shoulder designer gown with a full, floor-sweeping skirt—yards and yards and layer upon layer of gauzy, billowy tulle Jim Pinkston, a Hollywood journalist, editor, and historian, recalled, "I was but a few feet away from her, and my knees practically buckled when I saw her. I was unable to stifle an audible gasp, my mouth agape. When she heard it, she turned in my direction and flashed me a knowing smile that dazzled (me and everyone else!)."

The months after Richard's funeral were difficult for Elizabeth, though, as she tried to find her bearings not only in her life after Richard but also without alcohol and drugs. "Thank God I was clean and sober when he died," she would later say. "If not, I wouldn't be sitting here today. I would have totally destroyed myself out of grief."

There were a couple of missteps, of course. She filmed a campy television movie called *Malice in Wonderland* in which she played legendary gossip columnist Louella Parsons. It was an odd, poorly scripted undertaking that chronicled the rivalry and exploits of Parsons and Hedda Hopper, portrayed by Jane Alexander. Though it wasn't exactly a highlight in Elizabeth's career, she did get paid a million dollars for about three weeks' work, so it wasn't a total waste. Later that year, she also appeared as a madam in a Civil War period piece for television, *North and South*. One day's work for $100,000. It was a strange and somewhat melancholy experience for her fans to see Elizabeth now appearing in made-for-TV movies, such as the one she would make in a couple years' time, *There Must Be a Pony*, from the James Kirkwood novel and costarring Robert Wagner. Most of these films weren't very good, and it seems ironic in retrospect that even in her older years Elizabeth would not have the strong sense of self required to make better career choices. In her defense, though, it's also true that once an actress hits her fifties, good roles usually dry up anyway in Hollywood and her choices do become more limited. Elizabeth had long ago reconciled herself to the fact that her glory days on the silver screen were over. Hopefully her public would allow her an easy transition from that time in her life as well.

Also in 1984, she began dating Dennis Stein, a wealthy New York businessman her own age. By the end of the year, she was engaged to him and wearing a twenty-carat sapphire ring he'd given her. He accompanied her to Gstaad for Christmas. However, by January 1985, Elizabeth realized that she was about to make a mistake in the case of Stein—and fortunately came to her senses. It's safe to say that had it not been for her treatment at the Betty Ford Center, she might have had two more husbands added to the list of her spouses, Stein as well as Victor Luna. "Finally, I'm growing up," she said. Then, with a laugh, she added, "I think I have figured out that I don't have to marry every man I date." In the next five years, she would be linked with many interesting men, such as the millionaire financier and the publisher of *Forbes*, Malcolm Forbes (a constant companion for a number of years), and actor George Hamilton (with whom in 1987 she would make a western-comedy TV movie called *Poker Alice*). Both Forbes and Hamilton were dear friends; their fantastic and well-publicized exploits in the 1980s could fill an entire volume. In truth, though, no man would capture her heart—and a few with whom she were linked weren't even interested in attempting to do so—until 1989, when she would meet the man who would become her eighth husband.

Original television movies that offered her fans little and boyfriends that offered her even less had made Elizabeth feel much as she had when she was in Virginia and married to John Warner—a bit lost. Her life lacked focus, a sense of purpose. She remembered how much she had enjoyed being on the campaign trail with him, though, in the early days of their relationship, before he began to take her for granted. It had opened her up to the idea of giving to others. She remembered the personal satisfaction that she felt just in giving, in doing something that didn't involve her own career but yet mattered so much more. She didn't want to lose this new aspect of her character, and it had been years since she'd satisfied it. The challenge, as she saw it, would be to find a cause to which she could lend her name and her celebrity, which would benefit from the fact that she was Elizabeth Taylor, *star* . . . and not just Elizabeth Taylor playing a *role* for which she was ill-suited (such as a politician's wife).

Just as she was thinking about her life's goals and what she might do with the rest of it, a terrible crisis facing the world gave her an opportunity to really give of herself. In the next decade, her image would undergo a tremendous transformation, as would her personality and priorities. She would find not only that her public would never again think of her in the same way, but, much more important, she would never again be the same woman.

Part Seven

THE GLORY YEARS

"I Will Not Be Ignored"

It seems almost impossible to imagine that in the early 1980s, many people didn't know what AIDS was, or how it was contracted. AIDS—acquired immunodeficiency syndrome—was first reported in the United States in 1981. Actually, even before that time, gay men in the United States and Sweden—and heterosexuals in Tanzania and Haiti—had first begun showing signs of the disease. It was at first referred to as a "gay cancer" by a media grasping for a way to explain it to the masses. Everyone knew what cancer was, and the disease did seem to be striking, for the most part, homosexual men. Many gay men just assumed that they were probably infected and would die. The medical profession couldn't explain why the virus seemed to lie dormant for years only to suddenly become active. In January 1985, the world wasn't even clear as to what specific role HIV—human immunodeficiency virus—played in the passing on of AIDS, or even how it was transmitted. Could you get it, and AIDS, from casual contact? From kissing? It would be years before an HIV antibody test was widely available. There was discussion about experimental drugs. In 1980 and 1981, there were a combined 234 deaths in the United States attributed to the disease. In 1982, there were 853 deaths; it was the year the acronym AIDS was first used. In 1983, there were 2,304 deaths. In 1984, 4,251. In 1985, 5,636.

A press conference on October 15, 1982, would mark the first public mention of AIDS in the Reagan White House. Reagan himself did not mention the disease for three more years. In the next twenty years, AIDS would kill more than 30 million people worldwide, of both sexes and in all races and economic stations in life, almost a million of them in the United States.

In those early years of the epidemic, Elizabeth Taylor knew about as much about AIDS as anyone else in the entertainment community: that some of her closest friends were dying from it and that much of the world seemed indifferent to their loss. Over the years, many of her gay colleagues in the entertainment industry had suffered terribly in their private lives as a result of their true selves not being accepted in the business. She'd known many actors who'd been closeted, such as Montgomery Clift and Rock Hudson, and she had always reached out to them with friendship and a shoulder to cry on. It's easy to think that Elizabeth, as a movie star known as much for her excessive private life as for her film work, was a totally self-involved and egocentric woman. However, all one has to do is consider her close friendships with Clift, Dean and Hudson—not to mention so many others whose names would be unfamiliar but whom she'd taken under her protective wing—to know that her capacity for love and generosity knew no bounds. Remember also that she adopted a child at a time in her life when she really didn't need more responsibilities, and though she was taken to task for it—and by the Vatican, no less!—the reason she did it was because she wanted to *give*. Though the stress of her celebrity combined with certain very human weaknesses had caused her personal life to career out of control many times over the years, her sense of decency, generosity, fair play, and compassion for others was never sacrificed as a consequence. As a sort of mother protector to so many gay men over the years, she was confused, hurt, and angry when AIDS began to take her loved ones. She didn't know what she could do about it, but she sensed that she owed it to herself and her friends to become involved. "I felt early on that people needed to become better educated about the disease," she would later say. "I just couldn't sit back and watch this terrible sickness take so many of my friends without wondering if there was something I could do, though I couldn't imagine what that might be."

Elizabeth's publicist, Chen Sam, knew that Elizabeth had become deeply concerned about the growing AIDS epidemic by January 1985. Around that time, Sam was contacted by two men who were attempting to put together an organization that would offer assistance to AIDS patients, and they wanted Elizabeth Taylor's help. Bill Misenhimer, an AIDS activist, and Bill Jones, a Los Angeles caterer, had a vision they, along with five other gay men, would call AIDS Project Los Angeles (APLA), and they hoped to convince Elizabeth to become chairperson of the first major AIDS benefit, which would be called the Commitment to Life Dinner, the proceeds of which would go to benefit APLA. In meeting with Misenhimer and Jones, Elizabeth learned that celebrities were shunning the disease as if it didn't exist and didn't pose a huge danger not only to the gay population but to the world. She was shocked at first, but after thinking about it, she wasn't really surprised. No one wanted to be identified with this "gay epidemic." There had always been rampant homophobia in Hollywood, as much as it vexed her. She began polling her friends to see what kind of support she could get, and as she did she saw that the prejudice against homosexuality was, indeed, one of the chief reasons AIDS was being ignored. "I was so angry," she would recall. "The attitude that people had, the bigotry! Nobody was doing or saying anything and it incensed me. It offended my sensibility, my sense of fairness. I know so many homosexuals," she said. "I mean, let's face facts, shall we? There would be no art in America if it weren't for gays."

Frank Sinatra turned her down when she asked him to become involved with the dinner, telling her that it was one of her "lame dog causes" and that it would hurt her to become involved in it. She got a similar response from Nancy Reagan when, in January 1985 she attended President Ronald Reagan's second inauguration with Frank and Barbara Sinatra. Nancy didn't really want to discuss the matter. "No one really wanted to get into it with me," Elizabeth said years later. "I had to take the position, 'I will not be ignored, so get used to hearing about this from me because you will be, for a long time, or for however long it takes.' I started noticing that my calls weren't being returned. I must say, *that* was a first in my life.'"

At about this same time, Rock Hudson was undergoing secret treatment for AIDS in Paris, though no one knew at the time that this was his crisis. Elizabeth knew he was ill, and certainly knew he was gay. The last time they had worked together was in 1980 when they filmed *The Mirror Crack'd*. Although Amy Archerd, a columnist for *Daily Variety*, broke the news to the movie colony of Rock's AIDS diagnosis on July 23, it wasn't until Hudson's spokesman made the announcement on July 25 that the rest of the world learned of the actor's diagnosis. Elizabeth was crushed, more determined than ever to spread the word about the disease. Hudson was the first major celebrity to announce that he had AIDS, and that, combined with the public's leap to the conclusion that he was also homosexual—which happened to be accurate, but could just as easily have been wrong—was all stunning information to digest. So well loved in his youth as a dashing young matinee idol and for more than a decade at or near the top of Hollywood moneymakers, Hudson would unwittingly change the way the world viewed AIDS. He demystified it, gave it a face, an identity. When he returned to Los Angeles for further treatment, Elizabeth was the first to visit him at the hospital. "He knew that I knew," she recalled. "We didn't discuss it." She simply could not believe how ravaged he appeared from the awful disease. Her mind went back to the fun they had on the set of *Giant* so many years earlier, and as she would later recall, it was difficult to imagine that his life had turned out this way. "He's such a wonderful man," she said. "He deserved happiness in his old age, not this."

Seeing Rock Hudson and coming to terms that he truly was dying strengthened her resolve to do something about the disease that would claim his life. It was shortly after her visit with Rock that she decided to establish a national AIDS foundation that would fund scientific research on the disease. She, Misenhimer, and Dr. Michael Gottlieb, Hudson's doctor and an AIDS pioneer

who'd been warning about the disease since 1980, met over dinner in Santa Monica and decided, as she would later tell it, "that
we were going to make a difference. Goddamn, we would!"

In the summer of 1985, Elizabeth announced plans for the
Commitment to Life Dinner. "Never has a disease left so many
helpless," she said, "leaving loved ones and families reaching out
only to frustration and fear."

"The reaction was extraordinary. No one wanted to come to
this dinner," she told Whoopi Goldberg years later, in 1993. "I
made the phone calls myself. I've never received so many no's in
my life. I couldn't understand it and would ask why? And they said
well we give to cancer or whatever and we really don't want to be
involved in this particular charity. Other people would say, 'Drop
it, Elizabeth. It'll go away.' I would just lose my cool and say this
is not going away and it's going to become an epidemic. I didn't
know then it would become a pandemic. It actually was because
of Rock that I was able to get people to come to the dinner. The
town said, 'Oh one of our own has been stricken,' and then Hollywood really got their shit together."

In a couple of years' time, the epidemic would again strike
home for Elizabeth when her daughter-in-law Aileen Getty (married to but estranged from her son Christopher, and the mother of
two of her grandchildren), would confide in her that she was HIV
positive. Aileen would admit she'd had an unsafe sexual affair outside of her marriage in 1984, and through it had caught the virus.
She'd tell Elizabeth the terrible news in France in 1987, where the
two of them attended an AIDS benefit. Her friend the columnist
Liz Smith recalled, "Elizabeth said to me, 'Liz, this girl is like my
own child. She's the mother of my two grandchildren. How can I
do anything but everything I can do to save her life? *I am going to
save her.*'"

Previously, when Elizabeth had learned that Aileen was a drug
addict, she had supported her through a difficult recovery process.
Her HIV infection brought the two women even closer, but the
two had always had a special camaraderie, perhaps because they

shared such troubled lives. Aileen once said she was "victimized by my parents, by my legacy, by life. I'd been in seven institutions, I'd had twelve shock treatments, I had seven miscarriages. I was anorexic, a self-mutilator. I'd been there and back." She also said of her mother-in-law, a woman who'd also "been there and back," "It was always easy to talk to her. She taught me that I was still a beautiful person, that I could die with Mom [Elizabeth] and she would hold me safe and tight." (Aileen continues to keep a hospice near Los Angeles for people suffering from AIDS and also remains an active figure in amfAR—the American Foundation for AIDS Research. She has remarried, and remains close to Elizabeth.)

The Commitment to Life Dinner took place in the ballroom of L.A.'s Bonaventure Hotel on September 19, 1985. It was a huge success, generating more than a million dollars for APLA. During the proceedings, Burt Reynolds read a telegram from President Reagan in which Reagan acknowledged that the spread of AIDS was indeed a critical issue, marking the first time the President had made any public statement about it. (Two days earlier marked the first time Reagan mentioned the word AIDS in public, in response to a reporter's question.) Soon after, Elizabeth would join forces with Mathilde Krim, a doctor specializing in a form of biotherapy using interferons—a natural substance produced by the body in response to infection and disease. Mathilde, wife of Arthur Krim (who had been a major player in the motion picture industry), practiced at New York's Memorial Sloan-Kettering Cancer Center and had established the AIDS Medical Foundation. Dr. Krim and Elizabeth, along with businessmen such as Jonathan Cannon, Dr. Arnold Klein, Dr. Michael Gottlieb, David Geffen, Bill Misenhimer, and others founded amfAR. "The stakes are phenomenally high," Elizabeth said. "We hope the foundation will emerge as the national organization to support research, with the staying power to attract adequate financing and resources from the private sector. We plan to muster the talent and energy of America's brightest scientific and medical researchers to solve the mysteries of AIDS. We are prepared to do what it takes to find a cure."

Two weeks later, on October 2, Rock Hudson died, but with his tragic death came the emergence of a new and reborn Elizabeth Taylor. From this point onward in her life, she would have a cause that inspired more passion in her than anything else in which she'd ever invested herself, and considering the life she'd led up until this time, that was really saying a lot. In May 1986, Elizabeth testified before a congressional subcommittee in an effort to get more funding for AIDS research. "I will not be ignored," she said, repeating her motto. "And I will not go away. So . . . help me. Please."

Her longtime agent and friend Robert Lantz recalls, "She called me one day and said, 'We have a big dinner to raise money for AIDS, and I'm leaving many hours early to do some begging.' I asked, 'What are you talking about?' She said, 'We can't sell the tickets to anyone and so I'm going from studio to studio with these damn tickets until I sell every one of them.' And she did. And of course, she didn't need appointments. When Elizabeth Taylor arrived at a studio, she could see anyone she wanted to see."

Anyone who knew Elizabeth, who had tracked any portion of her sensational fifty-three years on the planet thus far, either from the intimate vantage point of a close friend or the distant one of just a fan, would have to marvel at the change in her as she entered this new and significant phase in her life as an AIDS activist and philanthropist. It's also interesting, in assembling the puzzle pieces of her life, that her time as a senator's wife is what really helped to prepare her for so much in-person, hands-on work as an AIDS activist. Without her experiences on the campaign trail, it's very likely that she would not have been able to connect to the public so easily and so genuinely.

Also, and it must be said—even at the risk of trivializing her very important work—that becoming an AIDS activist at this particular time in her life took her focus from the one thing that would surely have caused her despair had she begun to obsess over it—Richard Burton's death. She needed something else in her life at this critical time, something to hold on to and give her a sense of purpose—and how astonishing that it would turn out to be the sort of philanthropic work that would cause a veritable revolution in AIDS awareness, research, and care. It was almost as if she, on some level, decided that she would not waste another second being consumed by thoughts of Richard—that she would instead put her energy elsewhere. No doubt, his sudden death also served to remind her that her time on this planet was to be all to brief and that she needed to fill her days with something worthy of her time and attention.

Elizabeth Taylor's Passion

By the beginning of 1987 as she approached her fifty-fifth birthday, it was clear that plum film roles were no longer coming Elizabeth Taylor's way. Like many of her peers in Hollywood, she was obliged to adjust to—if not ever fully accept—the sexist and ageist attitudes of movie studios when it came to hiring actors, especially women, over the age of forty. Occasionally, an interesting part would be brought to Elizabeth, such as a role in Franco Zeffirelli's *Young Toscanini*, which, as it happened, would turn out to be one of his most obscure ventures. In a strange bit of casting, Elizabeth played a Russian soprano (her singing dubbed) who becomes involved with maestro Arturo Toscanini (played by C. Thomas Howell).

While the occasional film or TV role kept her from falling into creative atrophy, Elizabeth moved gracefully through this challenging time in her life. After all, she now had a life's purpose that was, in her view, much more important than making movies. She was fulfilled by her invaluable work raising not only the public's awareness about AIDS, but also raising millions for important scientific research about the disease. She also would branch out, in 1987, with an exciting new business venture that would lift even higher her public profile, generate many millions of dollars in the process, and also increase the "celebrity quotient" so beneficial to her when it came to her work with AIDS. She would license her name to a perfume company, the Parfums International division of Chesebrough-Pond, to market a fragrance that would be called "Elizabeth Taylor's Passion." Elizabeth would announce the new venture at a press conference in New York on January 14, 1987.

Photographer and reporter Tom Gates recalls, "The invitation to the press conference was very mysterious and simply stated that Elizabeth Taylor would be at a banquet room of the Palace Hotel in New York to make an announcement. A large card mounted near the elevator bank in the hotel lobby never mentioned Elizabeth by name, ostensibly to keep away the curious, but instead simply stated the particulars involving a 'Chen Sam Press Conference.' Once inside, Taylor's press agent, Chen Sam, gave members of the press their name tags and assigned seats. We were told that Miss Taylor would make her announcement and then answer questions. Looking spectacular in a fur hat and a fur-trimmed tweed coat, she came out and explained that she would be involved in every aspect of developing the scent. What would it smell like? 'It will have a violet aroma, of course,' she said. When Chen finally announced that Elizabeth would only take one or two more questions, I summoned up the courage to raise my hand. She pointed to me and I stood, stating, 'Hello, I'm Tom Gates and I'm with *Palm Beach Society* magazine.' At that point, she winked at me in recognition, which unsteadied me for a second, but I continued by asking if she had any prior arrangement with the one fragrance that she had been associated with up until that time, Jungle Gardenia, whose advertising slogan was 'The Perfume Worn by the World's Most Beautiful Woman.' She laughed and said, 'No, but I think they might have sent me a bottle once.' You instantly knew that she would love to have said, 'Those cheap bastards.'"

Passion's premiere to the world would be financed by a $10 million promotional investment from Chesebrough-Pond. Elizabeth would make appearances in department stores to promote the fragrance, as well as appear in a lavish television and print advertising campaign. With the passing of just a couple of years, Elizabeth Taylor's Passion would become the fourth-largest-selling women's perfume in America, grossing $70 million annually. The fragrance business would enhance Elizabeth's portfolio significantly; her net worth was nearly $100 million by the end of the 1980s, thanks in great part to Elizabeth Taylor's Passion.

On February 27, Elizabeth turned fifty-five. The next day, a party was hosted for her by songwriter Carole Bayer Sager and her husband, composer and arranger Burt Bacharach, at their Bel Air home. Attended by more than 150 of her friends, including Sydney Guilaroff, Joan Collins, Barry Manilow and Michael Jackson, it would become one of the most memorable nights of her life. "The theme of the party was diamonds," she once explained. "At the end of the party, each woman was given a ring, a cut-glass Cartier reproduction of the Taylor-Burton diamond, inscribed 'E.T./ 2/27/87/.' Can you imagine all of those flashing gigantic 'diamonds.' Camp, yes. But I loved it."

One of those present—indeed, one of the guests of honor—was sitting in a corner, holding court, surrounded by a group of people who couldn't seem to get enough of her. Michael Jackson recalled to the present author, "I was standing there looking at this wonderful older woman, who was talking in an animated kind of way, full of life. Elizabeth tapped me on the shoulder and said, 'Come with me.' She took me by the hand."

Elizabeth walked Michael over to the older woman, breaking through the crowd around her. "Michael, I would love for you to meet the most special person in my life," she said. "This is my dear mother, Sara. Mother, this is the fellow I have been telling you about. This is Michael Jackson."

Michael was speechless, as he recalls it. "I couldn't believe my eyes. This woman, who I later learned was ninety-one years old, was so beautiful. Elizabeth's essence was emanating from her, but she was actually the *origin* of that beauty, of that persona. I think I was more nervous about meeting her than I had even been about meeting Elizabeth. I didn't know what to say to her. I just stood there with my mouth open, thinking, '*My God, this is Elizabeth Taylor's mother!*'"

Finally, after a few moments of silence, Sara Taylor pointed a crooked finger at the pop star and said, "Speak up, Michael Jackson. What's the matter? Cat got your tongue?"

He and Elizabeth had to laugh. "That was so *totally* Elizabeth Taylor," he said of the moment. "I knew, then, where she got her personality from . . . and it all made sense."

Among the many celebrity guests was movie legend Bette Davis, who was escorted by Elizabeth's agent and good friend Robert Lantz. (Lantz also represented Michael Jackson on his memoir edited by Jackie Onassis at Doubleday, as well as Bette Davis.) At the end of the evening, as Lantz walked Davis to her car, Elizabeth and Michael came running out of the house. "Bette, Robbie, wait, wait!" she shouted at them. The two stopped and waited for Elizabeth and Michael to reach them. "Michael wants his picture taken with Bette," Elizabeth said. Michael stood behind her, looking embarrassed. "He didn't know how to ask, though. I told him to just *ask*, but . . . well, can we do this, please?" Bette smiled, graciously but, as Lantz later said, she really had no idea who Michael Jackson was. Michael handed Elizabeth his camera. He then stood next to Bette. The two smiled broadly. "Say cheese," said the one movie icon as she snapped a picture of the pop sensation with the *other* movie icon. "Wow," Michael exclaimed. "Me and Bette Davis. Who's gonna ever believe this!"

The AIDS benefits and fund-raisers continued through 1987— the year that both entertainer Liberace and Broadway director-choreographer Michael Bennett died of the disease—with Elizabeth totally immersing herself in her work for the important cause. A late but very welcome birthday present for her came in the form of a statement from President Ronald Reagan. He had not mentioned AIDS since a speech he gave back in February 1986. Now he appeared before the College of Physicians in Philadelphia to deliver his first major speech on the disease, calling it "public enemy number one." Vice President George H. W. Bush was later heckled when he called for mandatory HIV testing, a controversial issue at that time. Elizabeth, as amfAR's new chairperson, convinced the President to speak at the amfAR awards dinner in Washington in 1987. During his speech, Reagan also mentioned mandatory HIV testing. People began to shout at him and heckle him from the audience. Elizabeth sprang into action. "The President looked so bewildered," she later recalled. "I jumped up onstage and said, 'I don't care what your politics are. I don't care how you feel about the President or what he's not doing. He is still the President of the United States of America and you owe him some due respect so shut the bleep up!' And they did."

That same year, Sotheby's hosted a fund-raiser for amfAR called "Art Against AIDS," which was attended by more than a thousand people. Elizabeth, in a green, beaded silk gown, was radiant with diamonds on her ears, her neck, her wrists . . . it was difficult to find a place on her that wasn't sparkling under the lights. After accepting a check for $400,000 from gallery owner Leo Castelli, she posed for photographs with a long line of excited admirers. One of the advantages to having Elizabeth Taylor involved with any kind of fund-raiser—and a quality that would serve amfAR well for years to come—was always her easy manner with the public, her endless reserve of patience for her longtime fans and others who just wanted to shake her hand or take her picture so they would be able to always remember the moment their paths crossed.

Back at Betty Ford

The latter half of the 1980s had seen the stunning rebirth of Elizabeth Taylor as an AIDS activist and perfume business entrepreneur, but in the process of undertaking so many new challenges in her life she would find that her recovery as an alcoholic and drug addict would not be easy to preserve. First off, Richard Burton's and Rock Hudson's deaths had both taken their emotional toll. Then there was the tumult of strategizing her war against AIDS. On top of all that, her many appearances in conjunction with the perfume business also proved exhausting. For a woman who had never been in good health, this was a punishing time. Slowly, over a period of about five years, from 1982 to 1987, the stress in her life contributed to a variety of illnesses—such as osteoporosis, the crippling bone disease, which had begun to affect her pelvis and hips. Her doctors, wishing to ease her misery, prescribed a variety of medications for her. She began to depend on them, and before she knew it, she was addicted again.

Throughout the mid-1980s, she would spend many months in bed feeling very unwell, and taking a myriad of medications, including Percodan and Demerol. There were mornings when she would not be able to get out of bed, yet would have a full schedule of personal appearances with which to contend. Somehow, she had to get through it. She was in a wheelchair much of the time in 1987 and 1988, rising from it only for appearances.

On top of all of that, she continued to battle her weight. After leaving Betty Ford, she had decided to adopt a sensible eating regimen and stick to it as much as possible—but also, importantly, not to feel deprived or guilty when she would splurge. She wrote a book about her experiences with dieting and food rationing, *Elizabeth Takes Off*, which was a best-seller in 1987. Touring to promote the book posed a new set of problems, though. On the road, she was obliged to "openly" discuss her sobriety in press interviews, but was at the same time taking many prescription drugs just to get through the tour. It felt wrong and disingenuous, as she would later admit, and just added to the pressure in her life.

Meanwhile, Elizabeth was very concerned about her mother, Sara, now ninety-two.

In the fall of 1988, Sara was hospitalized with bleeding ulcers in the Eisenhower Medical Center, which happened to be adjacent to the Betty Ford Center. Margaret DeForest and Eleanor LaSalle, two women from Palm Springs whose mothers were friends of Sara Taylor's, both spent much time with Sara and, in the 1980s and 1990s, with Elizabeth when she would visit her mother in Palm Springs.

"I think what people don't know about Elizabeth is how utterly devoted she remained to her mother," says DeForest. "Yes, there was some frustration, especially when Sara got into her nineties. They had their share of mother-daughter battles, but they were absolutely in love with one another.

"One day in the summer of 1988, I was at Sara's with my own mother and she [Sara] announced, 'Elizabeth is coming by today, so I need to freshen up.' She went into another room with a live-in nurse—she was in a wheelchair at the time, very feeble—and was gone for about an hour. When she came back, she was all dolled up in a lovely lavender dress, her hair meticulously combed, makeup on. She always got dressed when Elizabeth came to visit. A few minutes later, there was a big commotion in the front entrance and, sure enough, Elizabeth had arrived with a group of gay men—about six—none of whom I knew, all fawning over her and carrying on about the two-hour drive from Los Angeles and the stifling desert heat. They had elaborately wrapped presents and bunches of exotic flowers and boxes of cakes and bags of cookies and . . . well, it was a big production. Elizabeth was very slim, I remember. I complimented her on it and she said, 'Thanks, honey. But all I want every minute of every day is a simple pepperoni pizza. That's really all I want. I mean, is that too much for a fading screen star to ask for, a simple pepperoni pizza?' We all laughed and she said, 'Now, see that! That's exactly the problem. Everyone thinks I'm joking. I'm not!'

"After saying hello, people scattered about, busying themselves in the kitchen, making desserts and mixing cocktails. All the while, Elizabeth was saying things like, 'Francesco, my mother likes chocolate, so make sure she has chocolate in her parfait, please, and hurry up, she's very old, you know?' It was a party, and Sara loved it. Through it all, she and Elizabeth were inseparable, holding hands and laughing. About an hour later, someone was buzzing at the door. It was a pizza delivery boy. One of her friends had actually ordered Elizabeth a pepperoni pizza as a surprise. She was delighted. 'See how lucky I am,' she told me. 'When you're a star, people do these kinds of things for you!' I've never seen a woman enjoy a slice of pizza as much as she did on that day. Then, after her one slice, she refused to eat another bite. "Get rid of it, quickly,' she said, 'before I just inhale the whole thing.'

"When Sara went into the hospital with the ulcers, it really scared Elizabeth. My mother told me that she thought it was the thing that put Elizabeth over the edge that year, the thought that Sara might die. Then, one morning in October [1988] my mother got a call from Elizabeth. 'No one can know this,' she told her, according to what my mom later recalled, 'but tomorrow I am going into the Betty Ford Center. Can you believe it?' She said she was totally addicted to painkillers again, because of her osteoporosis. Ironically, she had just been on a book tour saying how she was off drugs. She truly did not want people to know. She was afraid they would discount all of the valid information in her book about dieting if they thought she was fibbing about the drugs. She was very, very concerned about secrecy. 'I owe it to my public to try to be discreet about this goddamn thing,' she said. She just wanted my mom to know so that she could help her make certain arrangements at the hospital with Sara. I remember this as an extremely difficult time for everyone concerned."

Elizabeth felt she had no choice but go back into the Betty Ford Center for help. Her drug use was out of control, and now, she was even drinking again. However, she must have known that she would never be able to keep it a secret when she checked in on October 25, 1988. It was a nice coincidence that Sara was hospitalized just a few blocks away, on the same campus. Every day while Elizabeth was at Betty Ford for her second stint there, Elizabeth and her brother, Howard, would visit Sara in the hospital. One day, Eleanor LaSalle showed up with her mother to visit Sara. Elizabeth and Howard were present in the room. "It was a sad scene," Eleanor said, "Elizabeth was in a wheelchair because she could barely walk. She was trying to get off painkillers, but she was in excruciating pain. There she was, in the wheelchair, sitting next to Sara, who was lying in bed, quite ill, in and out of a coma. The two were holding hands and whispering back and forth to one another. It took my breath away, it was so moving. After a little while, I pushed Elizabeth out into the hallway and we waited there while Howard went to a telephone to tell the Center that he was returning Elizabeth to their care."

"Oh my God," Elizabeth told Eleanor, according to her recollection. "Getting old is such a bitch. I swear, I never would have believed *this* thirty years ago . . . me in a wheelchair? Osteoporosis? Damn those doctors," she exclaimed. She also said that she was under constant medical care, "and it's turned me into an addict." She added that it was difficult seeing Sara in such frail shape and added, "We were like two balls of fire in our day, you know? I mean, we were unstoppable."

For the next twenty minutes or so, Elizabeth regaled Eleanor with stories about dance classes when she was young, the audition gone bad for Hedda Hopper, and some of the other wild stories about Sara Taylor back in happier days, including the time she and Elizabeth met with L. B. Mayer and Elizabeth told the much-feared MGM boss to "go to hell."

"My poor father," Elizabeth said wistfully. She said that Francis did not know how to reconcile her childhood stardom, "so if it were not for my mother, I would never have become who I became."

"Well, I'm sure you had a little something to do with it, too," Eleanor told her.

"I may have," Elizabeth agreed with a smile. "But my mother started it all. My God, she was relentless, that woman. Sometimes, I wanted to kill her," she said with a chuckle. "Funny how life is, isn't it?" she asked. "Now, all I want is for her to live . . . just one more day." With that, Elizabeth took a deep breath and slumped forward slightly, as if suddenly overcome by emotion. The moment hung awkwardly. "Excuse me," she said. She then slowly rolled away in her wheelchair.

Larry Fortensky

Elizabeth Taylor's stay at the Betty Ford Center in the fall of 1988 was, in many ways, more difficult than the first time, five years earlier. She was paranoid and disoriented upon her arrival and it was clear that she was, at the age of fifty-five, suffering now more than ever. As in 1983, she stayed at the Center for seven weeks.

Amazingly enough, Sara Taylor recovered. At ninety-two, she seemed indestructible, leaving the hospital and returning to her home in Palm Springs. Elizabeth was having a more difficult time and when she left the Center on December 10, 1988, she was off alcohol but not the drugs. She would never be able to get off her medication completely, especially with her osteoporosis, but she was now taking it in a more controlled way. Still, a little poison as opposed to a lot of poison was still . . . poisonous.

One day at Betty Ford, Elizabeth noticed a man with long blond hair and hazel eyes whose personality she found amusing.

He was a tall, thirty-seven-year-old truck driver and construction worker named Larry Fortensky. Later, Elizabeth would tell one assistant that what most attracted her to him was that he had no idea who she was. Of course, he knew the name "Elizabeth Taylor"—he'd have to have lived on another planet for it to not ring a bell. He just didn't know that she was this woman with whom he was beginning to strike up a friendship.

During subsequent group therapy meetings, he watched her intently and became taken by her demeanor, a mixture of frailty and fortitude. They began having long conversations about life and love as he pushed her about in her wheelchair. There was a spark between them, and they both felt it. However, the patients at the Betty Ford Center were not supposed to become romantically involved with each other. In fact, such involvement for its patients—not just with one another but also with others outside the Center—was strongly discouraged, as it is in Alcoholics Anonymous, during the first year of recovery. Elizabeth and Larry didn't plan on romance anyway. It was just a friendship. Amusingly, paparazzi staking out the clinic took photos of a tall blond man pushing her chair, thinking he was an attendant, not a fellow patient, and certainly not a potential love interest. Noted photographer Alec Byrne almost threw away his pictures of Elizabeth and Larry, that is until sources at the Center revealed to him that there might be something between the two. Then, when he tried to sell the photographs of Elizabeth and her new friend, he was met with skepticism. It was a story too far-fetched even for the tabloids! Eventually, though, the editors were convinced—it probably didn't take much—and Byrne ended up making a fortune on these, the first photos of Elizabeth and her new beau.

Lawrence Lee Fortensky, born in 1952, was the eldest of seven children, three boys and four girls. He was raised in lower-middle-class Stanton, about an hour south of Los Angeles in California's Orange County. His parents divorced when he was five; his mother remarried. He dropped out of high school and began working odd jobs as a teenager.

By the time he met Elizabeth, Larry had been twice married, both times to women he'd known since high school. His first marriage, when he was nineteen, coincided with the day of his being drafted into the military during the Vietnam War. He was discharged several months later. The marriage lasted eighteen months and produced a daughter who still lives in Stanton. A year later, he married again, his wife just seventeen. During his second marriage, he began to work as a construction worker. His was a tough nine-to-five workday, making minimum wage. He was a hard worker who enjoyed getting his hands dirty. No backbreaking labor was too strenuous for him. One problem that he faced, however, was that he had been a heavy drinker. It had interfered with both his marriages.

For the first year that she knew Larry Fortensky, Elizabeth thought of him as a good friend and nothing more. One wouldn't think that an iconic film legend and a hardworking day laborer would have much in common, and in most cases, they probably wouldn't. The interesting thing about Elizabeth, though, is that she's a woman who can find common ground with most people, whatever their economic position or social status. With Larry, of course, the fact that both of them were trying to stay sober helped to establish a strong bond between them. They offered each other support and understanding during times of great stress in their individual recoveries. They also liked to eat, which provided a lot of laughs as Larry took Elizabeth to all of the greasy spoons he enjoyed in and around Stanton. Dressed in her black leather jacket and blue jeans with boots, her hair teased out in a biker style, she would always be a total astonishment to the other diners when entering those hamburger joints. She could be totally unpretentious when she wanted to be, dressed down and completely comfortable in any surroundings. She had kept her humanity, despite her worldwide celebrity. It's a side of her that often surprised people who just thought of her as a spoiled star.

Of course, Elizabeth was also a pampered celebrity, and there was no escaping that side of her, either. She would usually consider a man's bank account, his earning potential, and whether or not he could offer her an appropriate lifestyle before dating him. There'd been a few men over the years, though, who did not have great wealth and to whom she was attracted anyway, such as Max Lerner back when she was married to Eddie Fisher. For the most part, though, she was as practical as she was passionate, and liked to know exactly what she was getting into when she brought a man into her life. She was a very rich woman, after all. If she was going to become romantically involved with someone, he too would have to have considerable wealth. She was accustomed to being presented with expensive gifts from consorts such as Malcolm Forbes, who had recently presented her with a purple, custom-made Harley-Davidson motorcycle, dubbed *Purple Passion*. She returned the favor by hosting his seventieth birthday party in Morocco August 1989—to which Larry was not invited.

Tom Gates, by this time the New York editor for the *Palm Beach Social Pictorial*, attended the festivities and recalls, "As soon as we arrived in Tangier, we [the media] were told that Elizabeth and Malcolm would be holding a 9 a.m. photo shoot the following morning at the entrance to his Palace Mandaub, where the party would take place later that evening. Many of us arrived at seven or eight in the morning to get a good spot—and we waited, and we waited, and we waited. At around 10 a.m., we got a briefing that 'Miss Taylor was up and having her hair done.' An hour or so later, we were briefed that 'Miss Taylor is dressing and will be down shortly.' Finally, around lunchtime, Elizabeth and Malcolm arrived together, dressed very casually. They stood side by side for about . . . ten seconds. 'Oh, thank you all, so very much,' announced Elizabeth as she started to leave. There was almost a riot as everyone yelled for more pictures. She acquiesced and stood next to Malcolm for a while longer. At that point, Mr. Forbes told us that he had taken Elizabeth shopping in the Tangier bazaar for a pair of diamond-and-ruby earrings as a present, but that when either or both of them were recognized, 'there went our bargaining power.'

"The birthday party itself was the most festive and exotic event imaginable," Gates continues. "Seemingly hundreds of native musicians clad in white jelabas lined the path to the entrance of the palace, playing strange-looking and -sounding instruments, as native girls scattered rose petals along the path. Burly guards wearing harem pants and bearing swords stood at the entrance to most of the rooms that we were allowed entry to. The dinner actually took place on the beautifully manicured lawn of the palace under dozens of colorful tents. There was an enormous fishbowl that contained all of the seating assignments and guests chose their seats as randomly as one would a door prize. This very democratic way of seating was praised by some and ignored by others who insisted, 'I'm sitting with so-and-so, and that's all there is to it.' The press, however, was not eligible for the 'democratic seating process' and we were all together under one tent.

"The following day, at a luncheon hosted by the king of Morocco at the Tangier Country Club, I went about asking many of the boldfaced names, such as Barbara Walters, and Beverly Sills, and David and Helen Gurley Brown, and Dina Merrill and Ted Hartley, if they had ever been to anything as opulent. Everyone said no, absolutely never. At one point, I got Elizabeth's attention and she said, 'What are you doing here?' I explained that I was on assignment from *Palm Beach Society* and that 'now I get paid to follow you around!' She let out a little squeal and said, 'I think that's just wonderful; it's sort of come full circle, hasn't it?'"

The kind of excessive glamour Tom Gates describes was something Larry Fortensky knew very little about—and something at which Elizabeth Taylor excelled. During this same time, she introduced two new fragrances, White Diamonds for women and, for the opposite sex, Passion for Men. One launch party for the new perfumes was at the New York Stock Exchange. Her date? Saudi arms dealer Adnan Khashoggi. Earlier in the year, he had hosted her at his home in Cannes in the south of France, and a few years earlier she was his guest at his ten-bedroom home in Marbella, on Spain's Costa del Sol. At that 5,000-acre estate, he kept a pen of 70,000 of his own pheasants for shoots. He also had a stable of Arabian stallions. And those were just two of the twelve residences he owned. While in New York for the Stock Exchange party, Elizabeth stayed at Khashoggi's opulent $25 million apartment at the Olympia Tower on Fifth Avenue. The place had its own Olympic swimming pool, not to mention $30 million worth of artwork.

By contrast, Larry Fortensky lived in a modest two-bedroom apartment, which he rented. He couldn't offer her much more than a double cheeseburger with fries. Working in construction, he was a member of Teamsters Local 420 in Los Angeles and operated an off-road Caterpillar dirt compactor, making $18.50 an hour. His Teamsters insurance had covered the cost of his Betty Ford stay. Elizabeth viewed him as a good and hardworking friend, but with little to no potential as a romantic partner. She liked his company, though, and by early 1989 she was often inviting him to her Bel Air home for the weekend. He didn't feel he fit in very well, but he liked her too, and accepted her invitations.

Still, despite their obvious differences, there was something between Elizabeth and Larry. As their friendship progressed into 1989, she found a new and different level of intimacy with him because they had both been in the same group therapy. They had been revealed to each other during that process in a way that was unlike any other. "You get to know someone real fast when you are in a group therapy, in a recovery program. All the bullshit is stripped away," Elizabeth said. "We just started instantly to know each other. He knew I could see through him, and I knew he could see through me." He was also handsome with his Nordic features and rock-solid, muscled body. Elizabeth couldn't stop herself from falling for him and, in fact, she didn't wish to do it.

The power differential was obvious, yet somehow it seemed not to matter. Their relationship was played out in a way that was totally unique in the life of Elizabeth Taylor: She was sober for it. Therefore, the melodramatic nature of her previous seven courtships before marriage was missing from this one, and it opened up wonderful opportunities for them to pursue their relationship without the unpredictable interference of drug and alcohol abuse.

He was quiet and unassuming—or at least he was in the beginning of their relationship—and also very strong and dependable. She appreciated his grassroots common sense. He had no patience for the petty interpersonal politics of her business and was able to see people for who they were and not be swayed by whatever image they were putting forth. He was a strong judge of character, which she admired about him. He was also open-minded, or at least he tried to be. He'd not known a single gay man until he started socializing with Elizabeth, and then he quickly became exposed to that different way of life. It wasn't easy for him to adjust to some of the more flamboyant members of Elizabeth's circle, but, still, he tried. If he'd openly shown any prejudice or judgment toward her friends in front of her, he would have been out on his ear. He didn't, though. Soon he was working with an important AIDS community group in Los Angeles called Project Angel Food, taking meals to AIDS patients. He also cleaned the charity headquarters' large ovens twice a week.

As the year progressed, Elizabeth Taylor continued to work with amfAR and with her burgeoning fragrance business, as well as in television movies. She took the role of the failing and aging once-great star, Alexandra del Lago, in Tennessee Williams's *Sweet Bird of Youth.* Her younger lover, Chance Wayne, was played by *St. Elsewhere*'s Mark Harmon, the former UCLA quarterback turned "Sexiest Man Alive." Linda Yellen, the movie's executive producer, recalls, "*Sweet Bird of Youth* is about facing aging with pride and dignity and appreciation. I do recall that Tennessee wondered if people would totally believe that this was about a woman—Elizabeth—who had been the greatest star in the world. But our first and only choice was Elizabeth Taylor. Tennessee's writing was not always reality but a kind of heightened reality, a lyrical reality, and she's one of the few actresses who somehow made it believable. When you heard her speak it, it was just in perfect character. She understood what his rhythms were about."

During the filming of the movie, there were rumors swirling about Elizabeth and the much younger—twenty-one years—Larry Fortensky. Once again, her movies reflected her life. Or was it the other way around? After so many years and so many mirror images, which came first—her real life or her reel life—was always the subject of great discussion among aficionados of her work.

In the spring of 1989, Larry moved into Elizabeth's home. He came with one suitcase containing two pairs of worn-out blue jeans, three cowboy shirts, a pair of crusty old work boots, tennis shoes, underwear . . . and no socks. "Now, you'll sleep *here*," Elizabeth said cheerily. She showed him spacious accommodations she calls "the Yellow Room." It's one of the guest rooms. He unpacked and made himself at home.

One day, about a month later, Elizabeth's cook came out of the kitchen carrying a breakfast tray. She saw Larry and felt sorry for him. He seemed so out of place. What was he doing there, anyway? None of the staff knew for sure. Was he Elizabeth's boyfriend? Or just a visitor? "Here," said the cook, handing him the tray and putting him to work. "Why don't you take this up to Elizabeth." Instead of being insulted, Larry smiled, took the tray, and climbed the steps to the master bedroom. He knocked on the door, entered the room, and closed the door. Hours later, he came back out, went downstairs, gathered his belongings, and moved them all into Elizabeth's bedroom. He and Elizabeth had become lovers.

Needless to say, Elizabeth's protective circle was concerned about this surprising new plot twist in The Elizabeth Taylor Story. Who was this hard hat, how did he gain access to Elizabeth, and what was his true agenda? It took some explaining, but she was able to convince most of her concerned friends and family members that she knew what she was doing, and that even if she didn't she was too old, and too experienced, to be lectured about her choices. Meanwhile, Larry would keep his construction job. Yes, it was strange, but also very sweet and endlessly fascinating. She would awaken at 4 a.m. in order to have breakfast with him before he left for work. Then he would have his day and she would have hers. Finally, at 4 p.m., he would return, sweaty and tired, to his movie-star girlfriend's Bel Air cocoon, where he would then be pampered by her prodigious household staff as they exchanged details of their experiences in the outside world. Sometimes she would meet him at his construction site. Imagine how it must have made Larry look to his coworkers when Elizabeth Taylor would show up to bring him a bag of treats for break time. Typically, she would sit with the hard hats and try to get to know them because, as she put it, "Look, if he's going to get to know my friends, I am going to show him the same courtesy."

Benny Reuben worked with Larry in early 1990 on a construction site in Studio City, California. He recalls, "Man, we're working in the hot sun and at about 2 p.m. a white Mercedes pulls up and we're looking at it trying to see who it is, and, Jesus Christ if the door doesn't open up and it's Elizabeth Taylor. I'm thinking, 'What the hell is Elizabeth Taylor doing *here?*' I'm looking for the cameras, thinking we're on *Candid Camera* or something. She walks right over to Larry and plants a big one right on the kisser. And he says, 'Elizabeth, you can't be here without a hard hat.' He hands her one, and she puts it on. I'm thinking, okay, this is a dream. She turns to us and says, 'Hello, boys.' Most down-to-earth woman you'd ever want to meet. She brought doughnuts, coffee. Afterward, I said, 'What the hell, man? Why didn't you tell me you were dating Liz Taylor?' He said, 'You didn't ask.' Like I woulda asked, 'Hey Larry, you dating Liz Taylor?' Damnedest thing ever. She started coming round regularly after that. We'd be asking, 'So, Larry, is Liz comin' today?' He'd say, 'You call her Liz and she'll hit you over the head with that shovel.' So we always called her Elizabeth. Classy lady, all around."

At the beginning of 1990, Larry had to prove his mettle. First, Elizabeth's constant companion Malcolm Forbes died in February. She was crushed by the loss.

Then, a month later, in March, she became deathly ill. Larry learned that if a man wants to be with Elizabeth Taylor, he has to be the kind of person who won't run for the hills when she becomes ill, because her health is always an issue in their relationship. She contracted a simple virus infection that advanced into a pulmonary virus, causing her to have to be admitted to Saint John's hospital in Santa Monica. It was a terrible time. The doctors told her she was going to die—again! They wanted to put her on life support. She refused to allow it, afraid that she would end up a "vegetable," she said. Finally, a doctor got huffy with her and said, "Look, you are a dying woman, now sign this goddamn paper." (Some bedside manner!) She did, but she didn't like it. However, she was scared enough to first call her attorney and make out a living will that stipulated that if she was unconscious for more than two weeks, they would "pull the plug." Of course . . . she lived—but only after a very painful open-lung biopsy.

But then death struck another friend of hers: Her very good consort, Halston, succumbed to AIDS while she was in the hospital; he was just fifty-seven, the same age as she. She couldn't even attend his funeral. Then she was diagnosed with the fungal infection, candidiasis. The treatment was horrendous; it took months; she was hospitalized from March to June. Larry stayed at the Bel Air home while she was in the hospital, keeping the homestead running in her absence. Truly, she was able to depend on him, and his dependability made her feel that she wasn't alone in the world. Also, much of her lifestyle was new to him and she delighted in his discovery of so many things she'd been taking for granted for years. For instance, he'd never even been on an airplane until she took him to Gstaad for Christmas in 1990 to show how much she appreciated his help that year. Somehow he managed not to feel insecure around her, not to be intimidated by her worldliness and his apparent lack of sophistication. She appreciated that about him, and soon she was in love with him. He felt the same way.

Elizabeth's work for amfAR continued to be successful, and by 1990 the charity had collected $30 million, largely due, no doubt, to her involvement. In 1991 she established the Elizabeth Taylor AIDS Foundation, through which she would now channel her philanthropic work for AIDS research and care. "I want to know that all the money that's donated is going to patient care," she later told Charles Champlin of the *Los Angeles Times*, "whether it's counseling, legal help, food, needle exchange, condoms. Whatever it is, I tag it so it doesn't go into some executive's pocket or for office space. Those are things that have to be paid and I'm not knocking them. But I have no staff. I pay for all the underwriting myself, and I want the money to go to the *patient*."

That same year, the disease hit even closer to home for Elizabeth with the tragic death of her personal secretary, Roger Wall, who had worked for her for six years. Wall took his own life after learning that he had HIV. He was just forty-two. Elizabeth, who had given him about $40,000 toward his medical care, took it hard, saying it was "one of the biggest losses of my life . . . such a sweet, lovely man."

The years were flying by, and she was busy. Yet Larry didn't have a lot to do. He still had his job as a construction worker, but what about his weekends? He decided to have a new security system installed in the house in 1991, and Elizabeth agreed to it. Hers was woefully outdated. He began then to catalog her paintings, bronze statues, costly crystals, and rare books. Then he went to work on her expansive, and expensive, jewelry collection. He gave up on that, though. (It would have taken him a year to finish the job.) However, what he had finished, he carefully compiled into a catalog. But instead of putting the heavy journal into a safe, he proudly displayed it on a coffee table in the living room. When his friends came to visit, he used it to give tours of Elizabeth's home, as if it were a museum. "See this painting," he would say, pointing at a photo of it in the catalog, and then at the real thing on the wall. "It cost a million bucks. Wow, huh?"

Michael Jackson

The wedding invitation, which was designed by Cartier, was a simple and classic white card with black type:

> Mr. Michael Jackson
> *requests the pleasure of your company*
> *at the marriage of his beloved friend*
> Miss Elizabeth Taylor
> To Mr. Larry Fortensky
> *On Sunday, the sixth of October 1991*
> *at 5 p.m.*

A few months earlier, Elizabeth Taylor had asked Larry Fortensky to marry her. She actually hadn't asked a man to marry her since she was nineteen, when she had requested the hand of Michael Wilding. He was twenty years older than she. Now she was asking Larry the same question, and he was twenty-one years younger. He accepted. In the past, when she became engaged she always received an expensive and eye-popping bauble from her fiancé. Not this time. Instead, she took Larry's grandmother and aunt shopping for new dresses and shoes. Things were definitely changing in her life! In July, Elizabeth and Larry made the announcement that they would marry in October, and the ceremony would take place at her friend Michael Jackson's Neverland Valley Ranch. "After being together for four years, Larry and I finally decided we wanted to spend the rest of our lives together," the fifty-nine-year-old Miss Taylor said in a statement released by her publicist, Chen Sam. "Life is good and sweet and we love each other. I always said I would get married one more time and with God's blessings, this is it, forever." Elizabeth had been single for eleven years—"history-making for me," she joked—and was now ready to try marriage for the eighth time.

But how did Michael Jackson fit into this puzzle?

Elizabeth and Michael had been friends since the early 1980s. Michael once explained to the present author that he sent Elizabeth a dozen tickets to one of his Los Angeles concerts at Dodger Stadium in hopes that she might attend the performance. It had been a dream of his to meet her. "I didn't know it, but it was her birthday—February 27," Michael recalled. "I thought I was giving her great seats because they were in the VIP box. But when Elizabeth got there, she became angry because the seats were so far away from the stage. And she left, upset. The whole time I was performing, I was thinking, 'Oh my God, Elizabeth Taylor is watching me, *right now.*' But she wasn't even there. When I got offstage, they told me she had gone home, mad. The next day, I called her, and I cried because I felt so awful."

According to Michael's memory, Elizabeth was cordial but direct. "Michael," she said, "a star such as myself *never* sits in the cheap seats."

"After that, we talked on the phone every day, on every stop of my tour," Michael said. "She somehow got my schedule. I would be in Cleveland and the phone would ring. Elizabeth. Or I would be in Denver and the phone would ring. Elizabeth. And I thought, 'Wow. Doesn't she have other things to do? After all, she's Elizabeth Taylor!' At the end of the tour, I asked her if I could come by for tea. She said yes. I brought Bubbles, my chimp, along. She didn't mind."

When asked, Michael will always say that no one has been a better, more understanding friend over the years than Elizabeth Taylor. She can deal with any problem, he says, and is always available with a warm hug and an understanding ear. After getting to know him, she felt that he was terribly misunderstood. She took him under her wing, as she had so many emotionally wounded people over the years. She was concerned about his antisocial behavior and wanted him to become more outgoing, perhaps live a more normal lifestyle. He fought her every step along the way. (In the end, she would lose that battle.) Because both had been child stars, they understood each other's problems and commiserated about their lost childhoods. Theirs is a friendship that defies complete explanation, though. To say that she has mothered him over the years is reductive of what they share, yet theirs isn't a romantic love, either. In a sense, Elizabeth and Michael really are, as she has termed it, "soul mates."

"We had a similar type of childhood," Michael said, "without the opportunities enjoyed by others. We shared a quest, in search of acceptance from an adoring public who never really knew our inner turmoil. She's someone who knows and understands the loneliness of our business." Elizabeth put it this way to the *New York Times*: "He had one of the worst childhoods. I think I had the second."

With his kind of money, Jackson could pretty much do anything he wanted at Neverland, so he decided to turn it into his own private amusement park with a huge Ferris wheel, bumper cars, steam trains and a carousel. There was a zoo with a menagerie of alligators, giraffes, lions, and a twelve-foot albino python. There was also Cricket, a miniature stallion, and Petunia, the potbellied pig, and Linus, the two-foot-tall sheep. Of course, Bubbles the chimpanzee also lived there, often sitting in the forty-seat cinema with Michael, eating free candy from the sweets counter. There's a game room, a toy room, an arcade . . . all of it designed for the purpose of allowing Jackson to relive his childhood and also to entertain children there. Its existence would play a part in getting him into a nightmare of trouble in years to come, but in 1988 it was just a dream come true for him.

Overlooking the somewhat eccentric nature of what Jackson brought to Neverland, the property itself provides the perfect backdrop for a romantic, storybook wedding. It is verdantly green as far as the eye can see, countryside hills rising and falling in undulated sweeps, irrigated pastures stretching to the horizon, all of it reminiscent of the English countryside where Elizabeth was raised. Old-fashioned windmills dot the landscape. Thousands of trees gently shade superbly manicured grounds, which include a five-acre, man-made, ice-blue lake with a soothing five-foot waterfall and a graceful, inviting stone bridge. It would be here, amid the infinite silence of this gentle countryside, that Michael, thirty-three in 1991, would host the wedding of his friend, Elizabeth, fifty-nine, to Larry Fortensky, thirty-eight. Michael would personally plan every detail of the event. He gave his executive assistant, Norma Staikos, a million dollars and told her to do whatever necessary to make the day a memorable one for his good friend Elizabeth and her new husband.

Elizabeth Marries Larry

On October 6, 1991, a large, white gazebo festooned with ornate silk swags of green and decorated with huge arrangements of daisies and gardenias was set up out near the lake at Neverland. The day was, to say the least, memorable. Among 160 guests present were Quincy Jones, Brooke Shields, Merv Griffin, Gregory Peck and Franco Zeffirelli. Former president Ronald Reagan and his wife Nancy were also there. The chauffeurs of the invited guests had their own barbecue in a special area, with their own waiters bringing them drinks. Esteemed entertainment reporter Liz Smith, the only journalist present, documented the event in her column. Her stories about the event and Herb Ritts's photos were sold around the world, with all of the proceeds going to several AIDS organizations. In an interview with Ms. Smith, Elizabeth said, "I've been single for ten years now. I always thought, knowing my nature as a marrying kind of woman, that I would try, just one more time, before I die."

Before the wedding, Elizabeth's good friend José Eber did her hair. "She was like a teenager getting married for the first time," he recalls. "Very nervous and excited. She's always said that she loves being in love. But then again, she's a pro. I mean, this wasn't her first time, obviously."

At 5 p.m., Elizabeth's mother, Sara, was escorted in a wheelchair to the front row. She sat with Larry's mother; his father, from whom he was estranged, did not attend. Larry then walked down the aisle, wearing a white jacket with black trousers. He met his best man, Elizabeth's hairdresser, José Eber, at the podium. And then came the bride, the lovely Elizabeth, in a golden ankle-length gown, designed for her by Valentino at a cost of $30,000. She wore yellow roses in her hair and long diamond earrings of her own design, by Cartier. She had rarely been any slimmer, at just 110 pounds, and she looked smashing.

Michael Jackson was at her right side, an unusual substitute for the long-gone Francis Taylor, especially since her brother, Howard, was alive and present. Still, Elizabeth was delighted to have Jackson with her, and he looked dapper in a black suit with black gloves, a large diamond pin on his collar, and gleaming silver boots. Elizabeth's thirty-nine-year-old son Michael Wilding Jr. was at her left side.

Well-known New Age evangelist Marianne Williamson performed the ceremony, which was interrupted by airplanes and helicopters overheard containing paparazzi trying to get their photos as best they could. Indeed, the worldwide attention Elizabeth's wedding generated was stunning even to longtime followers of the actress. She was fifty-nine and had been a star for almost fifty years, yet there seemed no end to the public's fascination with her. At one point, a man with a parachute dropped out of one of the planes, almost landing on top of Gregory Peck. He was immediately tackled by one of Elizabeth's security team and quickly ushered off the property. Dozens of giant purple and yellow balloons were released into the sky as an effort to get rid of the aerial intruders. It didn't work. The noise was unbearable.

"Well, it was everything we expected," says José Eber, "because, let's face it, it *was* at Neverland and such an extravaganza, so of course people were going to be going crazy over it. So, everything that happened, we expected—helicopters, parachutists, whatever. You couldn't hear a thing, though. I was standing next to Larry, and, honestly, you couldn't hear one word Marianne Williamson was saying because of the helicopters."

"I heard a little of it," Liz Smith recalled, "but only because I went over to a loudspeaker and took my notes there. After all, I was supplying the whole world with the story of this wedding, I needed to at least hear it! But it was like Vietnam overhead!"

"Shall I speak louder so that everyone can hear me?" Marianne Williamson asked over the din.

"No," answered Elizabeth. "Why not just speak to me and Larry?"

"Larry and I decided to forget all about the helicopters and the noise," Elizabeth later recalled. "We looked into each other's eyes and quietly spoke our vows."

"From this day forward you shall not walk alone," they each said. "My heart will be your shelter, and my arms will be your home."

They then exchanged rings, a plain gold ring for him, hers a diamond. Marianne Williamson pronounced them man and wife.

Afterward, they exchanged a kiss, then strolled to the dining tent. There they sat with Michael. Elizabeth didn't throw any bouquets or garters, but she and Larry did the traditional cutting of a cake covered in white bows, and she fed him a piece. A steady stream of guests brought congratulations to their table, and the couple also stepped out for the first dance. The Fortenskys then spent their first married night together at the ranch, having spent the previous night there as well. The wedding cost Michael Jackson $1.5 million—$500,000 over budget—but, as far as he was concerned, it was worth every penny just to make his friend Elizabeth happy. The couple would honeymoon in Europe. Later that month, to show their appreciation to him, the Fortenskys would gift Michael with a rare albino bird from the Amazon . . . as well as a 70,000-pound elephant, named Gypsy.

The night of their wedding, after all the guests had departed, Michael arranged for Elizabeth and Larry to have some time alone. Though the two had changed from their formal wear into casual clothes—jeans and T-shirts with light denim jackets—Elizabeth's hair was still in its wedding-day bouffant, yellow roses in place. The newlyweds boarded one of Michael's golf carts with Larry in the driver's seat and Elizabeth in the passenger's. He leaned over and kissed the nape of her neck. She tousled his long blond hair with her fingers and touched his mouth to hers. Then he started the ignition and began to drive his new wife slowly into a night that was now, mercifully, filled with immeasurable silence. There were twinkling lights hanging in the trees and, above them, a sky that took on a soft, violet hue. A spectacular full moon had emerged, its warm and magical glow wrapping them and all of Neverland in its snug embrace. Even Michael Jackson with all of his millions couldn't have prearranged such a moon. Soft music emanated from the bushes. In the distance, a Ferris wheel turned and turned . . . with nobody on it. A few feet from it, a train chugged along, but with only its conductor . . . no passengers. The scene was lovely and peaceful.

An unlikely marriage had taken place on this day: A movie star who'd been one of the most famous women in the world for almost fifty years had wed a day laborer twenty-one years her junior, a man she'd met while waging battle with her worst demons at a drug rehabilitation center. Could such a union last? Who could predict what the future would hold for them? However, in this serene time and very strange place, Elizabeth Taylor was content with the seventh man to take her as his wife. Certainly, if there was one thing she'd learned in her sixty years, it was to enjoy the moment and not look too far into the future. She rested her head on Larry's shoulder. A small group of servants collected on one of the nearby patios to watch the couple. They pointed at them and cheered them on as the newlyweds' golf cart disappeared around a curve in the road, headed toward an unknown destination.

Re-creating Her Mother's Marriage . . . but Not Quite

On the first anniversary of Elizabeth Taylor's wedding to Larry Fortensky, a longtime assistant went to the elegant Hotel Bel Air, which sits on twelve very private and well-manicured acres of lush gardens, and paid $3,500 for one night in its most commodious space—the Presidential Suite. It's a two-bedroom, two-bath, well-appointed accommodation. The formal living room has a wood-burning fireplace and double French doors, which lead to a private garden patio and large outdoor spa. The assistant decorated the suite with fragrant lavender and bouquets of yellow roses. She then placed scented candles around the sunken tub in the bathroom. She also ordered an extravagant meal to be delivered that night: beluga caviar to start ($250), and roasted rack of Colorado lamb with Niçoise olives and fig jus ($44 a plate), with chocolate soufflés for dessert ($25 each). It was all to set the stage for the perfect celebration of one year of marriage for her employer, Elizabeth, and her new husband, Larry. That night Elizabeth and Larry happily left for the hotel to enjoy their evening.

The next morning, when the assistant came downstairs, she was stunned to find Larry lying on the couch in the living room, watching television. The entire household staff was concerned about what might have occurred to cut the romantic evening short. Before anyone had time to do any snooping, however, Elizabeth swept into the kitchen and announced, "We decided to come home because it was boring." Then she walked back out, as if she just wanted to quell the gossip, once and for all, and not hear another word about it.

Things obviously weren't going well . . .

Of course, it had been expected that there would be adjustments to be made when Elizabeth married Larry, especially considering their divergent stations in life, the huge disparity in their finances as well as the twenty-one-year difference in their ages. One of the more interesting developments in Elizabeth's marriage to Larry, and one that would prove to be a big challenge to their union, had to do with her sudden determination to try to remake him. She thought of him as a diamond in the rough, and wanted to polish him. A longtime connoisseur of expensive jewels, she knew a good one when she saw one. Larry had a way to go before he would be perfect, but she began the work she felt necessary in transforming him into not only the ideal husband but also the perfect social partner. In that first year, her capacity for making suggestions seemed to have no limit.

"You should always pick up both the champagne glass and wineglass by the stem," she would tell him before they would go to dinner.

"Don't name-drop in public. Those we meet socially need not know who else we've met along the way."

"Don't ramble on. If you get stuck and don't know what to say, allow the other person to talk. People love to talk about themselves."

"Don't slouch."

"Don't contradict me in public, it's embarrassing."

It wasn't that Elizabeth didn't love Larry just as he was, it was that she knew in her heart, as she would tell it, that he had the potential to be an even better, more well-rounded person. He wasn't as worldly as she, hadn't experienced as much, and didn't always understand the social interaction between people in high society or in show business—or the perfume business, for that matter. By this time, she was among the ten richest women in the world, according to *Forbes*, her fortune estimated at $150 million, in large part because of her fragrance business. She was one of the most sought-after celebrities in Hollywood, with a full social calendar that also involved Larry as her escort. All she wanted to do was whatever she could to make his new life easier for him. When she took him to a formal dinner at her friends Burt Bacharach and Carole Bayer Sager's home, he seemed not to fit in with the others there. She didn't even like the way his fingernails looked in comparison to the other men. She made a mental note, as she would later tell it, to make an appointment with a manicurist for him the next day. He also didn't know which fork with which to eat his salad. Something else to work on. When Burt asked him about a film, he responded by saying, "Oh, yeah. I seen that one." Elizabeth cringed.

It had finally happened. Perhaps it was inevitable. Maybe the only surprise was that it had taken eight marriages to seven men before it had unfolded: Elizabeth Taylor had re-created in her own life the marriage her mother once had with her father.

"I know what the problem with you is," Sara used to tell Francis, "and here's how to fix it." She meant well, even if she was overly assertive. In time, she would mold Francis from a shy and retiring person into a more outgoing, social man with whom she was proud to be seen. She had even transformed Elizabeth from a bashful, awkward little girl into an effervescent and charismatic young lady, imbuing her with the self-confidence necessary for her to stand before movie cameras and give performances for which she would always be remembered. However, there was one major difference between what Sara had done back then and what Elizabeth was doing now. Francis wanted to change and actually welcomed Sara's suggestions. In fact, he missed her coaxing of him when Sara suddenly shifted focus and began working on the transformation of their daughter. But Larry wasn't nearly as welcoming of Elizabeth's suggestions. Their biggest arguments in the first year of their marriage resulted from his taking umbrage at her ideas of how he might change.

In February 1992, for instance, Elizabeth celebrated her sixtieth birthday with a fantastic party at Disneyland with hundreds of guests. The one problem of the day concerned Elizabeth constantly trying to tell Larry how to pose for photographers. "You mustn't smile so broadly," she told him in front of several witnesses. "It causes lines to form around your eyes. You don't want lines, now, do you?" It must have been the proverbial straw breaking the camel's back because Larry snapped—and that was when Elizabeth first learned something about him she wasn't aware of in the past: his temper. "Stop picking at me," he told her angrily. "I mean it. Stop it, *now*." He stormed off. It could have been embarrassing, except that Elizabeth is a first-rate actress who knows how to act completely unperturbed. "Men!" she exclaimed, and then she went about the business of having fun.

In the intervening months, Elizabeth had Larry's hair restyled in a way she felt better suited him. She even started giving him speech lessons. One of her servants recalled, "Elizabeth summoned the top designers like Valentino, Versace, and Armani to customize a wardrobe for him. He had never owned a tuxedo in his life. He soon began to rebel against her attempts to dominate him."

For instance, he refused to stop smoking in the master bedroom. Elizabeth had given up smoking in 1990 after her terrible bout with pneumonia, and had asked him repeatedly not to smoke in the bedroom. It didn't say much for him that he refused to do it. In fact, it sent up the proverbial red flag for Elizabeth, who began to wonder why her husband would care so little about her health that he would do the one thing that could definitely cause her problems. Perhaps he viewed it as a way of seizing control, but his Marlboros in the bedroom were dangerous to his wife's health, and smoking them there wasn't much of a way to make the point that she didn't control him. Also—and this was minor but became an issue—he insisted upon eating in bed, getting crumbs all over the sheets. The more she asked him not to do it, the more he did it. Finally, Elizabeth is a light sleeper. He liked to have the television on all night, and refused to compromise his viewing habits. She wasn't going to tell him when he could watch TV. It was fairly childish, and in the end he lost. It had been her bedroom for a good deal many more years than it had been his, and one day she had all of his belongings removed from it. It was back down to the Yellow Room for Larry, from whence he came. When the press got wind of these arrangements, it was assumed that it was because of Elizabeth's health problems. It wasn't.

Larry continued to fight Elizabeth's domination of him, and even began using her household staff as his accomplices. "He wanted to be informed about every telephone call Elizabeth received," said a former household staff member of Taylor's. "Who was calling and why? The pharmacist would send over medication on a weekly basis. Suddenly, Larry demanded that we not take her medication up to her until he had examined the prescriptions and counted the pills. If he was not around, we were supposed to hold the medicine downstairs until he returned. We explained to him that he was putting us in a difficult position and he said, 'Look, I am doing this for her own good.' None of us believed that, though. We knew it was about control."

Brian Bellows is a friend of Larry's from Stanton who was invited to a cocktail party at the Fortenskys' hosted by Elizabeth to thank some of her wealthier friends for money they donated to the Elizabeth Taylor AIDS Foundation. Larry had invited Bellows and a few other friends of his so that he would, as he told them, have someone to talk to at the gathering. "I was amazed at how much Larry had changed," he recalled. "I hadn't seen him since the wedding. He looked great in his suit with his haircut, the whole bit, but he was quiet and seemed afraid to say anything or do anything. Not like the outgoing Larry I knew. He was just standing in a corner drinking a soft drink, taking in the view, watching people but not getting into the mix at all."

Bellows went over to Fortensky. "What's going on, man?" he said, extending his hand. "Looks like you're hiding, buddy."

"That's 'cause I am," Larry said, shaking his friend's hand. "It's best for me to stay out of the way."

"Why?"

"Big night here for the wife," Larry explained. "I don't want to screw it up for her. Plus, I gotta tell you," he continued, suddenly seeming very angry for no apparent reason, "I'm about to blow, man. I'm about to lose my cool, man. And if I do, man, I'm gonna' turn this whole goddamn house on its ear, man."

It was clear to Brian that something wasn't quite right with Larry.

At that moment, Elizabeth came sweeping into view looking elegant in a floor-length black evening gown, the Krupp diamond gleaming on her hand. Rarely did she ever wear it at home . . . this *was* a special night. "Oh, my *darling*. Why, I've been looking *everywhere* for you," she said with a flourish. "Michael's here. Michael Jackson!"

"No kidding?" Larry said, suddenly brightening up. "Mike's here?"

"Yes, he is," Elizabeth said. "But you must come quickly, because who knows how long he'll stay. Why, at any moment, he could simply *vanish* into thin air! *Poof!* You know Michael." She laughed merrily and disappeared into the other room.

As Larry left, he turned to his friend and muttered, "Finally, a *real* person I can talk to."

Part Eight

ALL WOMAN

"Sara S. Taylor—Loving Mother, Devoted Wife— 1895–1994"

Elizabeth's mother, Sara Taylor, had not been well in recent years. True to her nature, though, she still wanted to maintain her independence, and therefore insisted on keeping her condominium at the Sunrise Country Club in Rancho Mirage, California. One of her friends there recalls, "From her little home, she had a wonderful view of rolling green golf courses and lovely blue lakes. It was pristine, gorgeous. She just wanted to tend to her rose bushes, be with her friends in her ladies' bridge club, have her life. I would go to visit and she would complain about the dust on her white plantation shutters. 'It's so dusty here,' she'd say. 'This goddamned desert, I hate it. I'd like to live near Elizabeth in Beverly Hills,' she said, 'but I'm not leaving my friends, here. No way.' Living a full life had always been important to her, and I have to say that she did just that. She didn't hate the desert, not really. It was just her way, complaining. Elizabeth had hired an Asian family to move into the condo next to Sara's and take care of her, a very nice young couple with a baby girl. Elizabeth visited often. However, at the end, she wasn't able to come as much because of her own health issues.

"Sara looked at newspaper photographs of her unwell daughter and said, 'Look, she's sicker than I am. I'm the one who should be visiting her, not the other way around.'"

Indeed, Elizabeth had not been in good health for some time, and then, in December 1993, things took an even more dramatic turn for the worse when she took a fall at her chalet in Gstaad. She had just spent six months racing around the globe with Michael Jackson. He'd needed her assistance when, in the winter of 1993, he was accused of child molestation. She rose to the occasion and joined him on his concert tour to offer counsel and sympathy. She'd even managed to get him into a rehabilitation center in London, where he dealt with an addiction to pain medications. She put her health at grave risk to help someone who is not only a friend but also a fellow survivor of a childhood gone wrong. However, it had not been easy for her, and by the time she got to Gstaad for the holidays she was physically and emotionally spent. It was speculated by her friends that this was why she tripped and fell. Unfortunately, the accident aggravated the osteoarthritis condition in her left hip. She began the year 1994 crippled by terrible pain, and her doctors were conferring with her about possible hip replacement surgery.

Elizabeth and Sara spoke on the telephone as much as possible. By this time, Elizabeth's brother, Howard, was living with his family on twenty-three acres on a mountain near Taos Ski Valley, New Mexico. He and Sara also remained close, as he always had to Elizabeth. In recent years, Sara had said she wanted to be there for Elizabeth, to help her "bring the magic back," as she put it. Elizabeth, though, was less accessible to her mother later in her life—a fact that, while difficult for her to accept, Sara had come to terms with. As Elizabeth's mother and the woman who had once shaped Elizabeth's stardom, the desire to help her was second nature. Sara couldn't help but recall her glory days, when Elizabeth not only needed her help, but welcomed it. However, it just may have been Sara's modus operandi over the years that eventually helped to drive a wedge between them.

For instance, many years earlier, in the spring of 1982—after Elizabeth had returned from her disastrous birthday reunion with Richard Burton in London—Sara had visited her daughter and invited a small group of friends to join them for tea in Taylor's new home in Bel Air. Elizabeth and John Warner were separated at this point, and Elizabeth was, perhaps, at her heaviest. While she may have dressed to shield that fact from the world, Sara didn't hide her disappointment with her daughter for "letting herself go."

During the gathering, one friend recalled Sara turning to the group and asking, "Does everyone remember the last time you could be called gorgeous?"

It was an odd question, to be sure, but all present, most over seventy years of age, recounted their last stab at ultimate beauty. Sara mentioned a time when she had visited Elizabeth in Rome during the filming of *Cleopatra* and spent a day in the able hands of her daughter's grooming team. "I walked out of that hotel looking like a movie star," she said. "When I met Francis that evening he almost fell out of his chair."

Then, after all the stories of faded beauty but Elizabeth's had been shared, Sara turned to her daughter. "How about you, dear?" she asked pointedly. "Do you remember your moment?"

The uncomfortable pause ended with Elizabeth's hollow yet promising response. "My moment is yet to come, Mother."

Sara gleefully raised her glass and proclaimed, "I *knew* it! You'll be beautiful again! Prove them all fools," she said, referring to the press who had painted Elizabeth as a shell of her former self.

It seemed as though Sara had arranged the tea in order to send Elizabeth a message—in a way that only Sara could do. She had challenged her daughter to reclaim her glamour, while managing to sidestep an awkward conversation. At her heaviest, Elizabeth had generated riotous public scenes and scathingly cruel press. Sara felt that the only way for her prized daughter to squelch the vicious chatter was to bring the past back. Elizabeth may have been wise to her mother's tactics of manipulation, but if she was, it didn't stop her from pursuing that goal with gusto. Of course, as we now know, Elizabeth did drop the weight she had gained, publicly citing her questioning of her self-worth as one of the reasons for the transformation. But as had happened so many times before, it was also her mother's prodding that had helped Elizabeth achieve physical perfection—which, after her Betty Ford stay in 1982, she eventually did.

During one of her visits with her mother in the hospital, during Elizabeth's stay at Betty Ford, Elizabeth revealed her weight loss. Sara grabbed her hand and said, "You can always get the magic back, dear. Never forget that." It was a supportive, wonderful moment between mother and daughter, played out in front of witnesses. Then, as would often happen with Sara, she continued where she might better have ended: "And if you avoid letting it slip away in the first place you'll save us both a lot of trouble."

It was passive-aggressive statements like that one that may have set the tone for their relationship in the years that would follow. Elizabeth had a cordial, yet increasingly distant relationship with her mother. They would speak on the phone less frequently as time went by, but Sara's later life was made quite comfortable thanks to her daughter's generosity. Sara, however, often reminded interested parties that the career she had created for her daughter was what gave Elizabeth the means to be so generous.

In many ways, Sara Taylor had the spirit of a passionate artist whose vision had been successfully realized. The joy of knowing that her ultimate goal had been achieved brought her great joy— but what it had cost her and her family was something of which she was quite aware. Still, she had to admit that, on the whole, it was worth it. Or, as her Palm Springs friend observed, "Her love for her children, but particularly for Elizabeth, knew no bounds. There were pictures of Elizabeth carefully placed all over her condominium, in silver frames. One that she most cherished was of her with Elizabeth and her granddaughter, Maria, at the opening night of *The Little Foxes* in New York, in 1981. In it, Elizabeth is wearing a red shawl, a white gown by Halston, I believe, with a deep, plunging neckline and, of course, lots of diamonds and pearls. Sara would show it to me and say, 'Will you just look at my daughter. Now, if she is not the most beautiful woman in the world, then I don't know who is. Don't you agree?'"

Indeed, everything considered, Sara Sothern Taylor remained Elizabeth's biggest fan until the very end. She passed away quietly on September 11, 1994, at the Sunrise Country Club. She was ninety-eight. She was then buried next to Francis in twin crypts in the Sanctuary of Peace section of Westwood Memorial Park. The small golden plaque on her burial site reads: "Sara S. Taylor— Loving Mother, Devoted Wife—1895–1994"; his: "Francis L. Taylor—All Our Love—1897–1968."

Elizabeth and Larry End Their Marriage

Come with me," Elizabeth Taylor said to five members of her household staff. "Quickly, now. Hurry!" They followed her up the stairs and into her master bedroom. Once they were all inside, Elizabeth closed the door and locked it. "There," she said. "That should keep him out of here. We'll be safe here until he cools off."

One of the surprising—and disappointing—facts Elizabeth learned about Larry Fortensky over the first couple years of their marriage was that he had a temper, or, as one of her household staff put it, "He had fits of uncontrollable rage." Elizabeth certainly never could have imagined when she first met him at the Betty Ford Center that such a mild-mannered man had a flip side. After witnessing Larry's "uncontrollable rage" become a pattern for him, she had one of her doctor's prescribe Prozac for him in hopes that it might help his temper, but it didn't work. It just got worse over the years. It would be unfair, though, to blame only him. No doubt, he learned what six other men before him had known: Being married to Elizabeth Taylor is a challenge. He was, as he would put it, "pissed off on a regular basis," and often it had to do with her not putting much stock in his opinion or his advice. His pride had been whittled away over the years. Still, he knew what he was getting into when he married her. Wasn't he the one who showed up at her doorstep with no socks? Did he really expect that he would be the one running the household? In a sense, though, he may have felt that he was doing just that. After all, it did seem that he had one of the greatest movie stars of all time hiding in the bedroom with her entire household staff . . . and it was his temper that had put them there.

Don't misunderstand, though: Elizabeth Taylor was not scared of Larry Fortensky. She wasn't hiding from him. Rather, she was sick of him. She didn't want to put up with him any longer that day, and she also did not want her servants to bear the brunt of his anger. However, if he thought for even a moment that she was actually afraid of him, he would have been wrong. She'd dealt with Richard Burton for more than twenty years. In terms of working up a good fury, Larry was just a beginner compared to Richard.

It would be an hour before she would release her staff from the bedroom, and Larry ranted and raved in the living room . . . about what, no one was even absolutely sure. Elizabeth was adamant that her employees not suffer the consequences of her husband's temper, and she had begun to believe that he might even strike one of them. One day, she walked into the kitchen and happened upon him berating one of her female employees. He raised his hand to her. Would he have hit her? He'd never been physically violent in the past. Still, Elizabeth was alarmed enough by the possibility to immediately step between them. "Larry, I don't know how you treat your construction crews, but you will not behave this way to my staff," she said angrily. "They are more than employees. They're my family." One witness to the confrontation recalls, "Larry just stormed off and shut himself up in his bedroom, where he slept for three days straight."

Perhaps to exact his revenge on Elizabeth's loyal staff, all of whom he perceived as being against him, he began to treat them poorly. One recalled, "He wanted details of what we spent maintaining the household. He even restricted what we ate. Since there are no restaurants close to the house and because we rarely had time to take a lunch break when dealing with Ms. Taylor's business ventures, we were given carte blanche in the kitchen. Elizabeth always told us to make ourselves at home. We never abused this privilege. One day Larry decided the kitchen was off-limits to us. Wearing only his boxer shorts and with a cigarette in his hand, he called everyone into a meeting from the secretaries to the gardeners and said, 'From this day onward, you have a choice. You can either bring a packed lunch from home, or the cook will make you a tuna sandwich. And no more eating off our china. Use paper plates.'"

"Larry was always very protective toward Elizabeth," says his and Elizabeth's friend José Eber, in Fortensky's defense. "He was always on the lookout for people he thought were taking advantage of her. At the end, though, he did get a little obsessive, and it caused some problems." (Elizabeth elaborated to Larry King: "All of a sudden he had obsessive-compulsive disorder and didn't want to leave the house.")

As soon as Elizabeth heard about Larry's edict to her staff, she rescinded it, which only caused more problems between them.

There were other problems, some difficult even for the casual observer to reconcile. For instance, Elizabeth had a collie puppy, Nellie, descended from the legendary Lassie with whom she had starred when she was eleven in *Lassie Come Home*. She asked Larry to care for the animal while she was out of town on AIDS business. He took Nellie into his bedroom, but was negligent about taking her outside to relieve herself . . . and so she did so all over the room. He became angry and began cursing out the dog. He then locked her in her traveling container, which she had long ago outgrown, with no food or water. The dog whimpered for many hours until she was finally rescued by one of the household staff. When Elizabeth found out about it, she became extremely upset at Larry, and a big argument resulted.

Larry's temper and inconsideration weren't the only issues in the Fortenskys' marriage. There was Elizabeth's health as well. Earlier, in the winter of 1994, she had to undergo a complicated hip replacement operation, the possibility of which doctors had been discussing with her ever since she took that fall in Gstaad. Her recuperation continued to be long and difficult all the way into 1995, with Larry at her side the entire time. She would be confined to a wheelchair for much of the time, to her great exasperation. It was a shame; she had been doing so well in so many areas of her life. Her movie career had faltered, true. She would have a cameo in the movie version of *The Flintsones*, which starred John Goodman and Elizabeth Perkins, but it was just a fun send-up, nothing that anyone will ever remember in years to come. ("Oh, she just did it for fun," says Liz Smith, "and because they promised they would hold all of the premieres as fund-raisers for AIDS, and they did.") However, her perfume business was thriving—by the early 1990s it had grossed $500 million. All things considered, it had been a good time in her life. However, it would never be quite the same after the hip replacement surgery. There would be another operation on the other hip, then still yet another to repair residual damage. She'd never be able to fully bounce back. As her good friend José Eber so succinctly put it, "Her rehabilitation took forever . . . and ever."

She wasn't at her emotional best after the operation, either. Mostly, she didn't want to be seen in such bad shape, her pride overtaking her common sense where her husband was concerned. The two fought about her recovery, and Larry began to feel as Richard Burton once had (and even Michael Wilding before him), that Elizabeth really didn't want to get better, that she thrived on her illnesses. Of course, only Elizabeth knows in her heart whether this is true, but it certainly does fly in the face of her recuperative powers and her will to continue to live, despite her many health challenges along the way. In June 1995, things got even worse when she had surgery to replace the other hip, her right one. There was no way that her marriage would survive a second recuperation. "I was a cripple," she later told *People* magazine. "It was hard on me. It was hard on Larry. It was hard on our marriage."

In summer of 1995, she decided to end it with Larry. "I think it's time for you to go," she told him. "I'm not happy, and you're not happy."

"Larry didn't give up easily," said one of Elizabeth's staff members. "He convinced her to go to a marriage counselor with him, but their counseling didn't last long. The therapist was star-struck at having Elizabeth as a client." From the employee's tone, it's easy to see that Fortensky was not going to win any points in that household, no matter what he did. It was his own fault, though; he had poisoned them all against him with his temper. He was in therapy, though, which was admirable, and he wanted Elizabeth to join him. His offer could have been viewed as a willingness to save his marriage, but instead it was seen in a pejorative light.

Elizabeth later explained that when she and Larry went for counseling, she felt that her husband and the therapist had "a conversation which had become a sort of code. I felt left out. But we did it anyway. Got into the car. Did it. Then we wouldn't speak until the next appointment."

Brian Bellows, Larry's friend from Stanton, California, recalls, "Larry telephoned me in September of 1995 and said, 'Before you read it in the papers, I want you to know that Elizabeth and I are separating.' He sounded very depressed, unhappy. 'What the hell happened?' I asked him. 'You know what? She's set in her ways,' he told me. 'She's been her own woman for so long, she never really listened to one goddamn thing I ever told her. Guess I can't blame her,' he said. 'She's Elizabeth Taylor, for Christ's sake. Why would she ever listen to *me*, anyway?'

"My impression was that the two hip surgeries were what

ruined that marriage. He said, 'She's been hurting for so many years, it's just a place she's used to being in, and I can't handle it.' In a sense, I don't think he had what it took to get her through the health issues, and she was unwilling to be helped, I believe. She was sixty-three. He was forty-three. The older they got, I think the difference in their ages became more pronounced. It was a losing battle, I guess."

On August 30, 1995, Elizabeth called her good friend Liz Smith. "You were the only press person at our marriage," she told her. "And I would have preferred not to have to call and tell you this. Larry and I both need our own space now. So we have agreed to a trial separation. We both hope this is only temporary."

Liz asked how Elizabeth felt about the decision. Elizabeth sighed. "Obviously, I feel sad," she said. "I sincerely hope it will work out. This is a difficult conversation for me to have . . ."

Before she hung up with the world-famous columnist, Elizabeth seemed to steel herself for what was to follow Ms. Smith's announcement in the press the next day. "Let the tabloid games begin," she said wryly.

In October 1995, Elizabeth had to return to the hospital for hip adjustment surgery because one of the operations had left her with one leg shorter than the other. There seemed no end to her misery at this time.

In February 1996, she filed for divorce in Los Angeles Superior Court, citing "irreconcilable differences." She offered a one-sentence statement: "We were not able to communicate, and I am very saddened that it didn't work."

With the mention of their failure to communicate, a comment Elizabeth made during her marriage to Richard Burton comes to mind. "A woman will try and dominate a man," she said, clarifying the dominance theme of all of her relationships. "She will try and get away with it. But, really, inside herself, she wants to be dominated. She wants the man to take her. If he does lean on her, everything goes slightly off key, like a bad chord. She hopes it will pass, that the guy will come through. When he doesn't, she begins to needle him. If nothing happens, she goes on needling—until he stops listening. At that moment, she becomes bitter, and he goes deaf. Finally, there is no more dialogue, they have no rapport."

Elizabeth was surprised when Larry sued her for $5 million and attempted to invalidate their prenuptial agreement, claiming they were both represented by the same attorney when it was signed. She was angry, and probably felt the way she did when Eddie Fisher went after her for money so many years ago. ("Try working. Like the rest of us.")

During the Taylor-Fortensky litigation, details of Elizabeth's financial documents were produced to provide insight into her wealth at this time. Of course, one would imagine that Elizabeth Taylor would be a rich woman, but the exact details of her financial portfolio—as of 1994—were nothing short of stunning. Consider this: Her net worth was $608.43 million. Her properties around the world were valued at $127.45 million. Her art and jewelry was valued at $102.77 million. Her stocks and bonds, $274.21 million. Her interest-bearing bank accounts, $104 million. She was also making about $12 million annually from her perfume business. She'd recently cashed in stock in the Hilton hotel chain (acquired through her first marriage) for a profit of $21.7 million. Also, interestingly, she inherited $8.7 million from the estate of her close friend, publishing mogul Malcolm Forbes. Is it any wonder that Fortensky felt he was entitled to more than the $5,000 per month he was to be paid in a divorce settlement, as per the prenuptial agreement? "For Elizabeth, it wasn't really about the money as much as it was the principle," said one of her attorneys, repeating the age-old refrain of rich celebrities who find themselves caught in marital disputes over money.

A dramatic moment in the divorce proceedings occurred during a deposition in the office of one of Elizabeth's lawyers. Larry didn't know that Elizabeth would be present for it, or at least he probably hoped she wouldn't attend. When he walked into the room, she was already there, waiting for him. She then sat across from him looking like a million bucks in her lavender power suit and stared him down as he explained why he required more money from her. He made observations such as, "The suits I own cost several thousand dollars each. The Valentino sweaters I own, many of which were handmade, also cost several thousand dollars." He also said that, when he was working—and he wasn't at this time—he'd become accustomed to being driven to the construction site in a limousine, which seemed ludicrous but was apparently true. Even he couldn't pull it off, though, and he ended up fleeing from the conference room saying, "I can't do this with her sitting there. It's ridiculous."

In the end, Elizabeth did love Larry and decided to just work it out with him. They settled for more than a million dollars. In November 1996, they were officially divorced. The two are still friendly today.

Earlier in the year, she had lost another of her dear friends, her longtime spokeswoman Chen Sam, who had suffered from cancer. It was a terrible blow; the two had been very close. "These last couple of years have been hard," Elizabeth said at the end of 1996. "My marriage to Larry had come undone and I lost Chen Sam. Truly, she was my sister for more than twenty-five years. She died of cancer, here in my house. I had gone to her room to say good night and found her breathing laboriously. I kissed her and held her and talked to her. After a while, I left. Five minutes later, she was gone."

It was sometimes difficult for her to resist becoming very depressed, and she spent much of 1997 and 1998 at home, nursing her physical as well as emotional wounds. "I was agoraphobic for about two years," she recalled. "Didn't leave the house, hardly got out of bed. Rod Steiger got me out of here." Steiger, the famous movie actor, became a constant companion. On their first date, he took her out for hamburgers and fried chicken. They had a wonderful time, and became good friends. However, her marriage days were over. "If you hear of me getting married, slap me," she told Barbara Walters during a television interview.

At the end of 1996, Elizabeth began having terrible headaches and, much to her dismay, memory loss. "What fresh hell is this?" she asked one friend of hers. She was a woman who had done so much with her life despite many formidable physical challenges, yet the greatest one was ahead for her. As she approached the age of sixty-five, she would face her mortality like never before . . . and the greatest lessons of her life were about to be revealed to her.

Facing Her Mortality . . . Again

It was in early February 1997 when Elizabeth Taylor knew something was very wrong with her. She couldn't figure out how to use the telephone. "And who ever had used a telephone more than me?" she later asked jokingly. She'd been having headaches, loss of memory, dizzy spells. But that morning, staring at the telephone, she knew for certain that something was very wrong. She screamed for help. When a doctor arrived, she discovered that she couldn't walk. She was taken to a hospital immediately, and after a series of brain scans she got one of the most frightening diagnoses of her life, certainly one that would cause any person the greatest of panic: She had a brain tumor. It was large, possibly the size of a golf ball, on the lining of her brain, and would obviously have to be removed. The doctors were 99 percent sure it was benign, they said. "I just sat there," she later wrote for *Life* magazine.

"Speechless. In sheer terror. A brain tumor! They wanted to operate on my brain, on my emotions, my thoughts, my memories, my sense of poetry, my feeling for colors, my soul, my *self*. Afterward, even if I survived, would I still be me?"

This very serious operation was immediately scheduled to occur in two weeks, on Monday, February 17. Ironically enough, at this very same time, the ABC network was planning a sixty-fifth birthday celebration to honor her, which was to be video-taped before a live audience and later televised. Entitled *Happy Birthday Elizabeth: A Celebration of Life*, it was to be produced at the Pantages Theatre in Hollywood on . . . Sunday, February 16, the very day before her operation.

Entertainment reporter and producer Cathy Griffin worked on the television program as a consultant. She recalled that much of the planning for the special was done at Elizabeth's Bel Air home, just prior to her startling diagnosis. As the producers went through various topics, she said yes to just about every idea. "One thing that was a definite no, though, was the subject of Eddie Fisher," says Griffin. "She wanted no mention of him at all. 'Keep him out of it,' she said. And she meant it. Basically she approved everything else, even some ideas that were thought to be iffy, such as Roseanne Barr on a barge as Cleopatra. She loved it.

"She talked a lot about her life and times because, after all, that's what the show was to be about. It was clear that she was still madly in love with Richard Burton. 'What a shame that he couldn't be here for this show,' she said. Also, she wanted to make sure that Mike Todd was recognized. She felt that he'd often been overlooked in retrospectives about her, and she wanted to make sure that didn't happen."

Elizabeth's only requirement? That Michael Jackson appear on the program and sing. Without him, she said, there would be no show. Once he agreed to appear, it was smooth sailing for the producers.

That is, until Elizabeth got news of the pending brain surgery.

She was then understandably uncertain as to whether or not she wanted to proceed with the tribute. How macabre would it be to sit through a retrospective program about her life, immediately before having brain surgery? Moreover, could she enjoy even a single second of it knowing what awaited her the very next day? She telephoned one of the producers and, crying on the phone, said that she would probably have to cancel; they'd have to go forward without her. "Oh no," he exclaimed. "But can't you put off brain surgery for just a day or two?" He was joking and she had to laugh. In the end, she decided she would go through with it, but only because the audience's contributions, which could (and did) total more than a million dollars, were to be earmarked for the Elizabeth Taylor AIDS Foundation. "To back out is really chicken shit," she said.

The pending brain surgery—now postponed one day—made headline news instantly and was thus on the producers' minds as they put together the broadcast. Now more than ever, they wanted to do a good job. Cathy Griffin explained, "The biggest problem was in putting together the photomontages. While there was certainly no shortage of pictures from collectors, Elizabeth had very little personal memorabilia, just photographs of her and Richard—and one other that she was very proud of, with Queen Elizabeth, in a silver frame on her piano. All of her memorabilia was in a storage facility. When we got there, we found that none of it was organized—just stuff packed away in boxes. 'Living my life was tough enough,' she said. 'Did you expect me to make scrapbooks, too?' She's been the most photographed woman in the world but, really, she doesn't care much about it. She looks at her show business history as having been attached to a brand—the Elizabeth Taylor brand—which has little to do with who she is as a woman.

"Throughout my work on the program, she was nothing less than a fabulous, bawdy class act, all the way," Griffin recalled. "I've been a big fan of Elizabeth's since I was a youngster in Texas, so working on this big extravaganza to honor her in Hollywood was an unforgettable experience."

In the end, *Happy Birthday Elizabeth: A Celebration of Life* turned out to be a star-studded success, paying homage to, truly, one of the greatest film stars of our time, but also one of the most memorable personalities of the twentieth century. It was actually rendered even more nostalgic and significant by the pending life-or-death operation. Michael Jackson did more than just show up, he escorted Elizabeth—and also sang a song he had written for her, "Elizabeth, I Love You." ("You had grace and beauty, charm and talent, but they robbed you of your childhood," he sang, repeating, once again, his life's theme.) Most of her extended family—children and grandchildren included—were also present.

It was interesting, though, that so much attention was paid in the retrospective tributes to her tabloid past. It was affectionate and brilliant in its presentation, but Eddie Fisher *was* mentioned . . . and many times. It had been an executive producer's decision to include him, and, really he had no choice. Elizabeth talks about her marriage to Eddie as if one could never find a photograph of them smiling or clutching at each other. Don't forget, they *did* adopt a child together, so there is legitimate history there. Still, Elizabeth couldn't have been very pleased about his inclusion in her tribute . . . especially after having been so specific about wanting to exclude him.

Two days later, Elizabeth checked into Cedars-Sinai Medical Center. She had, of course, spent a great deal of time in hospitals—in this one, in particular—with serious illnesses, but this time there was something different about the experience. As a consequence of her time at the Betty Ford Center, her work on behalf of AIDS research, and, no doubt, of nothing more than just living long enough to learn certain lessons about life and love, she now had an inner life that had been missing in her younger days. She was able to find peace through prayer. "I pray to God all the time," she said. "We have a conversational relationship and those conversations calm my fears."

As she faced her own mortality, she couldn't help but think about those she'd loved and lost over the years. Mike Todd and Richard Burton, of course, came to mind. She realized that she'd taken so much of her life for granted. It's not that she didn't have a ball doing it. She certainly did. But at the age of sixty-five, she now wished to cling close to her children, all of whom were with her at the hospital, and to her many grandchildren—and her friends. She thought a great deal about her father during this time, as if attempting to put the pieces of her life together one last time, trying to make sense of it . . . and of him, and her complex relationship to him. She also missed her mother, she would often say, especially in these days before the brain surgery. However, she knew that she was imbued with Sara's indomitable spirit, just as she'd always been. Anyone who had known both women could see that Sara Taylor lived on in her daughter. "And I have *lived*," she said at the time. "If the knife slips while I'm on that operating table tomorrow and I never wake up in this world again, I'll die knowing I've had an extraordinary life. It's been filled with love. I've loved my husbands and they've loved me. And I've learned and grown because of the love we shared— though I do wish I'd had more patience, more of the wisdom that comes with age."

Of course, Elizabeth pulled through the delicate surgery. Could anyone have imagined otherwise? She was completely bald after having had her head shaved for the operation, but she didn't care. In fact, she liked it—and even posed for a picture for *Life* magazine. It was refreshing, in a sense, as if she had finally been stripped of all the unnecessary cosmetics of her life, most of which had been spent in show business trying to look her best for her public. So after the surgery, she was bald . . . and so what? It felt good, liberating, even. She had a seven-inch incision extending across the back of her head. "I look like an ax-murderer's victim," she joked. Since about 1982, she'd been accused of having had a face-lift. Now it was finally clear to everyone who cared to look, she said, that she had no telltale scars of any kind of cosmetic surgery!*

Elizabeth really had faced the beast of her own mortality, once again . . . and had survived it . . . once again. "I'm never going to count her out," Liz Smith told Cathy Griffin. "If she should ever die, I might not believe it. I'd have to be convinced by her being dead for several years, she's just that resilient."

It wouldn't be over for her, though. Indeed, there would be more battles to wage.

On February 27, 1998, on her sixty-ninth birthday, she took a fall while preparing for dinner with her son Christopher and his family. Though it seems impossible to imagine that her frail body could withstand more punishment, she broke her back in the fall—"a severe compression fracture of my first lumbar vertebra," she explained. She would be in a back brace for two months. The rest of 1998 would be hell for her. She had worked so hard all of her life—making fifty-five movies and nine television films, not to mention her theater work ("and I should have gotten a medal just for *Private Lives*," she said)—and had been present to care for so many people, such as Michael Jackson, that her friends and family felt it grossly unfair that she should have to suffer so much as she grew older. Her celebrity, her wealth, her . . . *life* . . . had certainly not made her exempt from the pain of advancing age, not

---

* Anyone who knows Elizabeth would know that she'd never have allowed a person who wasn't a trusted friend close enough for such inspection. Deny it she will, but people in her inner circle believe she's had more than the admitted "tiny chin tuck." In their opinion she's had a face-lift and then several "fine-tunings." However, many stars avoid admitting such things; Elizabeth would certainly not be the first to do it. More power to her if she can pull it off. (Michael Jackson says he's only had two such surgeries!) When she turned sixty, Elizabeth had Roddy McDowall photograph her the way he did when she was thirty-four, with a pink towel wrapped around her head and no makeup. When the photos are compared side by side, her features appear to have been altered. "She and Roddy were crazy to do it," said one observer. "I'll bet he was the one suggested it, the little imp."

that she ever expected that she would get any such break. "I've been in pain my entire life," she told friends in the hospital after breaking her back. "I certainly knew what to expect of old age. No, it's not easy, is it? However, it's better than the alternative, isn't it?" Then, with characteristic humor, she added, "Though I have to admit that there have been times, especially this week, when I think I might have welcomed that alternative."

Once home from the hospital, Elizabeth surrounded herself with her loved ones as well as a menagerie of rabbits, pheasants, peacocks, and, of course, her beloved Maltese, Sugar. (The dog died in 2005, leaving Elizabeth inconsolable.) By May 1998, she was feeling much better and even hosted a Memorial Day party for her family and many friends. She and Rod Steiger were still companions; he was an invaluable help to her during the dark days of 1997 and 1998, and would continue to be a close—and platonic—friend until his death in July 2002. Amazingly, in June 1998, she was wearing a back brace—she was still recovering from the back injury—but did not allow it to prevent her from socializing with friends, going out in public in the kind of long, flowing muumuus Halston had designed for her during the John Warner years—but this time wearing them to camouflage her brace, instead of her weight. "I haven't felt this good in years," she would say by the end of 1998. She was crushed, though, when her dear friend Roddy McDowall died at the end of the year, aged seventy, of lung cancer. Elizabeth and Sybil Burton, Richard's first wife, visited Roddy shortly before his death. These two women hadn't been in the same room since Elizabeth and Richard became involved in 1962. After a whirlwind three-week courtship, Sybil had gone on to a 1965 marriage with an actor and rock musician (from a group called the Wild Ones) named Jordan Christopher, twelve years her junior. Though the couple was estranged for much of their union, it actually did not end until his death in 1996. She owned Arthur, a successful discotheque, and then moved to Sag Harbor, on New York's Long Island, and made a success of herself in community theater. Even though theirs was an uneasy alliance because of their unpleasant history, Elizabeth and Sybil held hands as they sat with their dying friend. Their presence at Roddy's deathbed served as a reminder that no matter the extent of past hurts, time does pass—Elizabeth was sixty-six and Sybil sixty-eight—and, somehow, works its promised magic: It heals. After Roddy's death, Elizabeth hosted a private memorial service for him at her home. Though she would never be able to get over his loss, it did underscore for her the importance of living each day to its fullest.

Of course, as sometimes happens when people feel they may lose a loved one, there were those in Elizabeth's life who suddenly wished to cling to her. Larry Fortensky, for instance, told her that he now regretted the divorce and would be devastated had she died as a result of her recent travails. He suggested that they rekindle their relationship. She realized that his sudden proposal had to do with his fear of losing her from his life, not a romantic love for her. She said no, but encouraged him in their ongoing friendship. Even her former lover Victor Luna was back in touch to tell her that she had been the love of his life. "Well, *of course* I was," she said with a laugh. The communication with Fortensky and Luna served to remind Elizabeth of something she'd almost forgotten during these darker years. "I've had the love of so many wonderful men," she said privately. "Say what you will about them—and I have said a lot, myself—the men I have spent my life with have all been so lovely." Then, with a cackle, she added, "Except for Eddie Fisher."

On January 28, 1999, Elizabeth received the truly shocking news that Larry Fortensky had either fallen or was pushed down a seven-foot staircase in his home in San Juan Capistrano, outside of Los Angeles. He had landed on his head. His blood alcohol level when he was found was through the roof at .265. Doctors operated on him and did the best they could, but the damage done to his body was so severe—a broken neck and back as well as severe head injuries—that his prognosis was grim: He might never walk or even move again. Elizabeth was, of course, shocked. She immediately telephoned Larry's daughter, Julie, to comfort her. The two stayed in daily communication for the five weeks that Larry lay in a coma, dependent on breathing machines. He emerged from it in March, but would never be the same.

It was a horrible accident and Elizabeth had a difficult time reconciling herself to it. True, it hadn't worked out with Larry, but she did have wonderful memories of him. "You can't be with someone eight years and have loved them and shared a life with them and have it disappear like turning off a faucet," she told Barbara Walters. Rod Steiger, her constant companion during this time, helped her deal with the tragedy. She had seen so much in her life, and this latest event with Larry was one of the tougher ones.

"I talk to him from time to time," says Larry's friend Brian Bellows. "'Things didn't turn out as I expected,' he told me. 'But, hell, whose does? You get through it, somehow. You live your life. I had an amazing experience with Elizabeth, and I'll never forget it, or her. I still can't believe I was married to her. I can't believe she had me.'"

Six months later, on August 18, 1999, Elizabeth took another fall in her bedroom and, unbelievably enough, broke her back—again! This time, the pain was almost more than she could bear. It took months for her to heal. Though constantly surrounded by friends and family at the hospital, and then at home, it was difficult for her to keep her spirits up, and understandably so. She had to go through the misery with just moderate use of drugs, lest she become addicted again. It was hell. But she was used to hell, wasn't she? One had to wonder though why, at the age of sixty-seven, she couldn't be granted some respite from her suffering.

"Sometimes I get so angry at my body," she said at about this time. "Not many people have a medical history like mine. Pneumonia [too many times to count]. Back, eye, knee, and foot surgery. Appendectomy, tonsillectomy [twice], cesarean section [three times], partial hysterectomy, adult measles, dysentery. Not to mention two stays at the Betty Ford Center to beat my addictions to alcohol and prescription drugs. And now this—coming after a two-year stretch in which I had two hip replacements and a third operation to correct one that went wrong. I loathe physical therapy. I learned to walk as a baby. Why did I have to learn all over again—in my sixties?"

By the end of the year, though, she was somehow making public appearances again—a little worse for the wear, much weaker in body but certainly not in spirit. When she attended Andrea Bocelli's concert in Los Angeles in November, she was asked how she had survived the year. She responded in typical Elizabeth Taylor candor: "How the hell did I survive *any* year?" She then let loose with that self-mocking laugh of hers. "You just do it," she said. "You force yourself to get up. You force yourself to put one foot before the other, and God damn it, you just refuse to let it get to you. You fight. You cry. You curse. Then you go about the business of living. That's how I've done it. There's no other way."

Dame Elizabeth: Honor at Last

As a child star, Elizabeth Taylor had been naïve about the real world. She believed romance to be as it was portrayed in her early films—a fantasy of passion, melodrama, and conflict that would magically work itself out in the end, with everybody living happily ever after. However, it certainly wasn't to be that way for her, as she well discovered by the age of eighteen. Her first marriage to Nicky was abusive, her second to Michael all wrong. Her third to Mike genuine, but in the end tragic. Her fourth to Eddie, a messy mistake. Her fifth and sixth to Richard? An emotional roller coaster. Her seventh to John, a growing experience that set the stage for perhaps her greatest role, as an AIDS activist. Her eighth, to Larry, a final attempt to claim a simpler life, which ultimately just never felt like home. In her, the world found the perfect Hollywood ideal, a movie star like no other. From *Cleopatra* to *Virginia Woolf*, she breathed life into more than sixty-five characters. Some performances were simply watchable, others brilliant, but all eminently engaging simply because of her star power and charisma. She was always a star—from her first picture to her last, and one like no other before or after her. Heavy or thin, young or old, ailing or well, she suffered our condemnation and commanded our devotion in equal measure. Remember, even her onetime rival Debbie Reynolds had said of her at Oscar time, "Hell, even *I* voted for her."

Indeed, if ever there was an American princess, it would have to be the actress with the sapphire-blue eyes—pampered, beautiful . . . beloved, Elizabeth. Hers has been a life well lived with great and, often, maddening passion. She says she doesn't regret much of it, but she also doesn't speak of much of it, either. José Eber recalls, "A friend of mine who's a manager in Hollywood called me and said, 'Do you think that you can ask Elizabeth if she'd like to write another book, a real autobiography, her whole life with Burton, etc?' . . . He said, 'I can guarantee her $10 million for it.' So I went to Elizabeth and told her. Ten million dollars. Without thinking about it for a second, she quickly responded, 'Nope, not interested.'" Or, as Elizabeth so succinctly and firmly put it to Barbara Walters in 1987 when asked about her memories of Richard Burton: "They're wonderful memories. They're warm memories. And they're my memories."

By the power of her personality, the drama of her life, and the example of her philanthropy, she has seduced us, charmed us, and inspired our admiration. Indeed, because we've been so transfixed for decades by her talent and her beauty, we sometimes lose sight of what she has truly done. After years of struggle, she rose above her own limitations, both emotional and physical, and mobilized Hollywood to recognize a health crisis that had only previously been mentioned in hushed tones in the film industry. Her bravery and passion to that end proved to friends, family—indeed, the world—that Elizabeth Taylor had truly become an aware and compassionate member of society. No longer oblivious to the concerns of others, she had managed to merge the polite façade she and her mother had created in her youth with the purposeful woman she now was at her core. With no need to feign interest for the sake of appearances, she had landed in a comfortable place where genuine caring came easily to her. It was during this period of self-discovery that Elizabeth would learn that she was going to receive an honor even her mother couldn't have expected. Now, at the age of sixty-eight, as if to top it all off, she would become a Dame, recognized by the British royal family, whom Sara Taylor had held in the highest regard.

Elizabeth received the call in the winter of 2000 from Buckingham Palace: She and Julie Andrews were to be honored as Dame Commanders of the Order of the British Empire—the female equivalent of a knighthood—in the millennium New Year Honors List. Both were born in Britain in the 1930s, though they'd spent their working lives mostly in the United States. The ceremony was set for Tuesday, May 16, 2000. When she called Michael Jackson with the news, he was thrilled for her and agreed to accompany her to England. He also helped to make what was already certain to be a grand occasion even more spectacular. He offered to foot the bill with diamond distributor De Beers, Sky Televison, and the British Film Institute, in order to make the event as memorable as possible for his good friend. "She has done so much," Jackson said. "She changed the planet. That's the truth. And it all started by changing herself."

Along with her twenty-four pieces of luggage, Elizabeth was accompanied to England by an entourage that included her four grown children and their partners, attorney, agent, hairdresser, makeup artist, and also her trusted assistant Tim Mendlesen. It was clear to everyone around her that this time in her life would stand out as one of the most, if not *the* most, important. She made no secret of that fact, either. "It's the most exciting—and I do not exaggerate—day in my life," she told reporters. "I had no inkling. It was just like, '*Whaaaat?* I can't believe it. Me? Getting a Dame-ship?'"

An exhibition of portraits of Elizabeth was scheduled at London's National Portrait Gallery, and she would also be the guest of honor at a charity spectacular at the Royal Albert Hall to raise money for AIDS research. The British Film Institute also intended to honor her with a BFI Fellowship at a tribute dinner at the Dorchester Hotel. Another highlight of the planned series of events in her honor would be the National Film Theatre's program of a dozen classic Elizabeth Taylor movies, including the epic *Cleopatra*. Every event on her itinerary was important to Elizabeth, and she would even go out of her way to be early for some of them—very unusual for her—making time to greet fans who had congregated with only the hope of perhaps catching a quick glimpse of a movie legend.

Before the ceremony, as Elizabeth and Julie were being briefed about their roles in the proceedings, their instructor turned to Julie and asked her to "look after" Elizabeth, as if to say, "This one could be trouble, so keep an eye on her, won't you?" Elizabeth had to laugh: "As though I would possibly misbehave!" Indeed, her troublemaking nature was part of the legend of Elizabeth Taylor that had continued beyond its validity. Much of the public still viewed her as an unpredictable, moody, and demanding film star. The woman who was preparing to receive this great distinction, though, had become a different person altogether.

On the special day, Julie Andrews, sixty-four, was the first to receive her insignia, for services to acting and entertainment, at a ceremony in the ballroom at Buckingham Palace. Next came Elizabeth, sixty-eight, who received her Dame Commander's brooch in honor of her services to acting and charity—recognizing her fund-raising for AIDS research. With her head slightly bowed, Elizabeth accepted the honor as Queen Elizabeth pinned the official insignia on her blouse. "Today doesn't compare to anything else that's happened to me in my life," she said, nearly overcome by emotion. She looked regal, maybe even more so than the Queen herself, in a heavy pearl necklace and Van Cleef & Arpels pearl-and-diamond earrings that she designed for the occasion. The Krupp diamond from Richard Burton shone brightly from her right hand. With her hair in a teased-out bouffant, and wearing the color—lavender—she hadn't looked as good and vibrant in some time. It was wonderful for her loyal fans to see her well . . . indeed, to have her back, even if she was in a wheelchair for much of the time. Her children surrounded her: the salt-and-pepper-haired Michael, now forty-eight, with his wife, Brooke; Christopher, forty-six, and his wife, Margi; Liza, forty-three, and Maria, thirty-nine.

It's probably not surprising that there was one man on Elizabeth's mind on this memorable day: Richard. It had been back in 1970 when she and Richard Burton arrived at Buckingham Palace to accept his OBE—the title of Sir Richard. Elizabeth had worn a Russian-style fur hat on that day, looking stylish and proud on the arm of her flattered husband. She couldn't help but wonder now what his reaction would be to her own day of honor—the "what ifs" involving Richard had never faded over the years. As much as Elizabeth had tried, she'd not been able to get over his death. In fact, she finally decided that she really didn't want to, preferring instead to keep not only his memory alive in her heart, but also the sadness of his passing. She would remember many of the good times with him in her life, and very few of the bad. "I miss him so much," she said of Richard after receiving her honor. "Oh, how I wish he was here."

Of her sixty-eight years of experience, she told reporter David Wigg of the *Daily Mail*, "What I can't envisage is my life any other way than it has been. The pattern of my life was inevitable. If there hadn't been World War II, I probably would have been a debutante, lived in England, and married somebody very secure and staid. But you can't 'if' your way through life, can you? Each experience, each blow, each happiness, each magical moment— even each moment in the pits—has taught me something. The really bad moments taught me to rely on my inner strength and not to succumb. I don't believe in wallowing. I have no sympathy for self-pity. Oh listen," she continued, "I'll cry on a shoulder, and I don't mean that I'm totally encased in a shell. I'm not, at all. It's just that I've learned that you have to solve your inner problems yourself. Nobody else can do it for you. The magical moments have taught me to appreciate my life. Hang on to it and relish it— and not take even a second of it for granted."

When she got back to the United States after all of the festivities, Elizabeth hosted a small dinner party with some of her closest friends and family members, including her brother, Howard—who was seventy-one in 2000—and his lovely wife, Mara. Howard and Mara had been married since 1951—forty-nine years in all—and spent much of their lives together with their children in Hawaii and, more recently, La Jolla, California. It's difficult to resist the temptation to contrast Howard's sole long marriage to his sister's track record in that department, but Elizabeth would be the first to say that she always believed her brother had chosen the more sane lifestyle, one outside of show business. "How I admired Howard's disdain for the movies," she once commented.

On this night at the home of Elizabeth Taylor, with friends and family surrounding her, Richard was still on her mind, as was Mike Todd. She became emotional when talking about them, her eyes filling with tears. "You know, Mike didn't deserve to die that way," she said, her voice shaking. Her guests were surprised. It was rare for Elizabeth to bring up Mike's death; she usually only spoke of his life, not his tragic demise. However, the honor she'd received in England had stirred so many memories for her, and, inevitably, when she thought of Richard—as she so often had in recent weeks—she automatically thought of Mike. After all, they were the two loves of her life. "And why is it that I always have this Goddamned feeling that Richard Burton is going to walk right through that door at any minute and start giving me hell about something?" she asked one of the guests, seemingly bewildered.

Then with a laugh she concluded, "Somewhere, the two of them are probably having drinks, waiting for me to join them. And oh, the hell we shall cause in heaven if in fact that's where we end up, which," she concluded with a cackle, "I *highly* doubt."

"It's her desire to live that has pulled her though so many crises in her life," says Eber. "Who knows where that comes from? Maybe it's from actually being at death's door so many times and just realizing how precious life is, and not wanting to miss out on a second of it. Or it could be a positive outlook at her very core that pushes her onward. Or is it her mother, maybe?"

That evening, as she stood before her closest friends and family in her Bel Air home filled with free-flowing laughter and love, Elizabeth Taylor raised a glass of sparkling cider. "There's a woman who deserves our deepest appreciation," she began, slowly, "because if it weren't for her we'd all be somewhere else right now. She taught me how to be a different kind of dame," she added, prompting raucous echoes of laughter. "Let's all drink to my mother, Sara Taylor."

"Hear, hear!" shouted a guest.

"No!" she commanded, bringing the room to a hush. "Let's drink to two things."

All eyes were on her.

"To my mother," she said. "And forgiveness."

Appendices

Selected Cast of Characters

~

DAME ELIZABETH ROSEMOND TAYLOR

For the last six years, Elizabeth Taylor has lived a quiet life at her home in Bel Air, California, limiting personal appearances to a precious few a year in order to conserve her energy and preserve her health. "My body's a real mess," she told a reporter for W magazine in December 2004. "If you look at it in the mirror, it's just completely convex and concave. I've become one of those poor little women who's bent sideways. My x-rays are hysterical." She also told the reporter that she was suffering from congestive heart disease.

"The pain she suffers on a daily basis is, I'm sorry to say, unbearable, to the point where there are tears," says José Eber, who sees her almost every day. "It only seems to get worse. I was with her recently and she was crying. She was supposed to go to a doctor, but couldn't even get dressed. I said, 'Can't you find a new doctor? Someone who can actually help you?' She said, 'My God. I have been to every doctor in Los Angeles . . . maybe in the world!'"

Despite her body, so broken and beaten in more ways that can be counted over the last fifty years, Elizabeth's spirit remains unscathed. "When a great guy wants to take her on a date, she becomes like a teenage girl," says Eber. "She'll be gone in a second."

Elizabeth often sends first-class airline tickets to friends and family members who are having difficult times in their lives, usually with a simple note: "Join me. Love Elizabeth." Celebrities also come to her home to pay homage, obtain advice, and bask in her presence. "From Johnny Depp to John Travolta to Billy Bob Thornton to Demi Moore," says José Eber. "I've seen Madonna there. Nicole Richie, her father Lionel, all of them, they come just to be able to say they know her."

Of course, Elizabeth also entertains her four children, ten grandchildren, and four great-grandchildren. "Her family is everything to her, now," says Eber. "They visit, stay with her. You walk in on a Saturday evening, and you'll find her in bed with her grandchildren, watching movies. Also, she loves cutting their hair. She has a great sense with a scissors, loves doing her grandchildren's hair. 'If there's one thing I finally learned over the years,' she has told me, 'it's that when things are at their darkest, we always have our family. And that's a gift from God.'"

As of this writing, Dame Elizabeth Taylor is seventy-four years old.

⟶

HOWARD TAYLOR

Howard Taylor, Elizabeth's only sibling, lives with his wife, Mara Regan Taylor, in La Jolla, California. The two, married since 1951, have three grown children.

He is seventy-seven.

MICHAEL HOWARD WILDING JR.

Michael Wilding Jr—Elizabeth's firstborn son from her second marriage to the British actor Michael Wilding—lives quietly in Santa Fe, New Mexico. Wilding is the only Taylor offspring to have dabbled in acting and has had a few roles over the years, including that of Jesus Christ in the 1985 TV miniseries *AD*. Though he also appeared on the television series *Guiding Light* and *Dallas*, he hasn't done any acting in the last ten years. He has also worked as a real estate agent and a restaurateur.

Michael has a thirty-four-year-old daughter, Leyla, from his first marriage to Beth Clutter, and another, Naomi, who is now thirty. Wilding is now married to actress/producer Brooke Palance, daughter of Oscar winner Jack Palance. They have a son, Tarquin, who is sixteen.

He is fifty-four.

CHRISTOPHER EDWARD WILDING

Christopher Wilding—Elizabeth's second-born son, from her marriage to Michael Wilding—lives in Los Angeles, California. He has had a dramatic and often difficult life. At twenty-six, he married oil dynasty heiress Aileen Getty. Tragedy struck in 1985 when an affair left Aileen with the HIV virus. The marriage was not able to survive the strain, and Christopher was awarded custody of their two sons, Caleb (now twenty-three) and Andrew (twenty-one). Today, Christopher works as a movie and television program editor. He is married to his second wife, Margi, who works as a film editor. They have a son, Lowell, fifteen.

He is fifty-two.

LIZA TODD TIVEY

Liza Todd Tivey—Elizabeth's daughter from her marriage to Mike Todd—lives in upstate New York. She never knew her father, the colorful fifties impresario and film producer; she was just an infant when he died in a fiery plane crash in 1958.

Liza, an accomplished equine sculptor, married artist and teacher Hap Tivey in 1984. They have two sons, Quinn, twenty, and Rhys, fifteen.

She is forty-nine.

MARIA BURTON CARSON McKEOWN

Maria Burton Carson McKeown—Elizabeth's adopted daughter—lives in New Jersey and California.

As a young girl, Maria endured more than twenty operations to correct congenital defects in her hips. She has been fully recovered for years and is today a gorgeous and vital woman who's even worked as a fashion model.

Though Maria was originally adopted by Elizabeth and Eddie Fisher in 1961, Elizabeth was given full custody of her when the couple finally divorced in 1964. It was then that Maria took the name Burton.

In 1982, Maria married talent agent Steve Carson; the marriage ended in the early 1990s. They have a daughter, Eliza, twenty-two.

In 2001, Maria married Tom McKeown, a compliance officer with a Wall Street firm. During that very brief and extremely troubled marriage, she gave birth to a son, whom she named Richard after the only father—Burton—she'd ever known.

Maria Burton Carson, who is presently single, is devoted to several disabled children's charities.

She is forty-eight.

~

CONRAD NICHOLSON HILTON JR.

Elizabeth Taylor's first husband, Conrad Nicholson Hilton Jr.—Nicky—went on to a difficult life after his divorce from Taylor, battling alcohol and substance abuse for years. He dated Joan Collins and Natalie Wood in the 1950s. He is the great-uncle of the young socialites Nicky (named after him) and Paris Hilton. (Conrad Hilton, Nicky's father and the founder of the international chain of business hotels that bear his name, is their great-grandfather.)

Nicky Hilton died in Los Angeles of a heart attack in 1969. Not surprisingly, he and Elizabeth were not friendly at the time of his death.

He was forty-two.

~

MICHAEL WILDING

Michael Wilding, Elizabeth's second husband, died in July 1979 after a fall at his home in Chichester, England. Elizabeth, who had remained friendly with him over the years, attended the funeral. On his casket was a single spray of yellow roses and a standard that read, "For dearest Michael. Love always. Elizabeth."

He was sixty-seven.

⁓

MICHAEL TODD
(AVROM HIRSCH GOLDBOGEN)

Michael Todd, Elizabeth's third husband, was—as she still maintains—one of the two loves of her life, the other being Richard Burton.

Michael—Mike—Todd died in a plane crash in 1958. He and Elizabeth were married for thirteen months.

He was fifty.

⁓

EDDIE FISHER (EDWIN JOHN FISHER)

"She still hates me, doesn't she?" Eddie Fisher asked of Elizabeth when he was interviewed for this book. "Yeah, well . . . I did the best I could for the old girl."

If he could do it all over again would he do differently?

"Not a thing," he says.

Would he marry Elizabeth Taylor? "Well, I'm afraid so," he answered. "I don't think there was any way around it. Truth be told, once is never enough when it comes to Elizabeth, anyway. I may have even married her *again*, if I'd had the chance."

Why does he think Elizabeth is still so angry at him? "She's mad at me because I left her," he says. "She wanted both of us, me and Burton, to stay," he explains. "She is Elizabeth Taylor, isn't she? So, she *should* have two husbands at the same time, or at least that's how she saw it. Seriously, whatever she wants to remember now, the fact is that she loved me as much as I loved her."

If Elizabeth Taylor were to call him and say, "Eddie, it's me. I'm on my deathbed. I just wanted to say good-bye," what would be his response? "I'd say, 'Baby, remember a hundred years ago when you had to choose between me and Richard Burton? Well, you made a big mistake, baby. A *big* mistake!'"

Eddie Fisher has had five marriages, four ending in divorce and one by death. He is currently single. He's authored two books about his life, in 1982 and in 1999. It's clear from his writings that he's still fascinated by Elizabeth, even though he can be quite critical of her. He also holds the dubious distinction of being the only one of her seven husbands with whom Elizabeth still seems tremendously angry. "Still, I've been the luckiest guy in the world," he concludes. "I have no regrets. I'm too old for regrets. Life is not for regrets, anyway. Life is for living, isn't it?"

Eddie Fisher lives in Los Angeles.

He is seventy-eight.

RICHARD BURTON (RICHARD JENKINS)

Richard Burton—who was twice married to Elizabeth Taylor, in 1964 and 1975—died of a cerebral hemorrhage in 1984. Elizabeth says she will never really get over Richard . . . nor does she ever wish to do so.

He was fifty-eight.

SENATOR JOHN WILLIAM WARNER JR.

John Warner—Elizabeth's sixth husband—remains an active and influential United States senator, Republican from Virginia. He is also a key member of the Senate Committee on Homeland Security and Governmental Affairs.

In December 2003, Warner married his third wife, Jeanne Vander Myde, in Washington. It was his first marriage since divorcing Elizabeth Taylor, in 1982. He and Elizabeth have remained on friendly terms.

He is sixty-nine.

⌒

LARRY FORTENSKY

Larry Fortensky—Elizabeth's seventh husband in her eighth marriage—has recovered from his accident. He remains physically weak and unbalanced, however, and still suffers from memory and attention deficit. He lives outside of Los Angeles. He and Elizabeth have remained friendly over the years.

He is fifty-three.

⌒

SYBIL WILLIAMS BURTON CHRISTOPHER

Despite numerous preliminary conversations with her, Sybil Burton Christopher did not wish to speak for this book. Though she remarried in 1964 to the late pop singer Jordan Christopher, one would not be surprised if some of her memories of her years with Richard Burton remain painful. In that regard, Elizabeth Taylor says that one of her biggest regrets in life is that she and Richard hurt so many people in the early days of their love affair. "Such as Sybil Burton," Elizabeth explained in 2004. "I have been holding this regret with such deep pain. I mean, I broke up a beautiful marriage." She now believes that her subsequent troubles with Richard were related to their romance's scandalous beginnings. "You always get back what you put forth," she said, "and I should have known that I'd get back exactly what I had done myself. You get what you give." In making that observation, she was referencing what happened after she married Burton the second time. "Richard went off with another woman," she explained. Then, with an arched eyebrow, she added, "Sally-who-shall-remain-nameless." (Of course, she was referring to Burton's wife Sally Hay Burton.)

In the 1960s, Sybil and Jordan Christopher opened Arthur, one of the first discos in New York City. Since 1991, she's been the artistic director of the nonprofit and extremely successful Bay Street Theatre in Sag Harbor, New York, having founded it with Emma Walton (the daughter of Julie Andrews).

Today, Mrs. Sybil Christopher, who lives in New York, is strong, beautiful, and triumphant. As recounted in the text, she and Elizabeth reunited in Los Angeles in 1998 when their mutual friend Roddy McDowall lay dying. She long ago accepted Elizabeth's apologies.

She is seventy-seven.

⌒

DEBBIE REYNOLDS

Debbie Reynolds continues her performing career, working as an entertainer many months of the year, around the world. Since her marriage to Eddie Fisher, she's been wed three times. She is presently single and lives in Los Angeles.

Debbie says that she too long ago reconciled her emotions where Elizabeth is concerned. (As noted in the text, she and Elizabeth mended their relationship on a cruise ship in 1964.) "What kind of woman would I be if I held a grudge over something that happened a lifetime ago?" Debbie said when interviewed for this book. "You live, you learn, you move on. Elizabeth and I became great friends." She and Eddie, however, are not friends. "I chose a long time ago not to have him in my life, and I think that was the right decision," she says. "I don't wish him ill will, though. We all got through it and went on with our lives. I just never wanted him in my life again."

In February 2001, Elizabeth and Debbie appeared in a television movie together, *These Old Broads*. Elizabeth says the two "dished and dished" about Eddie, but neither could bear to speak his name. Instead, they referred to him as "Harry Hunter."

She is seventy-four.

Acknowledgments

⁓

ELIZABETH TAYLOR

To begin, I would like to thank Miss Elizabeth Taylor. The first time I met her was many years ago at a reception in Los Angeles, when she was promoting her book *Elizabeth Takes Off*. My time with her that day was so brief, I wouldn't want it to be misconstrued as an interview. It was more like a . . . close encounter. I remember it vividly, though, because there's no one quite like Elizabeth Taylor, and one's first time meeting her is bound to be memorable.

As I walked into the hotel suite in which she was welcoming visitors—journalists, friends, and others who were just curious and managed to get by security—I entered a dimly lit foyer. I then turned a corner and walked toward an area flooded by bright lights. There, surrounded by elaborate floral arrangements, stood a tiny woman talking to someone in an animated fashion, using her hands and nodding her head while laughing. At first, from a distance, I thought *she* couldn't be Elizabeth Taylor. After all, she was little more than five feet tall. I figured she might be one of her handlers, maybe a publicist. However, as I got a little closer, I realized it was the lady herself, looking wonderfully thin and healthy, at least twenty years younger than her fifty-five years.

She wore an ivory-colored blouse and skirt that spectacularly accentuated her tiny, cinched-in waist and set off her bronzy tan.

Her hair was a soft brunette with wisps of blonde running sparingly through it, a modified upsweep that ended in an elegant and full halo. Scarlet lips framed even, snow-white teeth. The amethysts and diamonds at her earlobes fought for attention with her eyes—and lost. Indeed, much has been said and written about Elizabeth's eyes. I can tell you that they truly are striking. Their violet beauty wasn't all that caught my attention, though. As she introduced herself, I was struck by their almost indescribable complexity. It was as if I had been immediately presented with a great riddle: What history had those eyes taken in over the last half century, and how did she really feel about it?

Even given the time constraints and the chatter around her, Elizabeth was eager to talk about her sobriety and weight loss, answering my few questions with self-deprecating humor and occasional laughter. I mentioned that I couldn't fathom how a woman so obviously large in character could be so slight of frame. "Oh, I get that all the time," she told me. "I think people expect me to be over six feet tall. Part of it is from looking up at me from a seat in a movie theater for more years than I care to remember. The rest, I guess, is from my image, my *life*." Indeed, in her presence, one truly does feel that he or she is in the company of a genuine movie star. When she turned to greet someone else, I watched as she moved like a queen, serene and confident in her awareness of the impact her presence had on everyone with whom she came in contact.

When she brought up her recovery at the Betty Ford Center, I asked how she felt about therapy. It's not for her, she said. "Because some of it has been so painful," she explained, "I couldn't relive it. It's one of the reasons I've avoided psychiatry. I couldn't go back to some of those places. Why, I'd go out of my mind. I look only to the future," she said, "never to the past. I'm always moving ahead. That's just the way I am." She then painted her history with a wide, sweeping brushstroke. "Listen, I've had a lifetime of love and laughter," she concluded, "and that, and *only* that, is what I choose to remember."

I have seen her around town many times over the years since then, at different functions in Los Angeles. She's always been gracious and sweet—and surrounded by a troupe of menacing-looking security guards with little walkie-talkies and earpieces, lest anyone get too close. One could forget about trying to ask any probing questions of her as she whooshes by at these kinds of events. I certainly never dreamed all those years ago when I had my brief audience with her that I would one day write a book about Elizabeth Taylor. Surely, if I had known, I would have insisted that she sit down and spend many hours with me and answer hundreds of questions about a life so fantastic it can hardly be fathomed. Well . . . I can dream, can't I? As it was, I was lucky to ask her just a few questions—and if she could have looked into the future to see that I would one day write a book about her, she might not even have answered those!

I'm being facetious, of course and, in truth, not giving her enough credit. Indeed, celebrities have understandably mixed reactions to the notion of an unauthorized biography. After all, no one sees a life quite like the person who actually lived it. However, Miss Taylor has an astute understanding of history and of her place in it. During the course of research for this book, I learned that her concern for accuracy far outweighs any interest she may have in trying to control the public's perception of her. Of course, she has lived a life that's been controversial. However, she long ago abandoned any emotional attachment to the public's view of it, or of her. Interestingly, she says that it's only because of her worldwide celebrity that she's been able to achieve success in what she considers her most important work, as an AIDS activist—and not just the aspects of that fame that she embraces, but also the parts she would just as soon reject. "I spent fifty years protecting my privacy," she said. "I resented my fame until I realized I could use it." I think that this is one of the reasons why Elizabeth did not feel the need to discourage anyone from participating in this book—and, in fact, she actually encouraged members of her inner circle to speak for it. Because we went for balance, a point that we were able to convey to Miss Taylor, we did not feel the need to sugar-coat any of the more provocative elements in her story. For that, I truly thank her.

~

THE AUTHOR'S SUPPORT TEAM

I would like to thank my venerable editor, Maureen Mahon Egen, president and COO of Warner Books. *Elizabeth* is our third book together, the first being *Jackie, Ethel, Joan: Women of Camelot*, followed by *Once Upon a Time: Behind the Fairy Tale of Princess Grace and Prince Rainier*. It's so wonderful to have an editor who truly believes in me as a writer and allows me to express myself freely. Writing a book such as *Elizabeth* is a collaborative effort. It's not just the author sitting down in front of his keyboard and hoping for the best. During the course of years of production on a project such as this one, many people become invested in the project, from copy editors and fact-checkers to lawyers and designers, and that chain of command at Warner Books starts with Maureen Egen. I also owe a debt of gratitude to those talented people who have contributed to this work, beginning with Warner Books publisher Jamie Raab, who has such brilliant vision. I'm so lucky to be even a small part of it. I am also grateful to the wonderful production team, which includes Michelle Bidelspach and Eve Rabinovits. Bob Castillo was the managing editor of this book and Roland Ottewell was the copy editor, and both did a wonderful job, as always. Thomas Whatley managed the interior production, and Anne Twomey designed the cover (and what a cover it is!), with help from her assistant, Elaini Caruso. Thanks also to those in Publicity, including Emi Battaglia and Jimmy Franco and Evan Boorstyn; and to those in the Rights departments, including Nancy Wiese and Rebecca Oliver. Also, I would like to express my gratitude to Harvey-Jane Kowal. Once again, I was so fortu-

nate to work with Warner's counsel, Heather Kilpatrick, a dedicated and precise attorney. In all, I just couldn't ask for a better
environment for my work than the one I have at Warner Books. I
look forward with great anticipation to our next project together.

My deepest appreciation also goes to my domestic agent, Mitch
Douglas. He has been an important person in my life and career
for ten years, and I thank him for his constant and enthusiastic
encouragement. He went the extra mile for me, especially in the
final stages of production of this book in dealing with photographs, and I want him to know how much I appreciate it.

Dorie Simmonds of the Dorie Simmonds Agency in London is
always there for me when I most need her during the development
and writing of any of my books. As well as being my capable rep-
resentative in Europe, she is a good and trusted friend and I so appreciate her dedication to me and to my work. Truly, she's a
resourceful woman who can get *anything* accomplished for me, and
she does . . . daily!

Without my extremely capable fact-checker and editor, James
Pinkston, I can't imagine what kind of book we would be publishing. Jim is tireless in his quest for accuracy, and working with him
on *Elizabeth* has been a true honor and joy. As always, Jim went
the extra mile on this, our fourth book together, and I am grateful
to him. As I often say, I would never consider writing a book without having Jim in my corner for it.

THE TRUE EXPERTS

Whenever I am at a book signing for one of my publications, inevitably a person best described as a wise guy will point a finger at
me and say, "Hey! What makes you think *you're* such an expert on
the life of [insert biography's subject here]." Once and for all, I'd
like to dispel the notion that I am an expert on *anyone's* life. I'm

just a writer who's been fortunate enough to be able to tell true stories about people who matter to me and to others. Where Elizabeth Taylor is concerned, this book is about her life as I see it and can report it, based on my years of research. I focused on the parts of her life I thought were the most telling, the aspects that told the best stories and illuminated her ever-evolving character and personality. However, during the course of researching this book, as with every one of my books, I actually did meet people who truly are, for lack of a better word, "experts" at understanding all things Taylor. In that regard, there are five gentlemen I would like to recognize. Each has a busy life and career and had better things to do, I am sure, than respond to my telephone calls and e-mails asking questions like, "How was the wedding gown she wore in *Father of the Bride* different from the one she wore in real life when she married Nicky Hilton?" However, respond they did, and without them this would be a very different—and, doubtless, not as accurate—book.

Thank you, first, to Denis Ferrara for his assistance in so many tangible and intangible ways, and for sharing his vast knowledge of Miss Taylor's life. Denis began as a fan chasing after Elizabeth's limousine, eventually becoming a journalist in 1981, writing with columnist Liz Smith, one of Taylor's chief chroniclers. In many ways, Denis has helped Ms. Smith continue the legend. His work with me and with Cathy Griffin on this book was invaluable, and I am deeply grateful to him.

Thank you, also, to Brad Geagley, a magnificent historian who shed light on so many elements of Taylor's career, and in particular, the history of *Cleopatra*. Brad also shared his memories of the many interviews he did over the years, including those with Richard Burton, Roddy McDowell, and Eddie Fisher. What a wonderful interview he gave to us!

A very special thank-you to Tom Gates, a wonderful friend of mine who has photographed Elizabeth for the last forty-plus years and whose work adorns the end pages of this book, as well as many of the interior photo spreads. Tom, who is New York editor for

Palm Beach Society and editor at large for *TravelSmart*, read this entire manuscript before it was copyedited and dutifully pointed out any errors in it before the ink had a chance to even dry. I am so grateful to him. He really devoted himself to this work, and all out of his deep affection for Elizabeth. His love and respect for Elizabeth is evident, I believe, in many of his photographs of her.

Thank you to Bill Goulding, who has followed Elizabeth's career since 1964 when she accompanied Burton to New York for *Hamlet*. He was very helpful in providing material and observations for background purposes.

Thank you, finally, to Michael Stevens, who sat with me for many, many hours going over seemingly countless interview transcripts to determine what mattered and what didn't in the telling of this story. Truly, if there is an expert on 1950s and 1960s pop culture, Michael is it, and I thank him so much.

THE RESEARCHERS

It is impossible to write accurately about anyone's life without many reliable witnesses to provide a wide range of viewpoints. I believe that a biography such as *Elizabeth* stands or falls on the cooperation and frankness of those involved in the story. I first started this book in 1995 and, as I do some of my books, put it aside in order that I might have a chance to consider the research and the angle of the story. I picked it up again in 1997 (right after I interviewed Elizabeth's first fiancé, William Pawley), in 2000 (when I first pitched the idea to Warner Books), and then finally in 2003, which is when I began to fine-tune the edition you now hold in your hands. Over the course of all of those years, a great number of people went out of their way to assist me in this endeavor: hundreds of friends, relations, entertainment journalists, socialites, lawyers, celebrities, show business executives and former executives, associates and friends as well as foes, classmates, teachers, neighbors, friends, newspersons, and archivists who were contacted in preparation for this book. It would be impossible for me to mention them all, but I am deeply indebted to them. Some are no longer with us; I pray that their memory is served well with their remembrances in this book.

Imagine the life of a person such as Elizabeth Taylor, and then try imagining how many people she must have touched along the way in a career that has spanned sixty years. It was a daunting task just to figure out who was who, and I never could have done it without so much help from my researchers. Though we had the opportunity to interview a wide range of sources, as always with my books, we decided to focus on those who had not previously told their stories. These people were interviewed for this work over a ten-year period either by me or my researchers.

I've had many investigators and researchers over the years, but none who have been as consistent as Cathy Griffin. Cathy is also a fine journalist in her own right. It would be easy with a subject as popular as this one to simply reinterview those who have told their stories to others, and hope for an occasional new angle. However, Cathy always manages to locate people who have new, previously untold stories. This particular work represents our sixth book together. I thank her for her assistance over the years, her tenacity, and, most of all, her friendship.

Also, I would like to thank Juliette Burgonde, Cloe Basiline, Maxime Rhiette, Suzalie Rose, and, especially, Babette Valmonde in France; Clarette Olsen-Smith and Mary Horby in South Wales.

I want to thank all of the people in Italy who assisted me in researching the *Cleopatra* years, including Nunziata Stornella, who organized the research team devoted to this work. Of that team, I must acknowledge Anne Edita and Elizabetta Renata for all of their assistance in Italy and for finding people to talk to me who were so difficult to locate. Also, regarding *Cleopatra*, thanks to Anthony Patrizia, Arnaldo Fiorella, Ysabella Donato, Stefano Rufina, and Anna and Giancarlo Oria for all of their help. I had such a wonderful Italian research team on this book, and I thank them all.

Some people we talked to have certainly told their stories from time to time but simply had to be included again in these pages. For instance, what would an Elizabeth Taylor biography be without Eddie Fisher and Debbie Reynolds? I do think, though, that even people such as Fisher and Reynolds who have been interviewed before were a little more forthcoming in this biography than they've been in the past.

LIBRARY AND
MISCELLANEOUS RESEARCH

To begin with, of course, I reviewed every one of Elizabeth Taylor's films, as well as all of her made-for-television movies and miniseries. I would not have had access to all of this material had it not been for Nick Scotti in the United Kingdom. I owe him a debt of gratitude for providing me with all of this material, much of which is simply not commercially available.

I must thank Marybeth Evans in London for her diligent work in the Manchester Central Library reviewing reams of documents for me there.

Thanks also to the staffs of the Hans Tasiemka Archives in London and the Special Collections Library of the University of California in Los Angeles.

Thanks also to Teri Donato for all of her research help in Italy, and for the tremendous amount of work she did regarding *Cleopatra*. I must also acknowledge Juliette Burgonde and Cloe Basiline for translating so many hundreds of pages of Italian interviews and other documents for me. I certainly would not have been able to manage so much of that material without them. Also, I would like to again thank Babette Valmonde, who conducted important interviews for me in France. She was determined to find just the right people to tell the right stories, and her persistence paid off in many ways. I thank her.

Suzalie Rose did much research for me in libraries in Paris and also translated all of her notes into English. Who could ask for more than that? I am deeply indebted to her and to Carl Mathers for their time and keen eyes for accuracy.

A special thanks to the fine folks at Photofest for providing so many of the wonderful photographs that are found in this book. I go to Photofest first whenever I begin the process of selecting pictures to illustrate my books. They always come through for me, and I am grateful to them.

I want to thank all of the fine and dedicated people who work at the Margaret Herrick Library of the Academy of Motion Picture Arts and Sciences for their assistance on this and all of my books. When a journalist asks to review "Elizabeth Taylor's files" at that facility, someone will disappear for a few minutes and then return with a cart upon which will be stacked what seems like hundreds of manila folders. "This is from 1942," she'll say. "Let me know when you're finished, and I'll bring out 1943." The entire collection goes to the year 2006. It could take years to go through it all. In fact, it *did*! I want to also thank Jim Pinkston for his research time at the Academy Library.

Numerous other organizations and institutions provided me with articles, documents, audio interviews, video interviews, transcripts, and other material that was either utilized directly in *Elizabeth* or just for purposes of background. Unfortunately, it is not possible to thank all of the individuals associated with each organization who were so helpful and gave of their time. However, I would at least like to express my gratitude to the following institutions: the American Academy of Dramatic Arts; the American Film Institute Library; the Associated Press Office (New York); the Bancroft Library at the University of California, Berkeley; the Billy Rose Theater Collection in the Library of the Performing Arts, Lincoln Center, New York; the Brand Library Art and Music

Center; the British Film Institute Library Archives; the *Boston Herald* Archives; the British Theatre Association Library, London; the Beverly Hills Library; the British Broadcasting Corporation; the University of California, Los Angeles; Corbis-Gamma/Liason; the Ernest Lehman Collection at the University of Southern California; the Glendale Central Public Library; the Hayden Library, Arizona State University; the Hedda Hopper Collection in the Margaret Herrick Library, Academy of Motion Picture Arts and Sciences, Beverly Hills; the Lincoln Center Library of the Performing Arts; the Joseph Losey Collection in the British Film Institute Informational Library, London; the Kobal Collection; the *Los Angeles Times*; the Los Angeles Public Library; the Louella Parsons Collection at the University of Southern California; the Manchester Central Reference Library, England; the Museum of Modern Art (Film Study Center, New York); the Museum of Broadcasting, New York; the former Metro-Goldwyn-Mayer studio archives, now part of the Turner Entertainment Group, Los Angeles; the National Archives and the Library of Congress; the New York City Municipal Archives; the National Film Archive Stills Library, London; the New York Public Library; the New York University Library; the *New York Daily News*; the *New York Post*; the *New York Times*; Occidental College (Eagle Rock, California); the Philadelphia Free Library (Theater Collection); the Philadelphia Public Library; the Philadelphia Historical Society; the *Philadelphia Inquirer* and the *Philadelphia Daily News*, the Time-Life archives and Library, New York; the Universal Collection at the University of Southern California; the Warner Brothers and Universal Pictures Collections in the Cinema and Television Library, University of Southern California; and finally, Rex Photos.

What goes into the production of a book of this nature really does at times boggle the mind. I could never do it alone, and if I forgot any single person who contributed in any way to the library research of this book—particularly those who are employed by my researchers and who I may not have even met—I am truly sorry. I am eternally grateful to all of the contributors.

Sources and Other Notes

Whenever practical, I have provided sources within the body of the text. Some people were not quoted directly in the text but provided observations that helped me more fully understand Elizabeth Taylor's life.

Also, in writing about a person as popular and influential as Elizabeth Taylor, a biographer is bound to find that many sources with valuable information prefer to not be named in the text. This is reasonable. Throughout my career, I have understood that for a person to jeopardize a long-standing, important relationship for the sake of one of my books is a purely personal choice. Nevertheless, I appreciate the assistance of many people close to Elizabeth who, over the years, gave of their time for this project. I will respect the wish for anonymity of those who require it, and as always, those who could be identified are named in these notes.

Since chapter notes are usually not of interest to the general reader, I have chosen a more general—and practical for space limitations—mode of source identification, as opposed to specific page or line notations. The following notes are by no means comprehensive but are intended to give the reader a general overview of my research. In some instances, I included parenthetically the year(s) interviews were conducted.

PART ONE: CHILDHOOD

I first have to also acknowledge the participation in this venture of one of Elizabeth's closest family members, a person who was key in confirming the material in this part of the book, as well as in the rest of this work. This person did not provide information as much as confirm what was obtained by independent research. However, without this person's thorough reading and evaluation of this book—a very time-consuming project for someone not compensated who did it strictly for accuracy's sake—I could not be as confident of the material contained herein as I am. This person asked not to be acknowledged for fear of opening the floodgates to other biographers wanting similar access. I understood as much, and agreed. I am so deeply grateful to my source. Thank you so much.

My interviews with the following people provided insight into Sara and Francis Taylor's early life together: Margaret DeForest, Tom Gates, Irene Massey, and Beatrice Edmonds. Thanks also to Edward Mitchell for the interview and for making available to me "A Look at the Real Elizabeth Taylor," Sunday *Chicago Tribune*, November 9, 1958.

I must give special acknowledgment to Marshall Baldrige and Stefan Verkaufen. Both of these marvelous gentlemen were interviewed back in the year 2000 when I first proposed the idea of an Elizabeth Taylor biography to Warner Books. They had never before been interviewed and were, understandably, reluctant to speak about their memories of Francis Taylor. Having written about complicated families in the past, such as the Kennedys and the Grimaldis, I recognize that nothing is ever simple when it comes to familial dynamics. I did my best to try to understand and relate the Taylor experience, and I hope my affection for all of them is clear in my work. I think it's safe to say that there is probably no one alive who knew Francis Taylor better than his friends

Marshall and Stefan, and so I am pleased and honored that both were involved in this project. This book could not have been done without their help.

The 1975 documentary *Elizabeth Taylor: Hollywood's Child*, produced by Jack Haley Jr., was most helpful. In it, Peter Lawford interviews some of those who've been closest to Elizabeth during her life and times. Some comments in this section of the book from Lawford, Richard Brooks, Rock Hudson, Roddy McDowall, Vincente Minnelli, and Sara Taylor were extracted from this documentary. It's poignant to note that the entire cast, every person who took part in this fascinating documentary, is now long gone, except for the woman they were all discussing—Elizabeth.

I also referred to my chief researcher Cathy Griffin's work on *Biography: Elizabeth Taylor*, an Arts and Entertainment documentary about Elizabeth Taylor. Cathy wrote and produced the program, which became, at the time of its broadcast in 1993, the highest-rated show in the history of A&E. Since then, it's been aired worldwide and even received high praise at the Cannes Film Festival. Cathy's persuasiveness in obtaining Elizabeth's blessing is considered by some an even greater coup than the documentary itself! Not by me, though . . . the documentary is probably the best thing ever produced about the star. Cathy personally interviewed the screen legend's closest friends: Michael Jackson, Robert Wagner, Roddy McDowall, and MGM's legendary hairdresser, Sydney Guilaroff, as well as the venerable entertainment columnist Liz Smith. She allowed me use of her original script (January 31, 1993), notes, and transcripts from her interviews for this book. (Cathy received a lovely letter of thanks from Elizabeth upon the show's completion.)

I also relied on two of Elizabeth Taylor's books, *Elizabeth Taylor* and *Elizabeth Takes Off*.

I utilized a three-part series Sara Taylor wrote for *McCall's*, "Elizabeth, My Daughter," in February, March, and April 1954. Also, I referenced a two-part series, again by Sara Taylor, "My Daughter Elizabeth," in *Good Housekeeping*, March and April

1989. Additionally, I utilized "Love and a Girl Named Liz," by Ann Macgregor, *Photoplay*, June 1949; "Glenn Davis, Southland Grid Hero to Wed Actress" (no byline), *New York Daily News*, March 10, 1949; "The Most Exciting Girl in Hollywood," by Elsa Maxwell, *Photoplay*, January 1950; "The Wild Welshman" (no author), *Look*, September 8, 1953. I also utilized Elizabeth's interview on the Louella Parsons radio show on ABC radio, in Los Angeles, broadcast on July 13, 1947.

PART TWO: FINDING HER WAY

Interviews with the following people provided insight into Elizabeth's early career days and her marriages to Nicky Hilton and Michael Wilding: Debbie Reynolds, Ivy Hewett, Paul Young, Mary Schaeffer, and Tom Gates. I also would like to acknowledge the assistance of Stacy and Marie Thomas, who actually attended Elizabeth's wedding to Hilton and subsequent reception and shared many memories for background purposes. Marianne Lincoln-Barstow worked for Francis Taylor in his Beverly Hills art gallery in her youth. I thank her so much for her tremendous contributions to this book. She spent many hours trying to remember details of a time so long ago, and I am very grateful. I relied on Stefan Verkaufen's memories for the anecdote about Howard Hughes and the Taylor family in Reno, Nevada. Also, Beatrice Lynn was a secretary to Jules Goldstone, Elizabeth Taylor's attorney during these years. She provided information concerning Francis Taylor's dealings with Howard Hughes on Walden Productions. Also, I interviewed William Pawley, who was such a charming man, for an early proposal of this book back in 1997. In this section and throughout the book, comments from James Bacon, Martin Landau, Liz Smith, Linda Yellen, and Austin Pendleton are culled from *Elizabeth Taylor: The E! True Hollywood*

Story, which was first broadcast in 1998. I also utilized Elizabeth's appearance on *The Tonight Show*, February 21, 1992.

I referred to Pandro S. Berman's Oral History, for which he was interviewed by Mike Steen, on deposit at the American Film Institute in Los Angeles. Also from AFI, I utilized their filing of "Michael Wilding: Second Husband of Liz Taylor Dies," *Los Angeles Times*, July 9, 1979.

Elizabeth's original contract and additional material regarding her deal with Universal Pictures can be found in the Universal Collection at the University of Southern California.

I also had a number of sources in the Hilton family and in the extended Taylor family who discussed Elizabeth's relationship to Nicky Hilton, all of whom asked for anonymity. I am, therefore, honoring their request and gratefully acknowledge their assistance with this very sensitive subject matter. I also referred to the public record: *Elizabeth Hilton, Plaintiff v. Conrad N. Hilton, Defendant*, Superior Court of the State of California, January 29, 1951.

Elizabeth Taylor has written about her first marriage in her two memoirs, and I culled some quotes from that source material. I also relied on "Liz: Ms. Taylor Will See You Now," by Paul Theroux, *Talk*, October 1999.

In 1994, when I was working on a biography of Frank Sinatra, I had the opportunity to interview Stanley Donen, who is mentioned in this book as having had a romance with Elizabeth. (Donen directed Sinatra's *On the Town*). "I thought she was a wonderful woman," he said, "and every second I had with her is one I cherish. As to what was going on in our lives at the time, of course I would never discuss that with you, or anyone else. A gentleman," he concluded with a smile, "never kisses and tells."

One of the best celebrity biographies ever published, at least in my opinion, is *Monty*, a biography of Montgomery Clift by Patricia Bonsworth. I referred to this excellent work for my research. Speaking of Elizabeth's relationship to Clift, director Franco Zeferelli, who worked with her and Burton in *The Taming of the Shrew*, tells a good story that didn't make it into this book's text.

It appeared in his tribute to her in the program for the American Film Institute Life Achievement Awards, which I attended on March 11, 1993: "We were filming in Italy when Monty was buried, and Liz's professionalism would not allow her to break the shoot. By the cruelest of ironies, the day of the funeral was ordained for one of the lightest, silliest comedy scenes in the entire story. One-shot Liz did the whole thing with unsurpassed humor. Only when filming was over did she allow Richard to hold her in his arms and comfort her as she wept for the handsome costar of her youth."

Obviously, a great deal has been written about Mike Todd over the years, and I referred to a good deal of it for this section of the book. I would like to thank Nicky Jackson, who is a huge fan of Todd's and who pointed me in the right direction when it came to unearthing material about the impresario, and well as people who knew him back in the day, such as Albert Skinner. And another special thanks to Mr. Skinner for his wonderful memories about Todd and for providing me with "Elizabeth Taylor Says She'll Reduce Film Activities If She Marries Again," *Los Angeles Times*, October 26, 1956; "The Woes of Elizabeth and Eddie," *Los Angeles Times*, August 25, 1959; "The Mike Todd Story—Three Great Loves Had He," *Los Angeles Herald & Express*, March 26, 1958; and "Liz Taylor Would Like to Wed Eddie in Vegas," *Los Angeles Examiner*, March 1, 1959; and "Mr. Edwin J. Fisher: Older, Wiser and Happier," *McCall's*, January 1962.

Of course, Debbie Reynolds and Eddie Fisher were both very important to all of the research concerning Mike Todd, and I would like them both to know how much I appreciate their assistance.

I also screened the 1956 documentary *Around the World with Mike Todd*. This TV special focuses on the production of the Oscar-winning movie *Around the World in 80 Days* and presents a rare look at its filming, and also of Todd. Narrated by Orson Welles, it features Elizabeth, David Niven, and Shirley MacLaine, among others. I am so grateful to Nick Scotti for locating it for me, and obtaining a copy of it. I also referred to *The Nine Lives of Mike Todd* by the late Art Cohn.

James Bacon's and Richard Brook's comments about Todd were culled from *Elizabeth Taylor: Hollywood's Child*. Elizabeth's comments about her condition after Mike's death were from an appearance on *Larry King Live* in February 2003. Sydney Guilaroff's comments are culled from interviews with the late hairstylist conducted in the fall of 1995 by his biographer (and my researcher) Cathy Griffin. Also, Shirley MacLaine's comments are from an interview with her, also by Cathy Griffin, in October 1995.

I want to thank all of the people in South Philadelphia who shared memories of Eddie with me. The people in South Philly—many of whom are in my own family—are as good as they come! Of course, I also referred to Eddie Fisher's two autobiographies: *Eddie Fisher: My Life, My Loves* (1984) and *Been There, Done That* (1999).

PART THREE: HER DESTINY

First of all, special thanks must be extended to actor and producer Chris Mankiewicz, Joseph's son, for sharing his memories of his and his dad's work on *Cleopatra*. I am very grateful to him for the time he devoted to this book. His multitalented, legendary father was, of course, the film's writer and director.

I'd like to also extend my sincere appreciation to Gary Springer, son of Elizabeth's and Richard's publicist, John Springer. Gary was also a godsend for this project. I would like to thank him for keeping alive the memory of his amazing father, and for speaking to us for this and other sections of *Elizabeth*.

To outline all of the published material I reviewed for the chapters concerning *Cleopatra* and the lives of Taylor and Burton during that time would truly take a volume in and of itself—the research was just that voluminous in nature. I am especially grateful to Nancy Marcus for proving me with "Cleopatra: The Trials and Tribulations of an Epic Film," by Walter Wanger and Joseph Hyams, *Saturday Evening Post*, June 1, 1963. I also referred to the excellent volumes *The Cleopatra Papers*, by Jack Brodsky and Nathan Weiss; *Confessions of a Hollywood Columnist*, by Sheila Graham, and *Pictures Will Talk: The Life and Films of Joseph L. Mankiewicz*, by Kenneth L. Geist.

I met so many people during the course of researching this book who were friends and confidantes of Taylor's and Burton's at the time their relationship first started. Some asked for anonymity and I am respecting their wishes here. I thank those people in Burton's circle for their help even if it went with a caveat of anonymity. Also, I would like to thank Patrick McMahon for his many recollections that I used in this and other sections of this book. And a special thanks to Hank Lustig for his memories and also for the many scrapbooks of his time on the set of *Cleopatra*. Thanks also to the wonderful actor Martin Landau for his remembrances of his work on *Cleopatra*. Thanks also to Stewart Wilson and Victor Zellman for their interviews. I also referenced Miss Taylor's first memoir, *Elizabeth Taylor*, for the chapter "A Turning Point in Gstaad." Also, I would like to thank Matissa Hart for sharing her wonderful reminiscences with me.

I was very sorry to not have been able to meet and interview Sybil Burton Christopher. After several conversations with my lead researcher, Cathy Griffin, she decided that she just didn't want to be interviewed. I certainly appreciate that she even considered as much and took the time to discuss it. She's a wonderful woman who has lived a courageous and dignified life, and I hope she feels she is well represented in these pages.

Thanks to all of those in Mering, Germany, who assisted me in obtaining information about the background of Elizabeth's adopted daughter, Maria. Because of the sensitive nature of this research, I am not identifying any of the informants here, but they know who they are and I am grateful to them.

Over the years, there have been numerous accounts of Elizabeth's apparent suicide attempts. For this volume, I relied on the verbal accounts of the man she was married to at the time, Eddie Fisher. What he said in his interview was exactly as he wrote about it in his book *Been There, Done That*. Numerous newspaper reports published at the time corroborated much of what he now recalls. Also, I relied on what Richard Burton wrote about this terrible time in his diaries, published in *Richard Burton: A Life*, by Melvyn Braag, particularly his memories of the attempt in Porto Santo Stefano.

When researching my Sinatra biography in 1996, I encountered many sources who knew Frank's second wife, Ava Gardner. Among them was the very lovely Lucille Wellman, who passed away a few years ago. She was a delight. I have included some of her memories of Elizabeth in the sections of this book concerning *The Night of the Iguana*. I know she would love being included in this text as she was such a fan of Elizabeth's and told her stories about her with such enthusiasm and love. I would also like to thank Tom and Lorraine Banks and Doris Rollins Cannon at the Ava Gardner Museum in Smithfield, North Carolina, who assisted my researchers.

I also referred to the following British interviews of Richard Burton: *In Town Tonight*, BBC-TV, December 24, 1955; *An Actor's Profile*, from the BBC Welsh Home Service, March 10, 1961; Burton with John Morgan on *Panorama*, September 12, 1966; Burton with Kenneth Tynan on BBC-TV, April 1, 1967; *Burton and Taylor at Oxford*, a TV special filmed at Merton College in Oxford on October 14, 1967; Burton with Barry Norman, BBC, September 1974; Burton with Vincent Kane, BBC, February 12, 1977; and an interview with Burton, BBC, December 5, 1977.

I also consulted the following features: "Playboy Interview: Richard Burton," by Kenneth Tynan, *Playboy*, September 1963; "Vatican Paper Rips Liz," UPI, *Los Angeles Herald Examiner*, April 12, 1962; "Elizabeth Taylor Talks about Cleopatra," by Jack Hamilton, *Look*, May 7, 1963; "A Moment by Moment Exclusive, Liz and Burton's Wedding," by Steve Brandt, *Photoplay*, June

1962; "All for the Love of Mike," by C. Robert Jennings, *Post*, October 9, 1965; "Does Liz Need a Spanking?" AP, *Los Angeles Herald Examiner*, April 4, 1962; "Liz Taylor Separation from Fisher Reported," by Hedda Hopper, *Los Angeles Times*, March 10, 1962; "Burton Tells Wife Love True Despite Kisses with Liz," by Raymond Palmer, *Los Angeles Herald Examiner*, April 4, 1962; "Deny Liz Taylor Eddie Near Rift," by Harrison Carroll, *Los Angeles Herald Examiner*, February 14, 1962; "Eddie Fisher Silent on Liz Love Rumors," by Daniel F. Gilmore, *Los Angeles Herald Examiner*, February 19, 1962; "Row Over Actor Ends Liz, Eddie Marriage," by Louella O. Parsons, *Los Angeles Herald Examiner*, March 9, 1962; "Liz, Burton in Photog Hassle," by Eddie Gilmore, *Los Angeles Herald Examiner*, December 6, 1962; "Liz Taylor, Co-Star Dick Burton to Wed," by Louella O. Parsons, *Los Angeles Herald Examiner*, January 17, 1963; "Whatever Happened to Elizabeth Taylor," by Adele Whitely Fletcher, *Family Weekly*, January 22, 1963; "Eddie is Stunned—Doesn't Know What It Means," by Earl Wilson, *Los Angeles Herald Examiner*, March 6, 1964; "20th Sues Liz and Dick for $50 Million," *Daily Variety*, April 23, 1964; "Elizabeth Taylor Fights Desperately for Life," UPI, *Los Angeles Times*, March 7, 1961; "The Rise and Fall of Elizabeth Taylor," by Lee Israel, *Esquire*, March 1967; "King and Queen—How They Rule Their Roost," by Jack Hamilton, *Look*, March 9, 1965; "Mr. Cleopatra," by John Morgan, *New Statesman*, Spring 1962.

And, finally, I also utilized *Elizabeth Taylor in London* (1963).

PART FOUR: "LIZ AND DICK," AND PART FIVE: CONFUSION REIGNS

Again, it would take a whole other volume just to list of all of the published material I and my researchers reviewed concerning Elizabeth's long relationship with Richard Burton. Suffice it to say, if it was published in the United States, Great Britain, France, or Germany I probably laid eyes on it somewhere along the line.

I want to thank Diane Stevens, who once worked for Taylor and Burton's publicist, John Springer, for her assistance on this part of the book—especially in the section concerning *Virginia Woolf*. Also, Ms. Stevens allowed me access to the many scrapbooks she meticulously compiled during those years. They were invaluable to my research. From her vast video collection, she also allowed me to utilize in my research her videotapes of *Richard Burton: In From the Cold* (1988), *TNT Extra: A Very Special Conversation with Elizabeth Taylor* (1993), and *Great Romances of the Twentieth Century* (1997), as well as Elizabeth's appearances on the *Today* show, broadcast on February 26, 1982; April 14, 1983; and February 2, 1988. Finally, it took her more than a year of searching to come up with a single article for me, which she was determined to find. It bears mentioning here: "Liz Taylor's Private Secretary Tells All," *Motion Picture*, August 1976. Thanks so much, Diane.

Also, I have to gratefully acknowledge the assistance of Rose Marie Armocida, who was the personal secretary to John Springer. Ms. Armocida did her best to remember stories she hadn't thought of in many years, and truly devoted herself to doing a good job at it for me and Cathy Griffin. What a fine woman she is. I so appreciate her effort. Her memories are found in this section as well as others in this book.

And, again, I must express my appreciation to Tom Gates, who had so many experiences with Elizabeth over the years, and whose memories helped to shape this section of the book. Also, Marshall Baldrige was, as mentioned earlier, important to shaping the chapter on Francis Taylor's funeral.

Marie Bentkover, who was a secretary to agent Victor French, was absolutely invaluable to my research in this part of the book, especially as it pertains to Burton's hemophilia. I personally had no idea that Burton was afflicted by this disease, and I may not have known about it had Ms. Bentkover not brought it to my attention, thereby putting into motion the research that went into corroborating the story. I am so indebted to her and to her family for so warmly receiving me. Thanks also to the fine people at the National Hemophilia Foundation who assisted me and my researchers.

And, again, my thanks to Debbie Reynolds for her memories, which were used in this section of the book.

Also, I would like to acknowledge the assistance of Michelle Griffin-Ayers and her memories of Dick Hanley, and also of her times with the Burtons. Her interviews were very important and I am grateful for her time.

I also want to sincerely thank Richard Burton's best friend and partner in crime, Joe Sirola, for all of his memories about "Rich," many of which can be found in this part of the book, as well as in other sections. It always means so much to me when a person who has had a close friendship with someone important to one of my books comes forth with such honesty and enthusiasm, eager to set the record straight and keep it clean. Joe was very forthcoming. I appreciate his trust.

I would also like to acknowledge the brilliant actor Michael York for his assistance and his memories of his work on *The Taming of the Shrew* (which happened to be his debut movie). Mr. York is a rare gentleman.

Over the years, I met many lawyers who worked alongside the Burtons' trusted attorney, Aaron Frosch, and I conducted informal interviews with most of them for background purposes only. Because of the sensitive nature of Mr. Frosch's work with the Burtons—especially as it related to their adopted child, Maria—these sources do not wish to be acknowledged in these pages, or even quoted in this book. For those who worked with Mr. Frosch, I respect their wishes and remain appreciative to them for the time they spent with me just so that I might have a better understanding of the Burtons' life and times. They know who they are, and know that this acknowledgment is directed at them.

Of course, I referred to Elizabeth's terrific book *Elizabeth Taylor: My Love Affair with Jewelry* in researching her vast collection of jewels.

My thanks to Sophia Loren's former personal assistant, Ellen Pallola, for her memories and the time she spent discussing the Burtons.

My thanks also to Giuseppe Patroni-Griffi, who directed Elizabeth in *The Driver's Seat*. Sadly, this talented man passed away in December 2005.

For anyone interested in seeing it, a DVD was released in the winter of 2006 of selected *Here's Lucy* programs, including the Burtons' appearance in 1970. It's actually quite funny. Interestingly, the "bonus features" include never-before-seen rehearsal footage of Elizabeth, Richard and Lucy during which the viewer can see Miss Ball in total control—and, in one scene, not particularly to Elizabeth's liking. It's worth purchasing.

I had a very important source for the chapters concerning Henry Wynberg, and who asked for anonymity. He knows who he is, and I thank him for his assistance. I also referred to an interview with Wynberg in the London *Mail on Sunday* magazine, *You*, published on October 21, 1990. And thanks to Beverly Wilcox for helping to sort out the shenanigans on the set of Burton's movie *The Klansman*. I also referred to *Marvin*, by Donald Zec (New English Library).

I would like to extend a special nod of gratitude to Robert Lantz, who was the Burtons' agent for more than fifty years. His assistance helped shape this and many other parts of the book, and truly I could not have done this without him. He represented first Burton, and then Burton and Taylor for many years, so his participation was vital and is very much appreciated.

Thanks again to Patrick McMahon for his assistance in this section as well. And I would also like to thank him for providing me with the very rare article "Can a Simple Welsh Lass of 36 Find Happiness with a Macedonian Rock and Roll Star of 24? Yes, says Sybil Burton Christopher. Hear, Hear, says the Author (Yeah,

Yeah!)" by Elaine Dundy, *Esquire*, December 1965. Also, Patrick made available to me Elizabeth's interview with Phil Donahue, which aired on February 15, 1988, and *America's All-Star Tribute to Elizabeth Taylor* (1989).

I also consulted "Elizabeth Taylor: She Insures Her Jewelry and Her Jewelry Insures Her," by Lloyd Shearer, *Parade*, May 3, 1970; "Burton and Taylor Must Go," by Wilfrid Sheed, *Esquire*, October 1970; "Three Queens Who Lost Their Thrones," by Liz Smith, *Pageant*, May 1970; "Elizabeth Taylor Talks About being a Mother," *Ladies' Home Journal*, March 1969; "Liz Has Mystery Operation," UPI, July 19, 1968; "Here Lies Elizabeth Taylor," by Terry O'Neill, *Ladies' Home Journal*, February 1973; "Liz Laughs at Rift Hint," UPI, August 20, 1968; "Liz in L.A. for Funeral of Father," *Los Angeles Herald Examiner*, November 22, 1968; "How Do I Love Thee? Let Me Count the Ways," by Joseph Roddy, *Look*, June 16, 1970; "Elizabeth Taylor Sees Red in The Blue Bird," by Rex Reed, *Ladies' Home Journal*, October 1975; "And So, It's Ten Years Since Scandal Time," by Romany Bain, *Cosmopolitan*, Spring 1972; "National Velveeta" by Aaron Latham, *Esquire*, November 1977; "Richard Burton—Back from the Brink," by Roderick Mann, *Los Angeles Times*, March 19, 1977; and "Is There Life After Liz," by Fred Robbins, *Playgirl*, Spring 1974.

~⁍

PART SIX: COMING TO TERMS,
PART SEVEN: THE GLORY YEARS,
AND PART EIGHT: ALL WOMAN

Thanks to Diane Stevens for her assistance on the chapters concerning Elizabeth's marriage to Senator John Warner, and also her coping with Richard Burton's untimely demise. She provided me also with many articles about those years, including "John Warner: Rally Round the Flag," by Sally Quinn, *Washington Post*, April 16, 1976; "The Farmer Takes a Wife," *McCall's*, January 1977; "Liz Taylor for the President's Wife," *Woman's Own*, May 20, 1978; "The Warner Touch," by Margo Howard, *New Republic*, February 7, 1983; and "Elizabeth at 60," by Vernon Scott, *Good Housekeeping*, February 1992.

My researchers in Virginia had many sources who have had and continue to enjoy close dealings with Senator Warner. Because of their ongoing relationships with him, they have asked for anonymity. I thank them for their cooperation and for all of the time they spent with those I charged with working on this book in Virginia and in Washington.

I also studied Elizabeth's book *Elizabeth Takes Off*, in which she wrote, I thought, very eloquently about the challenges she faced as a Senator's wife. Though it was heavily criticized in some quarters, I think that, as celebrity autobiographies go, this one is about as unsparing and objective as they come. I would definitely recommend it for further reading on the subject of Taylor's life away from Hollywood.

I would also like to thank the staff of the Palm Aire Spa in Pompano Beach, Florida, for their help on the sections of the book relating to Elizabeth's stay there.

Also, I should mention that a great deal of consideration went into the decision as to whether or not to include in this book entries from Elizabeth's private recovery journal. I decided that they should be included because she did allow them to be published in the *New York Times* feature "Elizabeth Taylor: Journal of a Recovery," by John Duka, on February 4, 1985.

A side note: I saw Elizabeth Taylor in 1981 in *Little Foxes* and again in 1985 with Burton in *Private Lives*, both in Los Angeles. One word to describe those performances: Wow.

Thanks again to Debbie Reynolds for her observations in this section of the book.

Sydney Guilaroff's comments are extracted from Cathy Griffin's interviews with him. I also read his autobiography, written with Cathy Griffin, *Crowning Glory: Reflections of Hollywood's Favorite Confidant*, published in 1996. Guilaroff's five decades in the motion picture business and intimate friendships with the biggest stars of Hollywood's golden era made his memoirs the most eagerly awaited autobiography of its kind. Cathy first met him in 1993 when she interviewed him for the previously mentioned A&E documentary on Elizabeth Taylor. She allowed me to review copious notes and transcripts from her work with Mr. Guilaroff.

Sally Burton exchanged a number of telephone calls with Cathy Griffin about cooperating with this book, but in the end she decided against it. "It's much too painful," she explained . . . and we certainly understood.

I also drew from interviews I have conducted with Michael Jackson over the years, and I would like to thank him, as well. I hope that he's found happiness during this time in his life. I would also like to acknowledge those who worked at Neverland during the Taylor-Fortensky years who shared so much with me, so many memories. Thanks also to the person who obtained for me *Michael Jackson's Private Home Movies* (2003), in which Elizabeth is featured.

Moreover, I would like to acknowledge the assistance of Margaret DeForest and Eleanor LaSalle, who helped me understand the complex nature of Sara Taylor, especially in her later years. Thank you so much, ladies. Also, Ms. LaSalle was gracious enough to give me her copy of a very rare videotape of the interview David Frost conducted with Elizabeth and Richard in Budapest, which was broadcast on March 19, 20, and 21, 1972.

Also, there are so many people in Larry Fortensky's family who assisted me in so many ways, and have asked not to be recognized in these pages. Truly, I could not have understood Larry and his marriage to Elizabeth without their help, and I would like to gratefully acknowledge as much here. Thanks also to Larry's friends Benny Reuben and Brian Bellows for the interviews they gave.

And, of course, thanks again to Tom Gates for his participation in this part of the book, as well.

Thanks also to Aaron Hill, who represented Richard Burton, for his time, energy, and memories and for making available to me the following important features, which I referred to in my research: "Elizabeth Taylor Loves Animals and Out-of-Doors," *Life*, February 26, 1945; "Honeymoon Unlimited," by Elsa Maxwell, *Photoplay*, September 1950; "Elizabeth Taylor Packs Up, Goes Home to Mother," *Hollywood Citizen-News*, December 7, 1950; "The Elizabeth Taylor Story," by Eleanor Harris, *Look*, June 26, 1956; "Elizabeth Taylor—The Men in Her Life," *Look*, July 10, 1956; "Men and Giddy Liz," by Arthur Halliwell, *People* (London), July 22, 1956; "Elizabeth Taylor," *Good Housekeeping*, April 1961; and "Elizabeth Taylor: The Endless Ordeal," by Liz Smith, *Good Housekeeping*, April 1974. Also, Mr. Hill allowed me to use the following videotapes from his vast collection: *A Closer Look: Elizabeth Taylor* (1991); *The Rosie O'Donnell Show*, September 24, 2001; *Cleopatra: The Film that Changed the World* (2001); *Headliners and Legends* (2002); and *Elizabeth Taylor: The E! True Hollywood Story* (1998).

Again, the Burtons' agent, Robert Lantz, was very instrumental in shaping the chapters concerning *Private Lives*.

I also referenced Burton's diaries, as published in *Richard Burton: A Life*, by Melvyn Braag. I also referred to *Richard Burton, My Brother*, by Graham Jenkins, for the sections on *Private Lives*, as well as on the death of Burton and Elizabeth's indecision about attending the services. Again, Patrick McMahon was very helpful in this regard, as well.

I would like to thank Bryan O'Neal for his memories of working with Elizabeth's son-in-law, Steve Carson. I am very grateful for his cooperation and also for providing me with the book *Burton*, by Penny Junior.

Elizabeth has talked extensively about her time at the Betty Ford Center in 1983, and written about it as well, in *Taking Off*. I referred to seemingly countless published source materials regarding this time in her life. I also finally had a chance to use the few quotes she gave me during my brief audience with her in 1987.

I thought long and hard about using information from sources who met Miss Taylor at Betty Ford, balancing the notion of privacy during such a time in a person's life with the objective of this book, which is to further our understanding of the subject. In the end, I decided to use only the memories that showed Elizabeth in the best light and would help the reader to understand the issues with which she was dealing at that time—especially since, as stated, Elizabeth has herself written about and talked about her recovery at great length.

I also referred to the eighty-seven-page probe of Taylor's three personal physicians, prepared by the Medical Board of California. I interviewed California deputy attorney general Earl Plowman, in 1994, and I referred to an article about the investigation published in *Time* on August 22, 1994. It was my decision not to name in this book the doctors who were under investigation. Though all three received written reprimands from the Medical Board, no charges were filed against them.

I also read "Elizabeth the Extraordinary," by Anne Edwards, *Ladies' Home Journal*, March 1986; "What Liz Taylor Has Gone Through," by Phyllis Battelle, *Ladies' Home Journal*, May 1984; and "The Red Queen," by Dominic Dunne, *Vanity Fair*, December 1985. Elizabeth also discussed her drinking and drug habits on an interview with Phil Donahue on February 15, 1988; during a week of segments on the television program *Hour Magazine*, August 21–25, 1987; and with Larry King on March 3, 1993.

The groundskeeper who worked for Elizabeth Taylor from 1980 to 1985 at her chalet in Gstaad asked for anonymity, and, given the circumstances of his employment, I granted it. I would like to thank him and his wife, though, for the hours they spent with me, and for all of the scrapbooks and other mementos they allowed me to borrow while I was researching this book. One of the many wonderful things about writing a book such as this one is that I have the opportunity to meet so many memorable people along the way, people whose lives intersected with the rich and famous for just a brief time and who are today all the better (rather than the worse) for it. This couple is a good example: They have the greatest affection for Miss Taylor. I have also found during the course of researching and writing more than a dozen books that when a celebrity employer treats her staff with dignity and respect, those employees spend the rest of their lives singing that famous person's praises. In this cynical day and age of celebrity journalism, that's nothing if not refreshing. It's a tribute, I think, to Elizabeth that I encountered so few former employees of hers with axes to grind—and the few disgruntled people seem to not blame Taylor herself for their dissatisfaction but rather whatever difficulty she was going through during that time in her life.

I would also like to thank all of the people at the American Foundation for AIDS Research who assisted me on this book in regard to Elizabeth's work as an AIDS activist. Elizabeth has talked in depth about her work in this respect, and I also culled many quotes from her press interviews, her speeches, and her television appearances.

José Eber has been Elizabeth's very good friend, as well as her hairdresser, for more than twenty years. Truly, he is the keeper of her secrets. I would like him to know how much I appreciate the interview he gave for this book, and his assistance in understanding the woman he knows so very well, especially in relation to her life during the Fortensky years. His assistance was absolutely vital.

My researcher Cathy Griffin worked as a consultant on the ABC-TV broadcast of *Happy Birthday Elizabeth: A Celebration of Life* and provided her many notes and memories from that experience.

I also referred to Barbara Walters's interviews with Elizabeth on ABC in 1987 and September 27, 2003; Elizabeth's appearance on Oprah Winfrey's interview with Michael Jackson, ABC, February 10, 1993; Nancy Collins's interview with Elizabeth on the *Today* show, NBC, June 18, 1986; Whoopi Goldberg's interview with Elizabeth on *Whoopi*, September 14, 1992; and Larry King's interviews with Elizabeth on his program, March 3, 1993, January 15, 2001; and February 3, 2003.

The Academy of Motion Picture Arts and Sciences has on file a very interesting interview with Elizabeth dated August 1, 1981. It can be found in the George Stevens Papers.

I also consulted: "Richard Burton: The Troubled Road Back to Camelot," by Barbara Gelb, *New York Times*, July 6, 1980; "In Remembrance of Richard Burton," by Steve Dougherty, *Los Angeles Herald Examiner*, August 24, 1984; "All The World His Stage," by Cecil Smith, *Los Angeles Times*, August 19, 1984; "An Olympian of the Stage," by Philip Dunne, *Los Angeles Herald Examiner*, August 12, 1984; "Richard Burton, 58, is Dead," by Maureen Dowd, *New York Times*, August 6, 1984; "Private Lives: Burton and Miss Taylor," by Frank Rich, *New York Times*, May 9, 1983; "MGM Vet Lucille Ryman Carroll Recalls the Reel Adventures of Liz, Rock, Marilyn and Nancy," *People*, November 2, 1987; "My adorable, difficult, fractious, intolerant wife—The Private Notebooks of Richard Burton," by Melvyn Bragg, *Life*, December 1988; "Richard Burton Dies of a Cerebral Hemorrhage" by Ted Thackrey Jr., *Los Angeles Times*, August 6, 1984; "Burton: A Talent Who Fizzled and Flared," by Peter Rainer, *Los Angeles Herald Examiner*, August 6, 1984; "Girl Talk with Elizabeth the Great," by Helen Gurley Brown, *Cosmopolitan*, September 1987; "Heartbreaker," by Katie Kelly, *Memories*, Spring 1988; "Taylor Fights to end Pain, Addiction," by Ann Trebbe, *USA Today*, December 9, 1988; "Elizabeth Taylor: Diet Tips on How to Become a Size 6," by Dena Kleiman, *New York Times*, May 23, 1986; "Stage: The Misses Taylor and Stapelton in 'Foxes,'" by Frank Rich, *New York Times*, May 8, 1981; "A Public 'Private Lives' for Taylor-Burton Fans," by Dudley Clendinen, *New York Times*, April 18, 1983; "Liz 'N' Dick Show Reprised," by Barbara Isenberg, *Los Angeles Times*, July 3, 1983; "A Broadway Party for Elizabeth Taylor," by John Duka, *New York Times*, May 8, 1981; "Liz Taylor Lightens Up," by Bob Sipchen, *Los Angeles Times*, January 25, 1988; "A Star is Reborn," by Elizabeth

Taylor, *People*, January 1988; "John Warner Describes the Cozy Caucus of Two . . . ," *People*, October 20, 1980; "At Last—Elizabeth Taylor's Broadway Debut," London *Sunday Times* magazine, May 17, 1981; "Elizabeth Taylor's Greatest Battle," by David Wallace, *Ladies' Home Journal*, September 1990; "The Elizabethan Age: 60 Years of Liz," by Ty Burr, *Entertainment Weekly*, March 13, 1992; "Queen of the Nile," by Simon Banner, *You* magazine, the *Mail on Sunday* (London), January 23, 1994; "Liz's AIDS Odyssey," by Nancy Collins, *Vanity Fair*, November 1992; "Liz: Larry's the Last," by Liz Smith, *New York Post*, September 1, 1995; "Liz Kin Trashes Book," by Stephen Schaefer, *New York Post*, April 17, 1995; "Farewell Fortensky," by Tom Gliatto, *People*, September 11, 1995; "Taylor Made Millions," by Kevin O'Sullivan, *New York Daily News*, June 16, 1996; "Liz and Larry Split," by Liz Smith, *New York Post*, August 31, 1995; "Life After Larry," by Charles Leerhsen, *People*, March 4, 1996; "Elizabeth Taylor—The Advocate Interview" (no byline), *Advocate*, October 15, 1996; "Liz on Liz," by Liz Smith, *TV Guide*, June 4–10, 1994; "Liz: Ms. Taylor Will See You Now," by Paul Theroux, *Talk*, October 1999; "Elizabeth Taylor's First Fiancé Reminisces—Interview with William Pawley Jr.," by J. Randy Taraborrelli, *Clue*, April 1997; "Pearls of Wisdom from Liz," by Charles Champlin, *Los Angeles Times*, March 31, 1996; "Elizabeth Taylor," by Brad Darrach, *Life*, March 1997; "Elizabeth—Triumphant," by Landon Y. Jones, *People*, December 10, 1990; "Here Comes the Groom," by Marjorie Rosen, *People*, October 7, 1991; "Way Off Broadway [Sybil Christopher]," by Bruce Weber, *New York Times*, August 2, 1994; "Elizabeth Taylor, the Movies," by Charles Champlin, *Los Angeles Times*, March 7, 1993; "Why Liz Had to Ditch Larry," by Cathy Griffin, *Here*, May 1995; "The Miz Liz Library," by Liz Smith, *New York Newsday*, September 12, 1995; "Liz in Hospital," by Wendell Jamieson and Helen Kennedy, *New York Daily News*, September 16, 1995; "Liz and Larry Separate," by Arlene Vigoda, *USA Today*, September 1, 1995; "Love-Rift Larry Goes for Liz's Loot," by Allan

Hall, *Daily Mirror* (London), September 1, 1995; "Divorce Elizabeth Style, Part 1," by Laura C. Smith, *Entertainment Weekly*, January 26, 1996; "If the knife slips tomorrow, I'll die knowing I've had an extraordinary life," by Elizabeth Taylor as told to Brad Darrach, *Life*, April 1997; "A First Class Affair," by Sam Kashner, *Vanity Fair*, July 2003; "Reunited at Last?" by Glenys Roberts, *Daily Mail* (London), October 15, 2005; "Good Times and Bum Ties, but She's Here," by Alex Kuczinski, *New York Times*, September 29, 2002; "Leave Sally Alone," by Marc Baker, *Wales on Sunday*, May 29, 2005; "Burton's Widow Reveals She's Unlikely to Marry," by Paul Turner, *South Wales Evening Post*, July 28, 2004; "My Sentimental Return to the Swiss Valley . . ." by Sally Burton, *Mail on Sunday* (London), July 28, 2002; "Living With a Legend Who Died 18 Years Ago," by Abbie Wightwick, *Western Mail* (Wales), January 26, 2002; "In The Court of Queen," by Chrissy Iley, *Australia Women's Weekly*, November 2003; "John Springer, 85, Hollywood Publicist, Dies," by Mel Gussow, *New York Times*, November 1, 2001; "Dame Liz Misses Her 'Sir,'" by Bill Hoffman, *New York Post*, May 17, 2000; "Hollywood Dames," by Paul Harris, *Daily Mail* (London), May 17, 2000; "Elizabeth Taylor," by Jon Clark, *Mail on Sunday* (London), May 28, 2000; "Dame Elizabeth," by David Wigg, *Daily Mail* (London), April 29, 2000; "Elizabeth—The Legend and the Lens," by Gabrielle Donnelly, *You* magazine, *Mail on Sunday* (London), May 14, 2000; "A Tale of Two Elizabeths," by Bryan Forbes, *Daily Mail* (London), May 16, 2000; The Birth of the Scandal," by Ryan Devlin, *Premiere*, May 2005; "Feud That's Tearing Liz's Family Apart," by Peter Sheridan, *Express* (London), May 29, 2004.

I also referred to "La Liz" by Christopher Bagley, *W*, December 2004, a very interesting interview with her that was also ominous in tone. It's the interview in which Elizabeth graphically described her poor health ("I've become one of those poor little old women who's bent sideways, a little old lady, bent all sideways"). Many of her fans were upset by her remarks and afraid for her. It was her friend Liz Smith who eventually put it all in perspective in her November 22, 2004, column: "This is ET's way. She's not ready to die right now, just not fearful of what comes to all—she has been near enough several times to not fear it. Just as she scribbled a dramatic note to the world when she and Richard Burton broke up, just as she risked her career to champion the AIDS fight, and just as she celebrated 'the child in me' at her Disneyland 60th birthday party, Elizabeth is the mistress of her own PR, still bold, honest and unafraid, living life on her own terms."

Once word got out that I was writing this book, many people contacted me and my researchers to tell me of their experiences with Elizabeth. It was impossible to work all of their stories into this book because of space considerations. I feel badly that they so graciously gave of their time, only to then not appear in the text. Therefore, I would like to acknowledge just a few of them here, and—who knows—maybe the paperback edition? Thank you for sharing with us your memories of Elizabeth: Lieutenant Douglas Coughlan (ret.), NYPD (whose father was a New York City police officer and driver for the Burtons' attorney, Aaron Frosch); Robert Forster (who costarred with Elizabeth in *Reflections of a Golden Eye*); Marvin Gillespie (who lived next door to Robert Burton in New York); Betty Warner (who was a close friend of Sybil Burton's); Jacqueline Burr (widow of Richard Burr, who was Burton's understudy in *Hamlet*); Martha Tyler (a friend of the Burtons' in Gstaad); and Christina Oxenberg (daughter of Her Royal Highness Elisabeth Princess of Yugoslavia, whose mother dated Burton).

⌐

RECOMMENDED READING

First of all, I don't think anyone could write about Elizabeth Taylor and Richard Burton without first studying Melvyn Braag's exceptional book *Richard Burton: A Life*. It really is definitive. I should also add that Brenda Maddox's and Donald Spoto's biographies of Elizabeth (*Who's Afraid of Elizabeth Taylor?* and *A Passion for Life*, respectively) are, in my opinion, the best two books about her. I would first turn to those for a good and sensible read about Elizabeth—after this one, of course! At any rate, here are other books about this and related subjects that I used in my research that I would recommend to the interested reader:

Elizabeth Taylor: The Most Beautiful Woman in the World, by Ellis Amburn (HarperCollins); *Hollywood Is a Four Letter Town*, by James Bacon (Avon); *Made in Hollywood*, by James Bacon (Warner Books); *Celebrity Register*, ed. Earl Blackwell (Simon and Schuster); *Miss Rona*, by Rona Barrett (Bantam); *Walter Wanger: Hollywood Independent*, by Matthew Bernstein (University of California Press); *Child Star*, by Shirley Temple Black (Warner Books); *Center Door Fancy*, by Joan Blondell (Delacorte); *Howard Hughes*, by Peter Harry Brown and Patte Barham (Dutton); *Clift*, by Patricia Bosworth (Bantam); *The Cleopatra Papers*, by Jack Brodsky and Nathan Weiss (Simon and Schuster); *A Christmas Story*, by Richard Burton (Morrow); *Meeting Mrs. Jenkins*, by Richard Burton (Morrow); *Richard and Philip: The Burtons*, by Philip Burton (Peter Owen); *Richard Burton: Very Close Up*, by Fergus Cashin (W. H Allen); *Elizabeth Taylor: The Illustrated Biography*, by James Christopher (André Deutsch); *The Nine Lives of Mike Todd*, by Art Cohn (Random House); *Mike Todd's Around the World in 80 Days*, ed. Art Cohn (Random House); *Holy Terror: Andy Warhol Close Up*, by Bob Colacello (HarperCollins); *Past Imperfect*, by Joan Collins (Coronet); *Dalton Trumbo*, by Bruce Cook (Scribner's); *Richard and Elizabeth*, by Lester David and Jhan Robbins (Funk and Wagnalls); *The Real and the Unreal*, by Bill Davidson (Harper and Brothers); *It's a Hell of a Life, but Not a Bad Living*, by Edward Dmytryk (Times Books); *The MGM Story: The Complete History of Fifty Roaring Years* (Crown); *Richard Burton*, by Paul Ferris (Berkeley); *My Life, My Loves*, by Eddie Fisher (W. H. Allen); *Been There, Done That*, by Eddie

Fisher with David Fisher (St. Martin's); *Pictures Will Talk*, by Kenneth Geist (Charles Scribner's Sons); *The Film Director as Superstar*, by Joe Gelmis (Doubleday); *The Fifty-Year Decline and Fall of Hollywood*, by Ezra Goodman (Simon and Schuster); *The Rest of the Story*, by Sheila Graham (Bantam); *The Eddie Fisher Story*, by Myrna Greene (Paul S. Erikson); *Merv*, by Merv Griffin with Peter Barsocchini (Simon and Schuster); *Don't Say Yes Until I Finish Talking: A Biography of Darryl F. Zanuck*, by Mel Gussow (Doubleday); *The Dress Doctor*, by Edith Head (Little, Brown); *The Whole Truth and Nothing But*, by Hedda Hopper with James Brough (Doubleday); *Rock Hudson*, by Rock Hudson and Sara Davidson (Weidenfeld); *Liz*, by C. David Heymann (Carol); *Olivia de Havilland*, by Judith M. Kass (Pyramid); *Richard Burton, My Brother*, by Graham Jenkins (Michael Joseph); *Burton: The Man Behind the Myth*, by Penny Junior (Sidgwick and Jackson); *Reeling*, by Pauline Kael (Little, Brown); *Elizabeth Taylor: The Last Star*, by Kitty Kelley (Simon and Schuster); *Mervyn Le Roy: Take One*, by Mervyn Le Roy and Dick Kleinser (Hawthorne); *Montgomery Clift*, by Robert LaGuardia (W. H. Allen); *Who's Afraid of Elizabeth Taylor?* by Brenda Maddox (Evans); *John Huston*, by Axel Madsen (Doubleday); *Elizabeth Taylor*, by Sheridan Morely (Pavilion); *Lana: The Public and Private Lives of Miss Turner*, by Joe Morella and Edward Z. Epstein (Citadel); *Elizabeth Taylor*, by Christopher Nickens (Dolphin); *The Hollywood Beauties*, by James Robert Parish with Gregory W. Mank and Don E. Stanke (Arlington House); *Letters from an Actor*, by William Redfield (Cassell); *Debbie: My Life*, by Debbie Reynolds and David Patrick Columbia (Morrow); *Bittersweet*, by Susan Strasberg (Putnam); *Heyday: An Autobiography*, by Dore Schary (Little, Brown); *The Genius of the System*, by Thomas Schatz (Pantheon); *Elizabeth* by Dick Sheppard (Doubleday); *A Passion for Life: The Biography of Elizabeth Taylor*, by Donald Spoto (HarperCollins); *John Gielgud Directs Richard Burton in Hamlet*, by Richard Sterne (Heinemann); *Michael Jackson: The Magic and the Madness*, by J. Randy Taraborrelli (Sidgwick and Jackson); *Sina-*

tra: A Complete Life, by J. Randy Taraborrelli (Carol/Harper-Collins); *Nibbles and Me*, by Elizabeth Taylor (Duell, Sloan and Pearce); *Elizabeth Taylor*, by Elizabeth Taylor (Harper and Row); *Elizabeth Takes Off*, by Elizabeth Taylor (Putnam); *Elizabeth Taylor: My Love Affair with Jewelry* (Simon and Schuster); *The Films of Elizabeth Taylor*, by Jerry Vermilye and Mark Ricci (Citadel); *Elizabeth*, by Andrew Walker (Grove); *Hollywood, England: The British Film Industry in the Sixties*, by Alexander Walker (Michael Joseph); *The Andy Warhol Diaries*, ed. Pat Hackett (Warner Books); *Confessions of an Ex-Fan Magazine Writer*, by Jane Wilskie (Doubleday); *Elizabeth Taylor: Her Life, Her Loves, Her Future*, by Ruth Waterbury with Gene Arceri (Bantam); *The Wilding Way: The Story of My Life*, by Michael Wilding (St. Martin's); *Liz: An Intimate Collection*, by Bob Willoughby (Merrell); *Shelly: Also Known as Shirley*, by Shelley Winters (William Morrow); *Shelley II: The Middle of My Century*, by Shelley Winters (Simon and Schuster); *Accidentally on Purpose: An Autobiography*, by Michael York (Dove Entertainment); *Portraits of Love* (no author) (Filipacchi).

~

PERSONAL ACKNOWLEDGMENTS

Special thanks to Stephen Gregory, not only for so many years of friendship but also for his extraordinary contributions to this work. It's truly difficult for me to even imagine what this book would be like if not for his input, which has been invaluable to all of my recent works. Without it, I am sure my research and writing would simply descend into chaos. I'm very grateful to him. He's an incredibly special and talented person. Having him in my life matters . . . and on a daily basis.

As I have often stated, without a loyal team of representatives, an author usually finds himself sitting at home writing books no one reads. Therefore, I thank all of those from "USA-Team JRT" who somehow mastermind the chaos in my office: attorneys Joel Loquvam, James M. Leonard, and James Jimenez; CPA Michael Horowitz, of Horowitz, McMahon and Zarem in Southern California, Inc; Michele Muico, also of Horowitz et. al.; and advisers Mike Johnston of Capital Lending and Doris Duke of Common Cents, Inc. I also owe a debt of gratitude to Buddy Thomas at ICM.

My sincere thanks to Jonathan Hahn, fellow author, personal publicist, and also close friend. Everyone should have someone like Jonathan in his corner. He's been so encouraging over the years and his support and abiding wisdom has meant everything to me. I would also like to acknowledge his lovely and immensely learned wife, Alysia Garrison, who has also been a loyal friend to me.

I thank, as always, Al Kramer, my trusted friend and writing colleague who has, for years, been there for me. Thanks, Al, for your continued friendship.

I want to thank Jeff Hare at Warner Bros. for being such a good and trusted friend and for always understanding and appreciating the work that I do.

Thanks also to Brian Evan Newman for his joyful outlook.

It means the world to me to be blessed with so many good friends, some of whom I would like to acknowledge here, including:

Richard Tyler Jordan, Steve Ivory, George Solomon, Iake and Alex Eisinmann, Hazel and Rob Kragulac, Frank Bruno, Jeff Cooke, Lisa Reiner, Steve Ridgeway, Andy Skurow, Billy Barnes, Scherrie Payne, Marvin Marshall, Freda Payne, Cindy Birdsong, Lynda Laurence, Rev. Marlene Morris, Kac Young, Jim Bzora, Dr. Jason Peters, Barbara Ormsby, Rick Starr, John Passantino, Linda DeStefano, Mr. and Mrs. Joseph Tumolo, Daniel Tumolo, Charles Casillo, John Carlino, Tony and Marilyn Caruselle, David Spiro, Mr. and Mrs. Adolph Steinlen, David and Frances Snyder, Abby and Maddy Snyder, Maribeth and Don Rothell, Mary Alvarez,

Mark Bringelson, Hope Levy, Tom Lavagnino, John Townsend, Matthew Barasch, Anthony Shane, Bethany Marshall, Dylan, and, of course, Yvette Jarecki.

During the third of four quarters of production on *Elizabeth*—a period from January to June of 2005—I was reporting on the Michael Jackson molestation trial in Santa Maria, California, for CBS News and Court TV. I met so many amazing people during that time, media colleagues, many of whom I now count as good friends of mine and who were supportive as I also worked on this book during a difficult time for us all. I would like to acknowledge just a few of them here: my very good friends Bruce Rheins and Dawn Westlake, Manuel Gallegos, Vince Gonzalez, Jennifer Sieben, Soshea Lebowitz, Jennie Josephson, Sherri Sylvester, Anne Bremner, Jim Moret, Michelle Caruso, Leslie Miller, Miguel Marquez, Quintin Cushner, Diane Dimond, Pat Ketchum, Savannah Guthrie, Dawn Hobbs, Stacy Brown, Andrew Cohen, Trent Copeland, Hal Eisner, Aphrodite Jones, Jane Velez-Mitchell, Roger Friedman, Jim Thomas, Dan Whitcomb, Steve Corbett, Frank Swertlow, Linda Deutsch, Tim Molloy, and Mike Taibbi. I apologize to anyone whose name is not on this list. What a strange, unique time we had in Santa Maria, and all while I was working on this book! Thanks also to Michael Jackson's team: Thomas Mesereau, Brian Oxmon, and Raymone K. Bain. Special thanks to Mike Lawler for his advice and support.

My thanks to Andy Steinlen for being such a great influence on me, for teaching me so much about life, for being my "sounding board" . . . and my ever loyal, ever true friend.

I have always been so blessed to have a family as supportive as mine. My thanks and love go out to: Roslyn and Bill Barnett and Jessica and Zachary, Rocco and Rosemaria Taraborrelli and Rocco and Vincent, and Arnold Taraborrelli. Special thanks to my father, Rocco, who has always been my inspiration. He has encouraged me in ways too numerous to mention.

My mom, Rose Marie, would have loved this book; she was

such a fan of Elizabeth Taylor's. She was also my biggest fan, and I was hers.

I must also acknowledge those readers of mine who have followed my career over the years. As I have said in the past, the reason that I write about people such Elizabeth Taylor is to bring about an exchange of ideas concerning how others have lived in the hope that we may learn by their choices. Never did I dream that I would have a global audience for such communication. I am indebted to every reader who has stuck by me over the course of my career. I receive so many letters from people who have enjoyed my books—as well as from those who have taken issue with aspects of my work. Whatever the response, I am eternally grateful to anyone who takes the time to pick up one of my books and read it.

Finally, I'd like to close this book with a comment from Roddy McDowall found in the previously mentioned program for the Life Achievement Award presented to Elizabeth in 1993 by the American Film Institute. I think it best sums up his good friend, the woman he always called "Bessie." Of her, he wrote: "Vulnerable, responsible, dedicated, awash with self-humor, kind, full of decades of woe and rapture, Elizabeth Rosemond Taylor emerges as a sort of elegant, rollicking Boadicea. A rainbow that arcs the travesties and triumphs of her time. She is an artist in both her craft . . . and her life."

J. RANDY TARABORRELLI
Spring 2006

Elizabeth Taylor Filmography

There's One Born Every Minute (1942)
Hugh Herbert, Tom Brown, Peggy Moran, Guy Kibbee,
Catherine Doucet, Edgar Kennedy, Carl "Alfalfa" Switzer,
Elizabeth Taylor (Gloria Twine)
Universal
ASSOCIATE PRODUCER: Ken Goldsmith
DIRECTOR: Harold Young
SCREENWRITERS: Robert B. Hunt, Brenda Weisberg

Lassie Come Home (1943)
Roddy McDowall, Donald Crisp, Edmund Gwenn, Dame May
Whitty, Nigel Bruce, Elsa Lanchester, Elizabeth Taylor (Priscilla)
MGM
PRODUCER: Samuel Marx
DIRECTOR: Fred M. Wilcox
SCREENWRITER: Hugh Butler

Jane Eyre (1943)
Joan Fontaine, Orson Welles, Henry Danielle, Peggy Ann
Garner, Margaret O'Brien, Agnes Moorehead, John Sutton,
Sara Allgood, Ethel Griffies, Elizabeth Taylor (Helen)
20th Century-Fox
PRODUCER: William Goetz
DIRECTOR: Robert Stevenson
SCREENWRITERS: Aldous Huxley, Robert Stevenson,
John Houseman

The White Cliffs of Dover (1944)

Irene Dunne, Alan Marshal, Frank Morgan, Roddy McDowall,
C. Aubrey Smith, Gladys Cooper, Dame May Whitty, Peter
Lawford, Van Johnson, June Lockhart, Elizabeth Taylor (Betsy)
MGM
PRODUCER: Sidney Franklin
DIRECTOR: Clarence Brown
SCREENWRITERS: Claudine West, Jan Lustig, George Froeschel

National Velvet (1944)

Mickey Rooney, Donald Crisp, Elizabeth Taylor (Velvet Brown),
Anne Revere, Angela Lansbury, Reginald Owens, Jackie "Butch"
Jenkins
MGM
PRODUCER: Pandro S. Berman
DIRECTOR: Clarence Brown
SCREENWRITERS: Theodore Reeves, Helen Deutsch

Courage of Lassie (1946)

Elizabeth Taylor (Kathie Merrick), Frank Morgan, Tom Drake,
Selena Royle, George Cleveland, Carl "Alfalfa" Switzer
MGM
PRODUCER: Robert Sisk
DIRECTOR: Fred M. Wilcox
SCREENWRITER: Lionel Hauser

Cynthia (1947)

Elizabeth Taylor (Cynthia Bishop), George Murphy,
S.Z. "Cuddles" Sakall, Mary Astor, Gene Lockhart, James Lydon,
Spring Byington
MGM
PRODUCER: Edwin H. Knopf
DIRECTOR: Robert Z. Leonard
SCREENWRITERS: Harold Buchman, Charles Kaufman

Life with Father (1947)

William Powell, Irene Dunne, Edmund Gwenn, Zasu Pitts,
Elizabeth Taylor (Mary Skinner), Martin Milner, Emma Dunn,
Moroni Olsen
Warner Bros.
PRODUCER: Robert Buckner
DIRECTOR: Michael Curtiz
SCREENWRITER: Donald Ogden Stewart

A Date with Judy (1948)

Wallace Beery, Jane Powell, Elizabeth Taylor (Carol Pringle),
Carmen Miranda, Robert Stack, Xavier Cugat, Selena Royle
MGM
PRODUCER: Joe Pasternak
DIRECTOR: Richard Thorpe
SCREENWRITERS: Dorothy Cooper, Dorothy Kingsley

Julia Misbehaves (1948)

Greer Garson, Walter Pidgeon, Peter Lawford, Elizabeth Taylor
(Susan Packett), Cesar Romero, Lucile Watson, Nigel Bruce
MGM
PRODUCER: Everett Riskin
DIRECTOR: Jack Conway
SCREENWRITERS: William Ludwig, Harry Ruskin, Arthur Wimperis

Little Women (1949)

June Allyson, Peter Lawford, Margaret O'Brien, Elizabeth Taylor
(Amy March), Janet Leigh, Rosanno Brazzi, Mary Astor,
Sir C. Aubrey Smith, Lucile Watson
MGM
PRODUCER/DIRECTOR: Mervyn LeRoy
SCREENWRITERS: Andrew Solt, Sarah Y. Mason, Victor Heerman

Conspirator (1950)
Robert Taylor, Elizabeth Taylor (Melinda Greyton),
Harold Warrender, Robert Flemyng
MGM
PRODUCER: Arthur Hornblow Jr.
DIRECTOR: Victor Saville
SCREENWRITER: Sally Benson

The Big Hangover (1950)
Van Johnson, Elizabeth Taylor (Mary Belney), Percy Waram,
Fay Holden, Leon Ames, Edgar Buchanan, Selena Royle,
Gene Lockhart
MGM
PRODUCER/DIRECTOR/SCREENWRITER: Norman Krasna

Father of the Bride (1950)
Spencer Tracy, Joan Bennett, Elizabeth Taylor (Kay Banks), Don
Taylor, Billie Burke, Moroni Olsen, Leo G. Carroll, Melville Cooper
MGM
PRODUCER: Pandro S. Berman
DIRECTOR: Vincente Minnelli
SCREENWRITERS: Frances Goodrich, Albert Hackett

Father's Little Dividend (1951)
Spencer Tracy, Joan Bennett, Elizabeth Taylor (Kay Dunstan),
Billie Burke, Moroni Olsen, Russ Tamblyn
MGM
PRODUCER: Pandro S. Berman
DIRECTOR: Vincente Minnelli
SCREENWRITERS: Frances Goodrich, Albert Hackett

A Place in the Sun (1951)
Montgomery Clift, Elizabeth Taylor (Angela Vickers),
Shelley Winters, Anne Revere, Raymond Burr, Keefe Brasselle,
Fred Clark, Frieda Inescort, Shepperd Strudwick

Paramount
PRODUCER/DIRECTOR: George Stevens
SCREENWRITERS: Michael Wilson, Harry Brown

Callaway Went Thataway (1951)
Fred MacMurray, Dorothy McGuire, Howard Keel, Jesse White,
Natalie Schafer. Guest stars (unbilled): June Allyson,
Clark Gable, Elizabeth Taylor, Esther Williams, Dick Powell
MGM
PRODUCERS/DIRECTORS/SCREENWRITERS: Norman Panama,
Melvin Frank

Love Is Better Than Ever (1951)
Larry Parks, Elizabeth Taylor (Anastacia "Stacie" Macaboy),
Josephine Hutchinson, Tom Tully, Ann Doran
MGM
PRODUCER: William H. Wright
DIRECTOR: Stanley Donen
SCREENWRITER: Ruth Brooks Flippen

Ivanhoe (1952)
Robert Taylor, Elizabeth Taylor (Rebecca), Joan Fontaine,
George Sanders, Emlyn Williams, Robert Douglas, Finlay Currie,
Felix Aylmer
MGM
PRODUCER: Pandro S. Berman
DIRECTOR: Richard Thorpe
SCREENWRITER: Noel Langley

The Girl Who Had Everything (1953)
Elizabeth Taylor (Jean Latiner), Fernando Lamas,
William Powell, Gig Young, James Whitmore
MGM
PRODUCER: Armand Deutsch
DIRECTOR: Richard Thorpe
SCREENWRITER: Art Cohn

Rhapsody (1954)

Elizabeth Taylor (Louise Durant), Vittorio Gassman,
John Ericson, Louis Calhern, Michael Chekhov, Barbara Bates
MGM
PRODUCER: Lawrence Weingarten
DIRECTOR: Charles Vidor
SCREENWRITERS: Fay and Michael Kanin

Elephant Walk (1954)

Elizabeth Taylor (Ruth Wiley), Dana Andrews, Peter Finch,
James Donald, Rosemary Harris, Abraham Sofaer
MGM
PRODUCER: Irving Asher
DIRECTOR: William Dieterle
SCREENWRITER: John Lee Mahin

Beau Brummell (1954)

Stewart Granger, Elizabeth Taylor (Lady Patricia), Peter Ustinov,
Robert Morley, James Donald, Rosemary Harris, Peter Bull
MGM
PRODUCER: Sam Zimbalist
DIRECTOR: Curtis Bernhardt
SCREENWRITER: Karl Tunberg

The Last Time I Saw Paris (1954)

Elizabeth Taylor (Helen Elswirth), Van Johnson,
Walter Pidgeon, Donna Reed, Eva Gabor, Roger Moore
MGM
PRODUCER: Jack Cummings
DIRECTOR: Richard Brooks
SCREENWRITERS: Julius J. Epstein, Philip G. Epstein,
Richard Brooks

Giant (1956)
Rock Hudson, Elizabeth Taylor (Leslie Lynnton Benedict),
James Dean, Carroll Baker, Mercedes McCambridge,
Jane Withers, Chill Wills, Dennis Hopper, Sal Mineo,
Rod Taylor, Judith Evelyn, Earl Holliman
Warner Bros.
PRODUCERS: George Stevens, Henry Ginsberg
DIRECTOR: George Stevens
SCREENWRITERS: Fred Guiol, Ivan Moffat

Raintree County (1957)
Montgomery Clift, Elizabeth Taylor (Susanna Drake),
Eva Marie Saint, Lee Marvin, Nigel Patrick, Rod Taylor,
Agnes Moorehead, Walter Abel, Tom Drake, Gardner McKay
MGM
PRODUCER: David Lewis
DIRECTOR: Edward Dmytryk
SCREENWRITER: Millard Kaufman

Cat on a Hot Tin Roof (1958)
Elizabeth Taylor (Maggie Pollitt), Paul Newman, Burl Ives,
Judith Anderson, Jack Carson, Madeleine Sherwood, Larry Gates
MGM
PRODUCER: Lawrence Weingarten
DIRECTOR: Richard Brooks
SCREENWRITERS: Richard Brooks, James Poe

Suddenly, Last Summer (1959)
Elizabeth Taylor (Catherine Holly), Katharine Hepburn,
Montgomery Clift, Albert Dekker, Mercedes McCambridge,
Gary Raymond
MGM
PRODUCER: Sam Spiegel
DIRECTOR: Joseph L. Mankiewicz
SCREENWRITERS: Gore Vidal, Tennessee Williams

Scent of Mystery (1960)
Denholm Elliott, Peter Lorre, Paul Lukas, Elizabeth Taylor
(The Real Sally Kennedy, unbilled)
A Cinerama/Michael Todd Jr. Release
PRODUCER: Michael Todd Jr.
DIRECTOR: Jack Cardiff
SCREENWRITER: William Roos

Butterfield 8 (1960)
Elizabeth Taylor (Gloria Wondrous), Laurence Harvey,
Eddie Fisher, Dina Merrill, Mildred Dunnock, Betty Field,
Jeffrey Lynn, Kay Medford
MGM
PRODUCER: Pandro S. Berman
DIRECTOR: Daniel Mann
SCREENWRITERS: Charles Schnee, John Michael Hayes

Cleopatra (1963)
Elizabeth Taylor (Cleopatra), Richard Burton, Rex Harrison,
Hume Cronyn, Roddy McDowall, Martin Landau,
Pamela Brown, Cesare Danova
20th Century-Fox
PRODUCER: Walter Wanger
DIRECTOR: Joseph L. Mankiewicz
SCREENWRITERS: Joseph L. Mankiewicz, Ranald MacDougall,
Sidney Buchman

The V.I.P.s (1963)
Elizabeth Taylor (Frances Andros), Richard Burton,
Louis Jourdan, Elsa Martinelli, Margaret Rutherford,
Maggie Smith, Orson Welles
MGM
PRODUCER: Anatole deGrunwald
DIRECTOR: Anthony Asquith
SCREENWRITER: Terence Rattigan

The Sandpiper (1965)
Elizabeth Taylor (Laura Reynolds), Richard Burton,
Eva Marie Saint, Charles Bronson, Robert Webber
MGM
PRODUCER: Martin Ransohoff
DIRECTOR: Vincente Minnelli
SCREENWRITERS: Dalton Trumbo, Michael Wilson

Who's Afraid of Virginia Woolf? (1966)
Elizabeth Taylor (Martha), Richard Burton, George Segal,
Sandy Dennis
Warner Bros.
PRODUCER/SCREENWRITER: Ernest Lehman
DIRECTOR: Mike Nichols

The Taming of the Shrew (1967)
Elizabeth Taylor (Katharina), Richard Burton, Michael York,
Cyril Cusack
Columbia
PRODUCERS: Richard Burton, Elizabeth Taylor, Franco Zeffirelli
DIRECTOR: Franco Zeffirelli
SCREENWRITERS: Paul Dehn, Suso Cecchi D'Amico,
Franco Zeffirelli

Doctor Faustus (1967)
Richard Burton, Andreas Teuber, Elizabeth O'Donovan,
Ian Marter, Elizabeth Taylor (Helen of Troy)
Columbia/Oxford University Screen Productions, et alia
PRODUCERS: Richard Burton, Richard McWhorter
DIRECTORS: Richard Burton, Nevill Coghill
SCREENWRITER: Nevill Coghill

Reflections in a Golden Eye (1967)
Elizabeth Taylor (Leonora Penderton), Marlon Brando,
Brian Keith, Julie Harris, Robert Forster

Warner Bros./Seven Arts
PRODUCER: Ray Stark
DIRECTOR: John Huston
SCREENWRITERS: Chapman Mortimer, Gladys Hill

The Comedians (1967)
Elizabeth Taylor (Martha Pineda), Richard Burton,
Alec Guinness, Peter Ustinov, Lillian Gish, Paul Ford,
Roscoe Lee Browne, James Earl Jones, Cicely Tyson
MGM/Maximillian/Trianon
PRODUCER/DIRECTOR: Peter Glenville
SCREENWRITER: Graham Greene

Boom! (1968)
Elizabeth Taylor (Flora "Sissy" Goforth), Richard Burton,
Noël Coward, Michael Dunn, Joanna Shimkus
Universal
PRODUCERS: John Heyman, Norman Priggen
DIRECTOR: Joseph Losey
SCREENWRITER: Tennessee Williams

Secret Ceremony (1968)
Elizabeth Taylor (Leonora), Robert Mitchum, Mia Farrow,
Pamela Brown, Peggy Ashcroft
Universal
PRODUCERS: John Heyman, Norman Priggen
DIRECTOR: Joseph Losey
SCREENWRITER: George Tabori

Anne of the Thousand Days (1969)
Richard Burton, Genevieve Bujold, John Colicos, Irene Pappas,
Anthony Quayle, Elizabeth Taylor (a courtesan, unbilled)
Universal
PRODUCER: Hal B. Wallis
DIRECTOR: Charles Jarrott
SCREENWRITERS: John Hale, Bridget Boland

The Only Game in Town (1970)
Elizabeth Taylor (Fran Walker), Warren Beatty,
Charles Braswell, Hank Henry
20th Century-Fox
PRODUCER: Fred Kohlmar
DIRECTOR: George Stevens
SCREENWRITER: Frank Gilroy

Under Milk Wood (1971)
Richard Burton, Elizabeth Taylor (Rosie Probert), Peter O'Toole,
Glynis Johns, Vivien Merchant, Sian Phillips, Victor Spinetti
Timon/The Rank Organisation
PRODUCER: Hugh French, Jules Buck
DIRECTOR/SCREENWRITER: Andrew Sinclair

X, Y and Zee (Zee and Co., U.K.) (1972)
Elizabeth Taylor (Zee Blakeley), Michael Caine, Susanna York,
Margaret Leighton, John Standing
Columbia
PRODUCER: Alan Ladd Jr., Jay Kanter, Elliott Kastner
DIRECTOR: Brian G. Hutton
SCREENWRITER: Edna O'Brien

Hammersmith Is Out (1972)
Elizabeth Taylor (Jimmie Jean Jackson), Richard Burton,
Beau Bridges, Peter Ustinov, Leon Ames, John Schuck,
George Raft
Cinerama Releasing Corporation
PRODUCER: Alex Lucas
DIRECTOR: Peter Ustinov
SCREENWRITER: Stanford Whitmore

Night Watch (1973)
Elizabeth Taylor (Ellen Wheeler), Laurence Harvey,
Billie Whitelaw, Robert Lang

Avco Embassy
PRODUCERS: George W. George, Bernard Straus, Martin Poll, David White
DIRECTOR: Brian G. Hutton
SCREENWRITER: Tony Williamson

Ash Wednesday (1973)
Elizabeth Taylor (Barbara Sawyer), Henry Fonda, Helmut Berger, Keith Baxter, Monique Van Vooren
Paramount/Sagittarius
PRODUCER: Dominick Dunne
DIRECTOR: Larry Peerce
SCREENWRITER: Jean-Claude Tramont

That's Entertainment! (1974)
Narration by: Fred Astaire, Gene Kelly, Elizabeth Taylor, James Stewart, Bing Crosby, Liza Minnelli, Donald O'Connor, Debbie Reynolds, Mickey Rooney, Frank Sinatra
MGM/United Artists
EXECUTIVE PRODUCER: Daniel Melnick
PRODUCER/DIRECTOR/SCREENWRITER: Jack Haley Jr.

Identikit (aka *The Driver's Seat*) (1974)
Elizabeth Taylor (Lise), Ian Bannen, Guido Mannari, Andy Warhol, Mona Washbourne
Avco Embassy
PRODUCER: Franco Rosselli
DIRECTOR/SCREENWRITER: Guiseppe Patroni-Griffi
CO-SCREENWRITER: Raffaele La Capria

The Blue Bird (1976)
Elizabeth Taylor (Queen of Light, Mother, Witch, Maternal Love), Jane Fonda, Ava Gardner, Cicely Tyson, Harry Andrews, Will Geer, Mona Washbourne, George Cole
20th Century-Fox

EXECUTIVE PRODUCER: Edward Lewis
PRODUCER: Paul Maslansky
DIRECTOR: George Cukor
SCREENWRITERS: Hugh Whitemore, Alfred Hayes

A Little Night Music (1977)
Elizabeth Taylor (Desiree Armfeldt), Diana Rigg, Len Cariou,
Leslie-Anne Down, Hermione Gingold
Sacha Film/S & T/New World Pictures
EXECUTIVE PRODUCER: Heinz Lazek
PRODUCER: Elliott Kastner
DIRECTOR: Hal Prince
SCREENWRITER: Hugh Wheeler

Winter Kills (1979)
Jeff Bridges, John Huston, Anthony Perkins, Sterling Hayden,
Elizabeth Taylor (Lola Comante, unbilled), Eli Wallach,
Dorothy Malone, Richard Boone, Toshiro Mifune,
Ralph Meeker
Avco Embassy
PRODUCERS: Fred C. Caruso, Daniel H. Blatt
DIRECTOR/SCREENWRITER: William Richert

Genocide (1979)
Narrated by Elizabeth Taylor, Orson Welles
A Simon Wiesenthal Center Release
PRODUCER: Marvin Segelman
DIRECTOR: Arnold Schartzman
SCREENWRITER: Arnold Schwartzman

The Mirror Crack'd (1980)
Angela Lansbury, Geraldine Chaplin, Tony Curtis,
Rock Hudson, Kim Novak, Elizabeth Taylor (Marina Rudd),
Edward Fox
EMI

PRODUCERS: John Brabourne, Richard Goodwin
DIRECTOR: Guy Hamilton
SCREENWRITERS: Jonathan Hales, Barry Sandler

Young Toscanini (1988)
C. Thomas Howell, Elizabeth Taylor (Nadina Bulichoff),
Sophie Ward, Pat Heywood, Franco Nero, John Rhys-Davies,
Valentina Cortese (unbilled)
Carthago Films
EXECUTIVE PRODUCER: Mark Lombardo
PRODUCERS: Fulvio Lucisano, Tarak Ben Ammar
DIRECTOR: Franco Zeffirelli
SCREENWRITER: William H. Stadiem

The Flintstones (1994)
John Goodman, Rick Moranis, Rosie O'Donnell, Elizabeth
Taylor (Pearl Snaghoople), Kyle MacLachlan, Halle Berry
Universal/Amblin/Hanna-Barbera
PRODUCERS: William Hanna, Joseph Barbera, Kathleen Kennedy,
David Kirschner, Gerald R. Molen, Bruce Cohen
DIRECTOR: Brian Levant
SCREENWRITERS: Tom S. Parker, Jim Jennewein,
Steven E. deSouza

TELEVISION MOVIES AND MINISERIES

Divorce His-Divorce Hers (1973)
Elizabeth Taylor (Jane Reynolds), Richard Burton, Carrie Nye
ABC-TV
EXECUTIVE PRODUCER: John Heyman
PRODUCERS: Terence Baker, Gareth Wigan
DIRECTOR: Waris Hussein
SCREENWRITER: John Hopkins

Victory at Entebbe (1976)

Elizabeth Taylor (Edra Vilnofsky), Helmut Berger, Theodore Bikel, Linda Blair, Richard Dreyfuss, Kirk Douglas, Helen Hayes, Anthony Hopkins, Burt Lancaster

ABC-TV

EXECUTIVE PRODUCER: David L. Wolper
PRODUCER: Robert Guenette
DIRECTOR: Marvin J. Chomsky
SCREENWRITER: Ernest Kinoy

Return Engagement (1978)

Elizabeth Taylor (Dr. Emily Loomis), Timothy Bottoms, Allyn Ann McLerie, Peter Donat

NBC-TV

PRODUCERS: Franklin R. Levy, Mike Wise
DIRECTOR: Joseph Hardy
SCREENWRITER: James Prideaux

Between Friends (aka Nobody Makes Me Cry) (1983)

Elizabeth Taylor (Deborah Shapiro), Carol Burnett, Barbara Bush, Henry Ramer

HBO

EXECUTIVE PRODUCERS: Robert Cooper, Marian Rees
PRODUCERS/WRITERS: Shelly List, Jonathan Estrin
DIRECTOR: Lou Antonio

Malice in Wonderland (1985)

Elizabeth Taylor (Louella Parsons), Jane Alexander, Richard Dysart, Joyce Van Patten

CBS-TV

EXECUTIVE PRODUCER: Judith A. Polone
PRODUCER: Jay Benson
DIRECTOR: Gus Trikonis
SCREENWRITERS: Jacqueline M. Feather, David Seidler

North and South (1985)
Kirstie Alley, David Carradine, Leslie-Anne Down, Genie
Francis, Patrick Swayze, Elizabeth Taylor (Madam Conti)
ABC-TV
EXECUTIVE PRODUCERS: David L. Wolper, Chuck McLain
PRODUCER: Paul Freeman
DIRECTOR: Richard Heffron
SCREENWRITERS: Douglas Heyes, Paul F. Edwards,
Kathleen A. Shelley, Patricia Green

There Must Be a Pony (1986)
Elizabeth Taylor (Marguerite Sydney), Robert Wagner,
James Coco, William Windom
ABC-TV
EXECUTIVE PRODUCER: Robert Wagner
PRODUCER: Howard Jeffrey
DIRECTOR: Joseph Sargent
SCREENWRITER: Mart Crowley

Poker Alice (1987)
Elizabeth Taylor (Alice Moffit), George Hamilton,
David Wayne, Richard Mulligan
CBS-TV
EXECUTIVE PRODUCER: Harvey Matofsky
PRODUCER: Renee Valente
DIRECTOR: Arthur Allan Seilelman
SCREENWRITER: James Lee Barrett

Sweet Bird of Youth (1989)
Elizabeth Taylor (Alexandra Del Lago, the Princess
Kosmonopolis), Mark Harmon, Rip Torn, Valerie Perrine
NBC-TV
EXECUTIVE PRODUCERS: Donald Kushner, Peter Locke, Linda Yellen
DIRECTOR: Nicholas Roeg
SCREENWRITER: Gavin Lambert

These Old Broads (2001)
Elizabeth Taylor (Beryl Mason), Shirley MacLaine, Joan Collins,
Debbie Reynolds, Carrie Fisher, Jonathan Silverman,
Peter Graves, June Allyson (unbilled)
ABC-TV
EXECUTIVE PRODUCERS: Ilene Amy Berg, Laurence Mark
CO-EXECUTIVE PRODUCERS: Carrie Fisher, Elaine Pope
DIRECTOR: Matthew Diamond
SCREENWRITERS: Carrie Fisher, Elaine Pope

Index